San Francisco

Bay Area & Wine Country

2009

A Selection
of ***Restaurants*** *&* ***Hotels***

Manufacture française des pneumatiques Michelin
Société en commandite par actions au capital de 304 000 000 EUR
Place des Carmes-Déchaux – 63000 Clermont-Ferrand (France)
R.C.S. Clermont-Fd B 855 200 507

Dépot légal Octobre 2008

Made in Canada

Published in 2008

Cover photograph : Getty Images / Rob Melnychuk

Please send your comments to:

Michelin Maps & Guides
One Parkway South
Greenville, SC 29615 USA
Michelinguide.com
Michelin.guides@us.michelin.com

Dear reader

We are thrilled to present the third edition of our Michelin Guide San Francisco.

Our teams have made every effort to update the selection to fully reflect the rich diversity of the restaurant and hotel scene in San Francisco and the Bay Area.

The Michelin Guide provides a comprehensive selection and rating, in all categories of comfort and prices. As part of our meticulous and highly confidential evaluation process, Michelin's American inspectors conducted anonymous visits to restaurants and hotels in the Bay Area. Our inspectors are the eyes and ears of the customers, and thus their anonymity is key to ensure that they receive the same treatment as any other guest. The decision to award a star is a collective one, based on the consensus of all inspectors who have visited a particular establishment.

Our company's two founders, Édouard and André Michelin, published the first Michelin Guide in 1900, to provide motorists with practical information about where they could service and repair their cars, and find quality accommodations and a good meal. The star-rating system for outstanding restaurants was introduced in 1926. The same system is used for our American selections.

We sincerely hope that the Michelin Guide San Francisco and the Bay Area 2009 will become your favorite guide to the area's restaurants and hotels.

The Michelin Guide

"This volume was created at the turn of the century and will last at least as long".

This foreword to the very first edition of the MICHELIN Guide, written in 1900, has become famous over the years and the Guide has lived up to the prediction. It is read across the world and the key to its popularity is the consistency in its commitment to its readers, which is based on the following promises.

→ Anonymous Inspections

Our inspectors make anonymous visits to hotels and restaurants to gauge the quality offered to the ordinary customer. They pay their own bill and make no indication of their presence. These visits are supplemented by comprehensive monitoring of information—our readers' comments are one valuable source, and are always taken into consideration.

→ Independence

Our choice of establishments is a completely independent one, made for the benefit of our readers alone. Decisions are discussed by the inspectors and the editor, with the most important decided at the global level. Inclusion in the guide is always free of charge.

→ The Selection

The Guide offers a selection of the best hotels and restaurants in each category of comfort and price. Inclusion in the guides is a commendable award in itself, and defines the establishment among the "best of the best."

How the MICHELIN Guide Works

→ Annual Updates

All practical information, the classifications, and awards, are revised and updated every year to ensure the most reliable information possible.

→ Consistency & Classifications

The criteria for the classifications are the same in all countries covered by the Michelin Guides. Our system is used worldwide and is easy to apply when choosing a restaurant or hotel.

→ The Classifications

We classify our establishments using XXXXX-X and 🏠🏠🏠-🏠 to indicate the level of comfort. The ✿✿✿-✿ specifically designates an award for cuisine, unique from the classification. For hotels and restaurants, a symbol in red suggests a particularly charming spot with unique décor or ambiance.

→ Our Aim

As part of Michelin's ongoing commitment to improving travel and mobility, we do everything possible to make vacations and eating out a pleasure.

Contents

How to use this guide

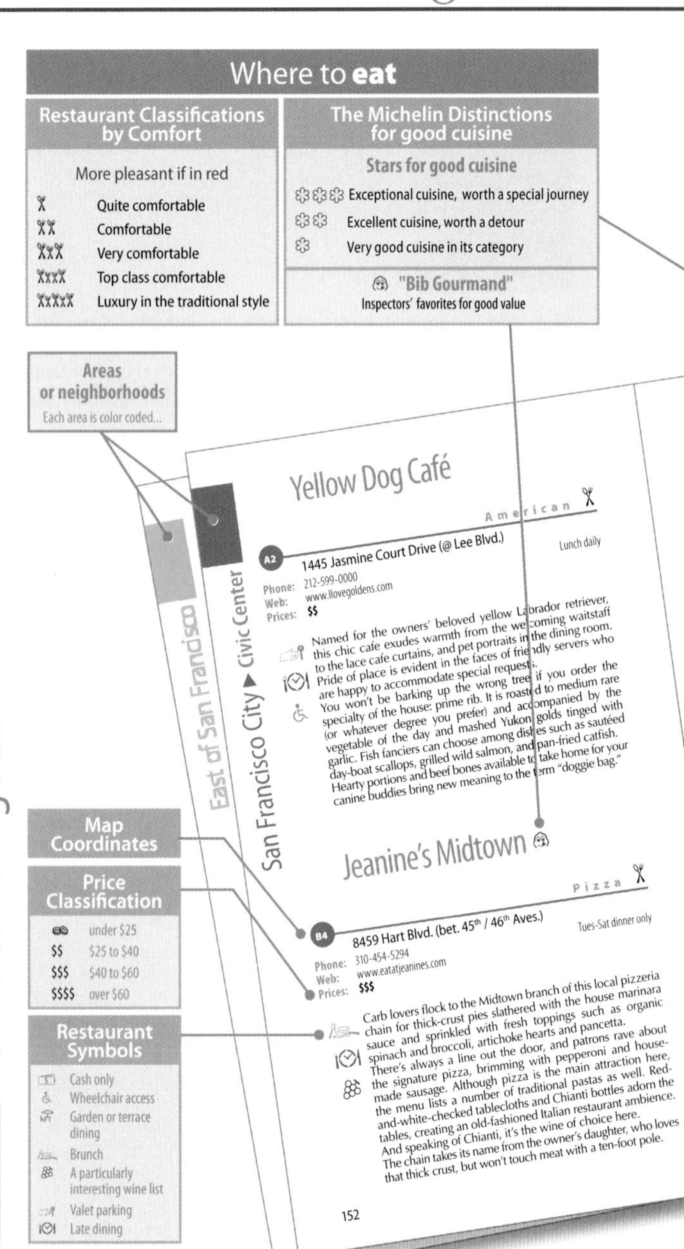

Where to eat
Restaurant Classifications by Comfort
More pleasant if in red
Quite comfortable
Comfortable
Very comfortable
Top class comfortable
Luxury in the traditional style
The Michelin Distinctions for good cuisine
Stars for good cuisine
Exceptional cuisine, worth a special journey
Excellent cuisine, worth a detour
Very good cuisine in its category
"Bib Gourmand"
Inspectors' favorites for good value
Areas or neighborhoods
Each area is color coded...
Map Coordinates
Price Classification
under $25
$$ $25 to $40
$$$ $40 to $60
$$$$ over $60
Restaurant Symbols
Cash only
Wheelchair access
Garden or terrace dining
Brunch
A particularly interesting wine list
Valet parking
Late dining
East of San Francisco
San Francisco City ▶ Civic Center
Yellow Dog Café
American
A2
1445 Jasmine Court Drive (@ Lee Blvd.)
Lunch daily
Phone: 212-599-0000
Web: www.llovegoldens.com
Prices: $$
Named for the owners' beloved yellow Labrador retriever, this chic cafe exudes warmth from the welcoming waitstaff to the lace cafe curtains, and pet portraits in the dining room. Pride of place is evident in the faces of friendly servers who are happy to accommodate special requests.
You won't be barking up the wrong tree if you order the specialty of the house: prime rib. It is roasted to medium rare (or whatever degree you prefer) and accompanied by the vegetable of the day and mashed Yukon golds tinged with garlic. Fish fanciers can choose among dishes such as sautéed day-boat scallops, grilled wild salmon, and pan-fried catfish. Hearty portions and beef bones available to take home for your canine buddies bring new meaning to the term "doggie bag."
Jeanine's Midtown
Pizza
B4
8459 Hart Blvd. (bet. 45th / 46th Aves.)
Tues-Sat dinner only
Phone: 310-454-5294
Web: www.eatatjeanines.com
Prices: $$$
Carb lovers flock to the Midtown branch of this local pizzeria chain for thick-crust pies slathered with the house marinara sauce and sprinkled with fresh toppings such as organic spinach and broccoli, artichoke hearts and pancetta.
There's always a line out the door, and patrons rave about the signature pizza, brimming with pepperoni and house-made sausage. Although pizza is the main attraction here, the menu lists a number of traditional pastas as well. Red-and-white-checked tablecloths and Chianti bottles adorn the tables, creating an old-fashioned Italian restaurant ambience. And speaking of Chianti, it's the wine of choice here. The chain takes its name from the owner's daughter, who loves that thick crust, but won't touch meat with a ten-foot pole.
152

Where to **stay**

Average Prices	Hotel Symbols	Hotel Classifications by Comfort
Prices do not include applicable taxes	149 rooms — No of rooms and suites	More pleasant if in red
$ — under $150	Wheelchair access	Quite comfortable
$$ — $150 to $250	Exercise room	Comfortable
$$$ — $250 to $350	Spa	Very comfortable
$$$$ — over $350	Swimming pool	Top class comfortable
	Equipped conference room	Luxury in the traditional style
Map Coordinates	Pet Friendly	

The Fan Inn

D1

135 Shanghai Road, Oakland

Phone: 650-345-1440 or 888-222-2424
Fax: 650-397-2408
Web: www.superfaninnoakland.com
Prices: $$

45 Rooms
5 Suites

Housed in an Art Deco-era building, the venerable Fan Inn recently underwent a complete facelift. The hotel now fits in with the new generation of sleekly understated hotels offering a Zen-inspired aesthetic, despite its 1930s origins.

A soothing neutral palette runs throughout the property, punctuated with exotic woods, bamboo, and fine fabrics. Off the lobby, the sultry lounge makes a relaxing place for a well-mixed cocktail or a glass of wine.

…e linens and down pillows cater to your comfort, while …reen TVs, DVD players with iPod docking stations, …ireless Internet access satisfy the need for modern …ies. For business travelers, nightstands convert to … tables and credenzas morph into flip-out desks. …printer, fax or scanner? It's just a phone call away. …quest, the hotel will even provide office supplies.

…half of the accommodations here are suites, where … factor ratchets up with marble baths, spacious …s, and fully equipped kitchens. Although the inn …e a restaurant, the nearby blocks hold nearly …ou could want in terms of food, from soup … haute cuisine.

South of San Francisco

419

…a's Palace

Italian

…uther Place (at 30th Street)
…5309
…nyasfabulouspalace.com

Dinner daily

San Francisco City ▶ Civic Center

Home cooked Italian never tasted so good than at this unpretentious little place. The simple décor claims no big-name designers, and while the Murano glass light fixtures are chic and the velveteen-covered chairs are comfortable, this isn't a restaurant where millions of dollars were spent on the interior.

Instead, food is the focus here. The restaurant's name may not be Italian, but it nonetheless serves some of the best pasta in the city, made fresh in-house. Dishes follow the seasons, thus ravioli may be stuffed with fresh ricotta and herbs in summer, and pumpkin in fall. Most everything is liberally dusted with Parmigiano Reggiano, a favorite ingredient of the chef.

For dessert, you'll have to deliberate between the likes of creamy tiramisu, ricotta cheesecake, and homemade gelato. One thing's for sure: you'll never miss your *nonna's* cooking when you eat at Sonya's.

Appetizers
- Crostini alla Toscana
- Antipasti della Casa
- Funghi con Polenta

Entrées
- Lasagna Bolognese
- Gnocchi alla Sorrentina
- Grilled Lamb Chops "Scotta Dita"

Desserts
- Panna Cotta
- Tiramisú
- Bombolini

153

How to use this guide

A brief History of San Francisco

You may well leave your heart in San Francisco as the song says, but be sure to bring your appetite. Cable cars notwithstanding, tasting your way around the city is the best way to sample much of its charm. Take the chill off the morning fog with a bowl of *jook* in Chinatown. Hit a Mission *taqueria* for lunch. Dine on a North Beach *cioppino* as the sun sets. Wherever you go, there's a story and flavor to savor.

GOLD RUSH, SLOW FOOD

By good culinary omen, the Spanish Mexicans who came for faith and fortune first called San Francisco *Yerba Buena* ("good herb") for the aromatic herb they found growing wild in the area. Despite the saintly renaming, fortune—or the hunt for it—prevailed during the 1849 Gold Rush. Gold panned out for some but others took up their pots to feed success. Elegant hotel and family-oriented restaurants sprang up as the rush slowed down and respectable business folk settled in. But dining kept a Wild West edge even as it grew more sophisticated. The gastronomic and other adventures to be had in Italian North Beach or even more exotic Chinatown were magnets for the city's first bohemian intellectuals and artists.

New immigrants nourished the Bay Area as cooks, restaurateurs and food artisans—chocolatiers Ghirardelli and Guittard, cheese and salami makers like the Molinaris. As farmers and marketers, they introduced vegetables and fruits from their homelands. Spanish missionaries had kept vineyards, but under

Brigitta L. House/MICHELIN

these newcomers wine production, well, fermented. The foodways that immigrants adapted have come to define San Francisco as well as feed it. Cioppino, the stew Genoan fishers concocted out of homesickness and whatever else they netted from the Bay, is one of San Francisco's iconic dishes. Sourdough bread, which the Boudin family started making here during the Gold Rush, is a real San Francisco treat.

THE GOOD HERB

Everything yet very little changed in the last century. The 1906 earthquake destroyed much of the old restaurant culture, although many that survived still open their doors to hungry diners (some of the doors are new). Posh theme dining and glamorous restaurants like Ernie's became the rage after Prohibition, and by the 1950s bohemian Beatniks were back in North Beach drinking in the cafe culture. Hippy health joints joined the fray in the '60s and '70s. A decade later, the dot-com boom financed new business, including a plethora of hip clubs and restaurants in SoMa.

The most earth-shattering trend of recent vintage began in the 1970s with idealist Alice Waters, whose radical approach to food recalls that of immigrants a century ago. With its epicenter in Berkeley, this movement's shockwaves reverberate across the Bay Area, the nation and into the future. Between its artisan bread, salami, cheese, chocolate, boutique wineries, farmers' markets and heirloom produce, San Francisco—America's most progressive food town—is still the "good herb."

Where to **eat**

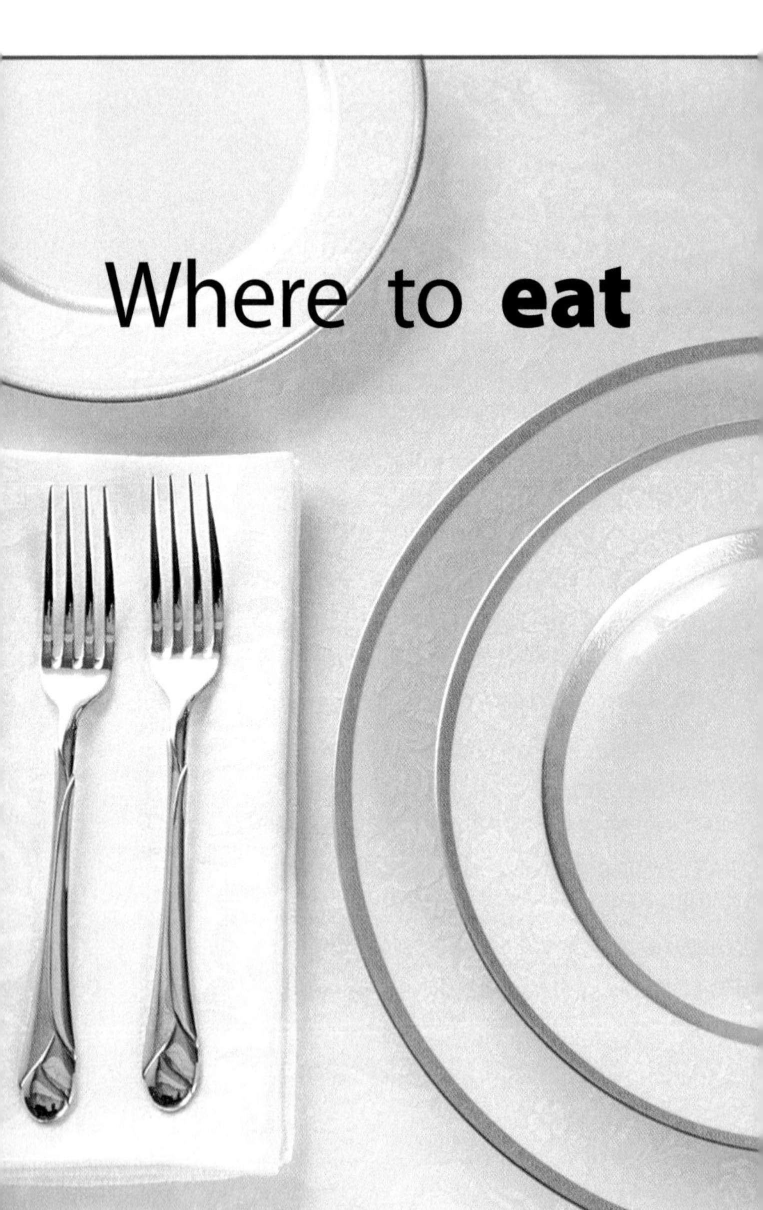

Alphabetical List of Restaurants

Restaurants by Cuisine type

bacar	XX	163
Bar Tartine ☺	X	105
Bay Wolf ☺	XX	185
Bistro Elan	X	226
Bistro Ralph	X	290
Boon Fly Café	X	264
Boulette's Larder	X	72
Boulevard ✿	XXX	164
Cafe La Haye	XX	290
Canteen	X	121
Chez Panisse ✿	XX	189
Citizen Cake	X	54
Coco500	XX	165
Dry Creek Kitchen	XXX	293
El Dorado Kitchen	XX	294
étoile	XXX	268
Farm	XXX	269
Farmhouse Inn & Restaurant ✿	XXX	295
1550 Hyde Cafe & Wine Bar	X	122
Fish & Farm	XX	75
Glen Ellen Inn	XX	294
Harvest Moon Cafe	X	296
Hurley's	XX	271
Jardinière	XXX	56
John Ash & Co.	XX	297
Julia's Kitchen	XX	271
Modern Tea	X	58
MōNO	X	193
Mosaic	XX	302
Murray Circle ✿	XXX	213
Navio	XXX	239
Nopa ☺	X	58
Olema Inn	XX	214
One Market ✿	XX	173
Oola	XX	172
PlumpJack Cafe	XXX	97
Ravenous Café	X	303
Rivoli	XX	195
Sent Sovi	XX	243
Serpentine	X	114
Slow Club ☺	X	114
Solbar	X	279
Syrah	XX	306
the girl & the fig	XX	307
25° Brix	XX	282
Universal Cafe ☺	X	116
Village Pub (The) ✿	XXX	246
Willow Wood Market Cafe	X	309
Wine Spectator Greystone	XX	283
zazu ☺	XX	310
Zinsvalley	X	284

Caribbean

Charanga	X	107

Chinese

Dragon Well	X	93
Eric's	X	46
Fook Yuen Seafood	X	230
Hong Kong Flower Lounge ☺	X	231
Hunan Home's	X	231
Koi Palace	X	234
Mayflower	X	150
Old Mandarin Islamic	X	151
Oriental Pearl	X	126
R & G Lounge	X	128
Shanghai 1930	XX	175
Tai Chi	X	129
Tommy Toy's	XXX	85
Ton Kiang	X	153
Yank Sing ☺	X	178

Contemporary

Restaurant	Comfort	Page
Ame ✿	XXX	161
Barndiva	X	289
Campton Place	XXX	73
Chez TJ ✿	XX	228
Circa	XX	92
Citron	X	188
Coi ✿✿	XXX	136
Conduit	XX	108
Cortez	XX	74
Cyrus ✿✿	XXXX	292
Dining Room at the Ritz-Carlton (The) ✿	XXXX	123
French Laundry (The) ✿✿✿	XXXX	270
Gary Danko ✿	XXX	137
John Bentley's	XX	232
La Toque	XXX	272
Luce	XX	170
Madrona Manor ✿	XX	300
Manresa ✿✿	XXX	237
Marché	XXX	238
Martini House ✿	XXX	274
Masa's ✿	XXXX	127
Meadowood, The Restaurant ✿✿	XXX	275
Mecca	XX	49
Michael Mina ✿✿	XXXX	79
Mustards Grill	X	276
Orson	XX	174
Picco	XX	215
Plumed Horse ✿	XXX	241
Postrio	XXX	81
Range ✿	XX	113
Redd ✿	XX	278
Saint Michael's Alley	X	242
Salt House	XX	174
Siena	XX	279
Silks	XXXX	83
Tanglewood	XX	245
Terra ✿	XX	281
Town Hall	XX	176
Trevese ✿	XXX	248
2223	XX	50
231 Ellsworth	XX	247
Willi's Wine Bar ☺	XX	308

French

Restaurant	Comfort	Page
Angèle	XX	259
Anjou	XX	69
Bistro Aix	X	91
Bistro Jeanty ✿	XX	263
Bistro Liaison	XX	186
Bouchon ✿	XX	265
Café de la Presse	X	73
Café Jacqueline	X	135
Chapeau!	XX	147
Chez Papa	X	107
Clementine	XX	147
El Paseo	XX	208
Fifth Floor ✿	XXXX	167
Fleur de Lys ✿	XXX	76
Fringale	XX	166
Grand Cafe	XX	77
ISA	XX	94
Jeanty at Jack's	XX	77
Jojo ☺	X	192
K & L Bistro ☺	X	298
La Folie ✿	XXX	125
La Forêt	XX	234
Le Charm ☺	X	169
Left Bank	XX	211
Le Papillon	XXX	235
Mirepoix ☺	X	301
South Park Cafe ☺	X	176

Fusion

Restaurant	Comfort	Page
Anzu	XX	69
Asia de Cuba	XX	71
bushi-tei	XX	91
Café KATi	X	92
Chaya Brasserie	XX	165
Pres A Vi	XX	97
Sutro's	XXX	153

Gastropub

Restaurant	Comfort	Page
Alembic (The)	X	44
Wood Tavern	XX	199

Greek

Dio Deka	XX	229
Evvia	XX	230
Kokkari Estiatorio	XX	139

Indian

Ajanta	X	185
Dosa	X	109
Gaylord	XX	210
Indian Oven	X	56
Indus Village	X	192
Junnoon	XX	233
Mantra	XX	236
Udupi Palace	X	197

International

Celadon	X	266
Foreign Cinema	XX	110
Kenwood	XX	298
Lalime's	XX	193
Underwood	X	307
Wappo Bar Bistro	X	283

Italian

Acquerello	XXX	120
Albona	XX	134
Americano	XX	160
Antica Trattoria	X	121
Aperto	X	104
A 16	XX	90
Bacco	XX	45
Bellanico	X	186
Beretta	X	105
Bistro Don Giovanni	XX	262
Caffè Verbena	XX	187
Cena Luna	XX	291
Cook St. Helena	X	267
Cucina	X	207
Cucina Paradiso	X	291
Delfina	X	108
Della Santina's	XX	293
Dopo	X	190
Farina	X	109
Florio	XX	93
Fork	XX	209
Frantoio	XX	209
Incanto	XX	48
Local	XX	170
North Beach Restaurant	XX	140
Oliveto	XX	194
Palio d'Asti	XX	80
Pasta Moon	XX	240
Perbacco	XX	80
Poggio	XX	215
Quince	XXX	98
Risibisi	XX	304
Rose Pistola	XX	141
Santi	XX	305
Scala's Bistro	XX	83
Sociale	XX	99
SPQR	XX	99
Sugo	X	306
Tommaso's	X	141
Trattoria Contadina	X	142
Tra Vigne	XX	280
Venticello	XX	130
Vin Antico	XX	218
Vivande	X	101

Japanese

Blowfish Sushi	X	106
Domo	X	55
Ebisu	X	148
Grandeho's Kamekyo	X	47
Hana	X	296
Hiro's	X	297
Kabuto	X	148
Kaygetsu	XX	233
Kiji	X	110
Koo	X	149
Kyo-ya	XX	168
Mifune	X	96
Naomi Sushi	X	238
O Chamé	X	194
Osake	X	302
Sakae	X	243
Sanraku	X	82

Latin American

Mediterranean

Mexican

Moroccan

Persian

Peruvian

Pizza

Portuguese

Seafood

Nick's Cove	X	212
Pesce	X	128
Plouf	X	81
Sea Salt	X	196
Spinnaker	XX	216
Tadich Grill	X	84
Waterbar	XX	177
Willi's Seafood & Raw Bar ☺	XX	308
Yabbies Coastal Kitchen	X	130

Southwestern

Loco's	X	273

Spanish

Bocadillos	X	72
Cascal	X	227
César	X	188
Iberia	XX	232
Laïola	X	95
Sabor of Spain	X	216
Zuzu	X	284

Steakhouse

ACME Chophouse	XX	160
Alexander's Steakhouse	XXX	225
Arcadia	XXX	225
Boca	XX	206
Cole's Chop House	XXX	267
Epic Roasthouse	XX	166
Harris'	XXX	124
Lark Creek Steak	XX	169
Press	XXX	277

Thai

Khan Toke Thai House	X	149
Manora's Thai Cuisine	X	171
Rin's Thai	X	303
Thep Phanom	X	62

Vegan

Café Gratitude	X	187
Millennium	XX	78

Vegetarian

Greens	X	94
Lettüs Café Organic	X	95
Ubuntu	XX	282

Vietnamese

Ana Mandara	XX	134
Annaliên	X	260
Bong Su	XX	163
Le Colonial	XX	78
Pagolac	X	59
Slanted Door (The) ☺	XX	84
Tamarine	XX	245
Vanessa's Bistro ☺	XX	198
Xanh ☺	XX	249

Cuisine by Areas

SAN FRANCISCO

Castro District

American

Burgermeister	X	45
Home	X	48

Asian

EOS	X	46

Chinese

Eric's	X	46

Contemporary

Mecca	XX	49
2223	XX	50

Gastropub

Alembic (The)	X	44

Italian

Bacco	XX	45
Incanto ☺	XX	48

Japanese

Grandeho's Kamekyo	X	47

Mexican

La Corneta	X	49

Peruvian

Fresca	XX	47

Seafood

Anchor Oyster Bar	X	44

Civic Center

American

rnm ☺	XX	61
Sauce ☺	XX	61
1300 on Fillmore	XXX	63

Asian

Poleng ☺	X	60

Barbecue

Memphis Minnie's	X	57

Brazilian

Espetus Churrascaria ☺	X	55

Californian

Citizen Cake	X	54
Jardinière	XXX	56
Modern Tea	X	58
Nopa ☺	X	58

Indian

Indian Oven	X	56

Japanese

Domo	X	55
Sebo	X	62
Yoshi's	XX	63

Mediterranean

Absinthe	XX	54
paul k	XX	60
Zuni Café	XX	64

Pizza

Little Star Pizza	X	57
Patxi's	X	59

Thai

Thep Phanom	X	62

Vietnamese

Pagolac	X	59

Financial District

American

Rotunda	XX	82

Californian

Boulette's Larder	X	72
Fish & Farm	XX	75

Chinese

Tommy Toy's	XXX	85

Contemporary

Campton Place	XXX	73
Cortez	XX	74
Michael Mina ✿✿	XXXX	79
Postrio	XXX	81
Silks	XXXX	83

French

Anjou	XX	69
Café de la Presse	X	73
Fleur de Lys ✿	XXX	76
Grand Cafe	XX	77
Jeanty at Jack's	XX	77

Fusion

Anzu	XX	69
Asia de Cuba	XX	71

Italian

Palio d'Asti	XX	80
Perbacco ☺	XX	80
Scala's Bistro	XX	83

Japanese

Sanraku	X	82

Mexican

Colibrí ☺	XX	74

Seafood

Aqua ✿✿	XXX	70
Bar Crudo	X	71
Farallon	XXX	75
Plouf	X	81
Tadich Grill	X	84

Contemporary

Dining Room at the Ritz-Carlton (The) ✿	XXXX	123
Masa's ✿	XXXX	127

French

La Folie ✿	XXX	125

Italian

Acquerello ✿	XXX	120
Antica Trattoria	X	121
Venticello ☺	XX	130

Japanese

Sushi Groove	X	129

Mediterranean

Frascati	XX	124
Luella	XX	126

Seafood

Pesce	X	128
Yabbies Coastal Kitchen	X	130

Steakhouse

Harris'	XXX	124

North Beach

American

Bix	XX	135

Asian

house (the)	X	138

Basque

Iluna Basque	X	138
Piperade	XX	140

Contemporary

Coi ✿✿	XXX	136
Gary Danko ✿	XXX	137

French

Café Jacqueline	X	135

Greek

Kokkari Estiatorio ☺	XX	139

Italian

Albona	XX	134
North Beach Restaurant	XX	140
Rose Pistola	XX	141
Tommaso's ☺	X	141
Trattoria Contadina	X	142

Persian

Maykadeh ☺	X	139

Vietnamese

Ana Mandara	XX	134

Richmond & Sunset

American

Park Chow	X	151

Asian

Namu ☺	X	150

Burmese

Burma Superstar ☺	X	146

Chinese

Mayflower	X	150
Old Mandarin Islamic	X	151
Ton Kiang	X	153

French

Chapeau!	XX	147
Clementine	XX	147

Fusion

Sutro's	XXX	153

Japanese

Ebisu	X	148
Kabuto	X	148
Koo	X	149
Sushi Bistro	X	152

Mediterranean

Troya	X	154

Moroccan

Aziza	XX	146

Pizza

Pizzetta 211	X	152

Thai

Khan Toke Thai House	X	149

South of Market

American

Jack Falstaff	XXX	168
TWO ☺	XX	177
XYZ	XX	178

Asian

Azie	XX	162

Australian

South Food + Wine Bar	XX	175

Californian

bacar	XX	163
Boulevard ✿	XXX	164
Coco500	XX	165
One Market ✿	XX	173
Oola	XX	172

Chinese

Shanghai 1930	XX	175
Yank Sing ☺	X	178

Contemporary

Ame ✿	XXX	161
Luce	XX	170
Orson	XX	174
Salt House	XX	174
Town Hall	XX	176

French

Fifth Floor ✿	XXXX	167
Fringale	XX	166
Le Charm ☺	X	169
South Park Cafe ☺	X	176

Fusion

Chaya Brasserie	XX	165

Italian

Americano	XX	160
Local	XX	170

Sonoma County

Starred Restaurants

Within the selection we offer you, some restaurants deserve to be highlighted for their particularly good cuisine. When giving one, two or three Michelin stars, there are a number of things that we judge, including the quality of the ingredients, the technical skill and flair that goes into their preparation, the blend and clarity of flavors, and the balance of the menu. Just as important is the ability to produce excellent cooking time and again. We make as many visits as we need, so that our readers can be sure of quality and consistency.

A two- or three-star restaurant has to offer something very special in its cuisine; a real element of creativity, originality or "personality" that sets it apart from the rest. Three stars – our highest award – are given to the very best restaurants, where the whole dining experience is superb.

Cuisine in any style, modern or traditional, may be eligible for a star. Because we apply the same independent standards everywhere, the awards have become benchmarks of reliability and excellence in more than 20 European countries, particularly in France, where we have awarded stars for almost 80 years, and where the expression "Now that's real three-star quality!" has entered into the language.

The awarding of a star is based solely on the quality of the cuisine.

Exceptional cuisine, worth a special journey.

One always eats here extremely well, sometimes superbly. Distinctive dishes are precisely executed, using superlative ingredients.

French Laundry (The)	XXXX	270

Excellent cuisine, worth a detour.

Skillfully and carefully crafted dishes of outsanding quality.

Aqua	XXX	70
Coi	XXX	136
Cyrus	XXXX	292
Manresa	XXX	237
Meadowood, The Restaurant	XXX	275
Michael Mina	XXXX	79

A very good restaurant in its category.

A place offering cuisine prepared to a consistently high standard.

Acquerello	XXX	120
Ame	XXX	161
Auberge du Soleil	XXX	261
Bistro Jeanty	XX	263
Bouchon	XX	265
Boulevard	XXX	164
Chez Panisse	XX	189
Chez TJ	XX	228
Dining Room at the Ritz-Carlton (The)	XXXX	123
Farmhouse Inn & Restaurant	XXX	295
Fifth Floor	XXXX	167
Fleur de Lys	XXX	76
Gary Danko	XXX	137
La Folie	XXX	125
Madrona Manor	XX	300
Martini House	XXX	274
Masa's	XXXX	127
Murray Circle	XXX	213
One Market	XX	173
Plumed Horse	XXX	241
Range	XX	113
Redd	XX	278
Terra	XX	281
Trevese	XXX	248
Village Pub (The)	XXX	246

Bib Gourmand

This symbol indicates our inspector's favorites for good value. For $40 or less, you can enjoy two courses and a glass of wine or a dessert (not including tax or gratuity).

Restaurant	Comfort	Page
Aperto	X	104
A 16	XX	90
BarBersQ	XX	262
Bar Tartine	X	105
Bay Wolf	XX	185
Bellanico	X	186
Betelnut Pejiu Wu	X	90
Burma Superstar	X	146
Cafe Gibraltar	XX	226
Cena Luna	XX	291
Colibrí	XX	74
Cook St. Helena	X	267
Cucina Paradiso	X	291
Delfina	X	108
Espetus Churrascaria	X	55
Farina	X	109
Fork	XX	209
Hong Kong Flower Lounge	X	231
Incanto	XX	48
Insalata's	XX	210
Jojo	X	192
Junnoon	XX	233
K & L Bistro	X	298
Kokkari Estiatorio	XX	139
Le Charm	X	169
Mamacita	X	96
Market	X	273
Maykadeh	X	139
Mirepoix	X	301
Namu	X	150
Nopa	X	58
Oliveto	XX	194
Osake	X	302
Perbacco	XX	80
Poleng	X	60
Risibisi	XX	304
rnm	XX	61
Sakae	X	243
Sauce	XX	61
Slanted Door (The)	XX	84
Slow Club	X	114
Sociale	XX	99
South Park Cafe	X	176
Tamarindo	X	197
Tokyo Go Go	X	115
Tommaso's	X	141
TWO	XX	177
Universal Cafe	X	116
Vanessa's Bistro	XX	198
Venticello	XX	130
Willi's Seafood & Raw Bar	XX	308
Willi's Wine Bar	XX	308
Xanh	XX	249
Yank Sing	X	178
zazu	XX	310

ROEDERER
en 1776

Where to eat for less than $25

← 000
WAYNE
TOW-AWAY
NO STOPPING
4 TO 6 PM
NO PARKING
ANY TIME
DIM SUM
MICHELIN

Where to have brunch

Restaurant	Comfort	Page
Absinthe	XX	54
Adagia	XX	184
Ad Hoc	X	259
Americano	XX	160
Angèle	XX	259
Anzu	XX	69
Aperto ☺	X	104
Arcadia	XXX	225
Asia de Cuba	XX	71
Barndiva	X	289
Bar Tartine ☺	X	105
Beretta	X	105
Bistro Liaison	XX	186
Boon Fly Café	X	264
Buckeye Roadhouse	XX	206
bushi-tei	XX	91
Café de la Presse	X	73
Campton Place	XXX	73
Canteen	X	121
Chez Papa	X	107
Circa	XX	92
Citizen Cake	X	54
Citron	X	188
Colibrí ☺	XX	74
Consuelo	X	229
Dio Deka	XX	229
Dosa	X	109
Dry Creek Kitchen	XXX	293
El Dorado Kitchen	XX	294
Epic Roasthouse	XX	166
Farina ☺	X	109
Farm	XXX	269
Fook Yuen Seafood	X	230
Foreign Cinema	XX	110
Fresca	XX	47
Gaylord	XX	210
Grand Cafe	XX	77
Greens	X	94
Home	X	48
Hong Kong Flower Lounge ☺	X	231
Insalata's ☺	XX	210
Koi Palace	X	234
La Forêt	XX	234
Lark Creek Inn	XXX	211
LaSalette	XX	299
Left Bank	XX	211
Lettüs Café Organic	X	95
Liberty Cafe & Bakery	X	111
Local	XX	170
Luce	XX	170
LuLu	X	171
Maverick	X	111
Mayflower	X	150
Modern Tea	X	58
Mosaic	XX	302
Murray Circle ✿	XXX	213
Namu ☺	X	150
Navio	XXX	239
Nick's Cove	X	212
Olema Inn	XX	214
Oriental Pearl	X	126
Paradise Bay	XX	214
Park Chow	X	151
Pres A Vi	XX	97
Redd ✿	XX	278
Rose Pistola	XX	141
Saint Michael's Alley	X	242
Sea Salt	X	196
Siena	XX	279
Slow Club ☺	X	114
Solbar	X	279
South Food + Wine Bar	XX	175
Spinnaker	XX	216
SPQR	XX	99

Where to have a late dinner

San Francisco

Castro District

Alembic (The)	X	44

Civic Center

Absinthe	XX	54
Nopa ☺	X	58
Poleng ☺	X	60
Sauce ☺	XX	61
1300 on Fillmore	XXX	63
Zuni Café	XX	64

Financial District

Asia de Cuba	XX	71
Bar Crudo	X	71
Bocadillos	X	72
Colibrí ☺	XX	74
Scala's Bistro	XX	83

Marina District

Circa	XX	92

Mission District

Beretta	X	105
Blowfish Sushi	X	106
Pancho Villa Taqueria	X	112
Taqueria Guadalajara	X	115

North Beach

North Beach Restaurant	XX	140

Richmond & Sunset

Sushi Bistro	X	152

South of Market

Jack Falstaff	XXX	168
Oola	XX	172
Orson	XX	174
Salt House	XX	174
South Food + Wine Bar	XX	175

East of San Francisco

À Côté	XX	184
César	X	188
Fonda	XX	191

North of San Francisco

Left Bank	XX	211
Spinnaker	XX	216
Sushi Ran	X	217

South of San Francisco

Cascal	X	227
Tanglewood	XX	245

Wine Country

Napa Valley

Bouchon ✿	XX	265
Hurley's	XX	271
Solbar	X	279

Sonoma County

Barndiva	X	289

Phillip H. Coblentz / SFCVB

San Francisco City

Castro District

Cole Valley - Haight Ashbury - Noe Valley

Epicenter of gay San Francisco, the Castro *(bounded roughly by Market, 22nd, Douglass, and Church Sts.)* hums with energy night and day along its central commercial corridor, **Castro Street**. This thoroughfare is also home to the 1922 **Castro Theatre**, San Francisco's grandest movie palace, along with a plethora of bookstores, bars, shops, and cafes. A universal symbol of gay pride, the rainbow flag is everywhere; it flies over the streets and adorns the district's vibrantly painted Victorian houses. Culinary styles as diverse as the neighborhood add spice to the Castro's restaurant scene.

The once quiet suburb called Eureka Valley adopted its present character in the 1970's, when enterprising gay designers began purchasing the Castro's 19th-century Victorians at rock-bottom prices and fixing them up. In 1977, residents succeeded in electing one of their own, Harvey Milk, to the city's Board of Supervisors. Slain by fellow supervisor Dan White the following year, Milk remains a revered figure for being the first openly gay elected official in U.S. history. The new biographical movie *Milk*, starring Sean Penn as Harvey Milk, wrapped up filming in San Francisco in early 2008, and is planned to be released in the fall.

HAIGHT ASHBURY

Although more than three decades have passed since the Summer of Love, a 1960's countercultural ethos still clings to the Haight, which borders **Haight Street** between Central Avenue and Stanyan Street, just west of the Castro. The stretch of Haight Street between Central Avenue and Stanyan Street, known as the **Upper Haight**, is packed with vintage boutiques and coffee houses, most of which cater to hip twenty-somethings with money to spend.

Near the southwest corner of **Golden Gate Park, Cole Valley** is a quiet upscale enclave known for its mom-and-pop bakeries, coffeehouses, and restaurants. Though Cole Valley is only a short walk from the Haight, you're more likely to see hybrid cars than tie-dyed shirts here.

NOE VALLEY

Once land used for cattle-ranching and sheep-grazing, the Victorian cottage-lined streets of neighboring Noe Valley are now largely populated by the stroller set. The area's colorful commercial thoroughfare **24th Street** *(between Dolores & Diamond Sts.)* overflows with designer clothing shops, bookstores, and wine merchants.

Brigitta L. House / MICHELIN

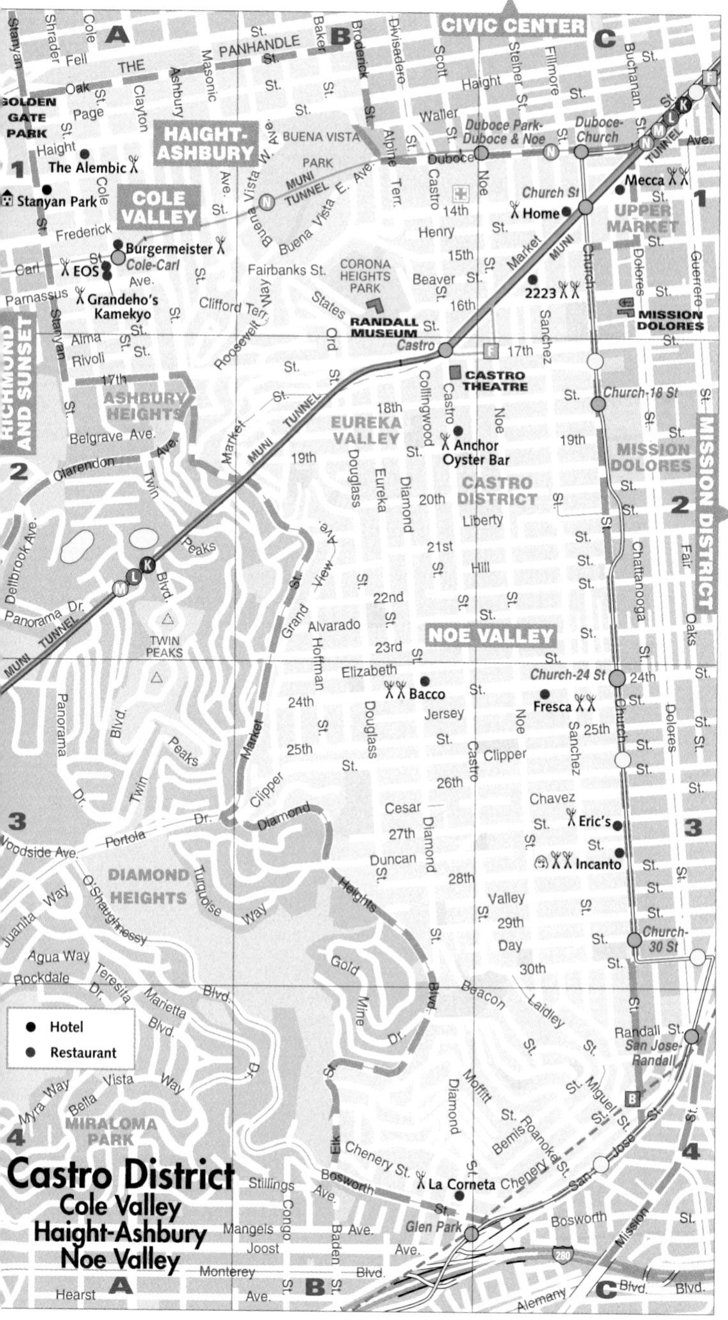
Castro District
Cole Valley
Haight-Ashbury
Noe Valley
Hotel
Restaurant
CIVIC CENTER
HAIGHT-ASHBURY
COLE VALLEY
UPPER MARKET
EUREKA VALLEY
CASTRO DISTRICT
NOE VALLEY
MISSION DOLORES
ASHBURY HEIGHTS
DIAMOND HEIGHTS
MIRALOMA PARK
GOLDEN GATE PARK
RICHMOND AND SUNSET
MISSION DISTRICT
THE PANHANDLE
BUENA VISTA PARK
CORONA HEIGHTS PARK
RANDALL MUSEUM
CASTRO THEATRE
MISSION DOLORES
TWIN PEAKS
The Alembic
Stanyan Park
Burgermeister
EOS
Grandeho's Kamekyo
Mecca
Home
2223
Anchor Oyster Bar
Bacco
Fresca
Eric's
Incanto
La Corneta
Duboce Park-Duboce & Noe
Duboce-Church
Church St
Cole-Carl
Castro
Church-18 St
Church-24 St
Church-30 St
San Jose-Randall
Glen Park
MUNI TUNNEL

The Alembic

Gastropub

A1

1725 Haight St. (bet. Cole & Shrader Sts.)

Phone: 415-666-0822 — Mon – Thu dinner only
Web: www.alembicbar.com — Fri – Sun lunch & dinner
Prices: $$

Local foods and fine moods characterize this tavern in the heart of the Upper Haight, where boards salvaged from the old Kezar Stadium top the bar, bare filament light bulbs hang above fat padded barstools, and mustard yellow colors the walls.

Kissed with local products, the changing menu takes small plates seriously. Moist bavette steak may couple with cumin-spiced carrots and bright, tangy chimichurri; fava beans, tomato, and shiso complement octopus carpaccio.

Over the bar, blackboards list artisanal, small-batch Bourbon, Scotch, and Rye—let the knowledgeable staff educate you on the selections. Talented bartenders mix creative cocktails, like the Boutonniere (Glentrothes special reserve Scotch with Nocino Della Cristina and a dash of bitters).

Anchor Oyster Bar

Seafood 

B2

579 Castro St. (bet. 18th & 19th Sts.)

Phone: 415-431-3990 — Mon – Sat lunch & dinner
Web: www.anchoroysterbar.com — Sun dinner only
Prices: $$

A neighborhood fixture since 1977, this pristine little oyster bar is a pearl in the eclectic sea of the Castro. Bivalve lovers pack the long marble-topped counter and the few stainless-steel tables like sardines, while a trophy marlin hanging on the wall surveys the scene.

You don't have to dive very deep to find good oysters here; a board above the bar announces the varieties along with the specials of the day. Served over a bowl of ice, fresh-caught oysters might include briny Beausoleil or Kuschi, depending on the season. Slurping them down is half the fun; the other half is starters such as milky New England clam chowder, seafood cocktails, or the abundant salads. Dungeness crab dishes, pasta, and steamed shellfish are specialties of the house.

Bacco

B3 — Italian XX

737 Diamond St. (bet. Elizabeth & 24th Sts.)

Phone: 415-282-4969 — Dinner daily
Web: www.baccosf.com
Prices: $$

From the staff to Chef/owner Vincenzo Cucco, who has presided over the kitchen since Bacco opened in 1993, everyone takes pride in this Noe Valley trattoria. Many regulars are greeted by name as they enter the warm yellow dining space, where arched openings, terra-cotta tile floors and Italian ceramics dish up a Tuscan feel.
Homemade potato gnocchi with fontina and black truffles, and prosciutto- and arugula-stuffed chicken breast served with creamy mashed potatoes and wilted Swiss chard are sure to please—but if you're not in a hurry, it's well worth the 30-minute wait for the made-to-order risotto of the day. Come Sunday through Thursday evening for the three-course prix-fixe option that allows diners to mix and match any of the menu items.

Burgermeister

A1 — American X

86 Carl St. (at Cole St.)

Phone: 415-566-1274 — Lunch & dinner daily
Web: www.burgermeistersf.com
Prices: ⊜

This family-owned Cole Valley burger joint is known for its big, juicy half-pound patties, made from humanely raised Niman Ranch beef. Toppings run from the expected, American cheese and chili, to the surprising, including sliced mango or grilled pineapple. Even the crisp fries are kicked up with roasted garlic, chili, or spices. Sure, there are other fine choices on the menu, such as Philly cheesesteak, fish & chips, or grilled chicken, but most come here for a burger. Vegetarians may indulge in a portobello burger with roasted red pepper mayo.
Beyond these offerings, Burgermeister has gone green with all natural products, bio-degradable packaging, and recyclable materials. Look for their other locations in the Castro, North Beach, and Daly City.

EOS

A s i a n

A1

901 Cole St. (at Carl St.)

Phone: 415-566-3063 — Dinner daily
Web: www.eossf.com
Prices: **$$**

The first decision you'll have to make at this Cole Valley corner restaurant and bar (near Haight Ashbury) is whether to eat in the celadon-green dining room, or at the seductive wine bar next door.

If you choose the former, plan to order several small plates to share. Spicy pan-fried Chinese long beans; Madras curry potato cakes with spiced pineapple and pink-peppercorn chutney; and hazelnut-crusted local halibut typify the selections onthe changing menu.

If you prefer to dine in the wine bar, you'll have access to the restaurant's menu, plus the same list of wines—which you can order by the glass, the taste, or the flight.

Served only from Sunday - Thursday, come indulge in happy hour specials like the $1 oysters and $5 wine and sake cocktails.

Eric's

C h i n e s e

C3

1500 Church St. (at 27th St.)

Phone: 415-282-0919 — Lunch & dinner daily
Web: www.erics.ypguides.net
Prices:

Eric's in Noe Valley dishes up fresh and flavorful Chinese cuisine at rock-bottom prices, so it is no wonder there is often a wait (they do not take reservations). Large framed mirrors ornament the yellow walls of the small, homey dining room, where lunch specials, including soup and green tea, are under $10. Dinner items are comparably priced, and portions are generous.

Hunan and Mandarin specialties share the menu with other favorites, and none contain MSG. Dishes include fried crabmeat Rangoon, triangular dumplings stuffed with crab and cream cheese, served with hot Chinese mustard and sweet-and-sour sauce; and rainbow fish with bell peppers and pine nuts in a white garlic sauce.

Fresca

Peruvian

3945 24th St. (bet. Noe & Sanchez Sts.)

Phone: 415-695-0549 Lunch & dinner daily
Web: www.frescasf.com
Prices: $$

Fresca's airy dining room, sun-yellow walls, arched ceilings and skylights emanate warmth. The front bar draws cocktail aficionados for Pisco Sours and other Latin libations, while the back of the restaurant highlights the raw bar and open kitchen.
The menu celebrates the cooking of Peru with the likes of *trucha*, skillet-roasted rainbow trout topped with caramelized tiger prawns; or pulled chicken stew with *aji amarillo* cream, Yukon potatoes, hard-boiled eggs, and steamed rice. Seafood starters include raw oysters and an array of ceviches, with combinations available.
For a Fresca fix elsewhere in the city, visit the restaurant's two other locations in the Pacific Heights and West Portal neighborhoods.

Grandeho's Kamekyo

Japanese

943 Cole St. (bet. Carl St. & Parnassus Ave.)

Phone: 415-759-5693 Tue – Fri lunch & dinner
Web: N/A Sat – Mon dinner only
Prices: $$

Grandeho's original location has satisfied Haight-Ashbury sushi lovers since 1996. A polished light wood sushi bar anchors the intimate dining rooms, while golden walls and a lavender ceiling warmly accent the minimalist décor.
Top quality fish make big waves here, and the warm, freshly-steamed sushi rice proves that the chefs take their craft seriously. Rather than limiting yourself, consider indulging in the many other fine examples of Japanese cuisine on the menu. Tempura and teriyaki share the limelight with udon or soba noodle bowls and wholesome hot pots, while Bento box specials offer economical samplings at both lunch and dinner. Several vegetarian choices are also available.
A sister restaurant resides in North Beach at 2721 Hyde Street.

Home

American

C1

2100 Market St. (at Church St.)

Phone: 415-503-0333
Web: www.home-sf.com
Prices: $$

Mon – Fri dinner only
Sat – Sun lunch & dinner

You'll find all the comforts of Home at the bustling intersection of Church and Market streets in the heart of the Castro District. Red banquettes and black lacquer chairs suggest a diner décor, while a roaring fire in the enclosed patio cuts the chill on those foggy San Francisco days. Walls of windows allow some of the best people-watching in the city.

Comfort food is key here, with the likes of Niman Ranch pot roast, buttermilk biscuits and gravy, and roasted Fulton Valley Farms chicken satisfying more than just hunger pangs. A peanut-butter-cup milkshake makes a perfect end to a meal or a night on the town (Home is open daily until midnight). Satisfy your wallet, too, with the three-course prix-fixe Early Bird Special (served from 5 to 6:00pm).

Incanto

Italian

C3

1550 Church St. (at Duncan St.)

Phone: 415-641-4500
Web: www.incanto.biz
Prices: $$

Wed – Mon dinner only

For nationally acclaimed Chef Chris Cosentino, good food is a family tradition—one that he now passes on to his patrons. The chef, who specializes in cured meats made in-house, doesn't leave any part of the animal unused. That means that the daily menu might feature pig's trotters with foie gras, bacon, and roasted figs; or beef tongue ravioli with Chianti brown butter.

A small room houses a collection of mainly Italian wines, many unfamiliar to all but the most dedicate oenophile. To help guests remember some of the obscure labels, a paper tag is slipped around the stem of all wines served by the glass.

Cosentino recently opened Boccalone Salumeria in the Ferry Building, featuring the chef's cured meats, fresh sausages, and cooked specialties.

La Corneta

Mexican 

B4

2834 Diamond St. (bet. Bosworth & Chenery Sts.)

Phone: 415-469-8757 — Lunch & dinner daily
Web: www.lacorneta.com
Prices:

The quaint neighborhood of Glen Park is not where one expects to find a great taqueria, yet here it is. Dishes are assembled fast at the walk-up counter, where meals are tailored to your liking, as the servers pile on and skillfully wrap the fresh, top-quality ingredients. The usual suspects appear on the large menu board in the airy dining room: tacos, nachos, burritos, and quesadillas—each with myriad variations. A word to the wise: anything described with the word "super" is a meal in itself. The super chicken taco, for example, is strictly a knife-and-fork operation—two corn tortillas brimming with beans, rice, stewed chicken, cheese, sour cream, and salsa.

A cash-only affair, La Corneta transports tummies to the multi-cultural heart of the Mission.

Mecca

Contemporary 

C1

2029 Market St. (bet. Dolores & 14th Sts.)

Phone: 415-621-7000 — Tue – Sun dinner only
Web: www.sfmecca.com
Prices: $$$

Mecca abounds with nightclub flair, from the oval bar in the middle room of this dim, 5,000-square-foot, industrial-chic space—where Castro's cool stay to drink, socialize and people-watch—to the sleek dining room with its spotlit black-and-white photographs, well-spaced tables and cozy curving booths. In June 2007, a fire sparked the renovation of Mecca, making it as much a nightclub as it is a restaurant.

The menu is inspired by regional American ingredients and the dishes are aimed to entice and satisfy. A selection of fresh oysters, Sonoma lamb rack, Dungeness crab, and local Petrale sole are just a sampling of what you might find on your plate. Be sure to order a side of satisfying Mecca fries, drizzled with truffled olive oil.

2223

Contemporary XX

C1

2223 Market St. (bet. Noe & Sanchez Sts.)

Phone: 415-431-0692
Web: www.2223restaurant.com
Prices: **$$**

Mon – Sat dinner only
Sun lunch & dinner

A slew of creative cocktails starts off an evening at 2223. Then it's on to favorites like herb-roasted Fulton Valley chicken and grilled double-cut pork chops, or perhaps chunks of tandoori-spiced leg of lamb served with grilled eggplant and summer squash atop a garlicky chickpea purée. Chef/owner Melinda Randolph lets the season dictate her menu; then she adds a dash of Asian, a pinch of Californian, and a soupçon of French influences.

Locals flock here for Sunday brunch, when they are treated to the likes of warm cinnamon rolls with toasted pecans, and a house-made chorizo and pepperjack scramble. Francophiles should drop by this honey-colored dining room on the *quatorze juillet* to partake of the prix-fixe Bastille Day tasting menu.

Good food without spending a fortune? Look for the Bib Gourmand ☺.

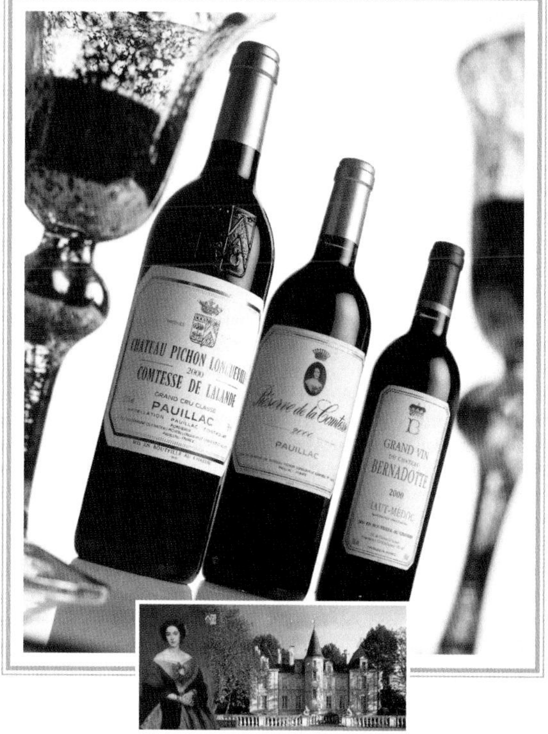

CHATEAU PICHON LONGUEVILLE
2000
COMTESSE DE LALANDE
GRAND CRU CLASSE
PAUILLAC
Réserve de la Comtesse
PAUILLAC
GRAND VIN
BERNADOTTE
2000

Civic Center

Hayes Valley - Lower Haight - Tenderloin

San Francisco's "town center" remains the sole remnant of a 1905 plan to remake San Francisco according to the principles of the City Beautiful movement—replete with wide boulevards and grand monuments that borrowed heavily from the aesthetics of the then contemporary Beaux-Arts movement. Among the movement's crowning achievements, San Francisco's magnificent **City Hall** stands out with its sparkling gold-leaf dome. This area is also home to several of the city's grandest performance spaces and cultural institutions, including the **San Francisco War Memorial and Performing Arts Center**, the gleaming granite **San Francisco Public Library**, and the stellar **Asian Art Museum**, home to one of the largest collections in the western world devoted exclusively to Asian art.

In 1945, Civic Center played its own role in world history. From April to June of that year, the United Nations convened in the War Memorial Opera House, and the UN Charter was signed in the **Herbst Theatre**. That said, Civic Center is not much of a neighborhood per se—its huge buildings and vast plazas (bounded by Market St., Van Ness Ave., and Golden Gate Ave.) did not leave much room for residential development, which mainly happened on its periphery.

Brigitta L. House/MICHELIN

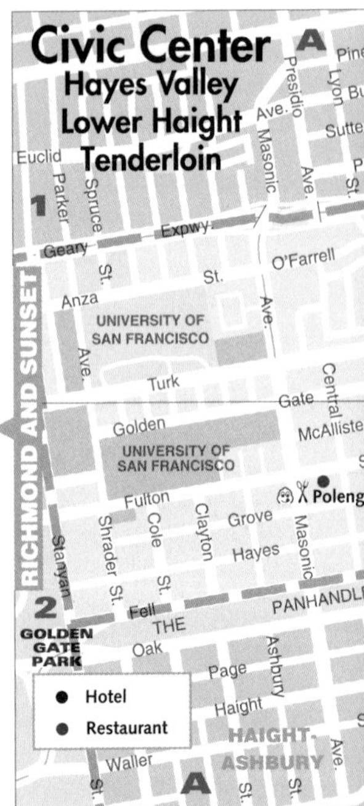

Civic Center has a split personality; during the day it's the bustling hub of local government, while at night it comes alive with chicly clad concert goers who flock to the area's popular restaurants and theaters.

TENDERLOIN

The most urban neighborhood within the city, the Tenderloin is located north of Civic Center in an area bounded by Geary, Jones, Mission, and Van Ness streets. Dubbed the Tenderloin (a reference to bygone days when policemen were paid more to cover the dangerous streets, thus they could afford more expensive cuts of meat), this area has a long and perilous reputation. Still there are some culinary gems to be discovered in the 'Loin, if you know where to look.

HAYES VALLEY

Just a few blocks west of Civic Center, Hayes Valley—centering on Hayes Street between Franklin and Laguna streets—profited in a way from the 1989 earthquake. After the Central Freeway was torn down due to damage by the quake, this once seedy section of the city morphed into a pedestrian-friendly neighborhood. Today Hayes Valley is chock-a-block with cafes, clothing boutiques, and funky art galleries. Keep in mind that most restaurants here require reservations between 6:00 P.M. and 7:30 P.M., peak hours for pre-performance dinners.

Bordering Hayes Valley on the west, the **Lower Haight**, as the area of Haight Ashbury between Divisidero and Webster streets is called, caters to a young crowd who favor its alternative nightclub scene.

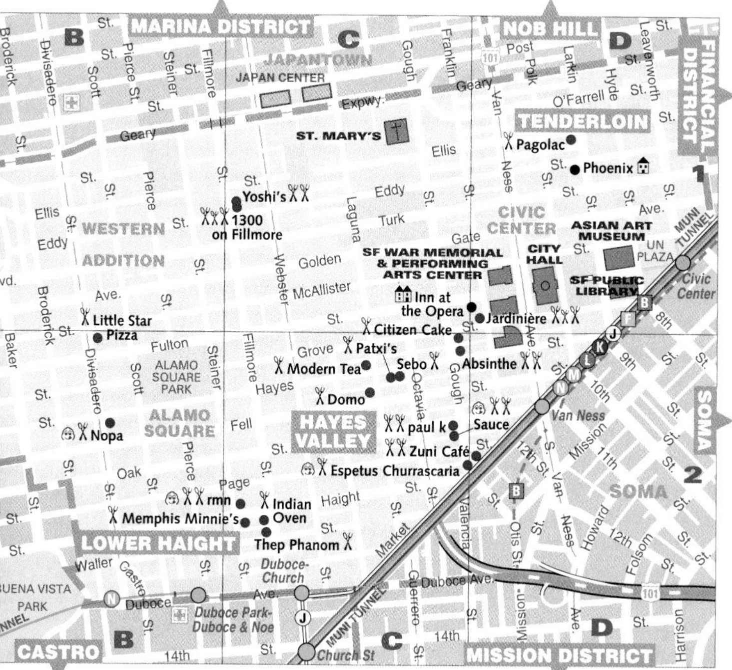

Absinthe

Mediterranean

398 Hayes St. (at Gough St.)

Phone: 415-551-1590
Web: www.absinthe.com
Prices: $$$

Tue – Sun lunch & dinner

This brasserie is known for its creative cocktails—which, thanks to recent legalization, can now incorporate the restaurant's namesake spirit. (The quaff of choice for artists in mid-19th-century France, absinthe was banned in 1912.) Lovers of the arts favor this Absinthe for its corner location near the performing-arts center, where it's a hotspot for a pre- or post-performance meal.

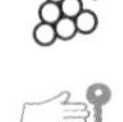

The theme of the menu is French, Californian, and Mediterranean notes play through. A riff on the classic frisée salad includes bacon, a fried duck egg, caviar, and baby leeks vinaigrette. Pizza topped with young dandelion greens, onion jam, and Cypress Grove goat cheese may solo as a small plate, while entrées like grilled halibut with piperade earn ovations.

Citizen Cake

Californian

C2

399 Grove St. (at Gough St.)

Phone: 415-861-2228
Web: www.citizencake.com
Prices: $$

Tue – Sat lunch & dinner
Sun lunch only

Elizabeth Faulkner's spiky hair and beaming smile are not the only factors in her rise to celebrity chef. Long known for her prowess with pastry, Faulkner expresses her artistry in Citizen Cake's pun-filled breakfast, lunch and dinner menus. Soup *du jour*, for example, is hailed as "a daily creation of a liquid variety from California's bounty." The Chef's interest in film accounts for the restaurant's name, and the plot thickens when it's time for dessert. Be sure not to fast-forward past the likes of a "bona fide citrus salad with olive oil gelato." You can take home one of the signature cakes and enjoy all the applause yourself.

Outtake Citizen Cupcake, is a great spot to pause for a snack; check out Orson, Faulkner's latest hotspot in SoMa.

Domo

Japanese 

511 Laguna St. (bet. Fell & Linden Sts.)

Phone: 415-861-8887 — Mon – Fri lunch & dinner
Web: www.domosf.com — Sat – Sun dinner only
Prices:

From the owners of ISA in the Marina, comes this diminutive new Hayes Valley eatery. Too tiny for tables, Domo seats 16 along the sushi counter, which wraps around to face the floor-to-ceiling windows in front.

In this Bento box-like setting, sushi specials and the fresh fish of the day are noted on the large mirrored wall. Don't overlook other more innovative items on the creative seafood-centric menu devised by Chef Kuo Hwa. Roasted wasabi peas or broiled salmon belly make a good start, while crudo selections—two for $5—amount to a bite of bliss in combinations like monkfish liver pâté with ponzu sauce, or a seared scallop with minced yuzu, tobiko, and Domo vinaigrette.

Given the limited seating, to-go orders are popular with the locals.

Espetus Churrascaria

Brazilian 

1686 Market St. (at Gough St.)

Phone: 415-552-8792 — Lunch & dinner daily
Web: www.espetus.com
Prices: $$

Meat, meat, and more meat is what you'll find at this authentic Brazilian "steakhouse," whose name translates as "skewer." Unlimited rounds of different cuts of meat—homemade pork sausage, chicken legs, beef sirloin, prime rib, pork loin, to name a few—are grilled on skewers oven an open fire and brought straight to your table by a waiter clad in *gaucho* garb. A small sign placed on your table will inform the staff of the state of your appetite: turn it green-side-up (*sim por favor*) if you want more; red-side-up (*nao obrigado*) will signal you are finished. The waitstaff will keep bringing food until you tell them to stop.

For accoutrements, there's a generous buffet with an array of mixed salads, fresh cut vegetables, and a host of other side dishes.

Indian Oven

Indian

C2

233 Fillmore St. (bet. Haight & Waller Sts.)

Phone: 415-626-1628 Dinner daily
Web: www.indianovensf.com
Prices: $$

Long a local favorite, Indian Oven dishes up an extensive menu of hearty Northern Indian cuisine. The plate of assorted appetizers makes a good place to start; it teems with a large, crisp samosa puff filled with spiced potatoes and peas; vegetable *pakoras;* and two flavorful pappadam wafers served with an array of chutneys and pickles. Entrées encompass classic tandoori chicken, spicy lamb vindaloo, *biryani,* seafood curry and chicken *tikka masala,* to name just a few.
Tables are cramped in the tiny downstairs dining room (some of the better seats here are next to the open kitchen); for a more intimate ambience, request a table upstairs.
Allow yourself extra time to park, since finding a space can be a nightmare in this Lower Haight neighborhood.

Jardinière

Californian

D1

300 Grove St. (at Franklin St.)

Phone: 415-861-5555 Dinner daily
Web: www.jardiniere.com
Prices: $$$$

Chef Traci Des Jardins and designer Pat Kuleto teamed to open this thriving supper club in 1997. Inside the landmark building, the stage is set for celebration with a golden dome shaped like an inverted champagne glass suspended above the oval bar.
Just a block from the Opera House, Jardinière appeals to wealthy opera and theater mavens seeking pre- or post-performance meals in an impressive setting. The noise level can be high when crowded, distracting diners from the piano music.

California cuisine is served with French accents, as in the house-made charcuterie plate, which may feature head cheese, saucisson de Lyon, and galantine of duck. The major growing regions of the world are showcased on the excellent but expensive wine list.

Little Star Pizza

B2 — Pizza

846 Divisadero St. (bet. Fulton & McAllister Sts.)

Phone: 415-441-1118 — Tue – Sun dinner only
Web: www.littlestarpizza.com
Prices: $$

This cash-only neighborhood pizza place in the Western Addition keeps fans of Chicago deep-dish pie right here in San Francisco, while also offering thin-crust versions, pleasing every pizza lover. The eponymous "Little Star" combines spinach, mushrooms, onions, garlic, ricotta, and feta cheese atop a thick cornmeal crust, and garners most of the attention; but the thin, crisp selections are not to be missed, such as the perfectly balanced gorgonzola, roasted garlic, and Italian sausage pie. Salads and do-it-yourself garlic bread (roasted bulb of garlic provided), add to the menu but should not distract from the main event.

Come early or late, or get takeout; otherwise, expect to wait. There is another location in the Mission District (*400 Valencia St.*).

Memphis Minnie's

C2 — Barbecue

576 Haight St. (bet. Fillmore & Steiner Sts.)

Phone: 415-864-7675 — Tue – Sun lunch & dinner
Web: www.memphisminnies.com
Prices: $$

The fire-truck red façade grabs your attention and sets the tone of this barbecue phenomenon in the Lower Haight. Inside, the carnivorous crowd is as eclectic as the narrow dining space, teeming with kitschy pig paraphernalia. However, the plate is all business, serving serious 'cue, pit-smoked up to 18 hours. Place an order, wait for your name to be called at roof-raising decibels, and choose from the Texas red, North Carolina vinegar, or South Carolina mustard sauces to accompany your meal. Sides include slaw with an abundance of fresh vegetables and beans with a subtle, smokey quality. For dessert, locals rave about the fried peach pies. Jars of sauce and meats are available by the pound, for those seeking a more subdued soul food experience

Modern Tea

Californian

602 Hayes St. (at Laguna St.)

Phone: 415-626-5406 — Wed – Sat lunch & dinner
Web: www.moderntea.com — Sun lunch only
Prices: $$

Tea salon and retail shop, Alice Cravens' Modern Tea is more than a place to chat with the girls over a cup of tea. As Executive Chef and owner, Cravens has crafted a cheery spot featuring an exhibition kitchen, worn wood floors, and undulating glass sculptures flowing through the room.

More important, that open kitchen turns out some nice dishes, while supporting local producers—and, of course, family-run tea farms. In addition to the expansive list of teas, patrons here enjoy plates such as chicken and sausage meatloaf with layered potatoes, or seared salmon over faro risotto.

Being good neighbors is important here; the restaurant participates in Modern Cooks, an after-school cooking program for neighborhood youths.

Nopa

Californian

560 Divisadero St. (at Hayes St.)

Phone: 415-864-8643 — Dinner daily
Web: www.nopasf.com
Prices: $$

Echoing the acronym for North of the Panhandle, Nopa is the quintessential neighborhood restaurant. The communal table teems with a lively mix of locals every night until closing, and a large wall mural depicts the environs.

Many of the Cal-Med items are prepared in the wood-burning oven or on the almond-wood-fueled rotisserie/grill. That means evolving seasonal fare such as flatbread topped with bacon, caramelized onions, radicchio, and Gruyere; and Mediterranean fish stew. Although this building once housed a bank, Nopa's modest prices won't require you to take out a loan.

Chef/owner Laurence Jossel plans to open a tapas place called Snack Bar in the Mission, as well as Nopalito, a quick-service Mexican spot on Broderick Street.

Pagolac

D1 Vietnamese

655 Larkin St. (at Ellis St.)

Phone: 415-776-3234 Tue – Sun dinner only
Web: N/A
Prices:

Located in the Tenderloin, Pagolac is a friendly, family-owned haven in an edgier part of town. The family honors the legacy of its late chef, Phuong Thi To, by consistently producing fresh and vibrant Vietnamese cuisine at bargain prices.

Getting into this popular pillbox-size restaurant may be a challenge, but once inside a feast awaits. For hands-on enjoyment, try the *Banh hoi* wraps, with mounds of garden-fresh lettuce, vegetables, rice-paper wrappers, and meats of your choosing. Adept servers provide some assembly guidance, but the rest is up to you. For a culinary adventure, try the "Seven Flavors of Beef"—a seven-course celebration of specialties where diners grill, steam, and roll food at the table. Much more fun than work, this is an experience not to be missed.

Patxi's

C2 Pizza

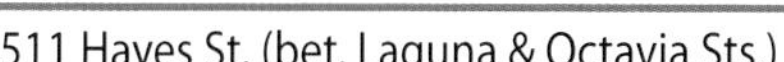

511 Hayes St. (bet. Laguna & Octavia Sts.)

Phone: 415-558-9991 Tue – Sun lunch & dinner
Web: www.patxispizza.com
Prices: $$

Chicagoans may argue that their city is home to deep-dish pizza, but owner Patxi (say PAH-cheese) Aspiroz is vying for that title both here and at the Palo Alto original (*441 Emerson St.*).

Hefty Chicago-style pies boast a rich two-inch-deep crust, stuffed with cheese and your choice of toppings, slathered with tangy tomato sauce—note that all the sauces and crusts conform to vegan diets. Try The Favorite (with pepperoni, mushrooms, and black olives) or go for a thin (or extra thin) cornmeal-crust pie.

With its skylight, concrete floor, and unadorned walls, Paxti's maintains a loud and lively vibe. Kids are welcome, but the deep-dish pies can take up to 40 minutes to prepare, so call ahead to pre-order your pizza—or bring patient children.

paul k

Mediterranean XX

199 Gough St. (at Oak St.)

Phone: 415-552-7132 Tue – Sun dinner only
Web: www.paulkrestaurant.com
Prices: $$

In 1999, when Paul Kavouksorian sold Picnix, the sandwich-and-salad place he had operated in the Presidio for 16 years, he moved to Hayes Valley to open this intimate neighborhood eatery. True to the owner's Armenian heritage, paul k blends exotic touches of the Middle East into its Mediterranean-accented fare. The likes of meze platters (in meat and vegetarian versions); duck breast rubbed with Syrian spices; grilled prime ribeye peppered with spicy harissa; and pressed sumac chicken fill the small, frequently changing menu.
A short but good selection of wines are whimsically classified under such headings as "pensive red beauties that blossom with our food," and "perfumed whites you can dabble behind your ears."

Poleng 

Asian X

1751 Fulton St. (bet. Central & Masonic Aves.)

Phone: 415-441-1751 Tue – Sun dinner only
Web: www.polenglounge.com
Prices: ◎◎

This May 2006 addition to the burgeoning Nopa (North of the Panhandle) neighborhood club and restaurant scene sizzles with island flair—the Indonesian islands, that is. From the batiks and Balinese driftwood to the trickling limestone water wall, Poleng exudes an exotic air.
The menu follows suit with small plates of tasty pan-Asian street food (half-moon Ahi poke; lemongrass satay *sampi*; Poleng curry), and a playful drink list that features tea elixirs, sake and *shochu*. End your meal with a cup of tea from the extensive selection (more than 30 types) of loose-leaf teas, served with a timer so you know how long to steep.
After 10pm, the Temple Room in back morphs into a nightclub, complete with a large dance area and a stage for live bands.

rnm

American XX

C2

598 Haight St. (at Steiner St.)

Phone: 415-551-7900 Tue – Sat dinner only

Web: www.rnmrestaurant.com

Prices: $$

Named after Chef/owner Justine Miner's late father, Robert, rnm is a swanky urban spot. This part of the Lower Haight can get a bit dicey after dark, but don't let that dissuade you from sampling Miner's carefully crafted small plates.

The chef justly honors her father in rnm's creative menu, which exhibits influences from Italy and France. A handful of artisanal pizzas hold their own against small plates like applewood-smoked pulled-pork barbecue served on a corn cake or a hearty parsnip soup topped with crispy pancetta and earthy chestnuts.

Hip and comfortable, the interior contradicts its edgier surroundings. A sophisticated taupe and eggplant color scheme renders the space warm and inviting, and the courteous staff makes you feel right at home.

Sauce

American XX

C2

131 Gough St. (bet. Oak & Page Sts.)

Phone: 415-252-1369 Dinner daily

Web: www.saucesf.com

Prices: $$

A California twist distinguishes home-style American fare at this Hayes Valley restaurant. Roasted chicken mac 'n' cheese, for example, is made with hand-rolled papardelle in a creamy four-cheese sauce topped with shredded chicken and peeled asparagus. Bacon-wrapped meatloaf or hanger steak & eggs will sate your appetite before or after (the restaurant serves until midnight; the bar is open 'til 2am) a performance at the Civic Center complex. Confections, like a Guinness milkshake topped with white chocolate and fresh cream, are sure to leave a sweet taste in your mouth.

Décor varies from minimalist hues of brown and yellow in the front room to a dark, supper-club vibe—complete with a shiny disco ball—in the back.

Sebo

Japanese

C2

517 Hayes St. (at Octavia St.)

Phone: 415-864-2122 Tue – Sat dinner only
Web: N/A
Prices: $$$

Serving a great variety of rarely offered fish, including seasonal and sustainably raised seafood, Sebo wins big in Hayes Valley for artfully presented sushi and sashimi. Try to get one of the six seats at the sushi bar in the back of the room and trust your meal to the chefs, who will be happy to describe the evening's fresh catch displayed in a case between the two work stations. The menu lists a different selection of remarkably buttery, delicate sashimi each night, but the wisest gourmets request an entire, personalized omakase. This allows guests to taste the freshest and most delicious cuts of fish as well as maki and hot dishes.

While a meal can be had for under $40, the little portions add up quickly if you are not careful.

Thep Phanom

Thai

C2

400 Waller St. (at Fillmore St.)

Phone: 415-431-2526 Dinner daily
Web: www.thepphanom.com
Prices: $$

Founded in 1986, this little place delivers big flavors. The extensive menu stays true to what the restaurant bills as "authentic Thai cuisine," but also leaves the kitchen leeway to be creative. Thus, the standards like Massaman and Panang curries and Pad Thai appear along with "Thaitanic" beef (a spicy stir-fry with a crunch of string beans and green peppers) and "Three's Company" (prawns, scallops and calamari in coconut sauce). The "dancing," "weeping," and "crying" ladies referred to on the Favorites menu are all edible and delicious.

Warmly lit and furnished with simple wood chairs and cloth-covered tables, the small dining room fills up fast. The bar in the back of the room usually bustles with locals coming 'round to pick up carry-out fare.

1300 on Fillmore

C1 — American XXX

1300 Fillmore St. (at Eddy St.)

Phone: 415-771-1700 — Mon – Fri dinner only
Web: www.1300Fillmore.com — Sat – Sun lunch & dinner
Prices: $$$

Christened the Fillmore Jazz Preservation District, this area is being revitalized with new jazz venues and restaurants. Chef David Lawrence fits right in at 1300, playing his own riffs on soul food in a high-brow setting.

The menu sings with Southern comfort, as the chef harmonizes his Jamaican ancestry, British upbringing, and French culinary training in freshwater shrimp hushpuppies, Bourbon-braised pork belly, and skillet-fried organic chicken. The likes of a sweet potato soufflé and "cast iron" cornbread bring it all down home.

Gauzy curtains filter urban views through the front window wall. In the comfy lounge, photos depict bygone decades when this neighborhood hosted jazz greats Billie Holliday, Duke Ellington, and Dizzy Gillespie.

Yoshi's

C1 — Japanese XX

1330 Fillmore St. (at Eddy St.)

Phone: 415-655-5600 — Dinner daily
Web: www.yoshis.com
Prices: $$$

Yoshi's has breathed some much-needed life back into this fringe area between Marina, Civic Center, and Japantown. During the 1940s and 1950s, it was known as the "Harlem of the West", with endless Jazz clubs and bars. In fall 2007, a $72 million dollar project opened in the Grand Heritage Center, including a 417-seat club with an ambitious program featuring the best the Jazz world has to offer.

You don't have to be a Jazz fanatic to enjoy dinner inside the upscale, strictly modern (outdoing its Oakland sister) 300-seat restaurant, with its glass enclosed communal table.

The menu is a bit pricy, but worthy with dishes that create new twists on Japanese classics, and exploit only the best, seasonal Bay Area and Japanese ingredients available.

Zuni Café

Mediterranean XX

D2

1658 Market St. (bet. Franklin & Gough Sts.)

Phone: 415-552-2522 — Tue – Sun lunch & dinner
Web: www.zunicafe.com
Prices: **$$**

One of the most beloved eating establishments in the city, Zuni Café occupies a triangular-shaped building on Market Street. Nooks and crannies in the quirky dining area create intimate spaces for seating, while exposed brick walls, a soaring ceiling, and a stone floor lend character to this San Francisco landmark.

Chef/owner Judy Rogers, who trained at Chez Panisse, has been overseeing the kitchen here since 1987. The changing menu of rustic dishes may include the roasted whole chicken for two (requiring an hour lead time); or *graisserons* (cubes of minced duck liver and gizzards) suspended in gelatin, served with a light slaw of radish, carrots, and frisée. Additionally, the brick wood-burning oven turns out savory thin-crust pizzas.

Do not confuse X with ✿! X defines comfort, while ✿ are awarded for the best cuisine. Stars are awarded across all categories of comfort.

Financial District

Embarcadero - Union Square

Contrary to its laid-back image, San Francisco does have a bustling business district—one that's ranked among the top five financial centers in the nation. During the 19th century, the area was part of a gold rush city, which also included **North Beach** and **Chinatown**. As the area was developed during the 20th century, several office buildings were built literally atop old abandoned ships. Nowadays, the weekday commute sees cars, buses, streetcars, pedestrians (some even wearing suits), and wildly pierced and tattooed bicycle messengers clogging the streets of the triangle bound by Kearny, Jackson, and Market streets. Lines snake out the doors of the better take-out sandwich shops and salad bars at lunch, and expense-account restaurants do a brisk business day and night.

SHAKING THINGS UP

The area has seen its share of natural disasters and boom and bust economies. The 1906

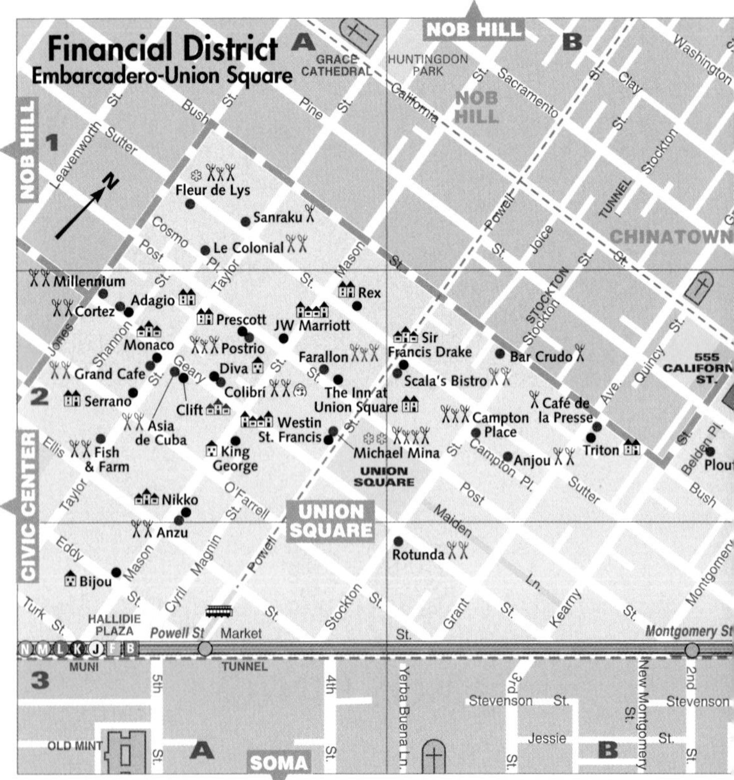

earthquake and fire destroyed this district, which was almost entirely built on landfill in the years following the **Gold Rush**. By 1909, however, the area was largely reconstructed, with many of the new buildings showing off the Classical style. The first skyscrapers started going up in the 1920's. By the 1970's, after the **Bank of America** *(555 California St.)*, **Park Hyatt** *(333 Battery St.)*, and **Transamerica Pyramid** *(600 Montgomery St.)* were erected, preservationists started to panic and strict limitations were placed on the height and bulk of new buildings. In recent years, these restrictions have been relaxed and a number of new towers, notably high-rise condominiums and hotels—leading to what is called the Manhattanization of San Francsico—have been added to the city's skyline. A cooling of the national economy in 2008 has manifested itself in the FiDi (as locals call the district), with a pronounced slowdown in the commercial leasing market.

EMBARCARDERO

The north end of the waterfront promenade known as the Embarcadero (boarding place in Spanish) has been reborn in recent years as a park paved with sidewalks and lined with palm trees. It is here, inside the soaring central arcade of the renovated 1898 Ferry Building *(at*

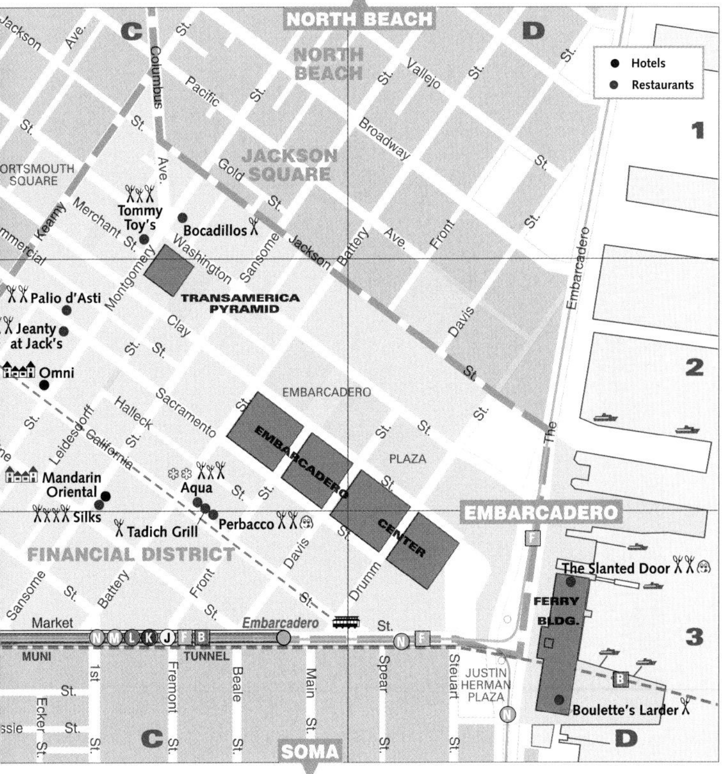

Market St.) that you'll find the **Ferry Building Marketplace**, an architecturally stunning showcase for local cheeses, gelato, exotic teas, and handmade chocolates as well as some great restaurants. On Tuesday and Saturday, check out the **farmer's market**—held on the building's front and rear plazas—for organic produce, mouth-watering baked goods, fresh pasta, and more.

UNION SQUARE

The first place any self-respecting shopper heads in San Francisco is the area bordering this formal park on the western edge of the Financial District. Named on the eve of the Civil War, Union Square lies at the center of the city's ritziest retail district. The Westin St. Francis Hotel (see hotel listing) presides over its western edge, with upscale department stores Saks, Macy's, and Neiman Marcus completing the square. Fashionistas flock here in search of a perfect handbag, a couture ball gown, or a diamond necklace; while foodies come for the area's profusion of gourmet restaurants.

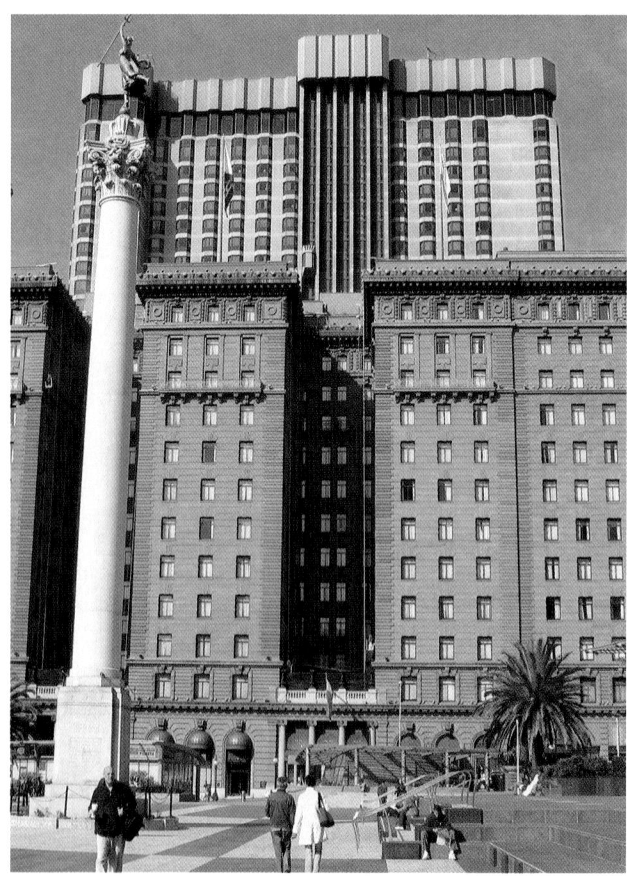

Brigitta L. House / MICHELIN

Anjou

French

B2

44 Campton Pl. (bet. Grant & Stockton Sts.)

Phone: 415-392-5373 Tue – Sat lunch & dinner
Web: www.anjou-sf.com
Prices: $$

Look for the yellow-and-white-striped awning hidden away in an alley off Union Square, where Anjou serves authentic bistro fare in a cozy ambience. The two-tiered dining room's exposed brick walls, skylight, and frosted-glass accents fashion a comfortable roost in which to savor French classics like foie gras, roasted chicken, or calf's liver; as well as more contemporary cuisine such as a warm salad of prawns and lobster scattered with artichoke hearts and pink grapefruit.
Named for the native region of Chef/owner Pierre Morin, Anjou may be off the beaten track, but at lunch the cadre of suits tapping on laptops is anything but out of touch. These patrons likely favor the express lunch, a choice of some 10 entrées served with soup or salad for $16.50.

Anzu

Fusion

222 Mason St. (bet. Ellis & O'Farrell Sts.)

Phone: 415-394-1100 Lunch & dinner daily
Web: www.restaurantanzu.com
Prices: $$$

Set on the second floor of the Hotel Nikko (*see hotel listing*), Anzu exhibits a minimalist style indicative of Japanese elegance. A lounge area with a long granite bar greets guests, while in the small dining room, low ceilings and a 10-seat sushi bar create an intimate feel.
At lunch, sandwiches and salads hold sway, in addition to a smattering of Asian noodle and seafood selections. In the evening, Anzu breaks out the linens and the raw fish. The kitchen brings new life to *hamachi crudo* with grapefruit, jalapeños, cilantro and grapefruit-ginger vinaigrette, as well as to hot dishes such as *shiso-* and garlic-crusted rack of lamb.
The hotel validates parking for up to four hours, so you have time to dine and take in a show at one of the nearby theaters.

Aqua 

Seafood 

C2

252 California St. (bet. Battery & Front Sts.)

Phone: 415-956-9662 — Mon – Fri lunch & dinner
Web: www.aqua-sf.com — Sat – Sun dinner only
Prices: $$$$

Aqua/Marleen Severijn

Fish is the name of the game at Aqua, but don't expect the usual suspects at this elegant oasis in the bustling Financial District. Chef/owner Laurent Manrique cut his teeth in France's Gascony region, and the result of all those hot hours toiling over French stoves is sublime seafood.

Settle into the sophisticated, yet relaxed, brasserie-style dining room—with its mile-high ceilings, enormous mirrors, and soft, earthy palette—and dig into soft piles of shredded Dungeness crab, gently wrapped in paper-thin cucumber leaves, and served over a bed of Meyer Lemon and ginger carpaccio. A fat slice of premium-grade Tombo Tuna might be paired with a tender veal cheek bourguignon, pocked with fragrant porcini mushrooms.

If you happen to be in the area for lunch, follow the lively power suit crowd to Aqua's $45 prix-fixe lunch, arguably one of the best deals in the city.

Appetizers

- Ahi Tartare, Moroccan Spices, Lemon Confit
- Trio of Foie Gras : Cured "Escabèche Style," Dashi Poached, Toasted Almonds Bombons

Entrées

- Chamomile-scented Hawaiian Walu, Frisée and Foie Gras Salad
- Olive Oil-poached Halibut, Crayfish-Yuzu Jus
- White Sturgeon Pastilla, Charmoula Vinaigrette

Desserts

- Milk Chocolate Mousse Bar, Caramelized Bananas
- Strawberry Gelée, Sorbet and Glacée, Mint-Basil Infusion
- Passionfruit Cream, Green Tea Anglaise, Lychee Gelée

Asia de Cuba

Fusion XX

495 Geary St. (at Taylor St.)

Phone: 415-929-2300 Lunch & dinner daily
Web: www.clifthotel.com
Prices: **$$$$**

Looking for a place to party? Head for the Clift Hotel *(see hotel listing)* near Union Square. Inside the sleek wonderland designed by Philippe Starck, you'll find Asia de Cuba. The San Francisco setting of Jeffrey Chodorow's successful restaurant concept attracts the young and the hip to its nightclub ambience. Glamour gleams in the moody lighting from Murano-glass lamps, and the cross-shaped communal table fashioned from a Venetian hand-etched mirror.
Fusing Asian and Latin cuisines, the food captures your palate as the décor does your eye. Tunapica, for instance, combines tuna tartare with Spanish olives, black currants, almonds and coconut, all tossed in soy-lime vinaigrette. Bring friends for sharing; the portion sizes match the hefty prices.

Bar Crudo

Seafood 

603 Bush St. (at Stockton St.)

Phone: 415-956-0396 Mon – Sat dinner only
Web: www.barcrudo.com
Prices: **$$**

Brothers Mike (chef) and Tim (manager) Selvera ride the crest of the crudo wave at their little place located next to the Stockton Tunnel. The raw bar is the focus here; in fact, it's the first thing you'll see upon entering. Though there are a few tables on the ground level, a more intimate perch is found upstairs.
Brushed-steel-topped tables form a pristine palette for the sashimi-style crudo combinations to come: Arctic char with horseradish cream; wasabi tobiko and dill; day-boat scallops with fava purée, chive blossoms, lemon, and olive oil. Can't decide? Go for the crudo sampler and you'll get four selections, each with their own flavorful accompaniments.
Heavy on Belgian imports, the beer list is an aficionados dream.

Bocadillos

Spanish 

710 Montgomery St. (at Washington St.)

Phone: 415-982-2622 — Mon – Fri lunch & dinner
Web: www.bocasf.com — Sat dinner only
Prices: ⓈⓈ

The name—Spanish for "little sandwiches"—describes the menu here, which focuses on diminutive sandwiches and tapas. Combinations may include sandwiches of 18-month-old Serrano ham with tomato rub; turkey, brie and cranberry sauce; double cheese, tomato and basil. However, tapas rule the evening, when Chef Gerald Hirigoyen stays true to the original Spanish concept with palate pleasers like house-made chorizo with sweet and hot peppers, and *patatas bravas* with romesco sauce.

A brick wall painted the color of *piment d'espelette* (a spice made from dried red Basque peppers) and a bar that runs around the periphery of the room foster a lively rustic-meets-metropolitan vibe. Groups should aim for the communal table near the entrance.

Boulette's Larder

D3

Californian 

1 Ferry Building (at the Embarcadero)

Phone: 415-399-1155 — Mon – Fri & Sun lunch only
Web: www.bouletteslarder.com
Prices: $$

The best reason for visiting the historic Ferry Building may be the marketplace occupying its central arcade—home to this European-style *épicerie*, named for owner Amaryll Schwertner's Hungarian sheepdog, *Boulette* (French for "little meatball").

The bulk of Boulette's business is in prepared, farm-fresh organic foods, such as composed salads by the pound, soups by the quart, gourmet entrées like ready-to-roast quails, and luscious desserts, such as an orange-olive oil chiffon cake. Those preferring to eat in will find communal seating inside or cafe tables just outside the shop. Once situated, indulge in smoky tomato soup drizzled with blood-orange oil or tender pork shoulder braised with *pimentón de la vera* and piled on a crusty roll.

Café de la Presse

French 

352 Grant Ave. (at Bush St.)

Phone: 415-398-2680 Lunch & dinner daily
Web: www.cafedelapresse.com
Prices: $$

From the rattan chairs surrounding marble bistro tables to the Gallic staff and patrons to the international newsstand, everything here whispers, "French." Naturally, the menu follows suit with classics such as a frisée salad tossed with lardons, petits croutons, dressed in a proper mustard vinaigrette, then topped with a poached egg; stuffed salmon roulades presented on sliced heirloom tomatoes; and profiteroles filled with hazelnut ice cream beneath chocolate sauce and candied hazelnuts for dessert.

Run by the same team that operates Aqua, the cafe profits from its location on a busy corner across from the Chinatown gate and next to the Hotel Triton. The restaurant is open for breakfast, lunch, dinner, and supplies room service for the hotel.

Campton Place

Contemporary 

340 Stockton St. (bet. Post & Sutter Sts.)

Phone: 415-955-5555 Lunch & dinner daily
Web: www.camptonplace.com
Prices: $$$$

You'll be swathed in soft lighting and hues of cream, gold and cocoa in this formal dining room, located off the lobby of Union Square's swank Campton Place hotel. Clean lines characterize this space, the centerpiece of which is a fanciful blown-glass flower suspended from the ceiling. Along the walls, framed collages add sparks of color.

While the décor hits its mark, the kitchen still seems to be finding its feet following the departure of Chef Daniel Humm. The menu presents a choice of three or four courses from the à la carte list, or a chef's tasting that might feature a composition of guinea hen with confit salad, galantine of breast, and foie gras terrine. Consider the wonderful selection of farmhouse cheeses as an added course.

Colibrí

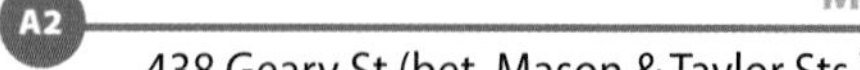

Mexican XX

438 Geary St (bet. Mason & Taylor Sts.)

Phone: 415-440-2737 — Lunch & dinner daily
Web: www.colibrimexicanbistro.com
Prices: **$$**

Sunny colors, wrought-iron detailing, and wagon-wheel chandeliers bring the soul of colonial Mexico alive in this pleasant bistro. Begin your sojourn at the long tequila bar, where you can catch a vintage Latino movie (with subtitles) while you sip a hand-shaken margarita.

In the cozy dining room, skillfully prepared dishes (*mole poblano* served over chicken; tender marinated pork *carnitas*; pan-seared catch of the day) can be accompanied by sides ranging from *frijoles negros* to a savory *torta* made with cornbread and chile pasilla.

Weekend brunch spotlights creative fare such as *huevos ahogados* (eggs baked in a clay pot with tomato-serrano sauce, panela cheese and cactus leaves) as well as more traditional Mexican offerings.

Cortez

Contemporary XX

550 Geary St. (bet. Jones & Taylor Sts.)

Phone: 415-292-6360 — Dinner daily
Web: www.cortezrestaurant.com
Prices: **$$**

Tucked inside the sleek Hotel Adagio, the Michael Brennan-designed Cortez packs a visual punch—with bold, futuristic orb lighting fixtures and painted walls sporting big squares of primary color straight out of a Piet Mondrian painting. A recent change of ownership brought with it another chef switcheroo. Chef Jenn Puccio (formerly of Ramblas) carries on the the Mediterranean fare where Seth Bowden left off.

The menu may include rings of sautéed calamari on a bed of cooked lentils and spaghetti squash; or a fresh slab of Arctic char, dotted with a purée of peas, and surrounded by peas, baby carrots, and spring onions. The service is a little young and chatty, and less than professional at times—but what can you do? Trendy is as trendy does.

Farallon

A2

450 Post St. (bet. Mason & Powell Sts.)

Phone: 415-956-6969 Dinner daily
Web: www.farallonrestaurant.com
Prices: $$$

Farallon must be seen to be appreciated. An undersea theme flows through partner Pat Kuleto's capricious design in which flamboyant glass jellyfish chandeliers hover over tables in the Jelly Bar, sea urchin fixtures light the Pool Room, and curving booths nestle in the Nautilus Room.

Named for the national wildlife refuge lying in a string of islands off the coast, Farallon features seasonal seafood crafted by co-owner and Chef Mark Franz. Dive into seared Hawaiian ono with celery root risotto and chanterelles or local Petrale sole poached in Champagne. Landlubbers will be well contented with the likes of grilled filet of beef or truffle-stuffed pheasant. No matter the origin of the dish, the cooking displays talent and highlights pure, fresh flavors.

Fish & Farm

A2

339 Taylor St. (bet. Ellis & O'Farrell Sts.)

Phone: 415-474-3474 Mon – Sat dinner only
Web: www.fishandfarmsf.com
Prices: $$

In true California style, Fish & Farm sources its sustainably harvested and farmed seafood and meats, as well as its organic produce, within a 100-mile radius of the restaurant. For Chef Jacob Des Voignes (formerly of Fifth Floor), that means his team works with the freshest ingredients. Diners can expect the likes of Tomales Bay oysters broiled Rockefeller-style with bacon vinaigrette, pickled shallots, and baby spinach; and flaky cracker-crusted Petrale sole laid over artichoke *barigoule* strewn with chunks of Dungeness crab, braised fennel, and fines herbes. The same care extends to the wine list.

Adjacent to the Mark Twain Hotel, the restaurant seats less than 50 guests in a narrow room decorated with brown leather banquettes and sea-blue walls.

Fleur de Lys 

French

A1

777 Sutter St. (bet. Jones & Taylor Sts.)

Phone: 415-673-7779 — Mon – Sat dinner only
Web: www.fleurdelyssf.com
Prices: $$$$

Bill Milne

Like so many city restaurants, Fleur De Lys's façade doesn't tell of the riches within. But brush past the lonely awning, and inside you'll find the kind of thoroughly romantic ambience slowly fading from the modern dining scene—waiters treading quietly under a tent of billowing velvet fabric, an enormous mound of fresh flowers anchoring a sea of white-cloth tables, all laid out with delicate china.

French-born owner and head chef, Hubert Keller, offers diners a rotating menu of French classics (there is a nice vegetarian tasting menu as well) cleverly tweaked to employ fresh, local California ingredients. A course might feature tender lamb loin cooked to perfection, garnished with a succulent side of lamb cheek sausage, and surrounded by bright vegetables. An elegant wine list teems with French labels, including a nice selection from the Chef's native Alsace region.

Appetizers

- Sweetbreads with Lobster Ceviche and Caviar
- Hazelnut-crusted Scallops, Truffled Gnocchi, Jus
- Oxtail & Truffle "Cappuccino", Jalapeño Brioche

Entrées

- Filet Mignon, Lobster Mac & Cheese, Bordelaise Sauce
- Wagyu Beef Cheeks, Pickled Onions, Juniper
- Salmon, Almonds, Lemongrass, and Scallion Sauce

Desserts

- Vanilla Cheesecake, Champagne Gelée
- Chocolate Mousse, Apple-Brioche Toast, Chocolate Donut
- FleurBurger: Chocolate Ganache, Banana Milk Shake, Fennel Ice Cream

Grand Cafe

French

A2

501 Geary St. (at Taylor St.)

Phone: 415-292-0101
Web: www.grandcafe-sf.com
Prices: $$

Lunch & dinner daily

"Grand" surely fills the bill given the elegant ambience of this restored turn-of-the-20th-century ballroom in the Hotel Monaco (*see hotel listing*). Art Deco splendor abounds, from the whimsical bronze sculptures to the soaring columns and the ornate gilded ceiling.

France provides the inspiration for the cuisine, which the kitchen executes with delicious results. For dinner, roasted wild Chinook salmon may be paired with creamy Brussels sprouts and a julienne of winter vegetables, while duck "coq au vin," cassoulet, and bœuf Bourguignon fill in the Gallic classics. Bistro fare makes a good showing at lunchtime too, between creative pizzas, salads, and steak frites.

Just inside the Geary Street entrance, adjoining Petite Café serves a bar menu all day.

Jeanty at Jack's

French 

C2

615 Sacramento St. (bet. Kearny & Montgomery Sts.)

Phone: 415-693-0941
Web: www.jeantyatjacks.com
Prices: $$$

Mon – Fri lunch & dinner
Sat – Sun dinner only

This may be the most charming Parisian-style brasserie in San Francisco. Philippe Jeanty (of Bistro Jeanty in Yountville) has transformed Jack's restaurant—a San Francisco institution since 1864—into a Belle Époque-style beauty. Lace cafe curtains, a black and white-tile floor, wood paneling, and sculpted relief on the walls keep the French décor à la mode. The ground level features the small bar, while the top (third) floor feels like an atrium, with natural light streaming through its glass ceiling.

Sole *meunière, coq au vin, ris de veau,* and cassoulet number among the authentic main plates. For dessert, the chocolate mousse crème brulée—a layer of perfect vanilla custard crowned with fluffy chocolate mousse—is sure to hit any sweet spot.

Le Colonial

Vietnamese XX

20 Cosmo Pl. (bet. Post & Sutter Sts.)

Phone: 415-931-3600 Dinner daily
Web: www.lecolonialsf.com
Prices: **$$$**

Fans of Trader Vic's will have no trouble finding Le Colonial, which fills the space once occupied by the legendary restaurant. Tucked down an alley off Taylor Street (look for the blue neon sign), Le Colonial is worth seeking out for its elegant ambience—featuring graceful rattan furnishings, tropical greenery, and lazily turning fans conjuring French colonial Vietnam—as well as its food.

The chef presents European style with exotic Asian flavors while creating dishes such as crispy turmeric rice crepes filled with lobster, prawns, and bean sprouts.

On weekends, the decibels climb as twenty-somethings gather in the upstairs lounge to listen to live music, sip tropical cocktails, and snack on Vietnamese street food. Valet parking is offered at the door.

Millennium

Vegan XX

580 Geary St. (at Jones St.)

Phone: 415-345-3900 Dinner daily
Web: www.millenniumrestaurant.com
Prices: **$$**

You don't have to be a vegan to appreciate Chef Eric Tucker's cuisine. He plumbs many different cultures for inspiration, creating food that's not only good for you but tastes good too. Organically grown ingredients that are free of genetic modification might yield a salad of grilled nectarines with sea palm, cucumber, and avocado as easily as a smoky black bean torte made with caramelized plantains, pumpkin-habañero *papazul*, cashew sour cream, and carrot escabeche. Believe it or not, coconut-crusted tofu bursts with flavor—try it for yourself and you may become a convert.

Speaking of which, vegetarians can bring their meat-loving buddies the second Wednesday of every month, when "Convert a Carnivore" evenings offer 25 percent off the price of dinner.

Michael Mina ✿✿

Contemporary XXXX

335 Powell St. (bet. Geary & Post Sts.)

Phone: 415-397-9222 — Dinner daily
Web: www.michaelmina.net
Prices: $$$$

Eric Laignel

An elegantly dressed, well-heeled crowd works the room at Michael Mina, which is tucked into the opulent Westin St. Francis hotel. And no wonder—the beautifully-appointed, spacious room exudes sophistication and grace, with its large columns, mile-high ceilings, and balcony overlooking the lobby. The service is on point, too, with a precise, uniformed brigade doling out Mina's signature trio dishes (one ingredient, done three ways), carefully prepared under Chef de Cuisine, Chris L'hommedieu.

Get things started with a super-fresh trio of tropical *crudo*, comprised of fluke (served with grilled pineapple and jalapeño gelée), konpachi (done in a coconut gelée and a curry marinade) and ahi tuna (with diced mango fruit and *Nuoc Mam Cham*).

Don't miss the impressive wine list, teeming with excellent Californian and French varietals and vintages.

Appetizers

- Hamachi Tartare, Uni Aïoli, Persian Mint; Albacore Tataki, Tempura Maitake, Marinated Mushrooms
- Ahi Tuna Tartare, Scotch Bonnet Pepper, Bosc Pear, Sesame Oil

Entrées

- Poussin Southern Style: Fried Leg, Mac & Cheese Croquette, Braised Collard Greens, Tea-brined Breast
- Maine Lobster Pot Pie, Brandied Lobster Cream, Vegetables

Desserts

- Chocolate S'more, Basil Marshmallow, Pistachio Purée
- Chocolate Ice Cream, Sesame Halva, Chocolate Streusel
- Devil's Food, Kalamata Olive, Juniper

Palio d'Asti

Italian XX

C2

640 Sacramento St. (bet. Kearny & Montgomery Sts.)

Phone: 415-395-9800 Mon – Fri lunch & dinner
Web: www.paliodasti.com
Prices: $$$

Colorful banners and coats of arms parade throughout this dining room, commemorating the famed bareback horse race that has been run each year since the 13th century in the Piazza Alfieri in Asti, Italy. Massive concrete pillars in this 1907 building take on a medieval look of their own, while a tiny bar near the entrance pours both Italian and Californian varietals.

The menu celebrates different regions of Italy, depending on the season. Main courses might run from fluffy gnocchi with roasted Muscovy duck to roasted Alaskan halibut with ratatouille. A freewheeling crowd comes in at happy hour for complimentary brick-oven pizzas.

Those in a hurry can grab panini to go at the two sister Paninotecas, nearby at 505 Montgomery Street, or on campus at UCSF.

Perbacco

Italian XX

C3

230 California St. (bet. Battery & Front Sts.)

Phone: 415-955-0663 Mon – Fri lunch & dinner
Web: www.perbaccosf.com Sat dinner only
Prices: $$

In October 2006, Perbacco took over the former Gold Coast Café in the heart of the Financial District. Gone is the Old San Francisco ambience; in its place reigns an urbane décor that incorporates high ceilings and one of the original brick walls from the 1913 Hind Building.

Northern Italian fare here highlights the dishes of Piemonte. For a quick bite, sit at the marble-topped bar, where you can wash down house-cured meats with a good selection of Italian wines by the glass. Prefer a hearty meal? House-made pastas (agnolotti filled with roasted veal and Savoy cabbage) and the likes of roasted monkfish in porcini *brodo* will do the trick. At lunch you might eavesdrop on some investment advice; after sundown the mood turns romantic.

Plouf

B2 — Seafood

40 Belden Pl. (bet. Bush & Pine Sts.)

Phone: 415-986-6491 — Mon – Fri lunch & dinner
Web: www.ploufsf.com — Sat dinner only
Prices: $$

In French, *plouf* is the sound that a stone makes when it drops into the water, and it makes an appropriate name for a restaurant whose angle is seafood with a French accent.

Don't spend too much time fishing around the menu. Go straight for the house specialty, steamed mussels and steamed clams. Both are offered in a variety of preparations (*marinière, Provençale, gratinée*); be sure to order a side of crispy fries. Other main-course offerings include excellent bouillabaisse and *fruits de mer* fresh from the market. To add to the seashore ambience, waiters dress in blue-and-white-striped shirts, and the walls are decorated with large trophy fish.

Grab a seat outside, where the view of the cafe-laden alley will seem like any place in France.

Postrio

A2 — Contemporary

545 Post St. (bet. Mason & Taylor Sts.)

Phone: 415-776-7825 — Dinner daily
Web: www.postrio.com
Prices: $$$$

Synonymous with its founder, Wolfgang Puck, Postrio is a San Francisco favorite. Taste Puck's stamp on the nightly changing menu, in roasted wild mushrooms with poached Maine lobster and a garlic-chile glaze, or perhaps a tempura-battered quail. The voluminous wine list adds a generous selection of half-bottles. At lunch, the bar/grill (the only midday dining option here) offers a limited menu including signature pizzas, salads, sandwiches, and a few grilled items. Designed with a sweeping staircase that leads from the casual bar area down to the main dining room, the restaurant is accessible off the lobby of the Prescott Hotel or via its own street entrance. Postrio opened in 1989 as Puck's first establishment outside southern California.

Rotunda

American

150 Stockton St. (at Geary St.)

Phone: 415-362-4777 Lunch daily
Web: www.neimanmarcus.com
Prices: $$

This four-story rotunda is all that remains of the beloved 1908 Belle Époque building replaced by Philip Johnson's boxy granite Neiman Marcus. Still, ladies who lunch love taking their midday meal on the top floor, beneath the marvelous oval stained-glass dome. Surrounded by gilded carvings of Poseidon, diners enjoy a visual feast, including a spectacular view of Union Square, before even looking at the menu.

There, the view focuses on American cuisine with seasonal touches. From Maine lobster spring rolls or ahi Niçoise salad to roasted free-range chicken and black truffle risotto, the upscale fare covers all the bases from light to hearty. Afternoon tea provides another languorous break from shopping.

Sanraku

Japanese 

704 Sutter St. (at Taylor St.)

Phone: 415-771-0803 Mon – Sat lunch & dinner
Web: www.sanraku.com Sun dinner only
Prices:

Regulars rave about this sushi spot, which stands out for its fresh fish in the neighborhood around Union Square. Simplicity is the keynote here, where a white wall cut out to form irregular columns divides the dining space from the sushi bar.

Smiling sushi chefs make conversation while they craft high-quality seafood into maki, nigiri and sashimi. For those who want a break from raw fish, the menu also offers a long list of cooked dishes including teriyaki, tempura, udon, and donburi. The best bargains at either lunch or dinner are the combination meals.

If you're wandering around SoMa, visit Sanraku's little sister at Metreon (*4th and Mission Sts.*), where video gamers meet sushi lovers in an airy space overlooking Yerba Buena Gardens.

Scala's Bistro

Italian XX

B2

432 Powell St. (bet. Post & Sutter Sts.)

Phone: 415-395-8555 — Lunch & dinner daily
Web: www.scalasbistro.com
Prices: $$

Adjacent to the St. Francis Drake Hotel, Scala's devises a contemporary bistro in this spacious, high-ceilinged room embellished with gold-framed mirrors and sepia-toned murals. Despite the French brasserie stylings, this is primarily Italian cuisine with Californian sensibility. Lunchtime features a roomful of office workers audibly discussing the day's doings between bites of wood-oven pizzas, panini, pasta, or entrées of grilled Italian sausages with gorgonzola polenta, and seared Loch Duart salmon with creamy buttermilk mashed potatoes. In case you forgot to leave room for dessert after that hefty plate of steak frites, many of the sweets on the menu are available in miniature portions, so you can have your cake and eat it too.

Silks

C2

222 Sansome St. (bet. California & Pine Sts.)

Phone: 415-986-2020 — Mon lunch only
Web: www.silksdining.com — Tue – Sat lunch & dinner
Prices: $$$$

For the perfect place for a power lunch or over-the-top dinner date, look no farther than the Mandarin Oriental Hotel (*see hotel listing*). In Silks' sleek second-floor dining room, the 13th-century journey of Marco Polo along the Silk Road to China imbues the décor with elegance—from the silk wall treatments and silk-draped chandeliers to colors inspired by exotic spices. The semi-circular booths against the wall are the best seats from which to appreciate the plush ambience. On the plate, looks occasionally trump flavor in presentations that can try a bit too hard to be creative. Yet the chef's passion and skill shines through in appetizers such as the whole roasted quail, sliced in pieces and stacked atop quinoa with rich foie gras.

The Slanted Door

Vietnamese XX

1 Ferry Building (at The Embarcadero)

Phone: 415-861-8032 Lunch & dinner daily
Web: www.slanteddoor.com
Prices: $$

San Franciscans hunger for Chef Charles Phan's take on Vietnamese street food. The original Mission District location moved to its current home in the restored Ferry Building. The well-appointed, glass-walled dining room has an outdoor terrace and offers expansive views of the Bay Bridge. The appetizing menu serves fragrant and flavorful dishes like the chicken claypot, sauced with red chili and ginger caramel. Pacific coast product at the raw bar, Niman Ranch shaking beef, and food presentations on locally produced ceramic, demonstrate the chef's dedication to utilizing locally sourced products in his operations.
Always a popular dining destination, those that can't snag a table, opt for carry out from one of Phan's "Out the Door" locations.

Tadich Grill

Seafood 

240 California St. (bet. Battery & Front Sts.)

Phone: 415-391-1849 Mon – Sat lunch & dinner
Web: N/A
Prices: $$

A San Francisco institution since the Gold Rush days, Tadich Grill has long been a family-run operation. The restaurant's precursor was a coffee stand on Long Wharf, started in 1849 by three Croatian immigrants.
A timeless atmosphere brings folks back to this landmark eatery. More than 150 years after it was established, Tadich Grill pays tribute to its history with dark wood paneling, bentwood chairs, and a pressed-plaster ceiling. The noise level is often deafening, the service gruff, and the menu an homage to recipes of yore.
Even so, the products are fresh, and seafood is available in a wide spectrum of preparations, including charcoal-broiled, pan-fried, sautéed, poached, and baked en casserole. Carnivores can prospect in the selection of steaks.

Tommy Toy's

Chinese XXX

C1

655 Montgomery St. (bet. Clay & Washington Sts.)

Phone: 415-397-4888 — Mon – Fri lunch & dinner
Web: www.tommytoys.com — Sat – Sun dinner only
Prices: **$$$**

Since 1986, this Financial District stalwart has made an equally elegant choice for power lunches or romantic dinners. Service is gracious and efficient in the formal, softly-lit room, which impresses with shimmering chandeliers, silk draperies, and framed antique tapestries. Porcelain votive lamps, fresh flowers, and silver-plated chargers accent tables.

The late Tommy Toy's menu of "haute cuisine Chinois" succeeds well beyond typical Chinese fare, to remain refreshing, pleasant, and consistently interesting. Wok-fried vanilla wasabi prawns are complemented by raisins and fresh melon, while Chinese fruits in cassis nectar finish the deep-fried pork tenderloin. Reasonable prix-fixe dining options include the Executive Lunch for less than $25.

The sun is out – let's eat alfresco! Look for a terrace.

Peter L. Wrenn/MICHELIN

2008
Olympic
THE LOUISVILLE RAILWAY COMPANY

Marina District

Presidio - Pacific Heights - Japantown

Extending from Pacific Heights to the northern waterfront, the Marina is a popular neighborhood for young, wealthy professionals. Visit on a sunny weekend and you'll see why—**Union Street** and **Chestnut Street** are both chock-a-block with chi-chi boutiques, bars, and wonderful restaurants. Outdoorsy types love to bike or jog along **Marina Green** past **Crissy Field** to the **Golden Gate Bridge** and beyond.

At the beginning of the 19th century, dairy farms covered the southern hills and valleys—present-day **Cow Hollow**.

PRESIDIO AND PACIFIC HEIGHTS

On 1,480 acres to the west, the Presidio lures visitors to its lushly forested expanse and its rich history as a military installation. Currently, the Presidio is maintained by the **National Park Service** and he face of this evolving quarter has changed in recent years with the addition of **The Letterman Digital Arts Center**, home to Lucasfilm Ltd. It's a self-contained community, with new condos and restaurants. The latest plans call for the creation of a winery—Foggy Bridge—the first to operate inside a national park.

Along a high east-west ridge between Van Ness Avenue and the Presidio sits **Pacific Heights**, a neighborhood synonymous with wealth. Great for strolling, eating, and shopping, this tiny residential enclave holds some of the city's finest houses and loveliest views—also some killer steep streets. **Fillmore Street** between Geary and Jackson is the place to go for perusing unique shops, and enjoying good cafes and restaurants. This vibrant area, with its bustling bar scene, is again becoming a haunt for jazz lovers.

JAPANTOWN

At the south end of Pacific Heights, in a part of the city known as the **Western Addition**, Japantown abounds with Japanese architecture and culture. This is the place to come for sushi, tempura, Korean barbecue, or donburi. At the heart of Japantown is the **Japan Center**, a complex of shops, sushi bars, theaters, and hotels. Crowned by a five-tiered pagoda, the center hosts celebrations like the annual **Cherry Blossom Festival**.

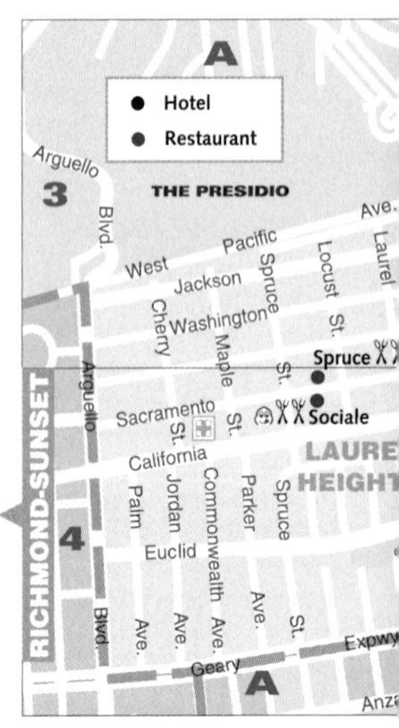

Brigitta L. House / MICHELIN

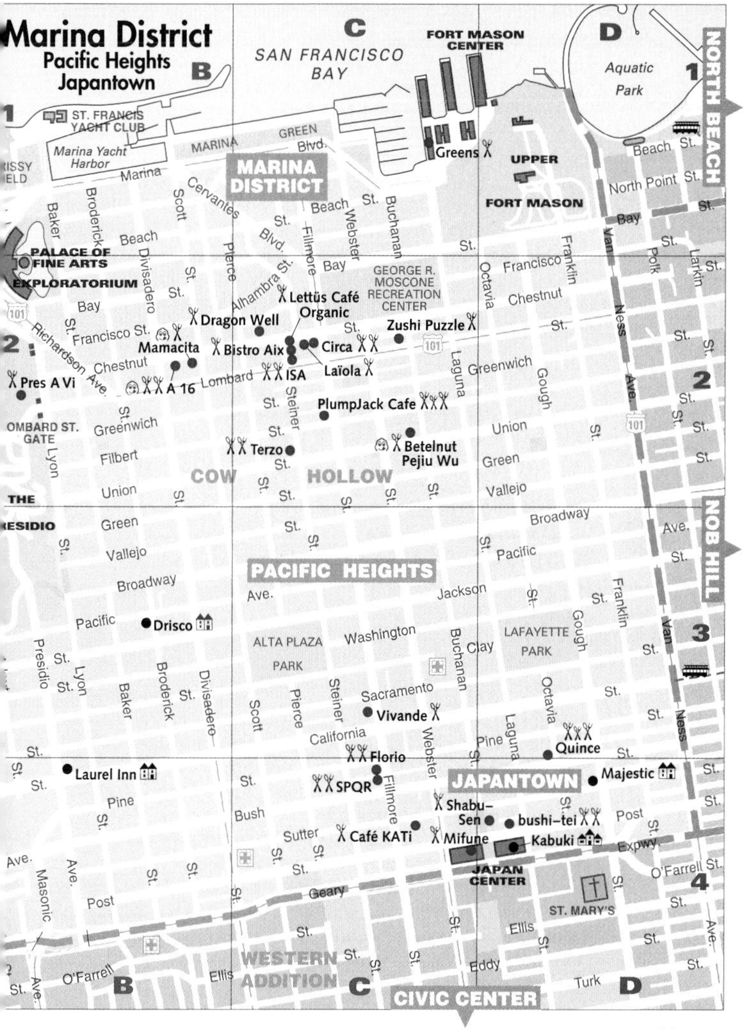

Marina District
Pacific Heights
Japantown

SAN FRANCISCO BAY
FORT MASON CENTER
Aquatic Park
NORTH BEACH
ST. FRANCIS YACHT CLUB
Marina Yacht Harbor
MARINA Blvd.
GREEN
MARINA DISTRICT
UPPER FORT MASON
PALACE OF FINE ARTS
EXPLORATORIUM
GEORGE R. MOSCONE RECREATION CENTER
LOMBARD ST. GATE
THE PRESIDIO
COW HOLLOW
PACIFIC HEIGHTS
ALTA PLAZA PARK
LAFAYETTE PARK
NOB HILL
JAPANTOWN
JAPAN CENTER
ST. MARY'S
WESTERN ADDITION
CIVIC CENTER

Greens
Lettüs Café Organic
Dragon Well
Mamacita
Bistro Aix
Circa
Zushi Puzzle
Laïola
ISA
A 16
Pres A Vi
PlumpJack Cafe
Terzo
Betelnut Pejiu Wu
Drisco
Vivande
Quince
Florio
Laurel Inn
SPQR
Majestic
Shabu-Sen
bushi-tei
Café KATi
Mifune
Kabuki

Beach St.
North Point St.
Bay St.
Francisco St.
Chestnut St.
Lombard St.
Greenwich St.
Filbert St.
Union St.
Green St.
Vallejo St.
Broadway
Pacific Ave.
Jackson St.
Washington St.
Clay St.
Sacramento St.
California St.
Pine St.
Bush St.
Sutter St.
Post St.
Geary Expwy
O'Farrell St.
Ellis St.
Eddy St.
Turk St.
Marina Blvd.
Cervantes Blvd.
Alhambra St.
Richardson Ave.
Baker St.
Broderick St.
Divisadero St.
Scott St.
Pierce St.
Steiner St.
Fillmore St.
Webster St.
Buchanan St.
Laguna St.
Octavia St.
Gough St.
Franklin St.
Van Ness Ave.
Polk St.
Larkin St.
Lyon St.
Presidio Ave.
Masonic Ave.

A 16 

Italian XX

B2

2355 Chestnut St. (bet. Divisadero & Scott Sts.)

Phone: 415-771-2216 — Wed – Fri lunch & dinner
Web: www.a16sf.com — Sat – Tue dinner only
Prices: **$$**

A perfect balance between stylish and warm, hip and comfortable, lively yet good for conversation—everything one could want in a restaurant is here. A 16 borrows its name from the autostrada that runs between Naples and Bari.

From a perch at the bar, the main dining room, or at the counter flanking the open kitchen, there's not a bad seat in the house. Menu decisions are also difficult. House-cured salumi is a tempting beginning, as are the mouth-watering pizzas, unique pastas (house-made chestnut tonnarelli with ragù bianco), or rustic entrées (scaloppini of Duroc pork shoulder with pickled peppers).

Street parking can by trying; an early arrival insures a few extra moments to peruse the extensive wine list, with terrific offerings by the glass.

Betelnut Pejiu Wu

Asian X

C2

2030 Union St. (bet. Buchanan & Webster Sts.)

Phone: 415-929-8855 — Lunch & dinner daily
Web: www.betelnutrestaurant.com
Prices: **$$**

From the enameled fire-engine-red bar to the bamboo ceiling fans, this Asian beer house, or *pejiu wu*, feels like a British Colonial movie set. Pull a stool up to the bar for a Tsing Tao or a sake flight, or grab a table in the dimly lit upstairs dining room, where the open kitchen offers counter seating for those who want to view the action.

The kitchen constantly plays to a packed room, serving up small plates that sing with the flavors of the Orient, such as minced chicken and *lup cheong* sausage in lettuce cups; Malaysian curry "laksa" with prawns, chicken, mint, and basil; and a host of other choices for the fireproof palate.

Plates arrive at the kitchen's whim and many are designed for sharing, so this is an ideal venue for a group.

Bistro Aix

C2 — French

3340 Steiner St. (bet. Chestnut & Lombard Sts.)

Phone: 415-202-0100 — Wed – Mon dinner only
Web: www.bistroaix.com
Prices: $$

Unpretentious Bistro Aix delivers friendly faces and budget-friendly European fare in the Marina District. True simplicity delivers in this no-frills restaurant, where white walls are embellished with black-and-white photographs, and the cozy bar invites guests to pull up a stool and chat with the staff.

Open since 1996, the bistro has become a neighborhood fixture. Chef/owner Jonathan Beard dishes up a modest menu of properly-prepared French favorites with a soupçon of Italian influence. Thus bouillabaisse and crispy duck leg confit might share a table with a cracker-crust pizza or orecchiette with pancetta, baby spinach, and tomato sauce. The best bargain is the two-course prix-fixe menu, served from 6 to 8pm Sunday through Thursday nights.

bushi-tei

D4 — Fusion

1638 Post St. (bet. Buchanan & Laguna Sts.)

Phone: 415-440-4959 — Mon – Sat lunch & dinner
Web: www.bushi-tei.com — Sun dinner only
Prices: $$$

Blend California ingredients, French cooking techniques, and Japanese flair, and you have the recipe for Bushi-Tei. Located in the heart of Japantown, this restaurant showcases the fusion fare of Executive Chef Seiji "Waka" Wakabayashi, who claims to give his customers "the world on a plate." He succeeds with the likes of herb-grilled John Dory over saffron potatoes; miso-marinated Wagyu beef with upland cress and French blue cheese; as well as black sesame blancmange.

Elements of old (wood panels removed from an 1863 house in Japan) and new (the sleek, 16-seat, half-wood, half-glass communal table) come together in the dining room. Now open for lunch and Sunday brunch, you no longer have to wait until dinnertime to experience this eclectic and tasty cuisine.

Café KATi

C4 — Fusion

1963 Sutter St. (bet. Fillmore & Webster Sts.)

Phone: 415-775-7313 — Mon – Sat dinner only
Web: www.cafekati.com
Prices: $$$

Nestled between Japantown and Pacific Heights, the intimate Café KATi has been pleasing area residents for over 15 years. Its cherry-red façade gives way to an intimate café of ten snug tables that sway from tranquil and romantic to busy and boisterous in a matter of moments. Chef Kirk Webber fuses a menu rich in Asian influence, adding dashes of French technique, with sensible California ingredient-driven cuisine. Although small, this operation clearly takes pride in both its food and gracious service.

The complimentary warm jalapeño cornbread with honey butter gives each meal a zippy start. Menu selections change daily, but may include the deep-fried pecan-crusted prawns served with *nam pla prik* and sweet chili sauces, representing the yin and yang of sweet and spicy flavors.

Circa

C2 — Contemporary

2001 Chestnut St. (at Fillmore St.)

Phone: 415-351-0175 — Mon – Fri dinner only
Web: www.circasf.com — Sat – Sun lunch & dinner
Prices: $$

CIRCA's playful, sensuous ambience befits its trendy Marina locale. Tones of black, gray, and brown are interrupted by strands of crystals dangling through rectangular openings in the velvet ceiling, while light boxes and narrow mirrors bring harmony to the polka-dot booths curving between close tables. Behind the hostess stand, a DJ spins tunes, transforming the space into a club for the young Marina set at night, who come to drink and nosh at the large square bar that consumes most of the room's space.

Chef Erik Hopfinger's versatility is evident in small-plate selections like the lobster and white truffle mac 'n' cheese; Dungeness crab and Ahi tuna ceviche; and chicken or Angus beef sliders (mini burgers). A mezzanine area is available for larger groups.

Dragon Well

Chinese 

2142 Chestnut St. (bet. Pierce & Steiner Sts.)

Phone: 415-474-6888 Lunch & dinner daily
Web: www.dragonwell.com
Prices:

Tucked among the posh boutiques and eateries on Chestnut Street, Dragon Well has been a Marina favorite for years. The narrow space, with its worn wooden-plank floor and neat rows of small, closely spaced tables is lit via skylights by day and pendant lamps by night.

Flavorful Chinese food is Americanized with delicious results. The freshest produce, meats, and seafood combine as Chinese eggplant gently stir-fried in a brown bean, scallion, and garlic sauce; or lightly battered prawns tossed in a sweet white sauce with a crunch of candied walnuts.

Dragon Well is open continuously from 11:30am to 10pm, so shoppers can drop by for a bite—to eat in or carry out—almost any time of day. These modest prices will leave cash in your pocket for more shopping.

Florio

Italian 

1915 Fillmore St. (bet. Bush & Pine Sts.)

Phone: 415-775-4300 Dinner daily
Web: www.floriosf.com
Prices: $$

Sequestered in a tiny alley in Pacific Heights, this bistro/bar oozes old-world charm with its cozy banquettes, dark wood paneling, black-and-white photographs, and crisp linens. Joseph Graham and Doug "Bix" Biederbeck founded this place in 1998, making it a neighborhood standby for the bustling bar, inviting feel, and simple fare (reservations are recommended).

Bouncing back and forth between Italy and France, the ever-changing menu jumps from pappardelle Bolognese with porcini oil to steak frites as entrées. The likes of chicken-liver pâté with fruit mustard, or locally cured Zoe's prosciutto plated with roasted pear, Grana Padano, and olive oil please palates for starters. Both Old and New Worlds are represented on the fairly priced wine list.

Greens

Vegetarian

Building A, Fort Mason Center

Phone: 415-771-6222 — Tue – Sun lunch & dinner
Web: www.greensrestaurant.com
Prices: $$

It's difficult to say which is the greater draw of this Zen oasis, the spectacular view or the inventive vegetarian cuisine. Occupying a former military warehouse at Fort Mason Center, Greens peers out over the marina and the Golden Gate Bridge beyond. Grab a table by the windows to take in the sunset, while you sip a glass of organic wine.

Established in 1979 by disciples of the San Francisco Zen Center, Greens gets its organic produce from the center's Green Gulch Farm. Healthy meals here don't require any badgering to get you to eat your veggies. From potato and poblano-chile griddle cakes to fresh pea ravioli, there's something to please every palate.

At the front of the restaurant, Greens To Go counter enjoys a brisk take-out business.

ISA

French 

3324 Steiner St. (bet. Chestnut & Lombard Sts.)

Phone: 415-567-9588 — Mon – Sat dinner only
Web: www.isarestaurant.com
Prices: $$

Set on a restaurant-rich block in the Marina, Isa borrows its name from owners Luke and Kitty Sung's daughter, Isabelle. New Age music soothes the sleek space while candlelight emits a warm glow. For an intimate meal, ask for a table on the covered patio, a quiet space away from the busy open kitchen.

A contemporary French slant infuses Chef Luke's cuisine, which hinges on small plates. Grilled honey-spiced calamari; baked Laura Chenel goat cheese topped with basil pesto and tomato concassé; and seared day-boat scallops alongside asparagus and potato purée all make good dishes to share. Go Monday through Thursday for the two-course prix-fixe menu; it's a deal at just under $23.

Recently, the Sungs opened a new sushi place, Domo, in Hayes Valley.

Laïola

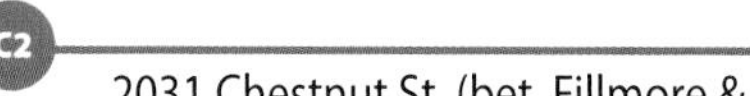

Spanish

C2

2031 Chestnut St. (bet. Fillmore & Steiner Sts.)

Phone: 415-346-5641 — Dinner daily
Web: www.laiola.com
Prices: $$

Wildly popular for both meeting and eating, Laïola burst on the San Francisco restaurant scene as one of the hotter spots to open. Credit the proprietors of the former Frisson in North Beach for this buzzing, warm L-shaped space, with pressed-copper ceiling and shimmering copper bar. Seating at the half bar/half kitchen counter is first-come, first-served, and no matter when you arrive, it's 100-percent loud.

A revolving selection of house-made charcuterie and terrines will kick things off. Keep the good times rolling by sharing a variety of small plates. From olive-oil-fried almonds and bacon-wrapped Medjool dates to Moorish-style lamb meatballs and cataplana of Willapa Bay clams, the flavors mainly hail from Spain. Ditto the list of wines.

Lettüs Café Organic

C2

3352 Steiner St. (bet. Chestnut & Lombard Sts.)

Phone: 415-931-2777 — Lunch & dinner daily
Web: www.lettusorganic.com
Prices:

This organic cafe in the heart of the Marina is perfectly suited to San Francisco's health-conscious lifestyle. Lettüs serves breakfast, lunch, and dinner, reminding us to always eat food that is as good for the body as it is for the earth—it is also delicious. Order and pay at the counter; the plates will be brought to your table.

Begin the weekend with fruit-stuffed brioche French toast or scrambled tofu; for lunch, try a garden burger or a barbecue tempeh panini. For those who want to cheat on their vegetarian diet, the dinner selection offers chicken and fish dishes. There's even a kids' menu for budding vegetarians.

Fresh-squeezed juices, smoothies, and organic free-trade coffees and teas share the beverage list with beer, wine, and sake cocktails.

Mamacita

Mexican

B2

2317 Chestnut St. (bet. Divisadero & Scott Sts.)

Phone: 415-346-8494 Dinner daily
Web: www.mamacitasf.com
Prices: $$

The lighting is low, but the volume is high in this upscale taqueria, where a cool, casual, and young Marina crowd gathers nightly for margaritas and Mexican fare. Small lacquered wood tables huddle under clusters of Moravian star lanterns, while lively Latin music sets the pace for bold flavors and changing California-style takes on South of the Border recipes.

Thus chipotle-agave nectar emulsion harmonizes beautifully with Ahi tartare; achiote chiles and green apple-mango salsa *verde* kick up the tempo on gulf prawns; and Oaxacan mole solos over braised tri-tip enchiladas. The crescendo builds as cinnamon- and sugar-dusted *churros* pair with *abuelita* hot chocolate in a sweet finale.

Little Asian sister, Umami, is located nearby on Webster Street.

Mifune

Japanese

C4

1737 Post St. (bet. Buchanan & Webster Sts.)

Phone: 415-922-0337 Lunch & dinner daily
Web: www.mifune.com
Prices: ⊜

Oodles of noodles are the star attraction at Mifune, located at Japan Center. Whether served cold with dipping sauce or in a bowl of steaming-hot broth, the house-made soba and udon noodles here are not to be missed. And if you're thinking that a bowl of noodles is a light meal, think again. You'll change your mind once you experience the massive portions at Mifune. The copious combination lunch, a steal at just over $10, includes sushi, a cut roll or don, and choice of soba or udon noodles.

Surrounded by Asian restaurants and gift shops in the Kintetsu Mall, this no-frills eatery is constantly packed. If Mifune is too crowded and you can't get a seat, go next door to little sister Mifune Don, which you'll find on the upper level of Miyako Mall.

PlumpJack Cafe

Californian XXX

C2

3127 Fillmore St. (bet. Filbert & Greenwich Sts.)

Phone: 415-563-4755 — Mon – Fri lunch & dinner
Web: www.plumpjackcafe.com — Sat – Sun dinner only
Prices: $$$

Service is friendly and intuitive at the classy Cow Hollow cafe, where wrought-iron sculptures frame banquettes covered in shimmering shades of violet, and a carved wood wine rack serves both a decorative and a practical function.

Kitchen changes have been rampant at this member of the PlumpJack group, which recently welcomed its fourth chef in three years. A San Francisco focus—season-driven cuisine made from local and sustainably produced ingredients—exhibits itself in the likes of handmade tagliatelle with smoked bacon, gulf shrimp, and artichokes; or a purée of corn soup topped with a dollop of crème fraîche and a warm mushroom salad. Dishes are designed to pair with the excellent and affordable wine list, which includes PlumpJack's own label.

Pres A Vi

Fusion XX

B2

1 Letterman Dr., Bldg. D (at Lombard St.)

Phone: 415-409-3000 — Lunch & dinner daily
Web: www.presavi.com
Prices: $$

In keeping with the forward-thinking spirit of the Letterman Digital Arts Center in which it is housed, Chef Kelly Degala and partners premiered this elegant restaurant in 2006.

Pres A Vi, sibling to Va de Vi in Walnut Creek, shares its older sister's culinary philosophy. The global menu embraces far-flung influences from the South Pacific, Asia, South America, and Europe. At lunch, it's all about hot and cold small plates and sandwiches. Dinner may offer Hawaiian mahi mahi with Thai red curry sauce. Note that they have recently added entrée-sized dishes to their small plate format.

A highlight, the wine list appeals with its serious selection and knowledgeable tasting notes. All wines are available by the bottle, the glass, or the 3-ounce pour.

Quince

Italian

1701 Octavia St. (at Bush St.)

Phone: 415-775-8500 Dinner daily
Web: www.quincerestaurant.com
Prices: $$$

Fans of Chef Michael Tusk's fine Italian cuisine are encouraged to know that the restaurant has a planned move in the coming months to a larger space in Jackson Square (*470 Pacific Ave*), formerly occupied by Myth. The community anticipates the same consistency and quality he and his wife Lindsay have presented through the years.

Chef/owner Michael Tusk is a Jersey boy, but his travels after culinary school introduced him to the rustic fare of Southern France and Italy, which provides his inspiration. He sources only the freshest products from a select network of producers, and the menu is updated nightly with original takes on Italian cuisine.

Quince's wine list contains a match for any dish, and the service is as smooth as butter.

Shabu-Sen

Japanese

1726 Buchanan St. (bet. Post & Sutter Sts.)

Phone: 415-440-0466 Lunch & dinner daily
Web: N/A
Prices: ⊛

You won't have to make many choices at Shabu-Sen. This inexpensive Japantown establishment only offers two types of dishes, shabu-shabu and sukiyaki—two preparations that derive from the Japanese practice of families gathering around a fire to warm themselves and make a meal together.

If you order shabu-shabu, you'll cook thin slices of beef, Chinese cabbage, shiitake mushrooms, tofu noodles and more in a pot of boiling broth at your table. You'll get two sauces (*gomadare*, with a sesame-and-peanut base; and *ponzu-shoyu*, with a base of soy sauce and vinegar) for dipping. Sukiyaki (vegetarian, beef or pork) is cooked for you in soy sauce enriched with sweetened sake and seaweed broth. It's served with fresh vegetables, udon, tofu and rice.

Sociale

Italian

3665 Sacramento St. (bet. Locust & Spruce Sts.)

Phone: 415-921-3200 Mon – Sat lunch & dinner
Web: www.caffesociale.com
Prices: $$

"Eat well, drink well, live well" are the three rules to follow at this Italian charmer, tucked away down an alley in Presidio Heights. It's worth seeking out, though, because once you're installed on the dreamy little patio out back, you'll feel miles away from the big-city buzz.

Sitting inside, where pastel hues set off black-and-white photographs of the Old Country, isn't so bad, either. Wherever you end up, you'll be treated to the same frequently changing Italian menu. The chef's discreet California twist stands out in the signature fontina-stuffed green olives, as well as in *concentrare* like grilled marinated quail with spicy ceci beans.

Just don't forget to make reservations, or you'll end up being anti-Sociale and eating at home.

SPQR

Italian

1911 Fillmore St. (bet. Bush & Pine Sts.)

Phone: 415-771-7779 Lunch & dinner daily
Web: www.spqrsf.com
Prices: $$

Friends, Romans, and Countrymen are all making their way to SPQR. This much-anticipated restaurant opened in fall 2007 in the former site of Chez Nous. Literally, the name means *Senatus Populusque Romanus* ("the senate and the Roman people"), but it may as well mean "wait in line," since this Pacific Heights darling takes no reservations.

Chef Nate Appleman, the tattooed wunderkind of A16, holds power in the kitchen. The simple spirit of Roman cuisine pervades modestly priced antipasti arriving hot (pancetta, cabbage, and farro soup), cold (sunchoke, radicchio, almond, parsley, and tangerine salad) or fried (Brussels sprouts with garlic, capers, lemon, and parsley). House-made pasta and rustic entrées complete the offerings in this petite place.

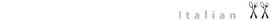

Spruce

Mediterranean XX

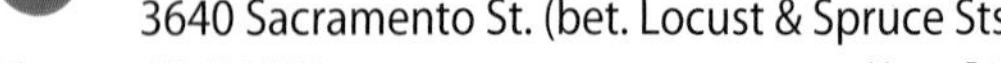

3640 Sacramento St. (bet. Locust & Spruce Sts.)

Phone: 415-931-5100 — Mon – Fri lunch and dinner
Web: www.sprucesf.com — Sat – Sun dinner only
Prices: $$$

Opened in late fall 2007 by the same folks who run the Village Pub in Redwood City, Spruce transforms a circa 1930s car garage in posh Presidio Heights into a luxurious den, done in shades of brown with textured faux-ostrich parlor chairs, mohair-covered walls, and large contemporary paintings.
A small cafe area to the left of the entrance offers take-out, including hot dishes from the kitchen. Better yet, stay and take in the swanky marble bar, the plush velvet loveseats and the upbeat music as you tuck into the best of the season: perhaps red pumpkin soup with chestnuts and sage, or crispy preserved duck leg with green lentils and sherry-glazed apples, in addition to an extensive list of international wines. Valet parking is offered at dinner.

Terzo

Mediterranean 

C2

3011 Steiner St. (bet. Filbert & Union Sts.)

Phone: 415-441-3200 — Dinner daily
Web: www.terzosf.com
Prices: $$

Sexy, sophisticated, and sometimes serene, Terzo is perfect for any rendezvous. The wood-burning grill's mouth-watering aromas escape from the open kitchen, as the list of Spanish-style tapas and tradtional entrée sized portions entice the appetite.
Flavors of the Mediterranean in grilled eggplant with red gypsy pepper and heirloom tomatoes; autumn chanterelles with crispy polenta and Pecorino Riserva; and chicken meatballs in *brodo* with braised chicories, pancetta, and parmesan. Add to that a fine international wine selection, with a generous ratio available by the glass.
Terzo ("third" in Italian) is the third San Francisco restaurant from Laurie Thomas and Nice Ventures, whose establishments also include Rose Pistola and Rose's Café.

Vivande

Italian 

2125 Fillmore St. (bet. California & Sacramento Sts.)

Phone: 415-346-4430 Lunch & dinner daily
Web: www.vivande.com
Prices: $$

Artisanal produce and authentic Italian products flavor the food in this neighborhood trattoria. Chef Carlo Middione, who opened Vivande in 1981, plumbs his Sicilian heritage for additions to the menu. Made fresh every day, the house fettucine appears at lunch in more than a half-dozen variations. House-made basil pesto; cream, butter, and parmesan; and fennel sausage, bell peppers, and marinara sauce (Salsiccia) will give you the mouth-watering idea. The wine list deftly balances offerings from the northern, central, and southern regions of Italy.
Brimming with bottles of olive oil and vinegar, jars of olives and jam, imported cheese and salami, and biscotti and amaretti, Vivande's take-out counter invites diners to take a taste of Italy home.

Zushi Puzzle

Japanese 

1910 Lombard St. (at Buchanan St.)

Phone: 415-931-9319 Mon – Sat dinner only
Web: www.zushipuzzle.com
Prices: 💰

Zushi Puzzle's diminutive façade is easy to miss as you're making your way down Lombard Street, but the cognoscenti know to head for this regularly packed Japanese place. Even solo diners are routinely turned away if they don't have a reservation.
What's the lure? Terrific fresh fish, and lots of it. Between the printed menu and the dry-erase board, the restaurant offers more than five dozen maki (think Romeo and Juliet: salmon and avocado topped with thinly sliced scallop, tobiko, and spicy sauce). Chef Roger Chong lords it the sushi bar—the best seats in the house—where freshly grated wasabi graces each plate.
Parking in this area can be a hassle, and often there's a line to get in, but a bit of advance planning brings its own reward here.

Mission District

Bernal Heights - Potrero Hill

This sunny southern neighborhood *(bounded by Duboce, Cesar Chavez, and Church Sts. and Potrero Ave.)* is San Francisco at its most bohemian, with artists, dot-commers, and activists coexisting with a vibrant Latino community. Aside from the historic **Mission Dolores**—the oldest building in San Francisco—there are dozens of good, cheap (and not-so-cheap) restaurants, and plentiful bars and nightspots that draw young hipsters. Funky art galleries stand shoulder-to-shoulder with thrift shops and used-book stores, while residential blocks are lined with pastel-painted Italianate row houses, some dating as far back as the 1870s. Throughout the area, you'll spot a large collection of Latino-themed murals.

Mission Dolores anchored a small village here in the early 1800s, but the area wasn't developed in earnest until after the Gold Rush. Some wealthy San Franciscans had weekend homes here, but by the turn of the 20th century, the neighborhood was mainly populated by European immigrants who worked in the warehouses, breweries and factories South of Market. Forced out of their homeland by the revolution, Mexicans began arriving in the 1920s. Central and South Americans have followed in the decades since.

Though gentrification has pushed many Latinos out of the area, the stretch of 24th Street between Mission and Potrero streets still dances to a salsa beat. Known as *El Corazon de la Misione*, or "the heart of the Mission," it's where the annual Carnaval festival takes place. To get a feel for the Latino art scene, check out the **Mission Cultural Center for Latino Arts** *(2868 Mission St.)*. Don't forget to sample some of the neighborhood's authentic taquerias.

BERNAL HEIGHTS

Crowning a steep, grassy hill at the southern end of the **Mission Valley**, this progressive urban community caters to families as well as price-conscious hipsters. These quiet streets once formed part of the *Rancho de las Salinas y Portrero Neuvo*. Bernal Heights takes its name from José Cornelio de Bernal, to whom the Mexican government granted the land in 1839. It's worth making the uphill trek for the cute cafes, local coffee shops, and neighborhood bars that center on the commercial hub of Cortland Avenue.

POTRERO HILL

Defined by Alameda, Third, and Cesar Chavez streets and Potrero Avenue, this quiet residential district was originally part of a land grant deeded to Don Francisco de Haro, who grazed Mission Dolores' cattle on the *potrero nuevo* (new pasture in Spanish). Small garden plots now provide a colorful counterpoint to the freeways that hem in this hill east of the Mission, where new office buildings and condos are cropping up. Look for shops and restaurants along the bohemian strip of 18th Street.

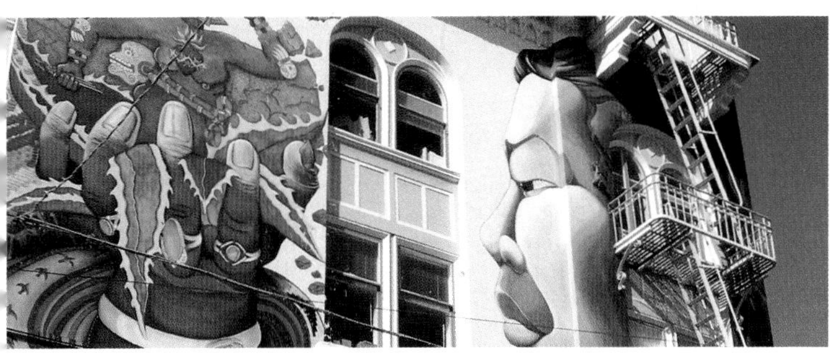

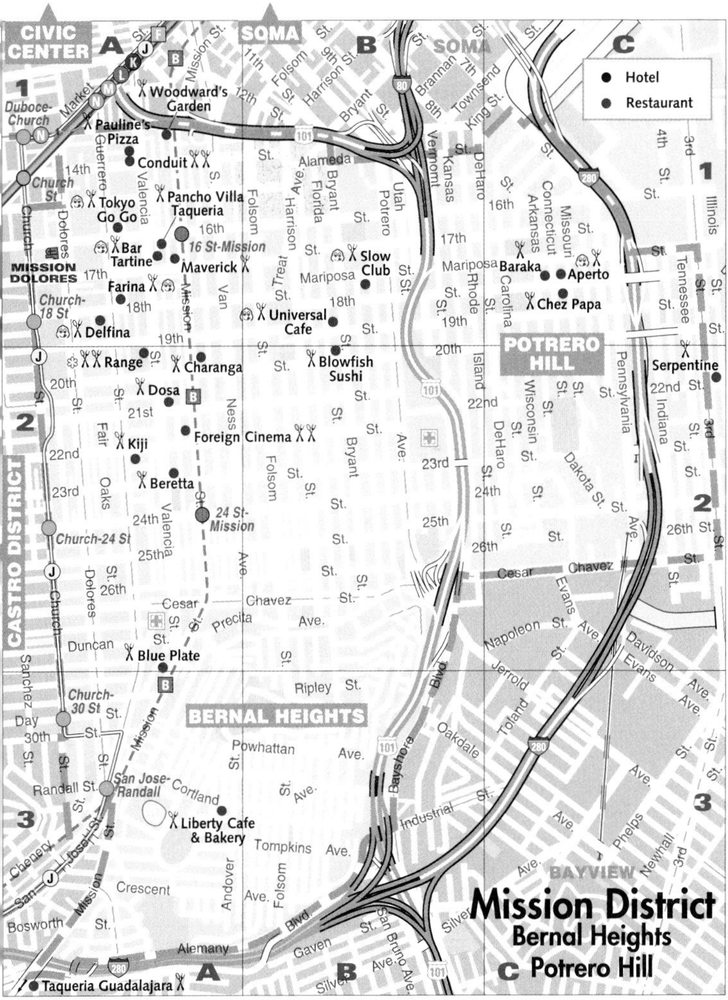

Mission District
Bernal Heights
Potrero Hill
Hotel
Restaurant
CIVIC CENTER
SOMA
MISSION DOLORES
CASTRO DISTRICT
POTRERO HILL
BERNAL HEIGHTS
BAYVIEW
Woodward's Garden
Pauline's Pizza
Conduit
Tokyo Go Go
Pancho Villa Taqueria
Bar Tartine
Maverick
Farina
Delfina
Slow Club
Universal Cafe
Range
Charanga
Blowfish Sushi
Dosa
Foreign Cinema
Kiji
Beretta
Blue Plate
Liberty Cafe & Bakery
Taqueria Guadalajara
Baraka
Aperto
Chez Papa
Serpentine
16 St-Mission
24 St-Mission
Duboce-Church
Church St
Church-18 St
Church-24 St
Church-30 St
San Jose-Randall
Market
Mission St.
Valencia
Guerrero
Dolores
Church
Sanchez
Folsom
Harrison
Bryant
Potrero
Vermont
Kansas
De Haro
Rhode Island
Carolina
Wisconsin
Arkansas
Connecticut
Missouri
Tennessee
Pennsylvania
Indiana
Illinois
Cesar Chavez
Precita
Alameda
Mariposa
Bayshore Blvd
Oakdale
Industrial
Tompkins Ave.
Alemany
Crescent
Bosworth St.
Napoleon St.
Evans Ave.
Jerrold
Toland
Phelps
Newhall
Ripley St.
Powhattan Ave.
Duncan
Randall St.
A
B
C
1
2
3

Aperto

Italian

C1

1434 18th St. (at Connecticut St.)

Phone: 415-252-1625 — Lunch & dinner daily
Web: www.apertosf.com
Prices: $$

From the open kitchen to its staff greeting guests with open arms, this little Potrero Hill Italian place is aptly named (aperto is Italian for "open"). And sister Bellanico is a welcome newcomer to Glenview in Oakland.
High-quality local and organic products add Californian touches to the distinctly Italian bill of fare. A chalkboard touts the daily specials, while the menu may list ravioli stuffed with cheese and sweet corn, topped with pancetta, fresh corn, pine nuts, and a white wine butter sauce; or a braised organic lamb shank served with summer ratatouille and natural jus. Dishes are nicely prepared and highlight fresh, well-matched flavors. Aperto is also happy to accommodate children, with its low-priced option of any shape of pasta served with roasted-tomato, butter, or cream sauces.

Baraka

Mediterranean

C1

288 Connecticut St. (at 18th St.)

Phone: 415-255-0370 — Dinner daily
Web: www.barakasf.net
Prices: $$

Quaint and cozy, Baraka beckons diners to this Potrero Hill corner with a large oxidized sign. A North African spirit pervades the place, founded by the same group that opened parents Chez Papa and Chez Maman nearby. Romance beckons in the candle-lit room, where red-orange walls, closely spaced copper-topped tables and red velvet cushions suggest romance.
Middle Eastern influences shimmy through the eclectic Mediterranean menu (think lamb tagine and paella), which changes with the season. Small plates hold sway at the bar, where guests team sangria and exotic cocktails with the likes of Moroccan-style meatballs with goat yogurt *fromage blanc*, and romaine heart salad with paprika croutons and shavings of Manchego cheese. Wine choices visit Spain, France and Italy, but call northern California home.

Bar Tartine

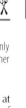

Californian

A1

561 Valencia St. (bet. 16th & 17th Sts.)

Phone: 415-487-1600 — Tue – Fri dinner only
Web: www.tartinebakery.com — Sat – Sun lunch & dinner
Prices: $$

An offshoot of wildly popular Tartine Bakery (nearby at 600 Guerrero Street), Bar Tartine has developed a following of its own. As parents of both places, Elisabeth Prueitt and Chad Robertson can be justly proud of their two culinary offspring. The narrow black and white dining room with its elk-antler chandelier has a contemporary bistro-meets-hunting-lodge vibe. Sit near the end of the Carrara marble bar that doubles as a prep area, if interested in cooking tips.

For dinner, enjoy the high quality ingredients and cooking in the likes of braised veal cheeks with heirloom broccoli and horseradish gremolata, or a house favorite: Marin Sun Farms bone marrow and grilled bread with persillade and arugula salad. Remember to save room for the delectable desserts.

Beretta

Italian

A2

1199 Valencia St. (at 23rd St.)

Phone: 415-695-1199 — Mon – Fri dinner only
Web: www.berettasf.com — Sat – Sun lunch & dinner
Prices: $$

Creative cocktails and artisan pizza pave the way for the latest Mission hotspot. The third in a string of restaurants by Ruggero Gadaldi (his others are Pesce and Antica Trattoria), Beretta occupies the space once filled by the Last Supper Club. The oxidized tin ceiling remains, but a long black communal table adds a trendy touch.

In addition to the star attraction—scrumptious thin-crust pizza—there is only one traditional main course offered each night. It may be lamb osso bucco on Thursday, cioppino on Friday; selections change per the day of the week. For a refreshing finish, go with the gelati and sorbetti.

Open until 1.00 A.M. every evening, Beretta lures nightowls from around the city with wine available by the taste, quartino, or bottle.

Blowfish Sushi

B2 **Japanese**

2170 Bryant St. (bet. 19th & 20th Sts.)

Phone: 415-285-3848 — Mon – Fri lunch & dinner
Web: www.blowfishsushi.com — Sat – Sun dinner only
Prices: ⊜⊜

With a name like Blowfish Sushi To Die For, this Japanese eatery is bound to raise expectations. Sit shoulder-to-shoulder at the concrete sushi bar and indulge in arresting items like the Godzilla Roll of sweet shrimp, mango, avocado, cashews, and coconut; the Fiesta Roll pairing tuna, avocado, cilantro, and salsa; or the Ménage à Trois of salmon, salmon skin, *ikura, masago, shiso,* and sprouts. Although the titles may sound gimmicky, their creations are exceedingly fresh, flavorful, and well presented.

The cool Tokyo vibe is enhanced by the hip and young yet professional staff, as well as the multiple screens featuring animé clips and art. Since the original Blowfish Sushi hit San Francisco, multiple outposts have emerged in California and as far away as Auckland, New Zealand.

Blue Plate

A2 **American**

3218 Mission St. (bet. 29th & Valencia Sts.)

Phone: 415-282-6777 — Mon – Sat dinner only
Web: www.blueplatesf.com
Prices: $$

Opened since 1999, this Bernal Heights bistro is as American as apple pie, starting with the blue neon sign that invites passersby to "EAT." Chef Cory Obenour crafts a new menu daily, focusing on the California formula of high-quality local and organic products. Mediterranean accents pepper a crispy-skinned Sonoma duck breast, fanned over a bed of fresh corn and potato hash with caramelized onions. Sides such as "taco truck" corn on the cob with *queso fresco,* lime, and chile salt; and macaroni and drunken Spanish goat cheese indicate the free-form nature of the kitchen.

If you have a choice, pick a table in one of the dining rooms rather than a seat at the counter facing the kitchen. The latter can get uncomfortably warm on a summer evening.

Charanga

Caribbean

A2

2351 Mission St. (bet. 19th & 20th Sts.)

Phone: 415-282-1813 Tue – Sat dinner only
Web: www.charangasf.com
Prices: $$

With a name that refers to both a Cuban dance party and a Latin flute-and-strings band, Charanga pulses with a lively atmosphere where neighbors enjoy good times and good food. Hemingway would have liked this Caribbean hideaway, with its weathered wood-plank floors, slowly turning ceiling fan, island music and mounted cigar boxes.

Billing itself as pan-Latin, the menu encompasses the cuisines of the Caribbean, Spain and Latin America. Think of Cuban-style roast pork leg (marinated in citrus, garlic and oregano) and *tostones a la tica* (fried green plantains layered with roasted-garlic goat cheese, pea shoots and black beans) as large tapas, and order several plates to share. Island-style libations like passionfruit mojitos, "guava-ritas" and caipirinha guajiros keep the party alive.

Chez Papa

French 

C1

1401 18th St. (at Missouri St.)

Phone: 415-824-8205 Lunch & dinner daily
Web: www.chezpapasf.com
Prices: $$

Everyone will feel at home at Chez Papa, where the relaxed atmosphere dreams up the South of France on Potrero Hill. In this corner bistro, zinc-topped tables and worn leather banquettes provide places to roost. Solo diners gravitate to the petit corner bar, while those preferring alfresco dining favor the sidewalk tables.

Family dinners *à la français* play up the simple cooking of Provence in such creations as *pissaladière*, lamb *daube*, and Loch Duart salmon with glazed endive. The staff convincingly fosters the warm vibe; guests can even break out their rusty school French without reprimand.

Owner Jocelyn Bulow, part of the team who also founded Chez Maman and Baraka, recently opened a branch of Chez Papa in the rejuvenated Mint Plaza in SoMa.

Conduit

Contemporary

280 Valencia St. (at 14th St.)

Phone: 415-552-5200 — Tue – Sun dinner only
Web: www.conduitrestaurant.com
Prices: $$

Construction conduit is typically used to conceal wiring, but there's no hiding the electricity that this newcomer is generating in the Mission. Designed by Stanley Saitowitz, the eye-catching décor incorporates steel and powder-coated conduit in its room partitions, bar, walls, and ceiling.

As arresting a first impression as this makes, it is Conduit's cuisine that leaves lasting memories. Chef Justin Deering's concise menu plays American chords with French and Italian riffs. Each item reads like an abbreviated recipe, as in game hen *sous vide*, green-pea ravioli, abalone mushrooms. Ask the convivial servers for more details about the dishes—and save room for dessert.

Opinions differ on the quirky co-ed bathroom with frosted-glass stalls.

Delfina

Italian

A1

3621 18th St. (bet. Dolores & Guerrero Sts.)

Phone: 415-552-4055 — Dinner daily
Web: www.delfinasf.com
Prices: $$

Craig and Anne Stoll continue to draw enthusiastic crowds to their Mission hotspot—still mobbed after all these years. The ambience is comfortably chic, uplifting, and lively (though loud), but the soul-warming Tuscan cuisine is the reason for the masses.

Here, a polite, and knowledgeable staff delivers true rustic fare: grilled fresh calamari with warm white bean salad; northern halibut with melted leeks and Meyer lemon-caper butter; brined and roasted Fulton Valley chicken plated beside mashed Yukon gold potatoes and earthy black trumpet mushrooms. A small front counter seats walk-ins, but it is best to reserve in advance.

Next door, Pizzeria Delfina shares the popularity, and has spawned a new sibling in Pacific Heights *(2406 California St.)*.

Dosa

Indian

995 Valencia St. (at 21st St.)

Phone: 415-642-3672 — Mon – Fri dinner only
Web: www.dosasf.com — Sat – Sun lunch & dinner
Prices: ⊜

A hotspot in the hub of the Mission, Dosa always seems to be bustling with activity. That's because fans of South Indian cuisine make a beeline for the boisterous dining room, where dangling pendant lamps cast a warm glow on tangerine-colored walls.
Savory dosas are the highlight of the menu; they're served filled (with mostly vegetarian ingredients), plain, or as open-faced versions called *uttapams*. All come with chutneys (coconut and/or tomato) and *sambar* (spiced lentils). South Indian curries, rice dishes, and traditional breads round out the offerings; the broad spectrum of spices is guaranteed to spark even the most jaded palate.
Good fortune for Marina dwellers: a second Dosa is slated to open at *700 Post St.* in late 2008.

Farina

Italian 

A1

3560 18th St. (bet. Guerrero & Valencia Sts.)

Phone: 415-565-0360 — Mon – Thu dinner only
Web: www.farinafoods.com — Fri – Sun lunch & dinner
Prices: $$

If first impressions rule, this new Mission restaurant will wow you. Its curving windowed façade reveals an eclectic design that incorporates elements of old and new into a sleek contemporary space.
Various cooking stations line the room. Pay particular attention to the pasta station, where chefs crank out silky handmade sheets of dough at a speed that is mesmerizing to watch. Paolo Laboa's Ligurian-accented menu changes daily, but the pastas are always winners (think delicate lasagna layered with a light creamy basil pesto). Warm *focacce*, like the focaccia di Recco—a simple Ligurian-style "sandwich" of Stracchino cheese melted between two thin layers of flaky and crunchy bread—will change your idea of a grilled cheese forever.

Foreign Cinema

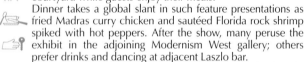

International

2534 Mission St. (bet. 21st & 22nd Sts.)

Phone: 415-648-7600 — Mon – Fri dinner only
Web: www.foreigncinema.com — Sat – Sun lunch & dinner
Prices: $$

A perennial favorite, Foreign Cinema elevates "dinner and a show" to new cultural heights. Foreign and independent films are screened on the white-washed brick wall of the enclosed courtyard while guests enjoy their meals.

Dinner takes a global slant in such feature presentations as fried Madras curry chicken and sautéed Florida rock shrimp spiked with hot peppers. After the show, many peruse the exhibit in the adjoining Modernism West gallery; others prefer drinks and dancing at adjacent Laszlo bar.

Although no movie is screened at weekend Picnic Brunch, the rough-hewn room is a pleasure in its own right. New Life Farm organic eggs star when served poached with Moroccan-spiced duck breast, or in a Champagne omelet studded with black truffles.

Kiji

Japanese 

1009 Guerrero St. (bet. 22nd & 23rd Sts.)

Phone: 415-282-0400 — Dinner daily
Web: www.kijirestaurant.com
Prices: $$

From the sushi chefs to the servers, a pride of place infuses this Japanese spot, which stands between the Mission District and Noe Valley. Pride shines through in the food as well. Raw offerings such as *toro* nigiri or konpachi carpaccio (Japanese amberjack arranged on a banana leaf and topped with thin slices of jalapeño, a drizzle of olive oil, and a crunch of sea salt) will satisfy sushi lovers, but the extensive menu goes way beyond sushi. Plump seared Hokkaido scallops, for instance, are flavored with a pleasant ponzu reduction, while black cod is marinated in sweet miso and broiled.

The varnished wood bar is the place to sit and if you want to go completely Japanese, complement your meal with a sampling from the well-stocked sake collection.

Liberty Cafe & Bakery

American 

410 Cortland Ave. (bet. Bennington & Wool Sts.)

Phone: 415-695-1223 Tue – Sun lunch & dinner
Web: www.thelibertycafe.com
Prices: $$

Opened in 1994, this cozy neighborhood favorite nestles among coffeeshops and bookstores on a quiet Bernal Heights street where parking is always a challenge. In the cafe's dining room, comforting entrées may remind you of food your mom used to make: chicken pot pie crowned with golden puff pastry; colorful seasonal salads; and pizzas with cracker-thin crusts.

Behind the cafe, the Cottage Bakery turns out breads and pastries—and it's open for breakfast to boot. The presence of the bakery also means that Liberty's desserts, like tangy/sweet raspberry-rhubarb pie and coconut-cream layer cake, are not to be missed.

From Thursday to Saturday evenings, the bakery area and back patio morph into a wine bar featuring an enticing menu of appetizers.

Maverick

American 

3316 17th St. (at Mission St.)

Phone: 415-863-3061 Mon – Fri dinner only
Web: www.sfmaverick.com Sat – Sun lunch & dinner
Prices: $$

Nonconformity can be a good thing—this is particularly true at Maverick, where innovative regional American cuisine arrives in bold flavors in a mod little neighborhood spot. Take a tour of the menu's playful combinations, from the Baltimore crab fluffs, to Southern fried chicken with Nora Mill "Georgia Ice Cream" grits, or Kurobuta pork cassoulet. With dishes such as duck confit hash, andouille sausage Benedict, and a fried-oyster po' boy, it is no wonder that Maverick's weekend brunch claims loyal fans.

Old "Maverick" beer cans on tables, and a hanging, backlit abstracted map of the United States offer a masculine, clubby feel to the space, though everyone is treated as a member. Drop by Monday night for 40 percent off any bottle of wine.

Pancho Villa Taqueria

Mexican

3071 16th St. (bet. Mission & Valencia Sts.)

Phone: 415-864-8840 — Lunch & dinner daily
Web: www.panchovillasf.com
Prices: ⊜

Located in the heart of the vibrant Mission District, this little taqueria features an extensive menu of fresh Mexican fare. Before you get in line, be sure to peruse the multitude of dishes on the enormous menu board. Once in line, you'll be pressed to make quick decisions on which (of the ten) meats, award-winning salsas, fresh condiments, types of beans, and cheese you want in your burrito. More decisions come at the end of the counter, where soda, *horchata*, *cerveza*, and glass barrels filled with fruit-flavored *aqua fresca* offer to quench your thirst.

The atmosphere is utilitarian dining hall with backless leather stools for seating, but that does nothing to dissuade the swarms of Mission denizens waiting patiently for an empty table.

Pauline's Pizza

Pizza

A1

260 Valencia St. (bet. Duboce Ave. & 14th St.)

Phone: 415-552-2050 — Tue – Sat dinner only
Web: www.paulinespizza.com
Prices: $$

Some darn good pizza can be found in the Mission at Pauline's. Crispy yet doughy handmade crusts can be strewn with "regular" (mushrooms, black olives, sausage, pepperoni) toppings or with seasonal "eccentric" ingredients (pancetta, artichoke hearts, goat cheese, house-made chicken sausage). The signature pie is slathered with pesto, and the chef offers a special "eccentric combination" each night in both meat and vegetarian versions. Try it with a glass of one of Pauline's private-label "pizza reds." For a sweet ending, how about homemade ice cream, chocolate mousse or butterscotch pudding?

Pauline's doesn't take reservations, and most nights, the line leads out the door. If all else fails, buy some of Pauline's frozen pizza shells to go.

Range ✿

A2 Contemporary XX

842 Valencia St. (bet. 19th & 20th Sts.)

Phone: 415-282-8283 Dinner daily
Web: www.rangesf.com
Prices: $$

♿

Rose Gray

Behind a small façade on a busy corner of the Mission District, a hip little trifecta of dining options awaits. You can sit in Range's shiny concrete bar, with its glowing lights and urban appeal. The room behind that has a modern feel, with small metal tables lining a long leather banquette, and bright oil paintings gracing the wall. The last room features exposed wood beams, and long narrow mirrors. Anywhere you sit, the goods are exactly the same—polished, but relaxed, service—and Chef Phil West's compact, but clever, menu that spins simple ingredients into sophisticated fare.

A fresh bass, for example, is cooked to golden exactness and set on a rustic mash of fava beans, chopped bacon, and baby white turnips. For dessert, a crisp puff pastry crust gets trumped up with sliced ripe aprium—an apricot/plum hybrid—and is topped with fresh cherries and ice cream.

Appetizers

- Roasted Spot Prawns, Herb Butter, Meyer Lemon
- Beets, Blood Oranges, Ancho Cress, Walnuts and Sheep's Milk Ricotta
- Lamb Sausage, Melted Endive

Entrées

- Vegetable Cassoulet with Portobello Mushroom Confit
- Oven-roasted Chicken, Caramelized Fennel, Olives, Pancetta
- Sirloin Roast, Creamed Leeks

Desserts

- Strawberry Shortcake, Lemon Cream, Rose Geranium
- Date Turnovers, Toffee Sauce, Crème Fraîche
- Chocolate Crêpes, Pink-Peppercorn Ice Cream

Serpentine

Californian

C2

2495 3rd St. (at 22nd St.)

Phone: 415-252-2000
Web: www.serpentinesf.com
Prices: $$

Tue – Fri lunch & dinner
Mon lunch only
Sat dinner only

Located on the flats of the eastern edge of Potrero Hill, the nine-square-block neighborhood called Dogpatch boasts a long and colorful past. Today, this district still has an industrial feel even while new condos rise on its borders.

Serpentine, an offshoot of Slow Club (below), named for the layer of rock that forms the foundation for many of the surrounding buildings, retains the stripped-down look of its once industrial space.

Chef Chris Kronner, who splits his time between the two siblings, may whip up a Tombo tuna salad, a savory bread pudding or a lamb meatloaf sandwich at lunch. For dinner he trots out the likes of crispy Hama Hama oysters, and buffalo bone marrow with a parsley and kumquat salad.

Slow Club

Californian

B1

2501 Mariposa St. (at Hampshire St.)

Phone: 415-241-9390
Web: www.slowclub.com
Prices: $$

Mon – Sat lunch & dinner
Sun lunch only

Slow Club's urban vibe and subtlety appeals to the hip SoMa set who are attracted by the moderate prices and the décor of varnished concrete and exposed black metal beams.

Carefully prepared dishes change daily on the menu. The best of the market's seasonal bounty composes dishes such as grilled pork loin with roasted butternut squash, sautéed radicchio, and pear compote; and pan-seared Coho salmon with avocado purée, roasted San Marzano tomatoes, wild arugula, and breakfast radishes.

Expect a wait; Slow Club doesn't take reservations and there aren't many other places on this block to vie for your dining dollars. Solo diners can grab a perch at the back bar—first come, first served.

New sister Serpentine is kicking up the scene in Dogpatch.

Taqueria Guadalajara

Mexican 

A3

4798 Mission St. (at Onondaga Ave.)

Phone: 415-469-5480 Lunch & dinner daily
Web: N/A
Prices: 

Bright painted murals adorn the interior of this tiny taqueria in the Excelsior neighborhood of the Outer Mission. Order at the counter, then claim a seat in the quaint dining area where you can watch Mexican *fútbol* on the flat-screen TV.

Tortillas here are grilled and come in wheat, spinach and sun-dried tomato; be sure to specify which you prefer, or you'll end up with the plain flour version. Char-broiled meats include *carne* and *pollo asada*, but regulars rave about the *lengue* (beef tongue) and *cabeza* (beef head). Since it lacks labels, the salsa bar can be a dangerous place. Beware of the orange-hued salsa—it's made with tongue-numbing habañeros.

Taqueria Guadalajara has a sister in the Inner Mission *(3142 24th St.)* that shows the same consistency.

Tokyo Go Go

Japanese 

A1

3174 16th St. (bet. Guerrero & Valencia Sts.)

Phone: 415-864-2288 Dinner daily
Web: www.tokyogogo.com
Prices: $$

Hip-hop and techno music set the pace of this cool, young place, styled after an *izakaya*. Chef John Park's menu is chockfull of innovative hand rolls from the sushi bar and hot plates from the kitchen. Baked spicy scallops rolled with wasabi tobiko are indeed Dynamite, while the Sunshine roll is brightened by *hamachi* and cilantro, and is topped with a raw quail egg. Hot entrées separate this place from the typical sushi bar, serving the likes of panko-breaded Tokyo garlic shrimp served with sweet eel *tsume* sauce and chili aïoli; or white tuna *escabeche* plated with shaved fennel, red onion, jalapeño and Thai chili.

Enjoy three dollar hand rolls and house cocktails during nightly happy hour from 5:30 to 7pm and on Sunday from 5 to 6:30pm.

Universal Cafe

B1 **Californian**

2814 19th St. (bet. Bryant & Florida Sts.)

Phone: 415-821-4608 — Wed – Sun lunch & dinner
Web: www.universalcafe.net — Tue dinner only
Prices: $$

This sparkling gem sits on the fringe of Potrero Hill, where the cognoscenti once happily kept it a secret. Word has slipped out, though, making reservations is difficult to attain. Plan to arrive early or wait elbow-to-elbow at the long Carrera marble bar that parallels the open kitchen.

Thanks to Chef/owner Leslie Carr Avalos, who forsakes a traditional toque in favor of a colorful kerchief, creative flavor combinations illuminate the daily menu. Flatbreads may be topped with porchetta, braised greens, and sheep's-milk ricotta; while soups pair the likes of fennel and Meyer lemon. Fans of the cafe's brunch come for seasonal blood orange or pomegranate mimosas, as well as fried eggs with linguica and Portuguese baked beans.

Woodward's Garden

A1 **American** 

1700 Mission St. (at Duboce St.)

Phone: 415-621-7122 — Tue – Sat dinner daily
Web: www.woodwardsgarden.com
Prices: $$$

A diamond in the not-so-rough Mission District, Woodward's Garden, is tucked under the 101 Freeway overpass, where owners Dana Tommasino and Margie Conard have run the quaint place since 1992.

Worn banquettes and small square tables offer an up-close and personal view of the kitchen, which is integrated into the front dining space. The menu serves up down-home comfort in a grass-fed hanger steak, served over a creamy gratin of sliced new potatoes, spring asparagus, and fava beans. Wholesome and delicious describes desserts like a cherry vanilla-bean brown-butter tart nestled in a shortbread crust.

In the mid-19th century, this was the site of an amusement park and gardens—the subject of Robert Frost's poem *At Woodward's Garden.*

MICHELIN

Nob Hill

Russian Hill - Chinatown

Three adjoining areas, Nob Hill, Chinatown, and Russian Hill, in the northeast corner of the city may share boundaries, but each retains its own distinct personality.

NOB HILL

Though it pokes into the sky like a knobby knee, Nob Hill was named for the titans of industry who once lived here (nob is a contraction of nabob, a term for European adventurers who made huge fortunes in India and the East).

These nabobs came in two waves. The first were the Big Four railroad magnates—Leland Stanford, Charles Crocker, Mark Hopkins and Collis Huntington—who built sprawling mansions atop Nob Hill in the 1870s. They were joined in the 1880s by two of the four Bonanza Kings,—James Fair and James Flood—who profited off Nevada's Comstock silver lode. Engineer Andrew Hallidie's Folly—the **cable car**—brought more development to the 376-foot summit after the establishment of the **California** (1878) and **Powell Street** (1888) lines.

Today residential Nob Hill *(edged by Polk, Geary, Mason & Washington Sts.)* is peppered with upscale restaurants, apartment buildings, and several of the city's most historic and posh hotels.

RUSSIAN HILL

Along with its knobby neighbor, Russian Hill offers some of the best views in the city. It wasn't until the 1880's, when the cable car provided easy access to its summit, that people started moving here en masse. The **Powell-Hyde** and **Powell-Mason** lines are still the best ways to get to the top.

Over the years, the swanky neighborhood defined by Francisco, Taylor, Pacific, and Polk streets has provided inspiration for many literary figures, from Mark Twain to Jack Kerouac. Today, it attracts thrill seekers and photographers to the 100 block of **Lombard Street**, where eight dramatic switchbacks mark the steep (16 percent) grade between Hyde and Leavenworth.

CHINATOWN

This densely populated and tight-knit community got its start around 1849 when thousands of Cantonese treasure hunters ventured up toward **Sutter's Mill** in search of gold. Today, Chinatown spills down the eastern slope of Nob Hill and bridges the Financial District and North Beach. Pass through the **Chinatown Gate** *(Grant Ave. at Bush St.)* and you'll enter a world of dim sum palaces, tea shops, vegetable markets, souvenir emporiums, and temples. **Grant Avenue**, Chinatown's main street, abounds in architectural chinoiserie, while on **Stockton Street** shoppers throng the produce, live-fish, and poultry markets flanking the blocks between Clay Street and Broadway. Marked by historic statues and plaques, **Portsmouth Square** lies at Chinatown's heart; the garage underneath the square provides parking for visitors.

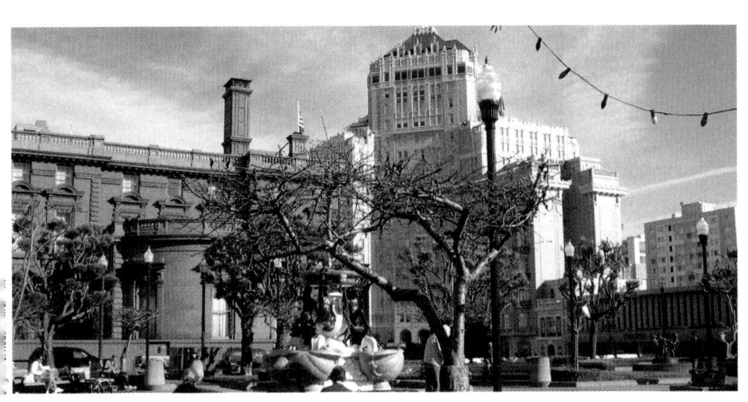

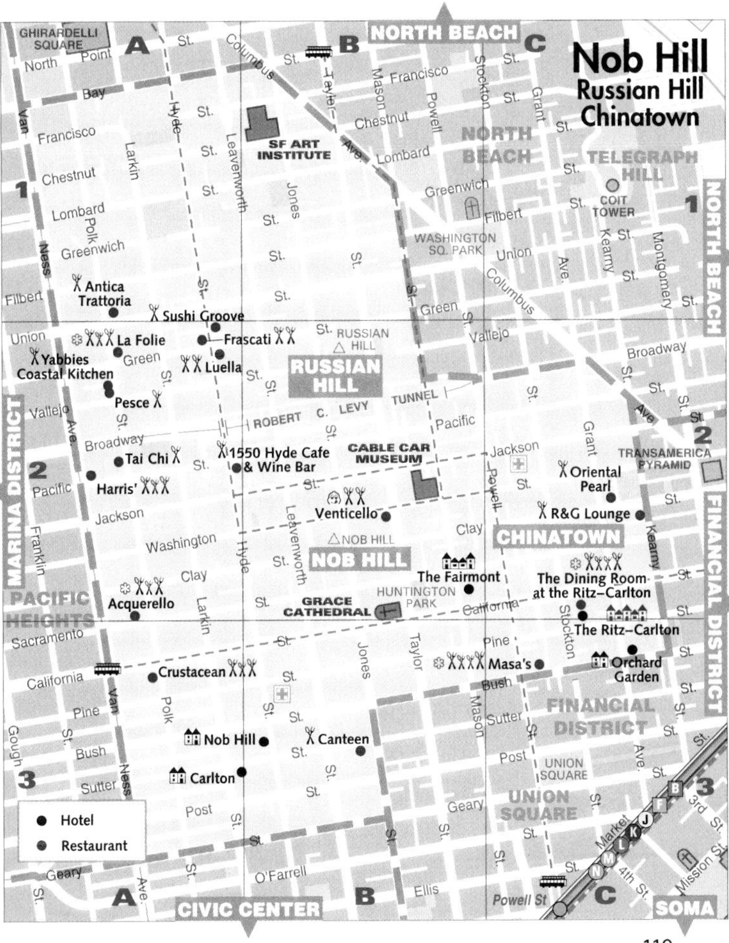

Nob Hill
Russian Hill
Chinatown
NORTH BEACH
CIVIC CENTER
SOMA
MARINA DISTRICT
FINANCIAL DISTRICT
GHIRARDELLI SQUARE
SF ART INSTITUTE
RUSSIAN HILL
NOB HILL
CHINATOWN
TELEGRAPH HILL
COIT TOWER
WASHINGTON SQ. PARK
CABLE CAR MUSEUM
GRACE CATHEDRAL
HUNTINGTON PARK
TRANSAMERICA PYRAMID
UNION SQUARE
PACIFIC HEIGHTS
ROBERT C. LEVY TUNNEL
Antica Trattoria
Sushi Groove
La Folie
Frascati
Yabbies Coastal Kitchen
Luella
Pesce
Tai Chi
1550 Hyde Cafe & Wine Bar
Harris'
Venticello
Oriental Pearl
R&G Lounge
The Fairmont
The Dining Room at the Ritz-Carlton
The Ritz-Carlton
Acquerello
Crustacean
Masa's
Orchard Garden
Nob Hill
Canteen
Carlton
Hotel
Restaurant
Van Ness Ave.
Columbus Ave.
Powell St
Market St.
Mission St.
3rd St.
4th St.

Acquerello ✿

A2 Italian XXX

1722 Sacramento St. (bet. Polk St. & Van Ness Ave.)

Phone: 415-567-5432 Tue – Sat dinner only
Web: www.acquerello.com
Prices: **$$$$**

The sun-soaked colored walls and whispering patrons lend a soothing beauty to this chapel-turned-restaurant, but dinner begins with a bang. Sink your teeth into fat, beet-soaked pockets of tortolloni, bursting with fresh spinach and beet greens and tossed in a delicate Gorgonzola sauce; then move on to fresh diver scallops, jacketed in crispy pancetta and laid over a mound of puréed squash and sautéed dandelion greens.

That's just a taste of what keeps the stylish crowd pouring in for Chef Suzette Gresham-Tognetti's upscale, contemporary Italian dinners, which, depending on your appetite, arrive in 3, 4, 5, or 7 courses. After dinner, lean back and soak in the high vaulted ceilings, lined with hand-painted wood beams, and let the soft thrum of music transport you to a small church in Tuscany. There is but one sermon in these hallowed halls—eat, drink, and be grateful.

Appetizers

- Lobster Panzerotti in Spicy Lobster Brodo with "Diavolicchio"
- Fennel Fettuccine with Moist Ragù of Wild Boar
- Parmesan Budino Topped with Shaved Asparagus Salad

Entrées

- Pork Chop, Grilled Radicchio, Parsnip-Potato Cake
- Boneless Rack of Lamb with Artichokes
- Halibut, Mushrooms and Green Beans with Saffron Sauce

Desserts

- Meyer Lemon Tartlet, with Italian Meringue and Citrus Salad
- Bourbon-Caramel Semifreddo with Amaretti Crumbs and a Drizzle of Chocolate Sauce

Antica Trattoria

Italian 

A1

2400 Polk St. (at Union St.)

Phone: 415-928-5797 — Tue – Sun dinner only
Web: www.anticasf.com
Prices: **$$**

Born and raised in a small town in northern Italy, Antica's Chef/owner Ruggero Gadaldi has been involved with food since he was a lad (his other local establishments include Pesce and Beretta). The menu at this rustic, no-frills trattoria, opened in 1996, shows off his commitment to fresh seasonal cuisine and Slow Food ideals with dishes such as light and fluffy *gnocchi con fonduta*, bathed in a creamy cheese fondue accented with earthy truffle oil; and *pollo al limone*, crisp-skinned chicken topped with bread crumbs, sliced almonds, and minced parsley.

Parking is nearly impossible in this area of Nob Hill, but you will forget that hassle as the friendly service welcomes you inside this popular neighborhood gem.

Canteen

Californian 

B3

817 Sutter St. (bet. Leavenworth & Jones Sts.)

Phone: 415-928-8870 — Wed – Sat lunch & dinner
Web: www.sfcanteen.com — Sun lunch only
Prices: **$$** — Tue dinner only

Next door to the erstwhile Commodore Hotel, this 20-seat diner seems an unlikely place to find the guy who took over Rubicon's kitchen from Traci Des Jardins. Yet at Canteen, Chef/owner Dennis Leary and his team dish up breakfast, lunch and dinner to savvy foodies.

The chef changes his menu weekly, offering perhaps a dozen dishes total. Though tender Parker House rolls are a staple, the likes of shrimp dumplings in a light, sweet-corn and chile broth are far from diner fare. Bare bulbs hanging from the ceiling light soft gray walls inset with bookshelves, giving the eatery a coffeeshop feel. Behind the bright-green counter, though, some big flavors come out of the galley kitchen.

Leary also mans the stove at his new breakfast and lunch spot, Sentinel, in SoMa *(37 New Montgomery St.)*.

Crustacean

Asian

1475 Polk St. (at California St.)

Phone: 415-776-2722
Web: www.anfamily.com
Prices: **$$$**

Mon – Sat dinner only
Sun lunch & dinner

Behind Crustacean there's a fairy tale come true about the Ans, a well-to-do Vietnamese family who was forced to leave their country in the wake of the Communist invasion in 1975. Mother Helene started the family's first epicurean venture at Thanh Long in San Francisco. Crustacean, the second in their string of restaurants, opened its doors in 1991.

Take the elevator to the third floor, where Crustacean creates an exotic world filled with bamboo, potted palms, whimsical lanterns, and large picture windows. In the locked kitchen within the kitchen, An family members prepare their "secret specialties," such as royal tiger prawns, tasty garlic noodles, and the much-ordered whole roasted Dungeness crab in garlic sauce.

1550 Hyde Cafe & Wine Bar

Californian

1550 Hyde St. (at Pacific Ave.)

Phone: 415-775-1550
Web: www.1550hyde.com
Prices: **$$**

Tue – Sun dinner only

Organic is the name of the game at this quaint Russian Hill cafe. Established in 2003 by Kent Ligget and Peter Erickson, 1550 Hyde fills its Cal-Med menu with sustainably raised, local, and organic products. Whether you crave grilled Pacific swordfish with faro salad; local sardines with sea beans, olives, and oranges; or a fried Hoffman Gamebird chicken, your palate is sure to be pleased.

As for the second part of the restaurant's name, there's a respectable list of more than 150 wines to pair with your meal. Why not be adventurous and introduce yourself to something new via the nightly "Flight Plan," of red and white flights?

With advance planning, you can avoid the parking hassles and play tourist by riding the Powell-Hyde cable car to dinner.

The Dining Room at the Ritz-Carlton

Contemporary

600 Stockton St. (at California St.)

Phone: 415-773-6198 Tues – Sat dinner only
Web: www.ritzcarlton.com
Prices: **$$$$**

Ron Starr/The Ritz-Carlton

It's true. You can get away with a ridiculously long name like this when you call the Ritz-Carlton home. Located in elegant Nob Hill, the Dining Room at the Ritz-Carlton is as luxurious and sophisticated as one might expect with such an impressive landlord, with warm, richly-patterned fabrics in gold and burgundy cloaking the room, gauzy window sheers hanging gracefully from the windows, and glowing chandeliers lining the walls. The crisply-suited service team (you'll be expected to wear a jacket too) also makes the grade, with a gracious, discreet tone and an eagle's eye for detail.

Chef Ron Siegel's contemporary menu runs the gamut, offering starters like silky strips of konpachi, topped with cool cubes of cucumber and a yuzu gelée; or an entrée of Japanese butterfish, pan-seared and gingerly placed on a sticky mound of short grain rice, and then ringed with pickled watermelon.

Appetizers

- Sashimi of Live Spot Prawns and Sauted heads and Yuzu Gelée
- Slow-cooked Veal Cheeks with Salad of Asian Pear & Ginger
- Big Fin Squid Noodles and Beech Mushrooms

Entrées

- Sansho-crusted Duck Breast, Mustard Rabe, Pickled Huckleberries
- Veal Chop, Asparagus, Morels, Artichoke Ravioli
- Diver Scallops, Green Sake Lobster Broth

Desserts

- Coconut Panna Cotta en Coupe, Milk Chocolate Ice Cream
- Chocolate Tower, Kirsched Cherries, Milk Chocolate Ice Cream
- Passionfruit Cake, Blood Orange Sorbet

Frascati

Mediterranean 

1901 Hyde St. (at Green St.)

Phone: 415-928-1406 Dinner daily
Web: www.frascatisf.com
Prices: $$

Big groups or single diners, all are welcomed as friends by Frascati's warm staff, as they have been since this charming restaurant opened its doors in 1987. Warm colors abound inside the high-ceilinged space, where those seeking a romantic soirée should request a table on the upstairs balcony.

French, Spanish, and Italian influences show up on the plates, be it in sweet-pea risotto studded with smoked salmon, melted leeks, mascarpone, mint, and gremolata; or an herb-crusted rack of lamb with potato purée, ratatouille, upland cress, mint oil, and lamb jus.

Parking spaces are scarce along these crowded Russian Hill streets. Instead of driving around hoping to find one, hop on the Powell-Hyde cable car, which stops right in front of the restaurant.

Harris'

Steakhouse 

2100 Van Ness Ave. (at Pacific Ave.)

Phone: 415-673-1888 Dinner daily
Web: www.harrisrestaurant.com
Prices: $$$$

Any doubts that this is a steakhouse will be dispelled once you spy the butcher counter just inside. From the entrance, the clubby Pacific Lounge beckons with its mahogany bar, classic martinis (shaken, not stirred) and live jazz music Thursday through Saturday nights. It's a fine place to sip a cocktail before adjourning to the skylit dining room decorated with Victorian-style brass chandeliers, curved leather banquettes, and a mural of the Kings River in California covering one wall.

This makes a fitting setting to carve into a wide selection of dry-aged midwestern Angus beef, ranging from the Harris steak (a thick, bone-in New York cut) to filet mignon Rossini (served with Sonoma foie gras, black truffle and Cabernet sauce).

La Folie ✿

French XXX

A2

2316 Polk St. (bet. Green & Union Sts.)

Phone: 415-776-5577 — Mon – Sat dinner only
Web: www.lafolie.com
Prices: $$$$

Dan Peak

Tucked into the patchwork of posh hotels and stylish eateries that is modern-day Russian Hill, you'll find perennial 'Frisco favorite, La Folie. This family-run mainstay, under the careful watch of Chef Roland Passot, has made its name turning out expertly-prepared classic French haute cuisine with a good dose of California sensibility (note the vegetarian tasting menu).

Having revamped its interior a few years back, guests can now expect to find soothing brown wood-paneled walls, long curtains in honey-hued fabrics, fresh-cut flowers, and velvet banquettes.

The tasting menus (offered in 3, 4, or 5 courses) change often, but might begin with crispy frog legs and frog leg mousse cannelloni, served with slices of wild mushrooms on a bed of bright green parsley coulis; or a pan-roasted cobia garnished with delta asparagus, pickled ramps, and morel mushrooms in a *beurre fondue*.

Appetizers

- Sautéed Burgundy Snails, Parsley and Bone Marrow Gratin
- "Tasting of Passot Roe", Sea Urchin Panna Cotta, Kona Konpachi Parfait, Lobster with Fennel Radish Salad

Entrées

- Butter-poached Lobster, Pea Raviolo, Almonds, Pea Tendril Salad, Carrot-Ginger Broth
- "Le Bœuf"-Tenderloin, Braised Short Rib, Burger Rossini with Madeira

Desserts

- Edam Cheese Soufflé with Fromage Blanc Sorbet, Crispy Bacon, White Sesame Tuile
- "Baked Alaska"-Huckleberries, Basil Crème Anglaise, Crème Fraîche Sorbet

Luella

Mediterranean 

1896 Hyde St. (at Green St.)

Phone: 415-674-4343 Dinner daily
Web: www.luellasf.com
Prices: $$

Finding a parking space in Russian Hill may be frustrating, but it's worth the hassle to experience the good food and hospitable service at this family-run restaurant. Ben and Rachel de Vries still operate the comfortable hotspot, bedecked with pebbled-leather booths and bamboo-framed mirrors.
Regulars clamor for the Coca-Cola-braised chicken and the orange-ricotta fritters, but dishes such as Ahi tuna tartare tacos and grilled local halibut with lemon beurre blanc are equally delicious. Bring the kids on Sunday night, when the Little Luella menu caters to diners under 10 with grilled cheese and French fries, chicken pot pie, and ice-cream sundaes for dessert.
Parking note: valet service is available on Polk Street, between Green and Union streets.

Oriental Pearl

Chinese 

760 Clay St. (bet. Grant & Kearny Sts.)

Phone: 415-433-1817 Lunch & dinner daily
Web: www.orientalpearlsf.com
Prices:

This pearl nestles in the heart of Chinatown, near Portsmouth Square. The stark white second-floor dining room is the place to come for noteworthy Hong Kong-style cuisine and genuinely friendly service—happy to offer unsure patrons a chopsticks lesson. Dive into refreshing, artistically presented dishes on the extensive menu. Choices include the house special chicken meatball, made of chicken, shrimp, mushrooms, and Virginia ham wrapped in an egg-white pancake dumpling. At lunch, try the inexpensive chef's specials or sample a set dim sum menu designed for two or more.
Mind that the restaurant only accepts credit cards for purchases over $15, as these low prices make it difficult to rack up much of a bill.

Masa's ✿

Contemporary ✗✗✗✗

648 Bush St. (bet. Powell & Stockton Sts.)

Phone: 415-989-7154 — Tue – Sat dinner only
Web: www.masasrestaurant.com
Prices: $$$$

If you were scurrying down Bush Street, just north of Union Square, you might miss the tiny glass awning that marks the entrance to Masa's. But behind the draped windows that frame this restaurant (connected to the Hotel Vintage Court), you'll find a gorgeously-appointed dining room filled with cushy mohair banquettes and enormous bright red lampshades. How's the food hold up under all that trendiness? Exceedingly well, thanks to the creative mind of Chef Gregory Short who spins a wide range of specialty ingredients into his contemporary, French-influenced fare.

The ever-changing nightly prix-fixe might include thick coins of grass-fed veal served over a tangle of roasted black trumpet mushrooms, freshly-shelled favas, and Perigord truffles; or tender New Zealand Thai snapper on a mound of sweet and creamy parsnip purée.

Don't miss the award-winning 900+ bottle wine list.

Appetizers

- Broccoli Velouté, Truffle-infused Custard, Broccoli Florets
- Crab and Avocado Salad, Tangerine Gelée, Red Shiso
- Roasted Maitake, Herbed Risotto Cake

Entrées

- Snapper, Parsnip Purée, Tempura of Spinach, Saffron-infused Broth
- Sautéed Quail, Chestnut-Pear Ragout, Poultry Jus
- Grilled Japanese Wagyu, Daikon

Desserts

- Brioche Brûlée, Orange Crème, Avocado Sorbet
- Pear-Rhubarb Crisp, Shortbread, Pineapple Sorbet
- Rum-soaked Apricot Custard, Puff Pastry, Cherry Sauce

Pesce

Seafood

2227 Polk St. (bet. Green & Vallejo Sts.)

Phone: 415-928-8025 — Mon – Fri dinner only
Web: www.pescesf.com — Sat – Sun lunch & dinner
Prices: $$

Most everything about Pesce is small, beginning with the dining room and ending with the *cichetti*, or small plates like those served at bars in Venice. Even the prices are relatively small, especially given the swanky Russian Hill neighborhood.

What's not small are the flavors. Ruggero Gadaldi (also owner of nearby Antica Trattoria and Beretta in the Mission), presides over this cozy self-styled "seafood bar" where *cichetti* are classified cold or hot. Among the former, you'll find house-smoked salmon, trout, and sturgeon; a Dungeness crab tower; and an oyster shot. The latter might include braised octopus salad, Sicilian swordfish rolls, and Merlot-braised lamb shank. For dessert, try the excellent tiramisu, creamy and redolent of liqueur.

R & G Lounge

Chinese 

631 Kearny St. (bet. Clay & Sacramento Sts.)

Phone: 415-982-7877 — Lunch & dinner daily
Web: www.rnglounge.com
Prices: $$

Savvy locals have been coming to R & G Lounge for quality Cantonese cuisine since 1985. Décor is contemporary in the deceptively small dining space, where dark wood paneling lines the well-lit room and a wavy metal "grid" covers the ceiling.

Start with one of the specialty martinis in watermelon, mango, or lychee, to name a few. Then move on to fresh seafood, much of which is scooped live from the aquariums around the restaurant. Chef's recommendations include deep-fried prawns with honey walnuts, and steamed clams with beaten eggs. Entrées like chicken with XO sauce and sautéed steak cubes with macadamia nuts are sure to satisfy. While many bargains abound, be prepared to pay top dollar for a bowl of the controversial shark-fin soup, the most expensive dish on the menu.

Sushi Groove

Japanese

1916 Hyde St. (bet. Green & Union Sts.)

Phone: 415-440-1905 — Dinner daily
Web: N/A
Prices: $$

You can take your pick of cuisine types in the posh residential Russian Hill neighborhood, but you can't beat Sushi Groove for good sushi at reasonable prices. Simple fresh nigiri is fine, but don't pass up the creative rolls—like the Jungle Roll with yellowtail, pineapple, and *tobiko*—or the poke salad made with diced Ahi tuna, mango, papaya, cucumber, and sesame-chili oil. Be sure to flip the menu over so you don't miss the multitude of other options—including the ever-changing specials—that are listed on the back. A word to the wise: the menu focuses on raw dishes, so if you're looking for cooked fare, you're better off just ordering a glass of sake and enjoying the conversation.
Ask about valet parking when you call to make your reservation.

Tai Chi

Chinese

2031 Polk St. (bet. Broadway & Pacific Sts.)

Phone: 415-441-6758 — Mon – Sat lunch & dinner
Web: N/A — Sun dinner only
Prices: ⊜

Neighborhood residents favor this popular, no-frills place for its copious portions of freshly prepared Chinese food and easy-on-the-budget prices. From cashew chicken to chow fun, there are plenty of options here. If your taste buds prefer fiery fare, seek the asterisk-marked menu items, like Hunan Mongolian beef (thin pieces of tender flank steak well-infused with heat from dried red chilies, and flavor from minced garlic and oyster sauce, are stir-fried with segments of pungent scallions).
The restaurant's location in residential Nob Hill, coupled with the lack of atmosphere in the plain canteen-style dining room, means that Tai Chi does a big take-out business. Unlike many of the area restaurants, this one is open for both lunch and dinner.

Venticello

Italian

1257 Taylor St. (at Washington St.)

Phone: 415-922-2545 Dinner daily
Web: www.venticello.com
Prices: $$

Venticello means "soft breeze" in Italian, and you'll be wishing for one after you scale Nob Hill to reach this rustic restaurant (if you don't savor hill-climbing, we recommend you drive to Venticello and avail yourself of the valet-parking option).
Inspired by farmhouses in Tuscany, the interior sets a warm tone with terra-cotta hues, an open kitchen, and a large wood-fired oven tiled in cobalt blue. From the latter come thin-crust pizzas and roasted meats, while the kitchen turns out the likes of spaghetti carbonara with homemade pasta, and *melanzane ripiene* (grilled eggplant rolls stuffed with ricotta and mascarpone and napped with tangy marinara).
As for *dolci*, you won't go wrong with the tasty tiramisu topped with fresh strawberries.

Yabbies Coastal Kitchen

Seafood

2237 Polk St. (bet. Green & Vallejo Sts.)

Phone: 415-474-4088 Dinner daily
Web: www.yabbiesrestaurant.com
Prices: $$

Weeknights are the best times to dine at Yabbies if you want a quiet meal. During the weekends, a crush of Russian Hill urbanites hovers around the seafood bar and the separate wine bar (the full menu is served at both). Simple paper dresses the tabletops, and a bustling ambience prevails.
Start by selecting some oysters on the half shell among the half-dozen kinds listed. If you have a party in tow, go for one of the chilled seafood platters, piled high with Dungeness crab, oysters, prawns, mussels and littlenecks (the larger, more expensive platters add Maine lobster to the mix). Besides the roster of predominantly seafood entrées, nightly specials—from fish and chips to a clambake for two—are offered Monday through Thursday.

North Beach Area

Fisherman's Wharf - Telegraph Hill

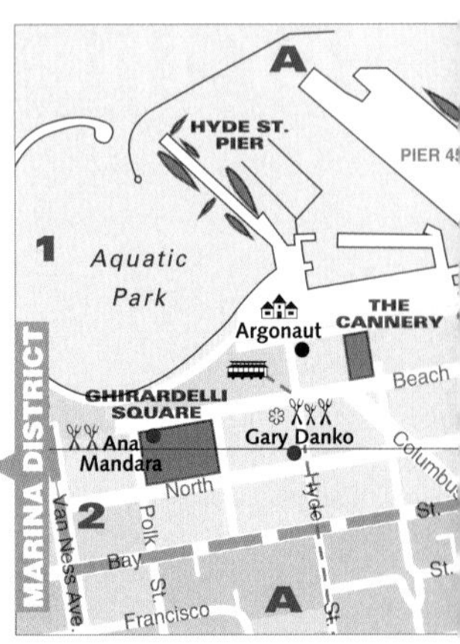

Nestled between bustling Fisherman's Wharf and the steep slopes of Russian and Telegraph North Beach is one of the sunniest and liveliest neighborhoods in the city. You can thank the Italians who came to dominate the area in the late 1800s. Though they're no longer in the majority, dozens of Italian restaurants and bars attest to their interpretation of the good life. Check out the Italian delis to supply a picnic in nearby **Washington Square Park**.

Today, the majority of North Beach's restaurants and bars lie along **Columbus Avenue**, which cuts diagonally from the **Transamerica Pyramid** to **Fisherman's Wharf**. Present and future establishments may be affected by a proposed alcohol ban (i.e., no liquor licenses) on all new businesses, a piece of legislation that also threatens to curtail beer and wine sales in this neighborhood.

FISHERMAN'S WHARF

Once an industrial zone, Fisherman's Wharf is San Francisco's most popular tourist destination. Six piers offer everything from carousel rides, shopping, and sea lions on **Pier 39**, to maritime history on **Hyde Street Pier**. Take a ferry to **Alcatraz** or **Sausalito**, or enjoy a sourdough bread bowl filled with chowder. Current plans call for a tax initiative to spruce up this area, adding more parks, open space, and seating for the public.

Lining the waterfront along land reclaimed from the bay, the **Embarcadero** was once the hub of San Francisco's shipping and transportation. Revitalization began after the 1989 Loma Prieta earthquake damaged the Embarcadero Freeway. Once the freeway was razed, massive redevelopment began, creating the palm-lined boulevard, airy plazas, and green spaces that define the area today.

TELEGRAPH HILL

Punctuating the eastern edge of North Beach, the abrupt 274-foot rise of Telegraph Hill is named for a long-vanished semaphore that used varicolored flags to signal the arrival of ships through the Golden Gate. Most of the early structures built on the hill were destroyed in the 1906 fire. Some on the eastern slope were saved by determined Italian Americans, who reportedly beat back the flames with blankets soaked in red wine. The svelte 180-foot-high column of **Coit Tower** tops Telegraph Hill. A climb to the top of the tower affords the best views in a city that, as Alfred Hitchcock said, doesn't have a bad angle.

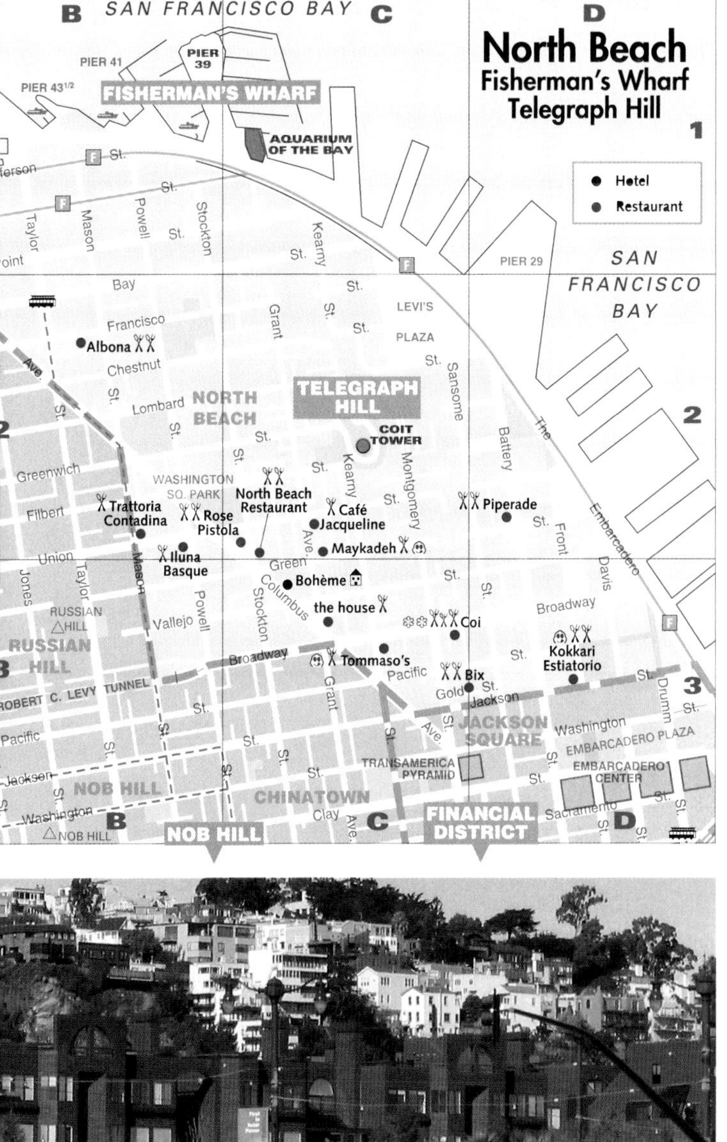
North Beach
Fisherman's Wharf
Telegraph Hill
Hotel
Restaurant
SAN FRANCISCO BAY
FISHERMAN'S WHARF
PIER 39
PIER 41
PIER 43 1/2
AQUARIUM OF THE BAY
PIER 29
LEVI'S PLAZA
TELEGRAPH HILL
COIT TOWER
NORTH BEACH
WASHINGTON SQ. PARK
RUSSIAN HILL
ROBERT C. LEVY TUNNEL
NOB HILL
CHINATOWN
JACKSON SQUARE
TRANSAMERICA PYRAMID
EMBARCADERO PLAZA
EMBARCADERO CENTER
FINANCIAL DISTRICT
Albona
Trattoria Contadina
Rose Pistola
North Beach Restaurant
Café Jacqueline
Piperade
Iluna Basque
Maykadeh
Bohème
the house
Coi
Tommaso's
Kokkari Estiatorio
Bix

Albona

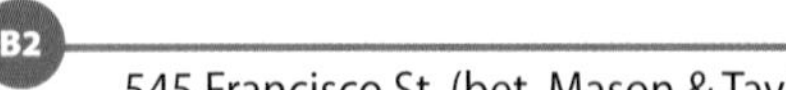

Italian

B2

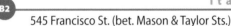

545 Francisco St. (bet. Mason & Taylor Sts.)

Phone: 415-441-1040 — Tue – Sat dinner only
Web: www.albonarestaurant.com
Prices: **$$$**

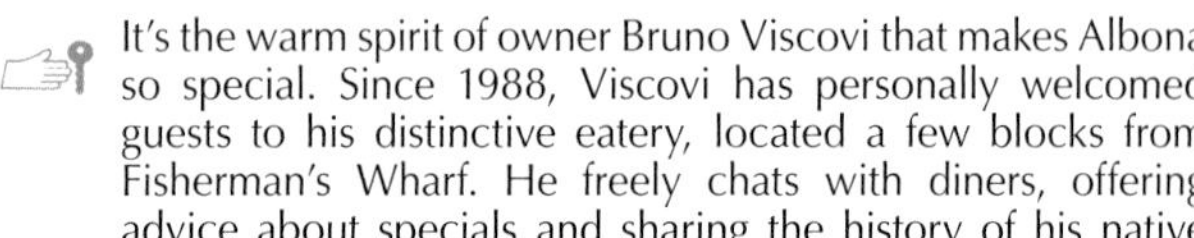

It's the warm spirit of owner Bruno Viscovi that makes Albona so special. Since 1988, Viscovi has personally welcomed guests to his distinctive eatery, located a few blocks from Fisherman's Wharf. He freely chats with diners, offering advice about specials and sharing the history of his native city, for which the restaurant is named.

This area near the intersection of Italy, Slovenia and Croatia shares its foodways and its geography with Eastern Europe. Along with northern Italian dishes such as the excellent *calamari al forno*, you'll find pork loin stuffed with sauerkraut, veal shank à la Triestina, and Adriatic fish stew. For dessert, the signature *crema di gelato* (creamy gelato mousse topped with brandy-soaked cherries) is a must.

Ana Mandara

Vietnamese

A1

891 Beach St. (at Polk St.)

Phone: 415-771-6800 — Mon – Fri lunch & dinner
Web: www.anamandara.com — Sat – Sun dinner only
Prices: **$$$**

Although its entrance lies on the bay side of Ghirardelli Square, Ana Mandara doesn't need a view to entertain. Its exotic ambience provides ample eye candy with a striking Vietnamese temple décor.

Populated by a chic cadre of diners, this restaurant is more than a "beautiful refuge," as its name translates. It's a stylish venue in which to relish the refined Vietnamese cuisine of Chef Khai Duong, whose Parisian training provides him with the technique on which he bases a ceviche of striped bass, cucumber, shallots and red-chile oil; or wok-fried beef tenderloin with sweet onions and peppercress.

Other reasons to go: validated parking for the Ghirardelli garage, and live jazz in the mezzanine lounge (Thursday through Saturday nights).

Bix

American 

56 Gold St. (bet. Montgomery & Sansome Sts.)

Phone: 415-433-6300 — Sat – Thu dinner only
Web: www.bixrestaurant.com — Fri lunch & dinner
Prices: $$$

Hidden in the dark narrow alley known as Gold Street, the brick façade of Doug "Bix" Biederbeck's restaurant would be easy to miss if not for the neon sign that advertises "Bix Here." Inside, this 20-year veteran shrugs off trendy in favor of a nostalgic supper-club décor recalling 1930s San Francisco. Mahogany paneling, baby grand piano, plush banquettes, and a long dimly lit bar dress the downstairs, while a sweeping staircase gives way to intimate booths in the mezzanine. Jazz music entertains diners nightly.

Servers clad in white tuxedo jackets and black bow ties deliver the likes of shrimp Louis, house-made papardelle with short-rib *sugo*, and steak tartare prepared tableside with an elegant flourish from hand-cut Creekstone Angus beef.

Café Jacqueline

French 

C2

1454 Grant Ave. (bet. Green & Union Sts.)

Phone: 415-981-5565 — Wed – Sun dinner only
Web: N/A
Prices: $$$

Those looking for a quick meal needn't read any further. This café specializes in slow food—soufflés to be exact. Seductively puffed and airy—and sized for two—these savory creations are flavored with ingredients such as gruyere cheese and white corn; brie and broccoli; and salmon and asparagus. While you're waiting for your soufflé to emerge from the oven, sample a salad or a bowl of the terrific French onion soup. Dessert brings more soufflés, these rich and sweet, heady with intense chocolate or Grand Marnier.

You have to walk through the kitchen on your way to the loo. There you'll see diminutive Chef Jacqueline Margulis passionately whipping up her signature dish—as she has for more than 25 years—kept company by an enormous bowl of fresh eggs.

Coi 

Contemporary XXX

C3

373 Broadway St. (bet. Montgomery & Sansome Sts.)

Phone: 415-393-9000 — Tue – Sat dinner only
Web: www.coirestaurant.com
Prices: **$$$$**

David Wakely

Other than the immediate locale, which is a touch on the seedy side, everything else about Coi (pronounced "kwa") is carefully calculated toward reaching foodie nirvana. From the polished, professional staff to the sleek, elegant room with its soothing earth tones and minimalist design, the backdrop of Coi is set up to let the undisputed star—in this case, Chef Daniel Patterson's creative, eclectic nightly tasting menus—take center stage.

Known for twisting impeccably fresh ingredients into inventive combinations, dinner might include a small tart of fresh, whipped goat cheese with a smear of magenta beet purée across the plate. For garnish, two small disks of cooked golden beets, tiny dill sprigs, and crushed caraway seeds. A silky bowl of chilled English pea soup might follow it, garnished with a dollop of fresh ricotta and a few clinging orange nasturtium petals.

Appetizers

- Grapefruit, Ginger, Tarragon, Black Pepper
- Earth & Sea - Potatoes, Cucumber, Sea Beans, Borage
- Squash in Different Forms

Entrées

- Butter-steamed Black Cod, Carrots, Peas, Sorrel
- Slow-cooked Prather Ranch Pork Belly, Sprouted Beans, Seeds, Nuts
- Grilled Porcini, Coconut Milk, Tapioca, Cilantro

Desserts

- Crème Fraîche Ice Cream, White Lady Peach, Almond, Thyme
- Carrot Cake, Carrot Ganache, Celery Sorbet
- Chocolate Ganache, Seascape Strawberries, Wild Licorice Anglaise

Gary Danko ✿

Contemporary

800 North Point St. (at Hyde St.)

Phone: 415-749-2060 — Dinner daily
Web: www.garydanko.com
Prices: $$$$

Step out of the fanny-pack parade that dominates San Francisco's beloved, but sometimes painfully touristy, Fisherman's Wharf, and into the stylish foodie haven that is Gary Danko. Named for the award winning chef who owns it, this airy brasserie is a world apart from the neighborhood it calls home—with its soft, inviting jazzy music, lively chatter emanating from the ever-filled room, and fresh-cut roses dotting the landscape.

As to the food, well, that's what Danko made his name on—working his technique into dishes like crispy, broiled Moroccan-spiced squab fanned over a rich stuffing of couscous and orange-cumin laced carrots.

The flexible menu offers a la carte offerings as well as tasting menus starting from 3-courses, and grape connoisseurs will want to take a second to check out the wine list, which plays patriot with a large American selection.

Appetizers

- Seared Foie Gras, Caramelized Onion, Rhubarb
- Lobster-Shrimp Risotto, Zucchini, Crispy Artichokes
- Glazed Oysters, Caviar, Zucchini Pearls and Lettuce Cream

Entrées

- Moroccan Spiced Squab and Orange-Cumin Carrots
- Roasted Loin of Bison with Trumpet Mushrooms and Herb Spätzle
- Lemon Herb Duck Breast, Duck Hash

Desserts

- Olive Oil Cake, Lemon Ice Cream, Berries
- Raspberry-Rhubarb Napoleon, Passion fruit Mousse, Thistle Honey
- Chocolate-Coffee Ganache, Chocolate Fudge Cake

the house

Asian 

1230 Grant Ave. (bet. Columbus Ave. & Vallejo St.)

Phone: 415-986-8612 — Mon – Sat lunch & dinner
Web: www.thehse.com — Sun dinner only
Prices: $$

Opened by Larry and Angela Tse in 1993, this tiny Asian eatery near the busy confluence of Broadway, Columbus, and Grant Avenues goes against the predominantly Italian grain of North Beach.

After taking a seat, a small plate of tangy marinated sesame cucumbers will arrive at your table. White shrimp and Chinese chive steamed dumplings with tangy soy-scallion sauce, wasabi house-made noodles with grilled pork, and a deep-fried salmon roll with spicy mustard are staples here, but wait for your server to rattle off the slew of specials before making a decision. Copious quantities, colorful presentations, and a good choice of beer and wine by the glass will encourage you to make this house your home for tasty and reasonably priced Asian fare.

Iluna Basque

Basque 

B2

701 Union St. (at Powell St.)

Phone: 415-402-0011 — Dinner daily
Web: www.ilunabasque.com
Prices: $$

Chef Mattin Noblia brings his Basque roots to the Italian enclave of North Beach. In 2003, at the tender age of 23, Noblia opened Iluna Basque, overlooking Washington Square. Since then, the restaurant has won acclaim as a place to go for late-night tapas and Spanish wine.

Small plates and *petite entrées* tempt diners with the distinguished specialties of southwestern France and northwestern Spain: seafood paella; piperade with sautéed Serrano ham and a poached egg; a hearty Basque chicken and chorizo sauté; and *gâteau Basque*, a rich almond cream cake.

Bordeaux-red walls, velvet curtains and candlelight accent the modern décor. A young crowd pours in beginning at happy hour, making the scene more rambunctious than romantic.

Kokkari Estiatorio

Greek

200 Jackson St. (at Front St.)

Phone: 415-981-0983 — Mon – Fri lunch & dinner
Web: www.kokkari.com — Sat dinner only
Prices: $$

Named for a small fishing village on the Aegean island of Samos, Kokkari transports diners to Greece with its rustic charms. Pick from the eye-catching taverna-style rooms: the front with its cavernous wood-burning fireplace, and the back with its communal table and view of the exhibition kitchen. A large copper urn filled with piping-hot sand stands at one end of the kitchen; it is used to heat pitchers of heady Greek coffee.

Courteous servers deliver the Mediterranean specialties such as grilled whole fish, moussaka, and grilled lamb chops with lemon-oregano vinaigrette. This *estiatorio* fills up fast, and reservations are recommended.

If you're in Palo Alto, Kokkari's successful sister, Evvia, is just as good.

Maykadeh

Persian

470 Green St. (bet. Grant Ave. & Kearny St.)

Phone: 415-362-8286 — Lunch & dinner daily
Web: www.maykadehrestaurant.com
Prices: $$

Think North Beach is all about Italian food? Think again. This Persian-style tavern (according to the definition of its name) sings a different tune. You'll be off to an excellent start with a copious plate of tender lamb's tongue in a sour-cream-based sauce with saffron and lime. Wonderful products turn a free-range baby chicken into a symphony: the bird cut into pieces; marinated in lime juice, onion, and saffron; roasted until crispy; and lined up artfully across the plate. Don't pass up *bastani* for dessert—Persian ice cream—scented with rosewater and studded with pistachios, vies with gelato any day of the week.

Valet parking here is a relief in a neighborhood where finding a place to leave your car nearby always presents a challenge.

North Beach Restaurant

Italian XX

1512 Stockton St. (bet. Green & Union Sts.)

Phone: 415-392-1700 Lunch & dinner daily
Web: www.northbeachrestaurant.com
Prices: $$$

Although oozing with Old World charm, North Beach Restaurant has always been ahead of its time. Partners Lorenzo Petroni and Bruno Orsi have been curing their own precious *salumi* since opening 1970—years before that practice came into vogue. Italian-American waiters clad in tuxedos cater to clients with the warmth typical of a family-run establishment. With its vaulted ceiling and cherry-wood paneling, the main dining room feels formal, yet comfortable.

The menu consistently focuses on simple, satisfying classics like veal saltimbocca, flavorful minestrone, chicken Marsala, lasagna made to order, and salmon poached in white wine with a lemon butter sauce.

Those seeking a late bite will appreciate that food service runs until 11:45 every night.

Piperade

Basque 

D2

1015 Battery St. (at Green St.)

Phone: 415-391-2555 Mon – Fri lunch & dinner
Web: www.piperade.com Sat dinner only
Prices: $$

The vibrant cuisine of the Basque region (straddling northwestern Spain and southwestern France) comes alive at Chef Gerald Hirigoyen's North Beach restaurant. Named for the traditional stew made with tomatoes, garlic, and sweet bell peppers, Piperade celebrates the chef's roots with a delicate sheep's-milk cheese and ham terrine drizzled in aged sherry; or a lamb *basquaise* chop with gigante beans dressed in "zikiro" vinaigrette. Savor the carefully chosen wine list of labels predominantly from France, Spain, and California.

The humble space also recalls the Basque countryside, where a communal farm table sits beneath an inverted cone holding empty wine bottles. Time stands still on the small patio, featuring an oversize antique clock with no hands.

Rose Pistola

Italian 

532 Columbus Ave. (bet. Green & Union Sts.)

Phone: 415-399-0499 Lunch & dinner daily
Web: www.rosepistolasf.com
Prices: $$$

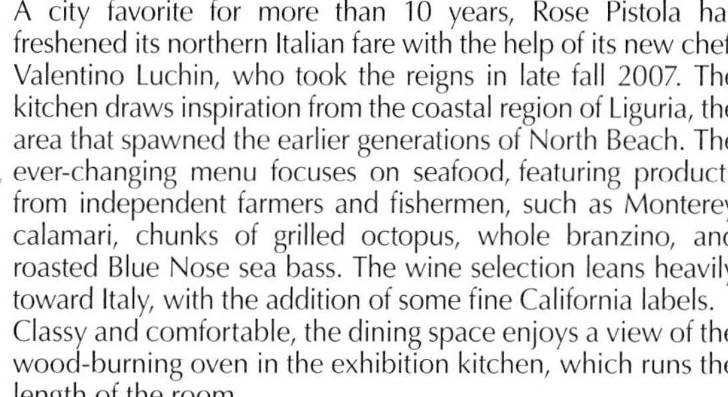

A city favorite for more than 10 years, Rose Pistola has freshened its northern Italian fare with the help of its new chef, Valentino Luchin, who took the reigns in late fall 2007. The kitchen draws inspiration from the coastal region of Liguria, the area that spawned the earlier generations of North Beach. The ever-changing menu focuses on seafood, featuring products from independent farmers and fishermen, such as Monterey calamari, chunks of grilled octopus, whole branzino, and roasted Blue Nose sea bass. The wine selection leans heavily toward Italy, with the addition of some fine California labels.
Classy and comfortable, the dining space enjoys a view of the wood-burning oven in the exhibition kitchen, which runs the length of the room.

Tommaso's

1042 Kearny St. (bet. Broadway St. & Pacific Ave.)

Phone: 415-398-9696 Tue – Sun dinner only
Web: www.tommasosnorthbeach.com
Prices: $$

A North Beach fixture since 1935, Tommaso's (originally known as Lupo's) has been dishing up consistently good cuisine for all these years. The speakeasy-style entrance leads to a long lower-level room lined with wood booths trimmed in white and decorated with a colorful mural of the Bay of Naples.
Specials change monthly, but other than that, the menu touts Neapolitan stalwarts—such as baked fresh coo-coo clams, homemade ravioli with marinara sauce, and stuffed manicotti with meatballs or sausage—as it has for more than 70 years. Locals in the know keep their eyes on the pies here, since Tommaso's lays claim to introducing wood-fired pizza to San Francisco. Toppings ranging from chicken and artichokes to sausage and prosciutto are offered.

Trattoria Contadina

Italian

B2

1800 Mason St. (at Union St.)

Phone: 415-982-5728 — Dinner daily
Web: www.trattoriacontadina.com
Prices: $$

Locals love this little corner trattoria, with its cramped dining room, warm service and simple décor. Though judging from the signed photos of celebrities that paper the walls, the place is no neighborhood secret.

Founder Dirk Correnti encourages patrons to leave their problems at the door and abandon themselves to copious quantities of Italian comfort food. House-made ricotta gnocchi in a tomato-cream sauce with asiago cheese; *rigatoncelli alla Carlesimo* (with pancetta and porcini in a spicy vodka-tomato sauce); and a grilled veal chop with a balsamic-vinegar reduction will stick to your ribs but won't put a big dent in your wallet.

Don't hassle with parking; the Powell-Mason cable-car line will drop you off right in front.

The ✿ award is the crème de la crème. This is awarded to restaurants which are really special for their cuisine.

Richmond and Sunset

Referred to locally as the Avenues, these two neighborhoods edging the Pacific Ocean remain residential havens where locals frequent their favorite ethnic restaurants. Richmond and Sunset share several traits in common. Both have a middle-class small-town feel; both are fog-shrouded; and their populations incorporate a cultural mix that is apparent in the area's myriad restaurants.

Where Richmond and Sunset meet the ocean, sit the **Lincoln Park Zoo**, **Cliff House**, the ruins of **Sutro Baths**, and the **California Palace of the Legion of Honor**. Follow the **Coastal Trail** along the shoreline for spectacular views of the Golden Gate Bridge and **Marin Headlands**.

RICHMOND

At the turn of the 20th century, Richmond's western reaches were condemned as the Great Sand Waste until the establishment of a railway along **Geary Boulevard** opened the district to settlement.

Today, Richmond's main thoroughfare, **Clement Street**, teems with shops and markets hawking everything from bok choy to flip-flops. Here, you can sup on a budget at your choice of Chinese, Thai, Burmese, Vietnamese, and Korean eateries. The stretch of Clement Street between Arguello and Park Presidio Boulevards rivals Chinatown for its concentration of Chinese restaurants. International is the key word here; a melting pot of cultures adds French bistros, Italian pizzerias, Japanese sushi bars and even Irish pubs.

SUNSET

South of Golden Gate Park sits the Sunset District, which was also a windswept region of sand dunes until developer Aurelius Buckingham built the first row houses on present-day Lincoln Way in 1887. With its global-village vibe amidst the perma-fog, the Sunset juggles a mix of mom-and-pop diners, coffee shops, and trendy new restaurants.

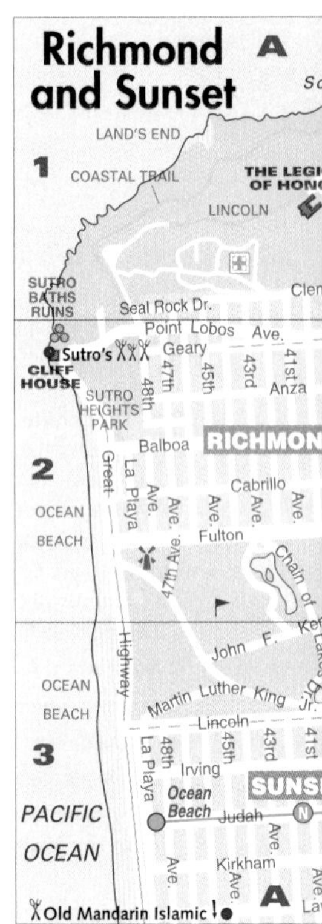

Brigitta L. House/MICHELIN

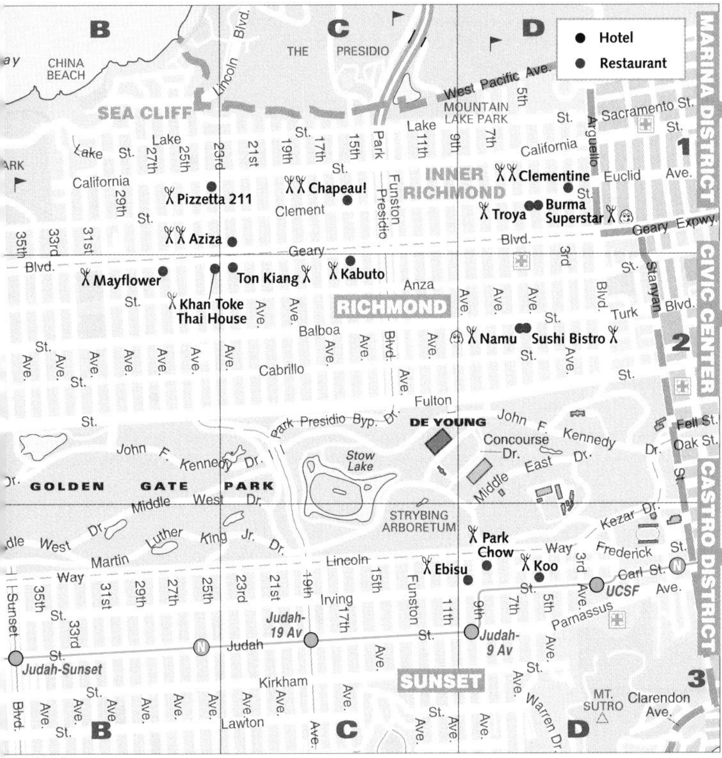

Aziza

Moroccan XX

C1

5800 Geary Blvd. (at 22nd Ave.)

Phone: 415-752-2222 Wed – Mon dinner only
Web: www.aziza-sf.com
Prices: $$

Aziza beckons like a desert oasis on this lively stretch of Geary Boulevard. Chef/owner Mourad Lahlou, who hails from Marrakech, honors his roots as he translates Berber tagines and Moroccan vegetable stews into modern Moroccan fare using prime California products (think seared Hokkaido sea scallops with warm Brentwood corn salad and Marash pepper).

You'll feel a sultry, North African vibe in the dining room, where sharply dressed servers and cool jazz pair with vibrant colors, decorated arches and candlelight. Cocktails are the beverage of choice at the bar. Will it be a "strawberry" (moscato d'asti), a "nutmeg" (a shot of espresso, Kahlua, Bailey's and brandy), or an "apple" (rosemary, maple sugar and tequila)?

Burma Superstar 

Burmese X

D1

309 Clement St. (bet. 4th & 5th Aves.)

Phone: 415-387-2147 Lunch & dinner daily
Web: www.burmasuperstar.com
Prices:

A little piece of Burma (now known officially as Myanmar) hides under an orange awning at the corner of Fourth Avenue. Blending in among the Asian restaurants that pack this part of Richmond, Burma Superstar always seems to draw a crowd.

The attentive and genuinely helpful staff is happy to assist guests unfamiliar with Burmese cuisine in navigating the exotic menu. Pumpkin pork stew, chili lamb, and the rainbow salad—with 22 ingredients (including four types of noodles) that play off each other in a perfect symphony of flavor—represent authentic dishes. Since Myanmar borders India, China, and Thailand, also uncover those influences in the shareable dishes here.

Success has spawned a little sister, B Star Bar, down the street at number 127.

Chapeau!

French

C1

1408 Clement St. (at 15th Ave.)

Phone: 415-750-9787 — Wed – Sun dinner only
Web: N/A
Prices: $$$

Boisterous and convivial, this bistro has been a Richmond fixture for years. When he's not at his latest acquisition, Clementine (below), owner Philippe Gardelle, a native of Toulouse, can be seen chatting with customers and offering wine suggestions in the butter-yellow dining room. Meanwhile, his wife, Ellen, manages the waitstaff and helps take food orders.

Tables crowd together at this casual place, where, to lay down your hat (*chapeau* in French), is to call the restaurant home. Roasted pork loin with French green lentils, coq au vin, and cassoulet *à la Toulousaine* constitute a sampling of the comforting French country fare.

Choose your courses à la carte, or select one of several prix-fixe menus. The "early bird" special is a real deal.

Clementine

French

D1

126 Clement St. (bet. 2nd & 3rd Aves.)

Phone: 415-387-0408 — Tue – Sat dinner only
Web: www.clementinesf.com
Prices: $$

Recently purchased by Chapeau owner Philippe Gardelle, Clementine was given a minor facelift and reopened in March 2008. Gardelle keeps the restaurant's tradition of hospitality alive, working the room to make sure his patrons are happy. A shiny copper-topped bar, decorative wall sconces and off-white color scheme enhanced by green trim are the most obvious changes.

Don't be surprised if the revamped menu echoes that of Chapeau, located a few blocks down Clement Street. Porcini-crusted veal sweetbreads, spinach- and mushroom-stuffed leg of Sonoma rabbit, and honey-glazed guinea hen are indicative of what you can expect.

Come early for the bargain three-course dinner menu; it's served from 5:00 P.M. to 6:00 P.M. Monday through Thursday.

Ebisu

D3 — Japanese

1283 9th Ave. (at Irving St.)

Phone: 415-566-1770 — Mon – Sat lunch & dinner
Web: www.ebisusushi.com
Prices: ⊜

Near Golden Gate Park on lively 9th Avenue in the Sunset district, Ebisu bears the name of the God of the kitchen, one of the seven Japanese deities of good fortune. Indeed, you'll consider yourself fortunate to discover this place, with its long and welcoming sushi bar offset by a smattering of tiny tables. An extensive list of daily specials fills the dry-erase boards near the sushi bar, augmenting the sizeable menu of sushi, rolls, and cooked dishes. Premium imported sakes have prices to prove their high quality (if you like to experiment, try one of the less-expensive sake samplers available in flights of three). Headed out of town? You can get one last Ebisu fix at San Francisco International Airport (in the food court in Terminal G).

Kabuto

C2 — Japanese

5121 Geary Blvd. (bet. 15th & 16th Aves.)

Phone: 415-752-5652 — Tue – Sat lunch & dinner
Web: www.kabutosushi.com — Sun dinner only
Prices: $$

Behind this tiny storefront façade hide some intriguing sushi creations. All the raw-fish dishes are made with pristine seafood, simply, and beautifully presented. However, it's the special sushi selections that set Kabuto apart. Regulars make a beeline here for such items as the Hot Apple (seared scallop, apple, and fruity mustard), the Ono grape (wahoo topped with grapefruit and basil cream), and the 16-20 Kiss (black tiger shrimp and avocado wrapped in paper-thin radish slices served with *abuto* chocolate sauce). The vast menu also cites a plethora of cooked dishes, from tempura to teriyaki. Sit at the varnished blond wood sushi bar for access to all the artistic action. You might even pick up a hint or two from the smiling *itamae* (sushi chefs).

Khan Toke Thai House

Thai

5937 Geary Blvd. (bet. 23rd & 24th Aves.)

Phone: 415-668-6654 Dinner daily
Web: N/A
Prices: $$

This slice of old Siam treats diners to authentic Thai food, music, and culture. Before entering, guests are asked to remove their shoes; sit cross-legged on floor cushions or legs dangling in wells below the hand-carved wooden tables.
Extensive, diverse, and unique, the menu travels through Thailand in the likes of *tom yam* soup with chicken, lemongrass, and cilantro; and *pong pang*, a combination of seafood sautéed with lemongrass, hot chilies, and the chef's secret spicy sauce. Neatly dressed servers can help guide you on your journey.
The ambience, set about with Thai artifacts and a lovely Asian garden out back, makes a perfect romantic rendezvous. Reasonable prices will leave you with enough money to tip the shoeman when you leave.

Koo

Japanese 

408 Irving St. (bet. 5th & 6th Aves.)

Phone: 415-731-7077 Tue – Sun dinner only
Web: www.sushikoo.com
Prices: $$

Located in quiet, and often foggy, Inner Sunset, Koo's tiny sushi counter and tastefully minimalist dining space fills on a regular basis with a coterie of connoisseurs.
Rolls, sized to be easily managed with chopsticks, such as the Tokyo Crunch (*hamachi*, *unagi*, cucumber, and *tobiko* covered by spicy *tenkatsu*) and the Best Roll (tempura asparagus and avocado wrapped in salmon and thinly sliced lemon) illustrate the tasteful tweaking at which Chef Kiyoshi Hayakawa excels. Tried-and-true plates of beef tataki and miso-marinated black cod are meant for sharing, while selections from the grill—marinated artichokes; jalapeño stuffed with *hamachi* and served with a side of lime aïoli—add a non-traditional twist not normally found in local sushi haunts.

Mayflower

Chinese

B2

6255 Geary Blvd. (at 27th Ave.)

Phone: 415-387-8338 — Lunch & dinner daily
Web: N/A
Prices: 

Easterners outnumber Westerners in this Cantonese dim sum house, and that's a good thing. That means that no matter their background, lovers of authentic Chinese cuisine will find marinated duck tongue and cold seasoned white chicken feet on the menu alongside tamer offerings such as steamed barbecue pork buns and crispy spring rolls. Much of the seafood served here swims in the aquarium tanks that flank the entrance.

Be aware that the pot of tea which appears on your table without you requesting it is not complimentary. Overall, however, prices are inexpensive, especially considering the copious portions (keep this in mind as you're ordering, in case your eyes are bigger than your stomach).

Visit Mayflower's other locations in Milpitas and Union City.

Namu

Asian

D2

439 Balboa St. (bet. 5th & 6th Aves.)

Phone: 415-386-8332 — Tue – Sun lunch & dinner
Web: www.namubar.com — Mon dinner only
Prices: $$

This zen-like oasis may be the spark that rekindles its Inner Richmond neighborhood. Incorporating natural slate and bamboo, the serene décor centers on a cypress bar made from a tree that once stood in Golden Gate Park—appropriate since the restaurant's name means "tree" in Korean.

Both Japanese and Korean dishes dominate the menu. Lunch brings an unexpected selection of sandwiches, like fish fillet with kimchee tartar sauce. At dinner, Japanese *sumi* charcoal fuels the fire that grills Hokkaido scallops and flavorful Kalbi-style skirt steak, cooked medium rare and glazed with Korean barbecue sauce.

Owners Dennis, Daniel, and David Lee simply ask that you leave with a "happy belly" (the name of their food-cart operation in Golden Gate Park).

Old Mandarin Islamic

Chinese

3132 Vicente St. (bet. 42nd & 43rd Aves.)

Phone: 415-564-3481 — Fri - Mon & Wed lunch & dinner; Tue & Thu dinner only
Web: www.oldmandarinislamic.com
Prices:

Neither pork nor alcohol is served, the décor centers around a few simple Chinese lanterns, and only cash is accepted. Yet devout foodies as well as pious Muslims seek this quaint eatery in "The Avenues" area of foggy Outer Sunset for the authentic, inexpensive halal cuisine ("permissible" under Islamic law) of northwest China. With more than 150 choices on the menu, sifting through the lists of hot pots, warm pots, dim sum, noodles, chow mein, and more can be overwhelming but are sure to quell any Chinese craving.
Once decided, expect dishes to be typically aromatic and very spicy. Intrepid diners should brave selections like Peking beef pancakes, hot braised lamb legs, or pan-fried seafood *bao*.

Park Chow

American 

1240 9th Ave. (bet. Irving St. & Lincoln Way)

Phone: 415-665-9912 — Lunch & dinner daily
Web: www.chowfoodbar.com
Prices:

Like her older sister, popular Chow in Castro, Park Chow has settled right into this Inner Sunset neighborhood as the affable girl next door to (a half block from) Golden Gate Park. Locals with their dogs flock to the sidewalk tables, while others chat away near the fireplace or bar inside or head up to the rooftop deck on sunny days.
Carefully prepared, the food here is eclectic, mostly diner-inspired comfort fare (pork chops over braised greens, pear cobbler) with nods to Italy and Asia in dishes like wood-fired eggplant parmesan and "smiling" noodles. A favorite is the fried-egg sandwich with ham and gruyère.
Casual-cool servers keep things coming in this frenetic-but-friendly gathering place. Call ahead to get on the "no-wait" list.

Pizzetta 211

Pizza

211 23rd Ave. (at California St.)

Phone: 415-379-9880 — Wed – Fri lunch & dinner
Web: N/A — Sat – Mon dinner only
Prices:

To call Pizzetta 211 small is generous. There is one cook, one person at the counter, and very limited seating. Still, the artisanal pies served at this shoebox of a restaurant deserve attention.

The short menu changes weekly but always features a handful of pizzettas, salads, and a daily cheeseboard. Place an order at the counter, pick up utensils, and wait for your food to be delivered to the table—provided you can get one. Local farms supply much of the organic vegetables and dairy products that create offerings such as golden beets with warm, herbaceous ricotta cheese. Thin, crisp pizzas are decked with such toppings as winter Bloomsdale spinach, red onion, and ricotta salata; or perhaps fennel, Meyer lemon, Niçoise olives, and Parmigiano Reggiano.

Sushi Bistro

Japanese 

D2

445 Balboa St. (at 6th Ave.)

Phone: 415-933-7100 — Dinner daily
Web: www.sushibistrosf.com
Prices: $$

Set on a quiet block in Inner Richmond, the discreet Sushi Bistro offers one of the best bargains in the city. Here, you can feast on a variety of fresh Japanese fare and still have money left over.

For something different try the Hot Love (baby lobster, avocado, and crabmeat rolled in whitefish and baked in a sweet and spicy sauce), or the 7-flavor Albacore Appetizer, a lightly seared albacore fillet peppered with seven types of spices. The wide range of chef's special rolls—from shrimp tempura to freshwater eel—will appeal to most everyone's palate.

Sunny colors and an affable vibe are but more reasons to visit. The one downside? It's nearly impossible to find parking. Look forward to their second location at *2809 24th Street* in the Mission!

Sutro's

Fusion

A2

1090 Point Lobos Ave. (at Ocean Beach)

Phone: 415-386-3330 — Lunch & dinner daily
Web: www.cliffhouse.com
Prices: $$$

Surf and sunsets compose Sutro's spectacular panoramic vista from the city's western-most point. Set within the 2004 incarnation of the 1909 Cliff House, this blufftop restaurant is as close as you can get to the Pacific, short of walking down the hill to Ocean Beach—which is where many find parking. The view from these multistory window walls, decorated with examples of modest 19th century swimwear and old time signage, also inspires the menu which dives into California seafood. Asian influence peppers both the "Thai-style" bouillabaisse as well as the macadamia-crusted local halibut served with coconut broth, pineapple chutney, and chile oil. Kurobuta pork and Wagyu beef add pedigree to the meat dishes. A Champagne buffet is offered on Sundays.

Ton Kiang

Chinese

C2

5821 Geary Blvd. (bet. 22nd & 23rd Aves.)

Phone: 415-752-4440 — Lunch & dinner daily
Web: www.tonkiang.net
Prices:

Upstairs or down, the focus here is on dim sum and Hakka cuisine. The Hakka people migrated across their country from northern China, many of them settling in the Guangdong Province near the Ton Kiang, or East River.

Once seated at a round table, equipped with a lazy Susan for sharing dishes, you'll be bombarded by a flurry of female servers proffering steamed, fried, blanched and roasted miniature delights with little explanation (though there is a diagram on each table to help you identify your choices). The density of the crowd, which gets chaotic on weekends, dictates the level of service.

No prices are posted for dim sum, but never fear; the total bill here may well add up to less than what you'd pay for just an entrée elsewhere.

Troya

Mediterranean

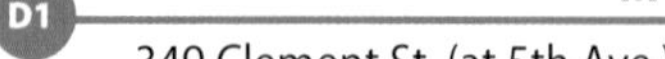

D1

349 Clement St. (at 5th Ave.)

Phone: 415-379-6000
Web: www.troyasf.com
Prices: ◎◎

Fri – Sat lunch & dinner
Sun – Thu dinner only

In late 2007, Chef Randy Gannaway (a former sous-chef at Aziza) took Troya's helm and steered the menu well beyond kebabs. Though his culinary journey still respects the Turkish traditions of the restaurant's original concept, the new chef has embarked on a more adventurous trek through the Mediterranean at large.

While the likes of chicken and lamb kebabs, or Turkish flatbread still hold their own here, *dolmas* (grape leaves stuffed with currants, pine nuts, and creamy feta), grilled sardines over local cress with sweet onions, and chicken *güvec* (crispy leg and thighs served with a spiced almond coriander sauce, parsnips, eggplant, and olives) illustrate how far the menu has traveled.The six-seat bar is the perfect perch for a mid-afternoon mezze break.

Feast for under $25 at all restaurants with ◎◎.

ubiubi
Discover. Indulge. Impress.
www.ubiubi.mobi
ubi
VENTO
MICHELIN
Italian | $$ |
Home > Dining > Vento > Reviews > Michelin
When the weather is warm and the breeze is coming off the Hudson river, there's no place lik
Vento's prime corner spot in the Meatpacking District to see and be seen. The menu is ideal for sharing, and a convivial meal materializes effortlessly from the small plates of cheeses, olives, and other Mediterranean starters. Wood-fired pizzas, house-made pastas, whole-roasted fish, and meats round out your family-style feast.
Menu
Back

South of Market (SoMa)

San Francisco's hardscrabble history meets its high-tech present in the large, heterogeneous region known as SoMa (for South of Market). During the Gold Rush days, SoMa was home to the town's wealthy and elite citizens. When the 1906 earthquake destroyed most of the area, followed by industries ascending on the area when it was rebuilt (for its proximity to the bay), displacing its residents to **Nob Hill**, this area bound by 12th, Market and King Streets, and the Embarcadero then became known as South of the Slot, a reference to its location on the wrong side of the Market Street cable-car track.

Today, all that has changed. Hundreds of thousands of conventioneers meet at the **Moscone Convention Center** each year. Over the past two decades, SoMa and **Yerba Buena** have transformed into an arts and cultural enclave and are home to such powerhouses as the **San Francisco Museum of Modern Art** *(151 3rd St.)*, five and a half acres that comprise the **Yerba Buena Gardens** *(Mission St., between 3rd & 4th Sts.)*, and its **Center for the Arts**, and the new Daniel Libeskind-designed home for the **Contemporary Jewish Museum** *(Mission St. between 3rd & 4th Sts.)*, as well as a "last Saturday" art walk to visit galleries in the area every month, which all draw throngs of visitors and locals. In between are scores of old warehouses, many converted into swank nightclubs, and some of the city's hottest new restaurants.

A NEW ANGLE

In 1847, city planner Jasper O'Farrell gave SoMa its distinctive look, making its streets twice as wide and its blocks four times as large as those north of **Market Street**, and setting the whole area at a 45-degree angle to the grid. The idea was to make room for industry, and it worked.

As manufacturing declined in the mid-20th century, architects, graphic designers, software companies, and publishers divvied up former industrial buildings and warehouses into loftlike offices. Then in 2000, the Internet bubble burst, leaving nearly half of the offices vacant.

SoMa is now booming again. This area has eclipsed the **Financial District** for new construction, as buildings including the 32-story InterContinental Hotel; the certified green, 18-story Federal Building; and luxurious residential towers such as the 22-story SOMA Grand, and the 60-story residential Millennium Tower rise on the skyline. The wide section of Jessie Street between 5th and Mint streets has been transformed into **Mint Plaza**, a lovely art- and greenery-filled public space lined with new cafes and restaurants. Once again, SoMa is the place where the new elite of San Francisco, who make their wealth in technology, are vying for space in one of nearly 50 newly constructed luxury buildings in the area.

As it has since the district's early days, Market Street still reigns as the city's major commercial thoroughfare. Shoppers make a beeline for the **Westfield**

San Francisco Centre *(between 4th & 5th Sts.)*, which added the largest Bloomingdale's store outside New York City, a handful of restaurants, and a nine-screen cineplex to the existing five levels of the **San Francisco Shopping Centre** anchored by Nordstrom. The mall is crowned by the 100-foot-diameter glass dome that once graced the 19th-century Emporium Capwell building.

Defining SoMa's southern border, breathtaking **AT&T Park**—the first major-league baseball stadium to use solar panels, is home to the **San Francisco Giants** baseball franchise. Just north of the stadium, the historic **South Park** centers on a grassy oval surrounded by townhouses, shops, and cafes.

Brigitta L. House / MICHELIN

South of Market
Hotels
Restaurants
NOB HILL
MARINA DISTRICT
CIVIC CENTER
MISSION DISTRICT
CHINATOWN
NOB HILL
UNION SQUARE
TENDERLOIN
CIVIC CENTER
Four Seasons
Fifth Floor
Palom
Zazil
The Mosse
Lark Creek Steak
OLD MINT
MOSCO CENTER W.
InterContinental
Luce
CALIFORNIA ACADEMY OF SCIENCES
ASIAN ART MUSEUM
CITY HALL
UN PLAZA
SF PUBLIC LIBRARY
SF WAR MEMORIAL & PERFORMING ARTS CENTER
Manora's Thai Cuisine
Powell St
Civic Center
Van Ness
TUNNEL
MUNI
UNION SQUARE

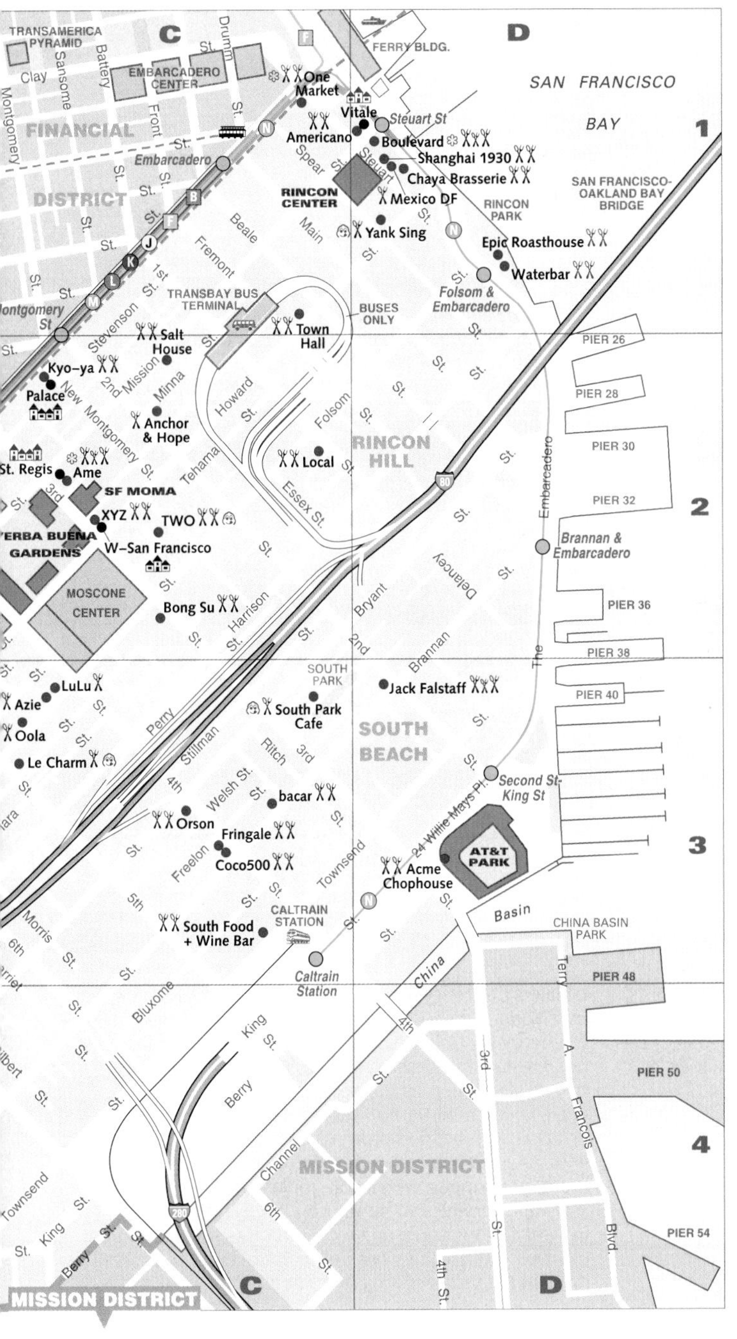

TRANSAMERICA PYRAMID
FERRY BLDG.
SAN FRANCISCO BAY
EMBARCADERO CENTER
FINANCIAL DISTRICT
One Market
Vitale
Americano
Boulevard
Shanghai 1930
Chaya Brasserie
Mexico DF
RINCON CENTER
Yank Sing
RINCON PARK
SAN FRANCISCO-OAKLAND BAY BRIDGE
Epic Roasthouse
Waterbar
Folsom & Embarcadero
TRANSBAY BUS TERMINAL
BUSES ONLY
Town Hall
Salt House
Kyo-ya
Palace
Anchor & Hope
Local
RINCON HILL
St. Regis
Ame
SF MOMA
XYZ
TWO
W-San Francisco
YERBA BUENA GARDENS
MOSCONE CENTER
Bong Su
Brannan & Embarcadero
PIER 26
PIER 28
PIER 30
PIER 32
PIER 36
PIER 38
PIER 40
SOUTH PARK
Jack Falstaff
LuLu
Azie
Oola
Le Charm
South Park Cafe
SOUTH BEACH
bacar
Second St-King St
Orson
Fringale
Coco500
Acme Chophouse
AT&T PARK
South Food + Wine Bar
CALTRAIN STATION
Caltrain Station
CHINA BASIN PARK
PIER 48
PIER 50
PIER 54
MISSION DISTRICT

ACME Chophouse

Steakhouse XX

D3

24 Willie Mays Plaza (at AT&T Park)

Phone: 415-644-0240 — Tue – Fri lunch & dinner
Web: www.acmechophouse.com — Sat dinner only
Prices: $$$

At AT&T Park, try Chef Traci Des Jardins' take on a ballpark restaurant that goes beyond hotdogs, popcorn and peanuts. ACME Chophouse hits a home run with its menu of natural meats (raised without hormones or antibiotics), local fish, and organic produce. A sandwich of thinly sliced house-cured pastrami and gruyere on rye, or a main plate of risotto with slow-cooked Petaluma chicken are both light years away from the usual game-day eats.

Handsome with rich wood tones and amber-hued light fixtures, the spacious dining room accommodates throngs of Giants fans. Here, cool jazz pinch-hits for organ music.

Take a seventh-inning stretch and pop down for seasonal sweets like a quince crostada or the ever-popular s'more sundae.

Americano

Italian 

D1

8 Mission St. (at The Embarcadero)

Phone: 415-278-3777 — Mon – Sat lunch & dinner
Web: www.americanorestaurant.com — Sun lunch only
Prices: $$$

Located on the ground floor of the stylish Hotel Vitale (*see hotel listing*), draped in earthy hues, and serving Italian cuisine meshed with Californian flair, Americano is not just another hotel restaurant. Dishes are stylish; they highlight clean, fresh flavors, and fine preparation. Choices may include a flatbread pizzetta with butternut squash, hazelnuts, pecorino, and drizzled with truffle honey; or buccatini "carbonara," tossed with sautéed spinach, cherry tomatoes, speck, parmesan broth, and topped with a soft-cooked egg.

Although service can be uneven, forgive the waitstaff's gaffs in light of the food's quality. When the weather is fine, opt to sit on the spacious outdoor terrace, order a cocktail, and drink in the views of the Bay Bridge.

Ame ✿

C2 Contemporary XXX

689 Mission St. (at 3rd St.)

Phone: 415-284-4040 — Dinner daily
Web: www.amerestaurant.com
Prices: $$$

Tucked into the hip St Regis hotel, Ame has the kind of sleek good looks one has come to associate with SoMa, where there are more hot new restaurants than you can shake a stick at. So what gives this joint a leg up from its trendy cousins? For starters, it's of excellent stock—Ame's parents happen to be husband-and-wife restaurateurs, Hiro Sone and Lissa Doumani, who also own Terra in Napa Valley. But don't take our word for it. Make your way into the handsome, paneled-wood room, with its Japanese lighting and custom-designed sushi bar, and see for yourself.

Chef Sone's fusion fare blends Japanese, Italian, and French seamlessly, with a little Asian sensibility thrown in for good measure. Tuck your fork into a smooth, delicate slice of trout, topped with crème fraîche and American sturgeon caviar; or dig into a crunchy rhubarb pie with a creamy swirl of ice cream and fresh strawberries.

Appetizers

- Chawan Mushi with Maine Lobster, Sea Urchin and Mitsuba Sauce
- Lissa's Staff Meal
- Sautéed Foie Gras, Duck Confit, Chestnut Flour Crêpe

Entrées

- Surf and Turf: Abalone and Wagyu Strip Steak
- Maine Lobster, Hokkaido Scallops, Leeks, Israeli Couscous
- Kurobuta Pork with Sweet Potato Cake and Manila Clams

Desserts

- Huckleberry Hand Pies with Lemon Curd Fool
- Green Tea "Affogato", Pistachio Ice Cream
- Chocolate Mousse Crunch ,Chocolate Sorbet and Cherry Compote

Anchor & Hope

Seafood 

83 Minna St. (at 2nd St.)

Phone: 415-501-9100
Web: www.anchorandhopesf.com
Prices: $$

Mon – Fri lunch & dinner
Sat – Sun dinner only

This East Coast-style fish house joins siblings Town Hall and Salt House as testimony to the success of Chefs Mitchell and Steven Rosenthal—along with partner Doug Washington. High spirits and high decibels go hand-in-hand under the 30-foot trestle ceiling of this converted turn-of-the-20th-century warehouse, whose beams are draped with thick ropes. A mounted gar turns an ominous eye on a bowl of goldfish behind the long zinc dining counter.

Nibble on some "fries with eyes" (fried smelts with remoulade) while perusing the chalkboard list of oysters and shellfish. Main courses flip from Smithwicks beer-battered halibut to the house lobster roll served with Old Bay-spiced chips.

Everything on the wine list is available by the glass, half-bottle, or bottle.

Azie

Asian 

826 Folsom St. (bet. 4th & 5th Sts.)

Phone: 415-538-0918
Web: www.azierestaurant.com
Prices: $$

Mon – Sat dinner only

Azie resulted from taking a basic SoMa warehouse, transfiguring it with posh fittings and bold colors, and mixing in contemporary Asian cuisine. It's clearly a recipe for success, starting with the cozy lounge where locals gather to soak up the hip ambience while they sip cocktails and nosh on Asian-inspired small plates like spring rolls brimming with salmon, trout, and crab.

Aside from the dramatic décor, Azie offers a literal taste of the Orient. Entrées roam from short ribs braised in coconut milk and Thai spices to steamed black cod with pea shoots, bok choy, ginger, and dashi broth.

If you have a romantic meal in mind, request one of the three booths equipped with curtains and dimmer switches for the ultimate in privacy.

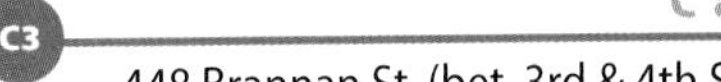

bacar

Californian

C3

448 Brannan St. (bet. 3rd & 4th Sts.)

Phone: 415-904-4100
Web: www.bacarsf.com
Prices: $$$

Sat – Thu dinner only
Fri lunch & dinner

At Bacar, a renovated brick and timber warehouse morphs seamlessly into a three-level dining space, its exposed brick walls and high arched windows creating a lofty look. The region's harvest shows up in entrées such as house-made fettucine with red wine-duck sugo, and Alaskan King salmon with borlotti beans, Brentwood corn, and King trumpet mushrooms. A five-course chef's tasting menu augments the à la carte. For a more casual option, sit at the bar and sample "bar bites," to pair with one of the many bottles that cool their heels in the glass-fronted cellar behind the three-story wine wall.

If you're looking for a midday meal, you'll have to go on Friday—the only day Bacar serves lunch. Live jazz bands entertain diners on weekends.

Bong Su

Vietnamese

C2

311 3rd St. (bet. Harrison & Folsom Sts.)

Phone: 415-536-5800
Web: www.bongsu.com
Prices: $$$

Mon – Fri lunch & dinner
Sat – Sun dinner only

Sultry and seductive, this SoMa beauty (sibling of Tamarine) takes its Vietnamese name from the plumeria flower that accents its design. Soft amber track lighting plays against hand-carved sandstone to enhance the sleek, romantic ambience. In the lounge area, a glassed wine cellar and illuminated bar add to the minimalist design.

Seasoning may be tempered for American palates, yet this is a restaurant where innovative and traditional cuisines blend well, with delicious results. Thus a Jungle Beef salad of grilled Angus skirt steak tossed with purple cabbage, sliced chilies, red pear tomatoes, and a julienne of green apples and carrots crowns a large leaf of butter lettuce. Ask the attentive staff about the fine selection of tea and cocktails.

Boulevard

Californian

1 Mission St. (at Steuart St.)

Phone: 415-543-6084
Web: www.boulevardrestaurant.com
Prices: $$$

Mon – Fri lunch & dinner
Sat – Sun dinner only

Boulevard

You may have left your heart in San Francisco, but many left their hearts at Boulevard. Now entering its sixteenth year and still going strong, this restaurant's popularity could be about its prime location on the ground floor of the old Audiffred Building, with its jaw-dropping view of the Bay Bridge. Or the killer interior design that manages to be not only warm and inviting, but roomy as well. It might be the gracious, attentive service team—always buzzing, but never hovering.

But no, more likely the loyalists pour in for Chef Nancy Oakes' delicious California cooking. Take a decadent butternut squash ravioli, simply garnished with fruity olive oil and fragrant black truffle shavings; or a tender, grilled Butterfish sporting perfectly-lined sear marks, and laid over a bed of wild rice pocked with tender cubes of sweet winter squash and silky trumpet mushrooms.

Appetizers

- Dayboat Sea Scallops, Grits, Ham Hock
- Squab, Organic Egg, Chanterelle Mushrooms, Squab Jus
- Monterey Abalone, Nettle Spaetzle, Sunchoke Meunière

Entrées

- Carrot-crusted Halibut, Carrot Vinaigrette, and Peppercress
- Suckling Pig, Gnocchi Carbonara, Caper-Raisin Agrodolce
- Lamb, Artichokes, Feta,Olives, Garlic Sauce

Desserts

- Carrot Sachertorte, Cognac Bonbon, Caramelized Hazelnuts
- Sticky Toffee Pudding with Caramel Custard, and Earl Grey Tea Ice Cream
- Almond-Butter Cake

Chaya Brasserie

Fusion XX

D1

132 The Embarcadero (bet. Howard & Mission Sts.)

Phone: 415-777-8688 — Mon – Fri lunch & dinner
Web: www.thechaya.com — Sat – Sun dinner only
Prices: $$

Opened in 2000 as the San Francisco satellite of a small chain of restaurants whose cousins live in Los Angeles and Venice Beach, Chaya fuses Asian cuisine with European elements. The bill of fare skews toward Japanese, with a substantial selection of sushi and maki, but entrées like roasted King salmon with cardoons, or red-wine-braised oxtail ravioli demonstrate continental notes. Desserts, such as warm chocolate croissant bread pudding, play a modern tune.

A long zinc-topped bar gives way to a formal carpeted back room. Local business folks favor this brasserie, and its bay views, for lunch.

Although the address is The Embarcadero, the valet stand is on Steuart Street, and a rear entrance at 131 Steuart Place is more readily accessible.

Coco500

Californian XX

C3

500 Brannan St. (at 4th St.)

Phone: 415-543-2222 — Mon – Fri lunch & dinner
Web: www.coco500.com — Sat dinner only
Prices: $$

Always abuzz, Coco500 packs 'em in for Chef/owner Loretta Keller's contemporary cuisine. "Small Starts" on her dinner menu may translate to mole tacos of braised beef cheek dabbed with avocado cream, while *"A la Plancha"* could feature sizzling shrimp with Spanish olive oil. "Wood Oven" means artisanal pizzas with toppings as varied as truffled mushrooms or pears and mountain gorgonzola. "California Dirt" stars local vegetables like organic beets, Star Route Farms swiss chard, and roasted celery root. Lunch choices skew more towards soups, sandwiches, and pizza.

In this 1906 building, chocolate, blue, and caramel tones color the pleasing décor, while the teak and Italian-glass-tile bar beckons with cocktails made from freshly-squeezed organic juices.

Epic Roasthouse

Steakhouse 

369 The Embarcadero (at Folsom St.)

Phone: 415-369-9955 Lunch & dinner daily
Web: www.epicroasthousesf.com
Prices: $$$

Designed by Pat Kuleto, this new power steakhouse offers fabulous views of the Bay Bridge and more. The space was modeled after the salt water pumping station that assisted the fire cisterns during the 1906 earthquake fires. The décor recreates this feeling with a wood wheel and ceiling pipelines, old wood, steel beams, and large picture windows.

A contemporary classic steakhouse menu is prepared from meats and ingredients, carefully selected from renowned California, Colorado, and Montana farms and ranches, in the custom built wood fire grill and oven. A casual lunch for $30 guarantees you'll be back to the office in 50 minutes.

Upstairs, a wine bar is a convivial spot to enjoy a drink and take in the fabulous waterfront view.

Fringale

French 

570 4th St. (bet. Brannan & Bryant Sts.)

Phone: 415-543-0573 Tue – Fri lunch & dinner
Web: www.fringalesf.com Sat – Mon dinner only
Prices: $$

Going strong since 1991, Fringale can attribute its longevity to friendly service and just plain good food. Though the cuisine speaks with an unmistakable French accent, all the fussy Gallic stereotypes are pleasingly absent here. Both food and service are unpretentious and approachable, and there's an obvious romance about the place. No wonder that Fringale is frequently packed, with a line of diners waiting outside for a table in the diminutive room.

Rustic and vibrant, the flavors of the Basque region embrace the dishes here. Spicy Monterey calamari "a la plancha" pairs with jalapeños and chorizo, while a portobello napoleon marries spinach, tomato, polenta, basil, and piquillo pepper. Consistency in this kitchen translates to quality on the plate.

Fifth Floor ✿

French XXXX

B2

12 4th St. (at Market St.)

Phone: 415-348-1555 — Mon – Sat dinner only
Web: www.fifthfloorrestaurant.com
Prices: $$$$

Fifth Floor/Justin Lewis

Those punching floor five in the Hotel Palomar elevator expecting to find the Fifth Floor restaurant of yesteryear will be surprised to find a revamped eatery in its place. Though the name remains, much has changed in the past few years, beginning with the banishing of the old animal print décor; in its place, a casually elegant dining room awaits, replete with a new wine room.

Even more importantly, Fifth Floor has a new power duo in the kitchen—Aqua's Laurent Manrique and Jennie Lorenzo (who cut her teeth as sous chef at Ame). Together, they're pushing out a menu inspired by the Gascony region of France—like a foie gras torchon starter that arrives Perigord style, dusted with coarse black pepper, and served with a biscuit covered in grapes and raw artichoke. For dinner, try an almond-crusted squab served over fresh celery sticks, and sided with small fingerling potatoes.

Appetizers

- Foie Gras Poached in Crushed Grapes, Artichoke and Black Truffle Salad
- Corn Polenta with Ossau-Iraty Cheese, Frog Legs and Artichokes
- "Thon Basquaise"

Entrées

- Poached Chicken with Foie Gras Stuffing, Herbed Vermicelli, Broth
- Smoked & Poached Halibut, Caviar, Oyster-Lemon Coulis
- Grilled Ribeye, "Pommes Paillasson"

Desserts

- Apple Crisp, Anise and Orange Blossom Syrup, Apple Sorbet
- Almond Cake with Black Cherry Marmalade
- Armagnac Baba with Crème Chantilly and Candied Violet

Jack Falstaff

American

D3

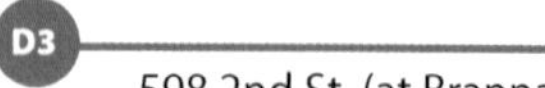

598 2nd St. (at Brannan St.)

Phone: 415-836-9239
Web: www.jackfalstaff.com
Prices: $$$

Mon – Fri lunch & dinner
Sat dinner only

This converted warehouse, located two blocks from AT&T Park, now masquerades as a swanky lounge with a lively evening scene. Inside, Chef Jonnatan Leiva's seasonal fare creates inventive American food. Sonoma quail and grits with shallots, grapes, and a balsamic glaze; Kampachi tartare; fennel stuffed Spanish mackerel; and a chocolate-nougat-peanut-butter-crunch bar highlight his eclectic flair. Bar noshes might include halibut and shrimp ceviche with mango, roasted *Pimiento de Padron* peppers with cracked sea salt; or mini burgers with garlic aïoli.

Its large covered space on the corner of Brannan Street is fully enclosed on chilly days, though when it is warm out, the plastic panels are removed in favor of fresh breezes.

Kyo-ya

Japanese 

2 New Montgomery St. (at Market St.)

Phone: 415-546-5090
Web: www.kyo-ya-restaurant.com
Prices: $$$

Mon – Fri lunch & dinner

Despite its separate entrance at the corner of Jesse Street, Kyo-Ya is part of the 1909 Palace Hotel (*see hotel listing*). The space is serene and tastefully done, with tables scattered throughout the nooks and crannies of the room. If you choose one of the seats at the sushi bar, you'll be dazzled by Master Sushi Chef Akifusa Tonai's deft knife skills as he prepares his trademark rolls. Many of these, such as the Celebration and the Volcano Ano, are wrapped with soy bean skin instead of the usual nori.

Kyo-Ya's proximity to the Financial District may influence its prices, but the selection and quality of the fish merit the higher price tag. The room is a bit quiet to discuss confidential business—unless the extensive sake list comes into play.

Lark Creek Steak

Steakhouse

845 Market St. (bet. 4th & 5th Sts.)

Phone: 415-593-4100 — Lunch & dinner daily
Web: www.larkcreeksteak.com
Prices: $$$

The Lark Creek Restaurant Group hopes to hook hungry shoppers at their comfortable steakhouse located in Westfield Centre. In the experienced hands of Chef John Ledbetter, succulent aged beef emerges from the kitchen in forms varying from a perfectly prepared 16-ounce bone-in ribeye to a red-wine-marinated hanger steak. Equal attention is given to vegetable selections, which are perfectly cooked and true to flavor. The menu succeeds in fusing the usual steakhouse fare with their characteristic seasonal, farm fresh carte.

Filled with natural light, the pleasant dining space (which offers views of the historic Emporium dome) could remedy mall mania. The solely Californian wine list of small producers and hard-to-find labels should remedy anything else.

Le Charm

French

315 5th St. (bet. Folsom & Shipley Sts.)

Phone: 415-546-6128 — Tue – Fri lunch & dinner
Web: www.lecharm.com — Sat – Sun dinner only
Prices: $$

Whether you're looking for a place for a brief business lunch or a venue for a romantic dinner, Le Charm lives up to its name. The lofty dining room with its poppy-colored walls has an intimate feel and a European flair, and the food is sure to satisfy any cravings for Gallic cuisine.

House-made *rillettes* and *saucisson* come with tiny cornichons and slices of toasted baguette; salt cod cassolette is blanked in a clam and mussel *velouté*; Spaetzle accompanies a confit of wild boar shoulder; juicy lamb chops are served with a mound of mesclun and thin, crispy frites. Can't decide? Go for the three-course prix-fixe dinner; it's a great value for $30.

The lush candlelit patio is de rigueur for an intimate tête-à-tête. That's Le Charm of it.

Local

C2 — Italian XX

330 1st St. (bet. Folsom & Harrison Sts.)

Phone: 415-777-4200 — Lunch & dinner daily
Web: www.sf-local.com
Prices: $$

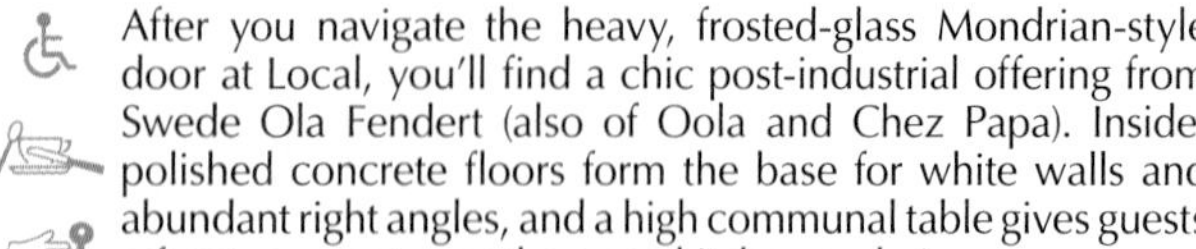

After you navigate the heavy, frosted-glass Mondrian-style door at Local, you'll find a chic post-industrial offering from Swede Ola Fendert (also of Oola and Chez Papa). Inside, polished concrete floors form the base for white walls and abundant right angles, and a high communal table gives guests a front-row seat near the open kitchen and pizza oven.

On the menu, Italian dishes from pizza to pan-seared mahi mahi exhibit a good dose of California savoir fare. The dessert docket shows off a few offerings that are largely unfamiliar in these parts, as in the cavoltini—an Italian take on profiteroles, filled with honey gelato and drizzled with lavender caramel. Stop in at the adjoining wine shop to stock up on wine and gourmet items to go.

Luce

B3 — Contemporary XX

888 Howard St. (at 5th St.)

Phone: 415-616-6566 — Lunch & dinner daily
Web: www.intercontinentalsanfrancisco.com
Prices: $$$

Located in the new InterContinental Hotel, Luce lies just beyond a series of lounges dressed in the same ultra-sleek, modern wardrobe. The effect is so slick and trendy, in fact, it can read a bit chilly—but the wood and marble floors, sheer drapes, and clean white linens do gather a little warmth as night falls. Italian staples mixed with a California sensibility defines Chef Dominique Crenn's menu, which might include a soft, warm risotto of English peas and saffron, with a dusting of parmesan on top; or a bitter chocolate *semifreddo* laced with fresh cream and sprinkled with pumpkins seeds.

If you happen to be doing some shopping in the area, Luce offers a good way to kick-start the day. Breakfast is served every day of the week, starting at 6:00 A.M.

LuLu

Mediterranean

816 Folsom St. (bet 4th & 5th Sts.)

Phone: 415-495-5775 — Lunch & dinner daily
Web: www.restaurantlulu.com
Prices: $$

With its soaring space, wide-open kitchen, and wood-burning oven and rotisserie as a centerpiece, LuLu has nothing to hide from the hip studio crowd that frequents this former warehouse. Wood-fired meats and fish cast enticing aromas around the room, tempting diners with the likes of rosemary-scented chicken and suckling pig with baby dandelions, roasted onions and fig balsamic vinaigrette. A different rotisserie special is offered each day. Fresh oysters and seafood platters kick off the menu, while the bartender mixes great cocktails, and a separate wine bar boasts one of the more extensive and interesting wine selections in the area.
If you're in a hurry, check out LuLu Petite in the Ferry Building for gourmet produce and deli items to go.

Manora's Thai Cuisine

1600 Folsom St. (at 12th St.)

Phone: 415-861-6224 — Mon – Fri lunch & dinner
Web: www.manorathai.com — Sat – Sun dinner only
Prices:

Open for more than 20 years, this unpretentious place still packs 'em in for good Thai food and rock-bottom prices. One of the better bargains in the city is Manora's lunch combination: a cup of lemon chicken soup, Thai fried jasmine rice, and a choice of two main-dish items for under $9. Chef's favorite dinner entrées include the Pooket skewer (char-broiled scallop, prawn and fish with veggies and two spicy sauces), and *Kai Yad Sai*, Thai-style omelets filled with crab, shrimp and chicken with a mixture of aromatic Thai herbs.
Though the dining room is small, there's a bar up front that accommodates solo diners. No matter where you sit, the colorfully clad and convivial staff proffer efficient service. Call ahead to avoid a wait for a table.

Mexico DF

Mexican

139 Steuart St. (bet. Mission & Howards Sts.)

Phone: 415-808-1048 — Mon – Fri lunch & dinner
Web: www.mex-df.com — Sat – Sun dinner only
Prices: $$

New to this restaurant-rich strip along the Embarcadero, Mexico DF evokes the *Distrito Federal* (known north of the border as Mexico City). This is where Chef Roberto Cruz finds inspiration for many of his dishes.

From the colorful, modern dining room, watch the *cocina* turning out fresh tortillas and many versions of creamy guacamole, including *classico*, mango, or shrimp and bacon. Tacos tempt appetites with the likes of barbecue goat and *nopales* (cactus), while succulent pork *carnitas* come by the half or full pound accompanied by a brightly flavored trio of house-made condiments.

And, yes, those digital pictures on the wall *do* actually change… but easy on the bar's ample selection of tequila, anyway. Takeout is available at the counter.

Oola

Californian

860 Folsom St. (bet. 4th & 5th Sts.)

Phone: 415-995-2061 — Dinner daily
Web: www.oola-sf.com
Prices: $$

This industrial-chic SoMa hotspot, with its sultry lighting and animated bar, appeals to the young and hip. Named for its Chef/owner, Ola Fendert (an original partner in Chez Papa, Chez Maman, and Baraka), Oola divides its soaring brick-walled space between booths on the ground floor and table seating on the mezzanine.

Market-fresh organic and sustainably raised products drive the menu, which focuses on sensible creations such as goat-cheese-stuffed salmon roulade, and coffee-roasted duck breast atop diced pears and fingerling potatoes. A long list of crafted cocktails with a separate section just for "shots" will start—or end—the evening with a bang. Check out Fendert's new venture, Local Kitchen & Wine Merchant *(330 First St.)*.

One Market ✿

Californian XX

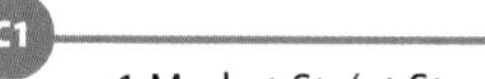

1 Market St. (at Steuart St.)

Phone: 415-777-5577
Web: www.onemarket.com
Prices: $$$

Mon – Fri lunch & dinner
Sat dinner only

John Benson

From its grand mile-high ceilings to its gorgeous stone-tile floors, this is one smart looking cookie. No wonder visitors to San Francisco's restyled waterfront area pour into this spacious brasserie—with its enormous windows facing the Bay Bridge and Ferry Building and cushy corner spot on bustling Market Street—this is prime real estate. But as most food critics will tell you, excellent location and breezy good looks don't always make for a good meal.

Not so at One Market, where the bustling, semi-exposed kitchen, is kept sharp as a tack by Chef/partner Mark Dommen, who packs his regional California menu with lots of creative surprises. A seemingly simple wild mushroom and baby mustard greens salad is topped with a warm, sweet-come-salty duck breast bresaola; while a creamy citrus-laced cheese cake is lidded with fluffy meringue and circled by puréed huckleberries.

Appetizers

- Smoked Sea Trout, Pancetta Vinaigrette
- Dungeness Crab Salad, Apples, Celery Root, Celery Sorbet
- House-made Duck Ravioli ,Foie Gras Emulsion

Entrées

- Bacon-wrapped Pork Tenderloin
- Rice Flake-crusted Sole, Fennel, Verbena-Shrimp Emulsion
- Duck Breast & Duck Leg Confit, Sweet Potato-Vanilla Bean Purée

Desserts

- Warm Apple-Rhubarb Galette, Creamsicle
- "Pavlova" Fresh Meringues, Tangerines, Crème Fraîche
- Valrhona Chocolate Soufflé and Cognac Chestnuts

Orson

Contemporary XX

C3

508 4th St. (at Bryant St.)

Phone: 415-777-1508 Mon – Sat dinner only
Web: www.orsonsf.com
Prices: $$$

Chef Elizabeth Falkner breaks out of her Citizen Cake and Cupcake mold in this eclectic eatery, set in an industrial section of SoMa. Lodged in a historic warehouse, Orson is part lounge and part restaurant. With its clubby atmosphere, artistic design, and pumping music, the place appeals to a trendy cadre of thirty-somethings.

In keeping with Orson's edgy theme, the cuisine is inspired and daring. Most of the time this works, but sometimes it doesn't; occasionally dishes suffer from pushing the envelope too far. Food here is meant to be shared, from "shorts" (a perfectly poached egg inside a crispy nori-tempura crust) and pizzas from the wood-burning oven to "premieres" (braised short ribs made smoky from espresso) and dishes sized for two.

Salt House

Contemporary XX

C2

545 Mission St. (bet. 1st & 2nd Sts.)

Phone: 415-543-8900 Mon – Fri lunch & dinner
Web: www.salthousesf.com Sat – Sun dinner only
Prices: $$$

A tavern feel pervades this narrow 1930s building, where exposed brick and oxidized-iron girders frame the kitchen; ovens and stovetops replace the printing press that once operated here.

The contemporary American fare changes daily, according to the whims of owners Mitch and Steven Rosenthal (of Town Hall and new sibling Anchor & Hope). Market permitting, Atlantic monkfish with veal cheeks and caramelized endive, or the Québecois favorite, *poutine* (made here with crispy potatoes, short-rib gravy, and fontina cheese), could grace the tables.

Salt House is wildly popular, so the noise level can escalate. It's a lively place to take a date—as long as you're not bent on conversation. No matter who you bring, be sure to make a reservation.

Shanghai 1930

Chinese

133 Steuart St. (bet. Howard & Mission Sts)

Phone: 415-886-5600 — Mon – Fri lunch & dinner
Web: www.shanghai1930.com — Sat dinner only
Prices: $$

Near the Embarcadero, Shanghai 1930 recalls the opulence of that city in the period between the two World Wars. The place takes on an underground nightclub feel, beginning with the staircase that leads down from the street. A long blue-lit bar and live jazz nightly take you back to the 1930s.
The menu roams the regions of China, bringing diners the different cooking styles of that vast country. At lunch, the set combinations are your best deal, but ask to see the à la carte menu too. Available all day, this bill of fare provides more variety. Firecracker chicken—presented in a mini wok—tangerine beef with celery hearts, and Sichuan braised chili fish will surely tempt your taste buds.
The wine list brags of more than 800 international labels.

South Food + Wine Bar

Australian

C3

330 Townsend St. (bet. 4th & 5th Sts.)

Phone: 415-974-5599 — Mon – Sat lunch & dinner
Web: www.southfwb.com — Sun lunch only
Prices: $$$

In collaboration with a few mates, celebrity Chef Luke Mangan brings this striking wine bar to SoMa, spotlighting and educating diners on the cuisine of Australia and New Zealand.
Wonderfully flavored and textured Maori bread (a cross between a biscuit and ciabatta) encases crispy tempura-fried New Zealand mussels, watercress, and garlic mayo at lunch, while New Zealand lamb and pan-roasted barramundi with Rozelle spices might inspire the dinner fare. Dessert offers a true black licorice parfait, a frozen confection sparked by lime zest, segments, and syrup.
To drink, South's exciting wine program complements the menu with a unique selection of labels not typically available in the U.S., exclusively from Australia, New Zealand, and South Africa.

South Park Cafe

French 

108 South Park Ave. (bet. 2nd & 3rd Sts.)

Phone: 415-495-7275
Web: www.southparkcafesf.com
Prices: $$

Tue – Fri lunch & dinner
Mon lunch only
Sat dinner only

A refreshing change from the warehouse-dominated areas of SoMa, the village of South Park clusters around a central green. This gem of a neighborhood, with its lovely town houses constructed mid-19th century, was modeled after a square in London.

The feel of a French cafe runs through the stone tile floors, transom windows, banquettes, and the long welcoming bar. Ditto for the food; this is good Gallic cuisine without the pretentious pricing and service. Locals turn out in the evening for classics like baked goat cheese with thyme and shallots, and roast rack of lamb with macaroni gratin and basil-almond pesto.

At lunch, the menu is more limited; it's basically counter service where you place your order from the chalkboard list of specials.

Town Hall

Contemporary 

342 Howard St. (at Fremont St.)

Phone: 415-908-3900
Web: www.townhallsf.com
Prices: $$

Mon – Fri lunch & dinner
Sat – Sun dinner only

Bright white wainscoting, exposed brick walls, and antiques purchased from a salvage yard in New York City lend Town Hall the look of an Adirondack eating hall. Housed in the beautifully renovated 1907 Marine Electric Building, Mitch and Steven Rosenthal's first restaurant venture still packs a trendy, very loud, and boisterous crowd.

From the different regions of the U.S. come tasty dishes like buttermilk fried chicken; seafood étoufée with crawfish, Dungeness crab, and shrimp; or slow-roasted duck with gingersnap gravy. It is well worth saving room for the sinful chocolate and butterscotch *pot de crème*.

A word to the wise: take a cab here in the evening. It can be a challenge to find parking and many of the nearby garages close at 7:00 P.M.

TWO

American 

C2

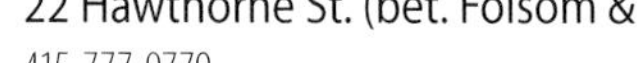

22 Hawthorne St. (bet. Folsom & Howard Sts.)

Phone: 415-777-9779 — Mon – Fri lunch & dinner
Web: www.two-sf.com — Sat dinner only
Prices: $$

This casual and affordable remake of Hawthorne Lane showcases a funky modern design complete with bright yellow tables, padded banquettes, and quirky shredded-coconut light fixtures above the elliptical copper-clad concrete bar.

Meals here start with warm, addictive Parker House rolls, but beware that only the first round is free. The reasonably-priced and often adventurous menu may include roasted striped bass with cannelloni bean ragout or house-made lasagna layered with sliced meatballs, fresh pasta, and a spicy tomato sauce. Meanwhile, whimsical desserts like the TWO cupcakes (one is peanut butter, the other double chocolate) or Sprecher's root-beer float with homemade ice cream are both creative, delicious, and fun endings to a lighthearted meal.

Waterbar

Seafood XX

D1

399 Embarcadero (at Harrison St.)

Phone: 415-284-9922 — Lunch & dinner daily
Web: www.waterbarsf.com
Prices: $$$

Another Pat Kuleto project (you can see more of the famed designer's work at Farallon, Jardinière, and Epic Roasthouse next door), Waterbar laps at the waterfront, just south of the Ferry Building. Although tall windows provide a great view of the Bay Bridge, there's more than enough inside to hold your attention. Twin 19-foot-tall cylindrical aquariums, and a hand-blown glass "caviar" chandelier over the raw bar paint an oh-so-chic picture.

Don't let all this eye candy distract you from the cuisine at hand, which—of course—is seafood flown in from around the globe. Chef and co-owner Mark Franz (also of Farallon) rides the tide with the likes of sea scallop ceviche; whole roasted Petrale sole; and rock cod Colbert, Waterbar's version of fish and chips.

XYZ

C2

American 

181 3rd St. (at Howard St.)

Phone: 415-817-7836 — Lunch & dinner daily
Web: www.xyz-sf.com
Prices: $$$

From its sleek design to the fine cuisine, the W Hotel is completed by XYZ. The restaurant's barrel-vaulted ceiling, high-backed circular booths, marble tables, and two-story windows framing Third Street echo the property's urban motif. Attentive, well-informed service and fresh ingredients complement the pleasant surroundings, the hues of which will change with the season.

The menu reveals each season's bounty, including *crab arancini* with persimmons, orange, and olive tapenade aioli; or pan-roasted salmon with frisée, shaved fennel, mizuna, and heirloom tomatoes. Desserts may include a chocolate caramel bar with candied peanuts, coffee sabayon and salted caramel ice cream.

The "W" may as well stand for wine, as XYZ offers over 600 labels from both new and old worlds.

Yank Sing

D1

Chinese 

101 Spear St. (bet. Howard & Mission Sts.)

Phone: 415-957-9300 — Lunch daily
Web: www.yanksing.com
Prices: $$

Dim sum at its finest—that's what you can expect at Yank Sing. Located in Rincon Center, this elegant restaurant explodes with patrons on weekends, changing the faces in the dining room from a weekday suit crowd to a lively social set.

If you come on a weekend, remember that the variety of dim sum offered is reduced by half in order to manage the crowds. No matter which day you eat here, the quality vies with the best dim sum halls in Hong Kong. Be sure to experience as wide a variety of items as your appetite can handle. And don't even think of passing up the terrific soup dumplings (called Shanghai pork dumplings here), or the perfectly pan-fried ground-pork potstickers—a far cry from the versions served elsewhere.

Zazil

Mexican

B2

845 Market St. (bet. 4th & 5th Sts.)

Phone: 415-495-6379 — Lunch & dinner daily
Web: www.zazilrestaurant.com
Prices: $$$

The word "clarity" (*zazil* in Mayan) often brings to mind images of clear, blue waters-just the tone that owners Eduardo and Sylvia Rallo (of Colibrí in the FiDi and Consuelo in San Jose) hope to set with the wavy banquettes and aquatic colors in their dining room on the fourth floor of Westfield Centre.

Clarity also shines through in the flavors of the traditional Mexican dishes. Many of these focus on seafood, as in the *axiote*-marinated grilled fish, stuffed Yucatan-style with black-bean purée and avocado.

Guacamole is served tableside, accompanied by a basket of fresh, warm tortillas in lieu of fried chips. Here, tequila trumps beer and wine, mixed in margaritas, or offered straight up from this selection of more than 280 different labels.

Look out for **red** *symbols, indicating a particularly pleasant ambiance at establishments.*

MICHELIN

East of San Francisco

East of San Francisco

Berkeley and Oakland

A short hop across the **Bay Bridge**—currently undergoing a $5.5-billion seismic retrofit scheduled for completion in 2013—or ride on the BART from San Francisco, the neighboring cities of Berkeley and Oakland have their own individual charms. Each is worth a visit in its own right—Berkeley for its storied university campus and its liberal attitude, and Oakland for its revitalized downtown.

BERKELEY

Synonymous with the renowned **University of California at Berkeley**, this bohemian college town is Oakland's erudite little sister—a small city with a big reputation for political activism. Though things have calmed down here since the Free Speech Movement was launched on Berkeley's campus in the 1960s, political protests are still not uncommon and the concepts of green and sustainable are taken very seriously. Cruise **Telegraph Avenue** to experience a slice of student life, and to check out the great book and music shops.

Berkeley has long enjoyed a reputation for attracting intellectuals, idealists, and eccentrics whose diverse tastes have left their mark on the city's history, architecture, and ambience. A New Jersey native who graduated from U.C. Berkeley in 1967, Alice Waters, changed America's food scene forever in 1971 when she opened **Chez Panisse** and gave rise to California cuisine. Today, Waters restaurant occupies the same Arts and Crafts-style bungalow on a bustling restaurant row on upper Shattuck Avenue *(between Rose & Virginia Sts.)* known as the *gourmet ghetto*. Along this avenue today, a handful of Chez Panisse alumni have opened their own places, dishing up fresh fare from pizza to paella.

OAKLAND

Named for its expansive growth of oak trees, Oakland was incorporated in 1852 as a quiet bedroom community for the woollier metropolis across the bay. Today, this workaday city is experiencing a renaissance. Businesses have replaced vacant warehouses on downtown blocks, and new office towers and condominium communities have sprung up—with more development on the way. The thanks go in part to former Mayor Jerry Brown, whose 10K Initiative catalyzed retail interest downtown. Here, a virtual gumbo of ethnic restaurants, cafes, and fine-dining establishments caters to taste buds as diverse as the city's population. Meanwhile, despite some persistent problems with crime, new nightclubs and bars, and revitalized shopping districts lure residents and visitors to the downtown core. Local farmers' markets eliminate the need for Oakland residents to cross the bay to buy fresh organic produce.

Another downtown draw is **Jack London Square**, a sparkling, pedestrian-friendly complex of shops, restaurants, and entertainment and cultural attractions that nestles along **Oakland Estuary** at site of the once-gritty dock area. The square is named for author Jack London, who spent his early years in Oakland. One of London's favorite watering holes, Heinold's First and Last Chance Saloon *(45 Webster St., in Jack London Square)* still operates as a bar. An influx of business in this area includes a six-story waterfront market encompassing local produce, fresh meat, and fish as well as a mélange of restaurants. It is slated to open in early 2009.

On Oakland's border with Berkeley, the upscale residential **Rockridge** neighborhood boasts a strip of trendy shops, gourmet markets and restaurants that makes a pleasant place to while away an afternoon.

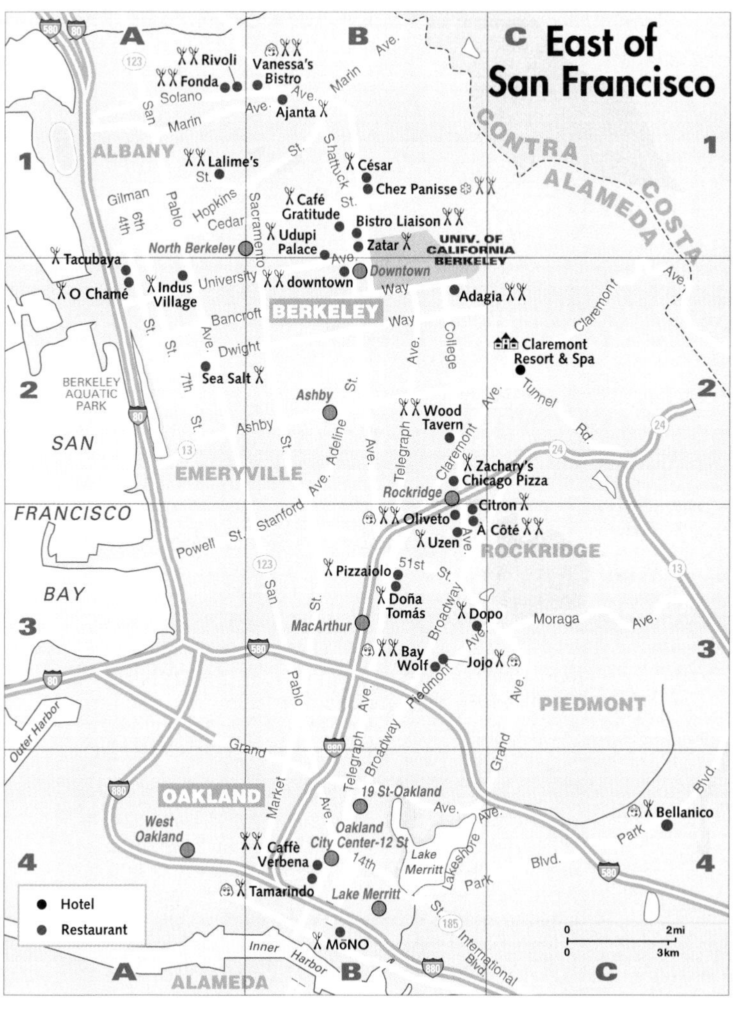

À Côté

Mediterranean XX

B3

5478 College Ave. (at Taft St.), Oakland

Phone: 510-655-6469 Dinner daily
Web: www.acoterestaurant.com
Prices: $$

Rockridge residents love this convivial place, where Mediterranean cuisine pairs with courteous service. Small plates hold sway here, in incarnations such as ricotta-stuffed squash blossoms, grilled duck sausage, and smoked trout salad with baby red mustard.

Take a seat at the communal table near the kitchen and its blazing wood-fired oven, or nosh at the bar while you sip one of the specialty cocktails or the 40 wines offered by the glass. During the warmer months, the sunny patio becomes prime real estate.

The restaurant sets aside a limited number of tables for reservations, but seating is primarily on a first-come, first-served basis. No worries: the adjacent blocks are chock-full of trendy boutiques to occupy you until your table is ready.

Adagia

Californian XX

B2

2700 Bancroft Way (bet. College & Piedmont Aves.), Berkeley

Phone: 510-647-2300 Lunch & dinner daily
Web: www.adagiarestaurant.com
Prices: $$

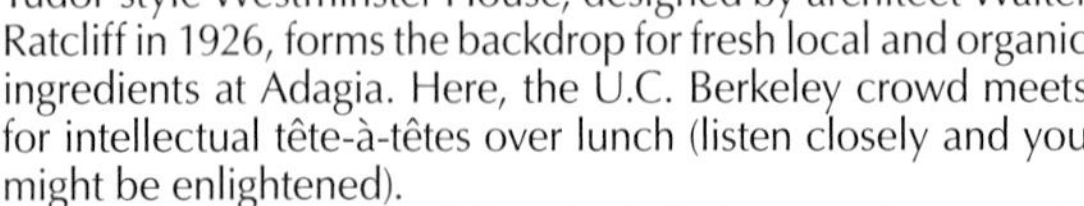

Tudor-style Westminster House, designed by architect Walter Ratcliff in 1926, forms the backdrop for fresh local and organic ingredients at Adagia. Here, the U.C. Berkeley crowd meets for intellectual tête-à-têtes over lunch (listen closely and you might be enlightened).

The wrought-iron chandelier, leaded-glass windows, rustic wooden tables, and huge fireplace recall Harry Potter's dining hall at Hogwarts, but the food here is far from institutional. Adagia's Cal-Med cuisine earns high marks, as in a tangy-sweet pulled-pork sandwich, or baked cannelloni with butternut squash. While these are fine for big appetites, a chicken Caesar salad—strewn with crumbled goat cheese, cranberries, and garlic crouton—-makes a meal for calorie-conscious co-eds.

Ajanta

B1

1888 Solano Ave. (bet. The Alameda & Colusa Ave.), Berkeley

Phone: 510-526-4373 — Lunch & dinner daily
Web: www.ajantarestaurant.com
Prices:

In an area of Berkeley where Indian restaurants abound, Ajanta stands out for its very pleasant, traditional, well-crafted regional cuisine. "As you like it" describes the heat levels here, which are adjusted to your preference—go for "hot" if you fancy spicier food. From Punjab comes tandoori game hen, marinated in yogurt, lemon juice, ginger, garlic, and spices; lamb *Do Pyaza*, a stew made with cubes of boneless Niman Ranch leg of lamb, hails from Delhi; green catfish curry, a recipe from Mumbai, simmers in a sauce made with coconut milk, green chiles, herbs, and cashew powder. The menu, which adds new dishes each month, specifies the origin of each entrée.
Enthusiasts can pick up a copy of Ajanta's cookbook and create some of these dishes at home.

Bay Wolf

Californian

B3

3853 Piedmont Ave. (at Rio Vista Ave.), Oakland

Phone: 510-655-6004 — Mon – Fri lunch & dinner
Web: www.baywolf.com — Sat – Sun dinner only
Prices: $$

This Oakland icon is set in a charming renovated Victorian house. Opened in 1975 by Chef/owner Michael Wild, Bay Wolf divides its dining space into two rustic rooms and the pleasant heated veranda, which is open all year.
Wild's monthly changing take on Cal-Med cuisine results in updated versions of recipes from Italy, France and Spain. The freshest local ingredients are interpreted simply in such entrées as coq au vin, pork pot roast, acorn-squash soufflé, and simple desserts (a refreshing Meyer lemon pudding cake or an apple and quince tart).
The serious young waitstaff knows the menu well and is happy to offer advice if you're wavering in your dinner decision. Elegantly presented dishes arrive at the table at a relaxed (not slow) pace.

Bellanico 

Italian 

C4

4238 Park Blvd. (at Wellington St.), Oakland

Phone: 510-336-1180 Tue – Sat lunch & dinner
Web: www.bellanico.net Mon dinner only
Prices: $$

A newcomer to the Oakland suburb of Glenview, Bellanico is the culinary child of Chris Shepherd and Elizabeth Frumusa (the duo behind Aperto in Potrero Hill). The space, once a flower shop, sports rust-colored walls and a granite-topped bar.

Chichetti—fava bean and English pea crostini; fried Sicilian olives—make a good segue into house-made pastas and *secondi* such as slow-braised lamb and roasted baby chicken. Many of the European varietals are served by the glass or the flight.

Having youngsters themselves—the owners christened this place in honor of their daughters Bella and Nico—they offer an inexpensive pasta option for kids. Despite the occasional bambino, the mainstay of Bellanico's crowd consists of sophisticated food lovers.

Bistro Liaison

B1

1849 Shattuck Ave. (at Hearst Ave.), Berkeley

Phone: 510-849-2155 Lunch & dinner daily
Web: www.liaisonbistro.com
Prices: $$

The story of Bistro Liaison began when Chef Todd Kneiss came to San Francisco in 1994 and began working for Roland Passot (of La Folie and Tanglewood) at the Left Bank restaurant in Larkspur. After years honing his skills cooking rustic French cuisine, Kniess opened this friendly neighborhood bistro in 2001.

What Kniess calls "French food for the soul" translates into favorites such as a *croque monsieur* sandwich, *bœuf Bourguignon,* and salad *Lyonnaise* (frisée tossed in warm shallot bacon vinaigrette and topped with a poached egg). For dessert, peruse the selections rubber-stamped onto the white butcher paper that covers your table.

A curving concrete bar divides the kitchen from the dining room, and outdoor seating attracts diners in warm weather.

Café Gratitude

Vegan

1730 Shattuck Ave. (at Virginia St.), Berkeley

Phone: 415-824-4652 Lunch & dinner daily
Web: www.cafegratitude.com
Prices: 

The Berkeley branch of a small chain of vegan eateries serving mostly raw foods, Café Gratitude nourishes both body and soul. Enjoy multiple levels of wellness as blissful, bohemian servers set down your plate, stating affirmations like "you are fulfilled," or "you are insightful" (no, they don't have ESP—these are the actual names of the dishes).

An environmentally conscious college set frequents the café for appetizing vegan food, smoothies, and elixirs. Solo diners may be seated at "shared" tables if there's no room at the bar. Be grateful that from an avocado stuffed with chipotle sunflower-seed pâté to "live" pizzas, no animals are sacrificed to feed you here.

Spreading the love, siblings are located in the Mission District, Sunset, and San Rafael.

Caffè Verbena

Italian

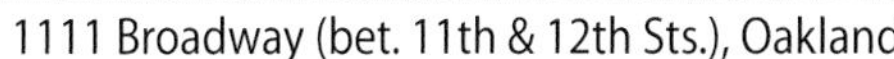

1111 Broadway (bet. 11th & 12th Sts.), Oakland

Phone: 510-465-9300 Mon – Fri lunch & dinner
Web: www.caffeverbena.com
Prices: $$

The Oakland Convention Center attendees are drawn with good reason to this spacious restaurant for Italian fare. Bright flavors highlight the Caffè's take on classic lasagna: three roulades of lasagna are napped with basil pesto and tangy tomato sauce. Traditional selections of antipasti, pizza, pasta, meat, and fish dishes round out the menu.

The large size of the restaurant and its location on the lobby level of the APL Building in downtown Oakland give it the feel of a hotel dining room. Even so, courtyard views outside the window-lined space feature a pleasant, grassy garden, enhanced by contemporary sculptures and a stone waterfall. After work, Caffè Verbena's bar brings in a lively crowd who sip cocktails and unwind.

César

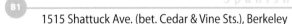

Spanish

1515 Shattuck Ave. (bet. Cedar & Vine Sts.), Berkeley

Phone: 510-883-0222 Lunch & dinner daily
Web: www.barcesar.com
Prices:

César was founded in 1998 by three Chez Panisse alumni, so it is no coincidence that this lively "gourmet ghetto" Californian tapas bar lives next door to its famous neighbor—and that its name is an homage to the same trilogy of films by Marcel Pagnol.

In the same spirit of offering incomparably fresh ingredients, César tempts with the likes of portobello mushroom *bocadillos* and fire-grilled shrimp *a la plancha*. Even the most ardent carb-counters will find it hard to resist the perfect mountain of fried potato ribbons dusted with herbs and sea salt, and accompanied by tangy garlic aïoli . A minimal and simple selection of sweets are also available.

In 2006, a second and much larger branch of César opened in Oakland *(4039 Piedmont Ave)*.

Citron

Contemporary

5484 College Ave. (bet. Lawton & Taft Aves.), Oakland

Phone: 510-653-5484 Tue – Sun lunch & dinner
Web: www.citronrestaurant.biz Mon dinner only
Prices: $$

International is too broad a label to put on a cuisine that jumps from Mediterranean to French to Californian. No matter its origins, the food here is fresh, expertly cooked, and full of flavor. At lunch, country pork pâté with dried cherries makes a worthy prelude to potato gnocchi with wild mushrooms, white corn, and parmesan; or even a barbecue pulled-pork sandwich with house-made *gaufrette* chips. A three-course prix-fixe meal offers good value for the budget-conscious.

Dinner reveals the same variety à la carte, featuring Creole-spiced prawns or grilled lamb sirloin with fall greens bread salad. Three- to five-course chef's tastings are also available. White linen tables, sultry jazz and blues music complement the upscale Rockridge neighborhood.

Chez Panisse ✿

B1

1517 Shattuck Ave. (bet. Cedar & Vine Sts.), Berkeley

Phone: 510-548-5525 Mon – Sat dinner only

Web: www.chezpanisse.com

Prices: **$$$$**

The word "locavore" may only be a few years old, but the roots of the movement date back to 1971, when Alice Waters—now one of the country's most influential chefs—and a few like-minded pals swung open the doors to Chez Panisse. It was history in the making, for the folksy bungalow with the warm, wood-paneled interior and bustling, open kitchen would quickly come to define California cuisine and ignite a movement that is still on fire almost four decades later. The concept was simple: employ premium ingredients from local farmers, ranchers and fisherman, and only serve whatever is market-fresh that day.

If you're planning on being in Berkeley, you can (and should) make reservations up to a month in advance for the dining room, where the fixed-price 4-course dinner (3-courses on Mondays) rotates nightly. Otherwise, a bustling upstairs cafe welcomes walk-ins.

Appetizers

- Tomato Salad with Herbs and Aïoli
- Blue Heron Farm Little Gems Lettuce and Figs with Grilled Duck Breast
- Roasted Tomato and Eggplant Soup with Fried Basil

Entrées

- Grilled Quail and Pork Belly, Peperonata, and Savory
- Farro Spaghetti, Shell Beans, Chanterelles, Escarole, and Parmesan
- Fried Shrimp with Frisée and Artichoke Salad

Desserts

- Pear-Huckleberry Tart, Vanilla Ice Cream
- Frog Hollow Farm Peach Cobbler, Vanilla Ice Cream
- Bittersweet Chocolate Custard, Buttered Pecans and Bourbon Cream

Doña Tomás

Mexican

B3

5004 Telegraph Ave. (at 50th St.), Oakland

Phone: 510-450-0522 — Tue – Sat dinner only
Web: www.donatomas.com
Prices: $$

A long wait lies in store for diners who don't reserve in advance here, but high-energy devotees are happy to sip tequila, margaritas, and specialty cocktails to while away the time. This very authentic, seasonal Mexican fare featuring the likes of butternut squash quesadillas; sautéed day-boat scallops "Veracruzano" in a butter sauce flavored with cherry tomatoes, capers, shallots, chiles, and cilantro; and *carne asada* made with grilled Niman Ranch beef keeps them on the hook.

Related to Tacubaya in Berkeley, this boisterous señora sits amid restaurants and shops in Oakland's Temescal district, which is quickly becoming the East Bay's next Gourmet Ghetto. The heated outdoor patio accommodates large crowds, but these tables cannot be reserved.

Dopo

Italian

B3

4293 Piedmont Ave. (at Echo St.), Oakland

Phone: 510-652-3676 — Mon – Sat lunch & dinner
Web: N/A
Prices: $$

Dopo's expanded space, with double the seating capacity of the original closet-size restaurant, allows for skylights and a long L-shaped counter that wraps from the open kitchen around the lacquered pine bar that was added in the renovation.

Very busy and still popular with the East Bay set, this five-year-old is perpetually bustling. Its daily menu may include a lunchtime assortment of antipasti, such as a salad of farro and roasted beets with mint, Meyer lemons, and walnuts; tuna confit, pickled red onion, egg, and mozzarella panini; or a thin, crisp pizza lightly layered in very fine toppings. Dinner is more adventurous, adding house-made salumi or tortellini with North Carolina white shrimp and chives. All items are available for takeout.

downtown

American XX

B2

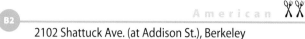

2102 Shattuck Ave. (at Addison St.), Berkeley

Phone: 510-649-3810 — Tue – Fri lunch & dinner
Web: www.downtownrestaurant.com — Sat – Sun dinner only
Prices: $$

Marked by a large angled façade on the corner of Shattuck and Addison, downtown restaurant sits in the liveliest part of Berkeley, across the street from the Berkeley Repertory Theatre and two blocks from the university. There's a big-city buzz in the high-ceilinged dining room, where a regular program of live jazz regales diners several nights a week (check online for schedule), and locals gather to nosh before and after the theater.

Chef/partner David Stevenson works magic with fish, grilling Bluenose sea bass with a Minneola citrus beurre blanc, roasting fish whole, and searing day-boat scallops. And his sleight-of-hand with braised lamb, brick-oven-roasted chicken and other meat entrées on the weekly changing menu wins applause too.

Fonda

Latin American XX

A1

1501 Solano Ave. (at Curtis St.), Albany

Phone: 510-559-9006 — Lunch & dinner daily
Web: www.fondasolana.com
Prices: $$

The Albany hotspot for sophisticated cocktails and gourmet tapas, Fonda Solana is indeed a "cafe on a sunny corner" as its Spanish name suggests. It's set on Albany's main street, where a cool East Bay crowd comes to drink in the festive atmosphere, while sampling the likes of sautéed prawns with *salsa negra*; duck and pomegranate tacos; and, to finish, perhaps a passionfruit crème brulée.

Portions may be small, but flavors are big (and the prices of all those small plates can add up fast). The kitchen's not afraid of using a generous dose of Mexican chiles and spices to wake up your taste buds. Luckily, Fonda offers a long list of inventive cocktails from mojitos to flights of tequila served with a glass of Fonda's zesty house-made sangrita.

Indus Village

Indian

A2

1920 San Pablo Ave. (bet. Hearst & University Aves.), Berkeley

Phone: 510-549-5999 Lunch & dinner daily
Web: N/A
Prices: ⊜

Vibrant murals depicting the desert life of Pakistan set the tone at this restaurant on eclectic San Pablo Avenue. Choose from the full menu of Pakistani cuisine or the white board at the entrance announcing the day's specials. Once decided, place an order at the counter, pay with cash (it's all they accept), then take a seat in one of the bright, high-backed, dowel-and-knob chairs that were handmade in Pakistan.

Chicken *tikka masala* pairs chunks of boneless meat with a rich, mild yellow curry sauce, while *paalak aloo* is a flavorful mélange of minced spinach, spices, and cubes of potato. Combination meals, served with basmati rice and delicious, tender naan flatbread, offer to take the guesswork out of ordering.

Jojo

French

B3

3859 Piedmont Ave. (at Rio Vista Ave.), Oakland

Phone: 510-985-3003 Tue – Sat dinner only
Web: www.jojorestaurant.com
Prices: $$

Gourmet French cuisine made with ultra-fresh products has been taking center stage at Jojo since 1999, courtesy of Chefs Curt Clingman and Mary Jo Thorensen, whose collective cooking credits include Zuni Café, Oliveto, and Chez Panisse. Thorensen also has experience in restaurant kitchens in Provence and Tuscany, so it's no surprise that the flavors of the Mediterranean dominate the couple's concise, ingredient-driven menu.

The kitchen ignores gastronomic fads in favor of rustic simplicity. While bistro fare such as steak frites with anchovy-mustard butter are staples, more contemporary dishes—a savory bread pudding with fresh-from-the-market vegetables—make excellent choices too. Be sure to save room for Chef Thorensen's mouth-watering desserts.

Lalime's

A1

International

1329 Gilman St. (bet. Neilson & Peralta Aves.), Berkeley

Phone: 510-527-9838 Dinner daily
Web: www.lalimes.com
Prices: $$

This Craftsman-style cottage blends into Berkeley's residential Westbrae neighborhood. Behind its picture-window façade, find the best of both worlds; a lively bar greets guests at the entrance, while a lower dining room fosters cozier meals *à deux*.

Cuisine at Cynthia and Haig Krikorian's place (whose relatives include Sea Salt and Fonda) celebrates the seasons with a menu that mixes numerous cultural influences, all with California flair. In summer, heirloom tomatoes could star with equal aplomb in a salad paired with tuna confit or grilled in a soup with bacon and garlic croutons. A poblano chile stuffed with chunks of zucchini in savory fromage blanc or a grilled Berkshire pork chop accented by apple-pear chutney is satisfying fare for cooler days.

MōNO

B4

Californian

247 4th St. (bet. Alice & Jackson Sts.), Oakland

Phone: 510-834-0260 Tue – Fri lunch & dinner
Web: www.monorestaurant.com Sat dinner only
Prices: $$

In the trendy Jack London Square, this historic structure, an erstwhile grocery company, is now a soon-to-be popular restaurant. This hip spot is run by husband-and-wife team Todd Wilson and Eloisa Castillo, and named after his pet name for her (monkey in Spanish).

Cement pillars and a cinderblock horseshoe-shaped bar define industrial-chic, while California-inspired small-plates highlight the menu. Organically grown and sustainably farmed products appear in the likes of grilled Castroville artichokes with Meyer lemon aïoli; or Ahi tuna *crudo* with preserved lemon, jalapeño granita, and soba noodles. Sangria and more than 100 wine labels provide perfect pairings. Glass-paned garage doors roll back to reveal a small patio, weather permitting.

O Chamé

Japanese

A2

1830 4th St. (bet. Hearst Ave. & Virginia St.), Berkeley

Phone: 510-841-8783 Mon – Sat lunch & dinner
Web: N/A
Prices: $$

Sandwiched between trendy home-furnishing stores in Berkeley's luxe 4th Street shopping district, O Chamé surprises as a Japanese restaurant. First of all, you'll find no typical Zen décor here; instead, sunny walls create a soothing tavern vibe and only Japanese lithographs here and there suggest the theme of the food.

Another surprise: they don't serve sushi. Grilled fish and a selection of noodles constitute the entrées on the concise, frequently changing menu. Soba and udon noodles fill bowls of clear fish broth, embellished with toppings like roasted oysters, pork tenderloin, wakame seeweed and shiitake mushrooms. Order yourself a bowl and enjoy it outside on the little sidewalk terrace, a great place to soak up the neighborhood scene.

Oliveto

Italian

B3

5655 College Ave. (at Shafter Ave.), Oakland

Phone: 510-547-5356 Mon – Fri lunch & dinner
Web: www.oliveto.com Sat – Sun dinner only
Prices: $$$

Located in the European-style Market Hall in Rockridge, Oliveto has a split personality. Downstairs, the trattoria-style cafe serves breakfast, lunch, and dinner. Up the winding staircase hides a more formal dining room with large windows that survey the streetscape. In the cafe, breakfast can mean anything from polenta to pastries, while lunch brings small plates, sandwiches, and pizzas; dinner adds pasta to the mix. More sophisticated fare rules upstairs, where a bruschetta of spicy Jones Farm rabbit confit, a *crespelle* of Dungeness crab and asparagus, and a spit-roasted leg of Watson Farm spring lamb team up for a gourmet trifecta.

Drop by for the popular seasonal menus, such as the tomato dinner in August and the whole hog dinner in February.

Pizzaiolo

B3

5008 Telegraph Ave. (bet. 49th & 51st Sts.), Oakland

Phone: 510-652-4888 Mon – Sat dinner only
Web: www.pizzaiolo.us
Prices: ⚭

Seek out Pizzaiolo in Oakland for good service, a lively atmosphere, and a daily changing menu of thin-crust, crisp, and delicately textured artisanal pizzas. From the wood-burning oven in the exhibition kitchen, pies are harmoniously decked with rapini and house-made sausage, delicata squash and gorgonzola, or maybe wild nettles and pecorino. If you require a prelude to your pizza, the handful of *primi* include salads crafted with the freshest seasonal produce, as well as regional Italian dishes such as *arancini* (Roman fried rice balls) or *ribollita* (a hearty soup from Tuscany). *Secondi* are also offered, but most are mesmerized by the pizza.

Low lighting and smooth jazz in the background make this a good casual option for a first date.

Rivoli

A1

1539 Solano Ave. (bet. Neilson St. & Peralta Ave.), Berkeley

Phone: 510-526-2542 Dinner daily
Web: www.rivolirestaurant.com
Prices: $$

Named for the Parisian *rue* where owners Roscoe Skipper and Wendy Brucker spent their honeymoon, Rivoli is a pleasant Berkeley boîte—and a certified green business to boot. A wine bar greets guests as they enter this little house, and a narrow hallway leads into the square dining area, lined with floor-to-ceiling windows.

Northern California products rule the menu, which is duly peppered with Italian gusto. The season dictates if you're feasting on saffron risotto with Dungeness crab, shrimp, and fennel; ricotta gnocchi with roast pears, fried sage, walnuts, and brown butter; or a grilled pork loin chop stuffed with prosciutto, fontina cheese, and sage.

New sibling Corso Trattoria (*1786 Shattuck Ave.*) also offers an intimate dining experience.

Sea Salt

Seafood

A2

2512 San Pablo Ave. (at Dwight Way), Berkeley

Phone: 510-883-1720 — Lunch & dinner daily
Web: www.seasaltrestaurant.com
Prices: $$

Cousin to Lalime's and Fonda, operated by Haig and Cindy Krikorian, Sea Salt serves some of the area's finest seafood. Arrive between 4-6pm daily for the $1 oyster special. Follow this with a bowl of exceptional white clam chowder, featuring fresh clams in a light, well-seasoned broth. The young, attentive staff is informative and well-versed in the menu, which changes seasonally but remains consistently fresh and well-prepared. Dishes may include a crispy, pan-roasted Alaskan black cod paired with white corn, cranberry beans, chanterelles, and tarragon crème fraîche.

Weekend brunch reels in such favorites as seared trout with red flannel hash and sunny-side-up eggs, or steamed lobster on a torpedo roll served with sweet butter and house-made potato chips.

Tacubaya

Mexican

A2

1788 4th St. (bet. Hearst Ave. & Virginia St.), Berkeley

Phone: 510-525-5160 — Wed – Mon lunch & dinner
Web: www.tacubaya.net — Tue lunch only
Prices: ⊖⊖

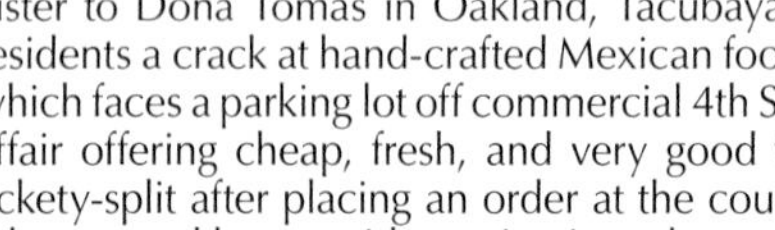

Sister to Doña Tomás in Oakland, Tacubaya gives Berkeley residents a crack at hand-crafted Mexican food. The taqueria, which faces a parking lot off commercial 4th Street, is a simple affair offering cheap, fresh, and very good food. Service is lickety-split after placing an order at the counter. Tables and a long wood bar provide seating in a cheery space animated by vivid primary hues.

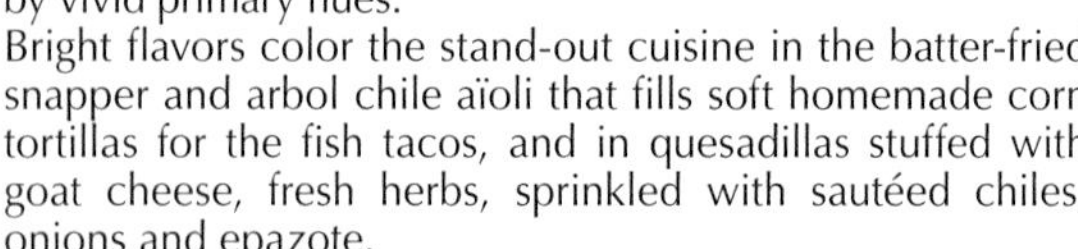

Bright flavors color the stand-out cuisine in the batter-fried snapper and arbol chile aïoli that fills soft homemade corn tortillas for the fish tacos, and in quesadillas stuffed with goat cheese, fresh herbs, sprinkled with sautéed chiles, onions and epazote.

Note that all sides (rice, black beans, or the crisp potato and cheese *papas con crema*) are priced separately.

Tamarindo

Mexican

468 8th St. (at Broadway), Oakland

Phone: 510-444-1944 Mon – Sat lunch & dinner
Web: www.tamarindoantojeria.com
Prices:

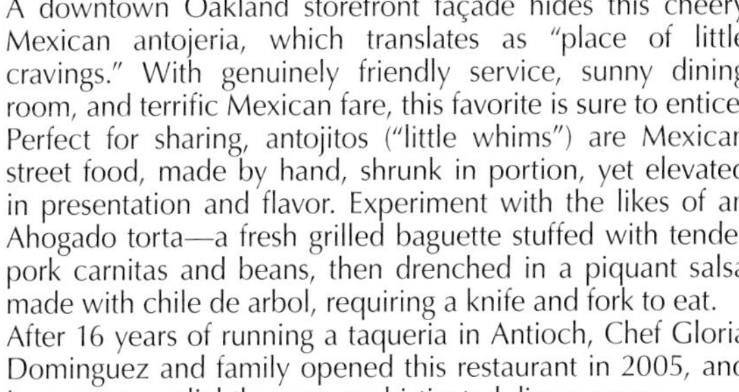

A downtown Oakland storefront façade hides this cheery Mexican antojeria, which translates as "place of little cravings." With genuinely friendly service, sunny dining room, and terrific Mexican fare, this favorite is sure to entice. Perfect for sharing, antojitos ("little whims") are Mexican street food, made by hand, shrunk in portion, yet elevated in presentation and flavor. Experiment with the likes of an Ahogado torta—a fresh grilled baguette stuffed with tender pork carnitas and beans, then drenched in a piquant salsa made with chile de arbol, requiring a knife and fork to eat.
After 16 years of running a taqueria in Antioch, Chef Gloria Dominguez and family opened this restaurant in 2005, and incorporate a slightly more sophisticated dinner menu.

Udupi Palace

1901 University Ave. (at Martin Luther King Jr. Way), Berkeley

Phone: 510-843-6600 Lunch & dinner daily
Web: www.udupipalaceca.com
Prices:

Students at U.C. Berkeley flock to the University Avenue location of this plain little place for its southern Indian vegetarian dishes. Several combinations at lunch ensure diners are back to class—or work—in a jiffy, and with money to spare. Just make sure to bring cash; Udupi doesn't accept credit cards.
Carnivores will never miss the meat in Udupi's piquant curries, with mixtures ranging from fresh eggplant, mashed tomatoes, and onions (*baigan bartha*) to potato, cauliflower, and spices (*Gobi masala*). Pronounced flavors enliven offerings like rich tomato soup accented by garlic and cilantro, or a vegetable samosa topped with tamarind sauce and minted yogurt.
Look for the newest location of Udupi Palace at *1007 Valencia Street* in San Francisco.

Uzen

Japanese

B3

5415 College Ave. (bet. Hudson St. & Kales Ave.), Oakland

Phone: 510-654-7753 — Mon – Fri lunch & dinner
Web: N/A — Sat dinner only
Prices: $$

Blending into a line of identical storefronts in Rockridge, tiny Uzen is easy to overlook. Inside the quiet, narrow space, rows of pew-like banquettes line the walls alongside a diagonal bar that serves wonderfully fresh seafood. Absent are the long lists of gimmicky rolls. Here, fresh, bright fish is skillfully cut, delicately prepared and best enjoyed as sushi. Several hot teriyaki dishes mollify those that prefer their fish cooked, and steaming bowls of thick udon noodles in savory broth, garnished with crisp tempura, make the ideal antidote for a gray, chilly day.

By day, skylights illuminate the diminutive space with natural light; at night, the bar's pendant lights flicker over the fresh fish. Note the $15 minimum charge if paying by credit card.

Vanessa's Bistro

Vietnamese

B1

1715 Solano Ave. (at Tulare Ave.), Berkeley

Phone: 510-525-8300 — Wed, Thu, Sun & Mon dinner only
Web: www.vanessasbistro.com — Fri – Sat lunch & dinner
Prices: $$

History brought together Vietnamese and French cuisines; Vanessa Dang adds Spanish tapas style and twists all her own to create original food.

Small (and some larger) plates include shaking filet mignon salad in garlic brandy-butter sauce; peanut-coated baby back ribs, fried and served with spicy pineapple beurre blanc; and crispy frogs' legs with garlic butter and spicy lime dipping sauce. Vegetarians surely aren't neglected with options like lemongrass tofu sautéed in a curry beurre blanc with roasted peanuts. Mouthwatering menu descriptions ring true on the beautifully arranged plates.

Though the bamboo-lined bar and red-clothed tables can fill fast, you'll want to bring along friends for sharing as much of this creative fare as you can.

Wood Tavern

Gastropub XX

B2

6317 College Ave. (bet. Alcatraz Ave. & 63rd St.), Oakland

Phone: 510-654-6607 — Mon – Sat lunch & dinner
Web: www.woodtavern.net — Sun dinner only
Prices: $$

Brought to you by restaurateurs Rebekah and Rich Wood, the former owners of Frascati on Russian Hill, Wood Tavern well exceeds the image its name may conjure. The tavern does foster its reputation as a popular neighborhood bar, but the décor showcases soaring sky-lit ceilings and a copper-lined bar, serving a fresh, seasonal cuisine that goes well beyond typical pub grub.

Picture house-smoked duck breast or crispy pork belly for starters. Follow that with a plate of fresh rigatoni topped with braised lamb *sugo*, or a grilled flat-iron steak with broccoli rabe and creamy parmesan whipped potatoes. Then, if you still have room, finish with profiteroles and homemade mint chocolate-chip ice cream, drizzled with chocolate sauce at the table.

Zachary's Chicago Pizza

Pizza X

B2

5801 College Ave. (at Oak Grove Ave.), Oakland

Phone: 510-655-6385 — Lunch & dinner daily
Web: www.zacharys.com
Prices: (bib)

The Windy City's signature dish has been enjoying success in Oakland since 1983 at this no-frills pizzeria (check out the other locations in Berkeley and San Ramon). Zachary's specializes in stuffed pizza: a satisfying deep-dish concoction made with a layer of dough on the bottom of the pan, filled with a copious helping of cheese and your choice among 19 ingredients, and topped by another layer of crust and flavorful fresh tomato sauce.

A few caveats: Zachary's doesn't deliver, and they don't accept reservations. In any case, you should be prepared to wait—it takes 20 to 40 minutes to prepare a pizza to order here. Otherwise, you can opt to pick up one of Zachary's half-baked pies; take it home and enjoy it hot from your own oven.

Zatar

B1

1981 Shattuck Ave. (bet. Berkeley Way & University Ave.), Berkeley

Phone: 510-841-1981 Wed – Thu & Sat dinner only
Web: www.zatarrestaurant.com Fri lunch & dinner
Prices: **$$**

Named for the traditional blend of thyme, sesame seeds, and sun-dried sumac berries commonly used in Eastern Mediterranean cuisine, eco-friendly Zatar complements its "green" Berkeley surroundings. Husband-and-wife chef team Waiel and Kelly Majid (also partners in Europa, which previously occupied this space) use organic milk for their house-made yogurt, free-range meats, eggs from their own hens, as well as organic fruits, vegetables, and herbs—much of which comes from their own garden.

This ensures the fresh and delicious flavors of grilled Niman Ranch lamb, freshly ground with shallots and spices, or a savory vegetable tagine slow-cooked in a clay pot and served over couscous. Enjoy the namesake spice mixture in several of Zatar's dishes.

Hotels and restaurants change every year, so change your Michelin Guide every year!

North of San Francisco

North of San Francisco

Marin County

Introduced by the windswept ridges, sheltered valleys, and sandy coves of the Marin Headlands, Marin County lies just over the **Golden Gate Bridge** from San Francisco. Here, surrounded on three sides by water, you'll find unparalleled natural sites such as the wave-lashed sands of **Point Reyes National Seashore**, the lofty peak (2,571 feet) of **Mount Tamalpais**, and the majestic stands of redwoods (one of only two stands of virgin growth in the National Park Service) at **Muir Woods National Monument**—named for Scottish immigrant, John Muir, the revered naturalist and pioneer in the U.S. forest conservation movement—which celebrated its 100th anniversary in 2008. All this natural beauty, coupled with the laid-back atmosphere of the county's' rural towns, provide a welcome break from the dynamism of the city. Not to mention the fact that this area makes a great launching point for exploring the wineries of the Sonoma Valley.

A favorite excursion for both residents and visitors, sophisticated **Sausalito** lies a short drive or ferry ride across the bay from San Francisco. Indeed, the most appealing way to get here—on a nice day—is to hop aboard a ferry from the city. Once you disembark, it's an easy stroll along **Bridgeway Boulevard**, the community's commercial spine. Here you'll find upscale shops, gorgeous views, and eateries galore. What better place to enjoy seafood than in a restaurant by the water, enjoying vistas that stretch across the blue bay to **Tiburon** and **Angel Island**? On the land side, tiers of pricey private residences climb down the steep slopes to the bay.

Keep traveling north on Highway 101 and you'll discover charming towns like chi-chi **Mill Valley** or lovely **Larkspur**, whereas a detour along the coast will bring you to tiny **Inverness** and bohemian **Tomales Bay**. Exuding the quaint feel of a European village, Mill Valley's lush hilly landscape sits in the shadow of Mt. Tamalpais. The action here revolves around **Lytton Square**, edged by stylish boutiques and good restaurants. Queen Anne Victorians distinguish the architecture of Larkspur, a place whose entire downtown is listed on the National Register of Historic Places as a model turn-of-the-20th-century village. Antiques buffs should head for the historic railroad town of **San Anselmo**.

Marin County's northernmost city, **Novato** is located about 29 miles north of San Francisco. Downtown's restored Grant Avenue beckons with shops and restaurants, and nearby sites that preserve Novato's past. **San Rafael** wins the prize as Marin's oldest and largest city. It grew up around the **Mission San Rafael Arcangel**, established in 1817 as the 20th of California's 21 missions along *El Camino Real*. It was originally a place for ailing neophytes (Christianized Native Americans) to convalesce. Today, San Rafael's downtown shopping district blends retail, ethnic restaurants, and Victorian architecture.

North of San Francisco

0 8 mi
0 12 km

A B C
1 2 3

Nick's Cove
Nicasio Res.
Point Reyes Station
Nicasio
Lucas Valley Rd.
Olema Inn
Olema
Sir Francis Drake Blvd.
Shoreline Hwy.
Lagunitas
MARIN COUNTY
Novato Blvd.
Novato
Novato Cr.
Taki
Boca
Ignacio
Miller Cr.
San Pablo Bay
POINT REYES NATIONAL SEASHORE
Drakes Bay
GOLDEN GATE NATIONAL RECR. AREA
Kent L.
Alpine L.
Cucina
Fork
Insalata's
San Anselmo
Marché aux Fleurs
Ross
Lark Creek Inn
Left Bank
Picco
Larkspur
Sabor of Spain
Vin Antico
San Rafael
San Quentin
Corte Madera
Mill Valley
El Paseo
Bungalow 44
San Francisco Bay
Tiburon
Marin City
Sausalito
POINT BONITA
Golden Gate
PACIFIC OCEAN
SAN FRANCISCO

0 1 mi
0 1 km

Frantoio
Buckeye Roadhouse
Richardson Bay
MARIN CITY
BELVEDERE
Fish
Paradise Bay
Bridgeway
Spinnaker
Sushi Ran
The Inn Above Tide
Casa Madrona
Poggio
Gaylord
SAUSALITO
Murray Circle
GOLDEN GATE NATIONAL RECR. AREA
Bunker Rd.
GOLDEN GATE BRIDGE

● Hotel
● Restaurant

Boca

B1 Steakhouse XX

340 Ignacio Blvd. (bet. Alameda Del Prado & Enfrente Rd.), Novato

Phone: 415-883-0901 — Mon – Fri lunch & dinner
Web: www.bocasteak.com — Sat – Sun dinner only
Prices: $$

Jersey boy George Morrone heads this ranch-style steakhouse. A northern California restaurant with a South American twist, Boca ("mouth" in Spanish) honors the chef's Argentinean heritage from its cuisine to the music. Grass and grain-fed beef form the core of the menu in a variety of cuts that are grilled over blazing hardwood, served with basil and smoked paprika chimichurri sauces, and accompanied by piping-hot baked potatoes. A good selection of fresh seafood entrées is also available. For lunch, "Boca dillios" sandwiches with duck-fat fries will satisfy any hungry cowpoke.

Boca's ranch-like ambience employs timber, rawhide, and leather placemats to create a home on the range. Ride over on Tuesdays to take advantage of half-price wine bottles.

Buckeye Roadhouse

A2 American XX

15 Shoreline Hwy. (west of Hwy. 101), Mill Valley

Phone: 415-331-2600 — Lunch & dinner daily
Web: www.buckeyeroadhouse.com
Prices: $$

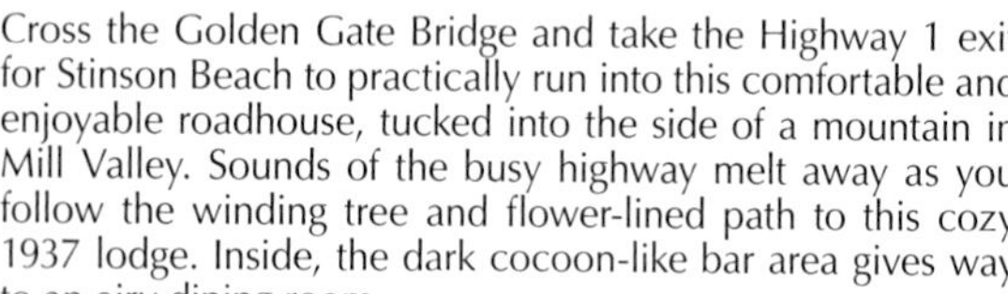

Cross the Golden Gate Bridge and take the Highway 1 exit for Stinson Beach to practically run into this comfortable and enjoyable roadhouse, tucked into the side of a mountain in Mill Valley. Sounds of the busy highway melt away as you follow the winding tree and flower-lined path to this cozy 1937 lodge. Inside, the dark cocoon-like bar area gives way to an airy dining room.

The quality of this cooking results in consistent, very good food. Entrées range from the Mongolian-spiced pork chop with peach chutney and curried mashed potatoes to the juicy chili-lime "brick" chicken served with a cheese-stuffed pasilla pepper and avocado salsa. Delectable sweets like the towering wedge of fluffy coconut-cream pie are reminders to save room for dessert.

Bungalow 44

American XX

B2

44 E. Blithedale Ave. (at Sunnyside Ave.), Mill Valley

Phone: 415-381-2500 — Dinner daily
Web: www.bungalow44.com
Prices: $$

Comfy booths and earth tones harmonize here with a menu that sings with American comfort food. Sibling to Buckeye Roadhouse, Bungalow 44 dishes up such wholesome and familiar fare as fried chicken, meatloaf, and braised short ribs. But defined and balanced California flavors come through in offerings such as wild mushroom flatbread with bacon, leeks, and fontina cheese, or zesty bisque made with fresh lobster and Dungeness crab meat.

This is a popular Marin gathering place, so be sure to make reservations or settle in for a long wait for a table—of course, you can always join the lively crowd who congregate around the bar. When it's cold, the second dining room warms diners with a fireplace; in fair weather this area morphs into an outdoor patio.

Cucina

Italian X

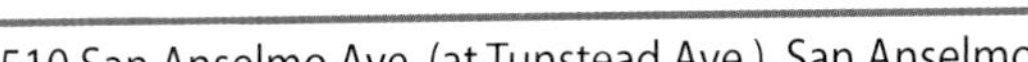

B2

510 San Anselmo Ave. (at Tunstead Ave.), San Anselmo

Phone: 415-454-2942 — Tue – Sun dinner only
Web: www.cucinarestaurantandwinebar.com
Prices: $$

Yellow walls, tile floors, and a wood-burning pizza oven near the kitchen form a simple but charming setting for a family-friendly trattoria in downtown San Anselmo. This is where you'll find—across from the Town Hall—Chef/owner Jack Krietzman's bustling Cucina (Krietzman also runs Jackson Fillmore).

The nightly changing menu presents a generous slice of Italian fare, including homemade pasta and gnocchi, and entrées such as mahi mahi *Fra Diavolo*; *salsicce* (spicy sausage with cannellini beans); and *pollo alla Siciliana*. If you're primed for pizza, don't come to Cucina on Friday or Saturday night—they are humming on these nights and the menu doesn't offer it. However, come to savor the wine list (most of it Italian) at their cozy wine bar.

El Paseo

B2 — French

17 Throckmorton Ave. (bet. Blithedale & Sunnyside Aves.), Mill Valley

Phone: 415-388-0741 — Wed – Sun dinner only
Web: www.elpaseorestaurant.com
Prices: $$$$

A curving, brick-paved alleyway lures you off one of Mill Valley's main streets into an Old World atmosphere punctuated by a series of small dining rooms. The overall feel oozes rustic charm between the exposed brick walls, the wooden ceiling beams, the high-backed leather chairs, and the warming fire in winter.

Don't let the Spanish name or the Japanese chef and owners confuse you. The heart of this menu is classically French, from duck confit to profiteroles. Even so, chef Keiko Takahashi puts an Asian spin on the likes of sea eel tempura and Washu beef carpaccio.

Across the alley, you can see the restaurant's extraordinary wine collection displayed in a glassed-in cellar. The superb list contains some surprisingly moderate pricing.

Fish

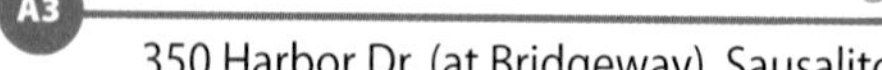

A3 — Seafood

350 Harbor Dr. (at Bridgeway), Sausalito

Phone: 415-331-3474 — Lunch & dinner daily
Web: www.331fish.com
Prices: $$

The name says it all. From white or Portuguese red chowders and ceviche to an organic tuna melt or Saigon salmon sandwich, this seafood is fresh and plentiful. Place your order at the counter, grab a number, and take a seat. Then tuck into grilled fish tacos with roasted tomatillo and lime *crema*, or peruse the daily specials posted on the blackboard. Offerings are abundant and creative here. You can even buy fish to cook at home.

Outdoor dining at this former bait and tackle shop is hard to beat. The picnic table seating and beverages in Ball jars may not add frills, but this grand Sausalito harborside setting amid yachts of all shapes and sizes adds luxurious embellishment. Although credit cards are not accepted, there's an ATM on site.

Fork

Italian

B2

198 Sir Francis Drake Blvd. (bet. Bank St. & Tunstead Ave.), San Anselmo

Tue – Sat dinner only

Phone: 415-453-9898
Web: www.marinfork.com
Prices: $$

Fork's co-owners Oliver Knill and Charles Low have been fortunate to attract a string of talented chefs to their San Anselmo eatery. The latest, is Nathan Lockwood, former chef de cuisine at Acquerello on Nob Hill. Lockwood imports his own version of seasonal Italian fare and presents it in a series of reasonably priced fixed-menu options, beginning with an early-bird three-course dinner for just $27 (served Tuesday to Friday from 5:30 P.M. to 6:15 P.M.). That's a bargain any way you slice it.

The owners constantly work the room, proudly delivering dishes—such as squid-ink tagliatelle with cuttle fish, and potato-crusted halibut atop a bed of flowering mustard rabe and caramelized red endive—to their guests seated in the three modestly decorated dining areas.

Frantoio

Italian

A2

152 Shoreline Hwy. (Stinson Beach exit off Hwy. 101), Mill Valley

Dinner daily

Phone: 415-289-5777
Web: www.frantoio.com
Prices: $$

Frantoio (Italian for "olive press") is a gem among Italian restaurants. They make their own state-certified extra virgin olive oil in an on-site facility. At the back, behind a large window, is the highlight of this lofty and expansive dining room. There lies the actual press, a contraption with two large granite wheels used to crush the olives. After you are seated, expect to be served a fine botle of golden olive oil with some bread on the side, but don't fill up. The wood-oven-fired pizzas, house-made pastas, and grilled fish and meats will surely tantalize your taste buds.

To watch the contrivance in action as you meander through a languid dinner, visit between December and February because the wheels are in motion then, no pun intended!

Gaylord

Indian XX

201 Bridgeway (on 2nd St. at Main St.), Sausalito

Phone: 415-339-0172 — Tue – Sun lunch & dinner
Web: www.gaylords.com — Mon dinner only
Prices: $$

Dining here by day may offer glimpses of harbor seals frolicking in the warm bay waters; by night, the San Francisco skyline glitters in the distance. Relocated from Ghiradelli Square, the restaurant now sits at the southern end of Sausalito's scenic boardwalk and gazes across to Tiburon, Angel, and Alcatraz Islands through its tall glass windows.

Tear yourself away from the view for a while to enjoy classic Indian fare including spiced chicken and lemon mulligatawny soup, 32 different curries, 14 types of breads, and a host of tandoor specialties. Three modestly priced set menus (one a vegetarian option) may assist with the tough decisions amid the varied Indian delicacies. Thursday through Sunday dinners are accompanied by live Indian music.

Insalata's

Mediterranean XX

120 Sir Francis Drake Blvd. (at Barber Ave.), San Anselmo

Phone: 415-457-7700 — Lunch & dinner daily
Web: www.insalatas.com
Prices: $$

Tastes of the Mediterranean sparkle inside the sunny vine-covered façade of Insalata's, where Chef/owner Heidi Insalata Krahling takes inspiration from Italy, Provence, Spain, Portugal, Greece, Morocco and the Middle East.

Set in downtown San Anselmo, this attractive spot with its larger-than-life paintings of fruit and vegetables is a local favorite, and for good reason. Middle Eastern couscous heaped with lemony lentils, roasted acorn squash, spinach, Moroccan spiced onions, Turkish yogurt and tomato-pistachio relish; and roasted eggplant Muhammara (mixed with red peppers, garlic and herbs, and served with warm pita) are just a couple of the draws.

If time is an issue, you can order your meal to go from the deli counter in back.

Lark Creek Inn

American 

234 Magnolia Ave. (at Madrone Ave.), Larkspur

Phone: 415-924-7766
Web: www.larkcreek.com
Prices: $$$

Mon - Sat dinner only
Sun lunch & dinner

Venerable redwoods shade this yellow 1888 Victorian, located a half-hour north of San Francisco. Opened in 1989, Lark Creek Inn was the first star in a constellation of restaurants owned by the Lark Creek Restaurant Group, headed by restaurateur Michael Dellar and Chef Bradley Ogden.

Commitment to a local network of organic farmers and producers of all-natural meats and seafood infuses the market-driven menu with premium ingredients like Marin Sun Farms Angus beef, Star Route arugula, Berkshire pork, and Fulton Valley Farms chicken. Of course, good food deserves good wine, something you'll have no trouble finding on this list with its deference to California vintners.

Sunday brunchers favor the cool (as in shady) patio in summer.

Left Bank

French 

507 Magnolia Ave. (at Ward St.), Larkspur

Phone: 415-927-3331
Web: www.leftbank.com
Prices: $$

Lunch & dinner daily

The name leaves no surprises as to what type of cuisine is served. The location, in the historic Blue Rock Inn in downtown Larkspur, may be a far cry from the Rive Gauche in Paris, but French comfort food such as bouillabaisse, coq au vin, *blanquette de veau*, and *tarte au citron* stay as true to tradition as any you'll find along St. Germain des Près.

Chef Roland Passot started this venture with partner Ed Levine in 1994. Recently, they've brought on Chef Scott Howard to energize the menus for the small chain (Menlo Park, Pleasant Hill, San Jose, and San Mateo). Echoing the atmosphere found in brasseries in Passot's Lyon hometown, Left Bank is outfitted with French advertising posters, a cherrywood bar, and a stone fireplace.

Marché aux Fleurs

Mediterranean

23 Ross Common (off Lagunitas Rd.), Ross

Phone: 415-925-9200 — Tue – Sat dinner only
Web: www.marcheauxfleursrestaurant.com
Prices: **$$$**

In the tiny hamlet of Ross in Marin County, Marché aux Fleurs evokes the farmers' markets in the South of France that inspired the restaurant's name. Look for the hand-painted sign and manicured shrubbery outside. A Provençal décor colors the interior, while the brick patio lures diners to tables dappled by rays of sunlight that shine through the canopy of trees overhead.

Chef Dan Baker, who runs the place with his wife, Holly, favors seasonal products from small local growers in entrées such as crispy Sonoma duck confit and house-made spinach pappardelle with Bellwether Farms ricotta meatballs. Thursday is hamburger night, when a half-pound burger topped with Carmody cheese, bacon, and grilled onions rings up at less than $15.

Nick's Cove

Seafood

23240 Hwy. 1 (near Miller Park), Marshall

Phone: 415-663-1033 — Lunch & dinner daily
Web: www.nickscove.com
Prices: **$$$**

On the reinvigorated shores of Tomales Bay, the new Nick's Cove has reinvented this 1930s settlement. The restaurant, an hour north of the Golden Gate Bridge, is not close to anything but oysters. That's great for the menu; the briny bivalves, a specialty of the house, are harvested fresh from Tomales Bay. Beyond oysters, there are Monterey sardines and Bodega Bay Dungeness crab, as well as sophisticated dishes made from the likes of Washington Arctic char, Maine diver scallops and Cape Cod clams.

This nostalgic spot, recreated by designer Pat Kuleto, retains a hunting-lodge feel along with great bay views. For those who would rather not jump back on the winding coastal highway, Nick's offers 12 rustic—but only on the outside—cottages on the beach.

Murray Circle ✿

Californian ✕✕✕

601 Murray Circle (at Fort Baker), Sausalito

Phone: 415-339-4750
Web: www.cavallopoint.com
Prices: $$$

Lunch & dinner daily

A romantic sense of history flows through this charming restaurant, part of the new Cavallo Point Lodge at Fort Baker. To get here, you'll wind along a road on the north side of the Golden Gate Bridge, savoring striking panoramas of the Bay, the city, and the Marin headlands en route.

Housed in one of the white Colonial-style wood buildings that line a looping drive through the fort grounds, Murray Circle shows off its early-19th-century heritage in its meticulously redone pressed-tin ceilings, leaded-glass windows, wood wainscoting, and wagon-wheel-inspired light fixtures.

Thoughtful and balanced compositions mark the cuisine of Chef Joseph Humphrey, late of Meadowood in Napa Valley. A shining example of farm-to-table Californian cuisine, courses here artfully and skillfully marry local ingredients to herbs, spices, infusions, and emulsions that spark their natural flavors.

Appetizers

- Halibut Grilled in Fig Leaves, Sassafras, Fennel "Brandade"
- Morels, Pappardelle, Duck Prosciutto
- Prawns, Little Gem Lettuces, Natural Vinaigrette

Entrées

- Quail, Romesco, Swiss Chard, Olives, Arugula
- Petrale Sole, Charred Squid, Garlic-Saffron Emulsion, Bacon
- Bluefoot Chicken, Cabbage, Mustard Seed Vinaigrette

Desserts

- Malt Waffle, Roasted Bananas, Coconut Sorbet, Candied Macadamia Nuts
- Petit Pot de Crème with Crunchy Peanut Butter Cookies
- Chocolate-Espresso Tart

Olema Inn

Californian 

A1

10,000 Sir Francis Drake Blvd. (at Hwy. 1), Olema

Phone: 415-663-9559 — Mon – Fri dinner only
Web: www.theolemainn.com — Sat – Sun lunch & dinner
Prices: $$$

Olema Inn sits high above Highway 1, in a tiny blip of a town (population: 55) that caters to folks headed for Point Reyes National Sea Shore. Owners John and Carole Wiltshire took the space over in 2007, beautifully renovating the quaint 19th century farmhouse, and handing the culinary reins over to her son, Chef James Wong.

The bulk of his ingredients—Hog Island oysters served eight different ways, succulent Marconi Cove mussels, or a fresh steak from Marin Sun Farms—are caught or grown within 50 miles of the Inn. But he's been known to let a few delicious exotic ingredients slip in here and there. A fittingly relaxed approach for a place where sitting on the shady porch and enjoying the country breeze for hours on end is de rigueur.

Paradise Bay

American 

A3

1200 Bridgeway (at Turney St.), Sausalito

Phone: 415-331-3226 — Lunch & dinner daily
Web: www.paradisebaysausalito.com
Prices: $$

Aptly named, this casual dining room overlooks Sausalito's placid harbor (with a dock available for short-term boat "parking"), with retractable doors opening onto a heated waterfront patio.

Despite its bayside location, the restaurant broadens its menu of contemporary American cuisine to include options as varied as Buffalo burgers, lemongrass-marinated chicken breast, or tamarind-glazed double pork chops. Cornmeal-battered halibut fillets served with fresh coleslaw and garlic fries; "Duck Trap" smoked salmon stack with pickled cucumbers, gaufrette potato chips, arugula, and horseradish cream; and a lobster maki roll assure a sea-loving component.

Cure whatever may ail you with a weekend brunch on the waterfront deck in the open, salty air.

Picco

Contemporary XX

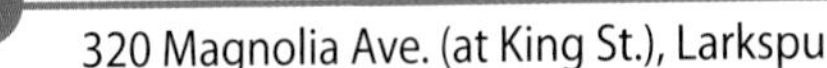

B2

320 Magnolia Ave. (at King St.), Larkspur

Phone: 415-924-0300 Dinner daily
Web: www.restaurantpicco.com
Prices: $$

"Taste more—dare to share" is the motto at this Larkspur restaurant. In an atmosphere of exposed rafters, brick walls and earth tones, Chef Bruce Hill crafts an eclectic menu of small plates that reads like a world tour. Recipes mix flavors from California, Asia, Italy, France and Morocco.

The intriguing wine list is a roster of some 300 selections grouped under such zany headings like—It's School Night, Wacky Wines, and Wine Geeks to Gurus. "Marin Mondays" focuses on products from Marin County farms and vineyards. Some classics are the ahi tuna tartare with apple, shiso, sesame, soy, and sticky rice cakes. For a quick bite, adjoining Pizzeria Picco can satisfy your craving with wood-fired pizzas and soft-serve ice cream—a local favorite.

Poggio

Italian XX

A3

777 Bridgeway (at Bay St.), Sausalito

Phone: 415-332-7771 Lunch & dinner daily
Web: www.poggiotrattoria.com
Prices: $$

Located along quaint Sausalito's main thoroughfare, this "special hillside place" (*poggio* in Italian) nestles on the ground floor of the Casa Madrona Hotel and Spa (*see hotel listing*). Mahogany-lined archways and terra-cotta tiles create a warm feel in the dining room. In fair weather, the doors and windows are flung open, bringing you closer to the serene yacht harbor right across the street.

A pleasant waitstaff delivers a roster of northern Italian dishes that changes daily, but always features several versions of thin-crust wood-oven-roasted pizza and rotisserie items. Among the other courses are perhaps oak-grilled, whole branzino, a roasted half-chicken marinated in yogurt, or house-made spinach and ricotta gnocchi with beef ragù.

Sabor of Spain

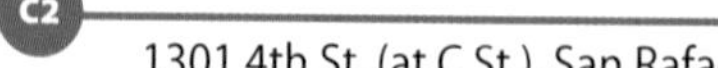

C2 **Spanish**

1301 4th St. (at C St.), San Rafael

Phone: 415-457-8466 Tue – Sun dinner only
Web: www.saborofspain.com
Prices: **$$**

At this vinoteca, you'll be immersed in the sights, sounds and, of course, *sabors* (flavors) of Spain, even though you're sitting in the center of San Rafael. Tapas portions of *albondigas* (beef meatballs in a wine-spiked tomato sauce); empanadas; assorted Spanish cheeses and cured meats; and seafood-stuffed *piquillo* peppers share the menu with more elaborate *raciones*, or main dishes. The latter might include paella; pistachio-and-almond-crusted baked salmon; and medallions of pork tenderloin.

All the wines here—more than 100 selections—come from Spain. You can order by the glass (more than 30 choices), by the bottle or by the flight; the latter is a good option if you're interested in discovering the regional vintages of Spain.

Spinnaker

A3 **Seafood** 

100 Spinnaker Dr. (at Anchor St.), Sausalito

Phone: 415-332-1500 Lunch & dinner daily
Web: www.thespinnaker.com
Prices: **$$**

Panoramic views of Richardson Bay, Tiburon, Belvedere Island, Alcatraz, and the Bay Bridge alone merit the price of admission at this Sausalito dowager (a $14 minimum charge discourages those seeking only to indulge in the spectacular scenery).

Picture windows lining three sides of the dining room are the most noteworthy aspect of the décor. This place draws crowds of tourists who love to capture the marine backdrop on film.

Steady as she goes, the time-honored menu brims with seafood, from rich bowls of spaghetti with prawns, flavorful crab pot stickers on a bed of frisée, to a Petrale sole sauté. Smartly dressed servers keep a friendly mien, no matter how packed the place may become. Every table here gets a warm sourdough baguette, butter, and a view.

Sushi Ran

Japanese

A3

107 Caledonia St. (bet. Pine & Turney Sts.), Sausalito

Phone: 415-332-3620
Web: www.sushiran.com
Prices: $$

Mon – Fri lunch & dinner
Sat – Sun dinner only

Sushi Ran is housed in twin wood bungalows (one open daily, the other reserved for dinner and private parties) along one of Sausalito's lively main streets, and near the waterfront. Chef/owner of this friendly spot, Yoshi Tome, invites guests to eat at the sushi bar, which occupies half the main room. In a more serene room located at the back, locals mingle with tourists and enjoy the inventive fusion fare.

The menu offers a good selection of *nigiri* sushi and maki rolls. A fresh assortment of salmon, maguro, yellowtail, red snapper, and mackerel are cut into thick, large slices, and served with perfectly cooked sushi rice. Pacific Rim and European-influenced dishes are also available, as is a sufficient selection of sake and wine to complement a meal.

Taki

Japanese

B1

452 Ignacio Blvd., Novato

Phone: 415-883-2423
Web: N/A
Prices: $$

Tue – Sat lunch & dinner
Sun dinner only

Despite the restaurant's name (which is Japanese for "waterfall"), there is none here, yet stepping into this pleasant space washes away all traces of the strip mall outside. Welcoming waters prevail in the indoor koi pond, and the current of hospitality is evident in the wall of personalized sake cups kept behind the bar for the crowd of faithful regulars gathering here at lunch.

This menu of enticing Japanese specialties includes sushi and maki, along with combination meals that showcase light, crisp tempura paired with sashimi or salmon teriyaki, accompanied by savory and satisfying miso soup. Groups can enjoy traditional floor seating behind rice-paper walls, with pits beneath the low tables to let feet comfortably dangle.

Vin Antico

Italian XX

881 4th St. (bet. Cijos St. & Lootens Pl.), San Rafael

Phone: 415-454-4492
Web: www.vinantico.com
Prices: $$

Tue – Fri lunch & dinner
Sat – Sun dinner only

Rustic northern Italian cuisine steals the limelight at Vin Antico. Grab a seat at one of the small, dark wood tables or at the white marble chef's counter (great for solo diners) that faces the open kitchen. Your mouth will water at the sight of blistered-crust *pizzettine* and *schiacciata* (thin, herbed flatbread), topped perhaps with garlic purée, gorgonzola, or arugula salata and served piping hot from the brick oven. Equally tempting are antipasto platters teeming with house-made bresoala, prosciutto *cotto*, mortadella mousse, and pickled fennel, or entrées of moist herb-coated chicken breast with roasted baby artichokes.
The restaurant, which occupies a historic building in the San Rafael business district, also features an inviting wine bar.

Couverts (X... XXXXX) indicate the level of comfort found at a restaurant. The more X's, the more upscale a restaurant will be.

NO
PARKING
ANY
NO
PARKING
ANY
TIME

Peter L. Wrenn/MICHELIN

South of San Francisco

South of San Francisco

The Bay Area bedroom communities, south of San Francisco, range down the east side of the Santa Cruz Mountains sandwiched between US-101 and I-280. From north to south, Millbrae, Burlingame, San Mateo, Redwood City, Palo Alto, Mountain View, Los Altos, and Santa Clara stretch down toward San Jose, California's third-largest city, located in the Santa Clara Valley along Coyote Creek and the Guadalupe River. The self-proclaimed capital of Silicon Valley, San Jose was founded in 1777 as El Pueblo San José de Guadalupe, by Lieutenant José Joaquin Moraga on order of the Viceroy of New Spain, as the first civilian settlement in Nueva California (later Alta

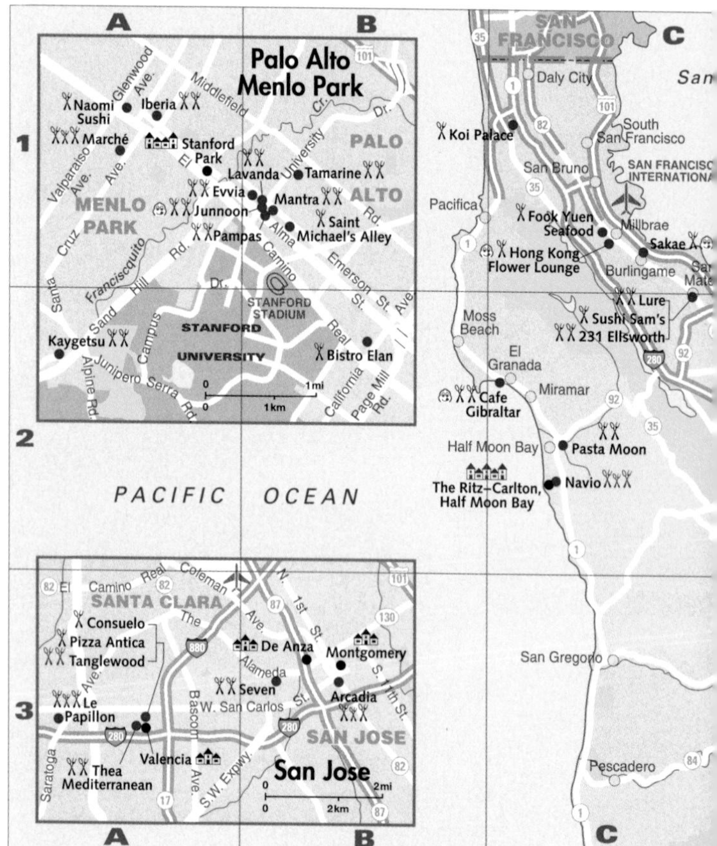

California). Then, it served as an agricultural community providing fruit, vegetables, wheat, and beef during the Spanish colonial and Mexican periods to the military personnel at nearby Presidio of San Francisco and **Presidio of Monterey**.

SILICON VALLEY

Agriculture remained the city's chief industry from the 1850s until the mid-20th century. After World War II, a population explosion in the area spurred rapid development and urbanization. By the 1950s, electronics industries began to supplant the orchards and ranches. Beginning with the development of the semiconductor industry in the mid-20th century, innovative new enterprises arose in the Bay Area to fill the growing demand for electronic products. By the 1970s, Silicon Valley, which included such computer giants as Hewlett-Packard, Apple Computer, Intel, and a host of semiconductor laboratories, had moved well beyond their humble garage beginnings to become the dominant industry in San Jose and the neighboring communities.

In the late 1990's, a new breed of technology-based companies came to town. Known as dot-coms, these Internet companies and their stock prices rocketed in the short term, making millionaires of many investors as well as many stock option-holding employees, until the bubble burst in March 2000. Today, IT professionals in the Silicon Valley—home to giants like Yahoo, NetFlix, eBay, Oracle, and Google, to name just a few—rank as the highest paid in the country. The area is gaining jobs and venture capital again, along with a more recent boom in the emerging solar- and renewable-energy sector. San Jose, meanwhile, boasts the largest concentration of tech companies around, with more corporate headquarters attracting young digerati into downtown.

The local braintrust includes **Stanford University** in Palo Alto, with its lovely Richardsonian Romanesque-style buildings roofed with red tile and surrounded by eucalyptus, bay, and palm trees. Established by railroad magnate Leland Stanford in 1891, Stanford University boasts a distinguished tenure-line faculty of 1,829, whose members include 16 Nobel laureates, 4 Pulitzer Prize winners, and 20 recipients of the National Medal of Science.

VISITING THE VALLEY

Cutting-edge technology is far from the only reason to visit this area. San Jose offers a wealth of cultural attractions from the downtown historic district—which dates back to 1777—to the 132,000-square foot **Tech Museum of Innovation**. If your interests are more commercial than cultural, the upscale European-style shopping and residential complex called **Santana Row** will surely appeal. The future promises professional sports, as the **Oakland Athletics** plan to relocate to **Fremont**, and the **San Francisco 49ers** are building a new 68,000-seat stadium in Santa Clara; both moves are currently slated for 2012. Of course, there's plenty of good eating here too. The word on the street is that some San Francisco restaurants are packing up and moving south to get in on the influx of the next new wave of money to Silicon Valley.

MICHELIN

Alexander's Steakhouse

Steakhouse 

E3

10330 N. Wolfe Rd. (at I-280), Cupertino

Phone: 408-446-2222 Dinner daily
Web: www.alexanderssteakhouse.com
Prices: $$$$

A boon for South Bay food lovers, Alexander's is far from your run-of-the-mill steakhouse. The Asian twist that runs through the wide-ranging menu is a creative surprise. Japanese Kobe appears alongside prime beef dry-aged on the premises. Chef Jeffrey Stout, whose heritage is half American and half Japanese, interprets surf and turf—called Cow and Crustacean here—as a petite filet mignon with lobster *kushiyaki* and shimeji mushrooms. Fish is given equal play, in small-plates such as *hamachi* shots—an intriguing mélange of *hamachi* sliced sashimi-style with red chili, frizzled ginger, cubes of avocado, and truffled ponzu.
A wall of wine and a decanting area in the middle of the room bear testimony to Alexander's award-winning wine program.

Arcadia

Steakhouse 

B3

100 W. San Carlos St. (at Market St.), San Jose

Phone: 408-278-4555 Lunch & dinner daily
Web: www.michaelmina.net/arcadia
Prices: $$$

Airy and spacious with its exhibition kitchen and wall of windows, Arcadia falls under the umbrella of the Mina Group, managed by Michael Mina (whose eponymous restaurant graces San Francisco's Westin St. Francis Hotel). Its location off the lobby of the Marriott hotel in downtown San Jose is convenient to the McEnery Convention Center, right next door.

Arcadia recently revamped its dinner menu to feature steakhouse fare, concentrating on steaks and chops, as well as a selection of seasonal fresh shellfish. But Mina fans, never fear; the chef's signature lobster potpie is still an option, along with house "classics" like the whole fried chicken for two, served with truffled mac & cheese. A kids' menu caters to families staying at the hotel.

Bistro Elan

Californian

448 California Ave. (near El Camino Real), Palo Alto

Phone: 650-327-0284 — Tue – Fri lunch & dinner
Web: N/A — Sat dinner only
Prices: $$

Attention to detail marks this welcoming bistro, from the long dining room decorated with mustard-yellow walls and black-and-white photographs, to the charming back garden. If weather permits, this tiny area shrouded with greenery makes a fantastically private setting for a meal.

California soul infuses such preparations as spaghetti carbonara, the Roman classic made here with blanched asparagus, caramelized spring onions, and cracklings of smoky cured pork. Moist pan-fried fillets of Petrale sole profit from a light, fragrant *pistou* scented with lemon. For dessert, berry sorbet explodes with flavor atop creamy panna cotta.

With service so gracious and warm, Bistro Elan should be the standard bearer for the Palo Alto area.

Cafe Gibraltar

Mediterranean

425 Avenue Alhambra (at Palma St.), El Granada

Phone: 650-560-9039 — Tue – Sun dinner only
Web: www.cafegibraltar.com
Prices: $$

Located on the San Mateo County coast, Cafe Gibraltar makes a pleasant excursion from the city. From the cheery sun-filled dining room, you'll have a view of the blue Pacific and of the open kitchen where Chef/owner Jose Luis Ugalde holds sway.

Although Ugalde is Mexican, he realizes scrumptious dishes from around the Mediterranean with ease and expertise. You can see him working in the kitchen, infusing complex layers of flavor into combinations like lamb with pistou, or *cassola*, an herb-scented seafood stew. Every week a new prix-fixe menu adds options to the à la carte fare, while pizza, noodles, and couscous on the kids' menu whet young appetites.

Another Ugalde restaurant, Chez Shea, opened in Half Moon Bay *(408 Main St.)* in summer 2006.

Cantankerous Fish

E2

420 Castro St. (bet. California & Mercy Sts.), Mountain View

Phone: 650-966-8124 — Mon – Sat lunch & dinner
Web: www.thecantankerousfish.com — Sun dinner only
Prices: $$

This fish may be a bit less cantankerous, thanks to a remodel in fall 2007. Now a prize catch with more than double its original space, the restaurant added a long granite bar and cocktail lounge, where small plates complement the discounted happy hour libations. Large, colorful canvases on the walls swim with a variety of denizens of the deep.

"Fresh Feisty Fish," as the menu bills its offerings, emerge from the open kitchen in preparations that would make Neptune proud. Bold creations could include spicy salmon fried wonton rolls, shellfish, and seafood corn dogs, and crab-encrusted Idaho trout. "More Grounded" dishes are available for those who prefer that their food have four legs.

The front patio reels in schools of diners when the weather permits.

Cascal

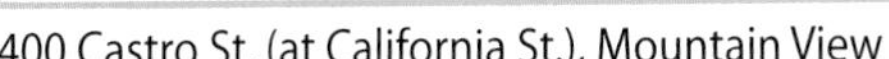

E2

400 Castro St. (at California St.), Mountain View

Phone: 650-940-9500 — Lunch & dinner daily
Web: www.cascalrestaurant.com
Prices: $$

Cheery and casual, this popular restaurant in Mountain View occupies a voluminous space on the main floor of an office building. Adorned in Spanish style with arched openings, wrought-iron fixtures and a high coffered ceiling, Cascal draws a large business crowd for lunch and after-work cocktails. Vivid splashes of red, gold, blue and green kick up some Latin panache in the room.

Tapas top the menu, which also features entrées, like paella, that are meant for sharing. Either way, Latin American flavors will tango with your taste buds in such vibrant dishes as a pair of bowl-shaped masa *sopes*, both filled with a base of earthy black beans. Spicy chicken *picadillo* crowns one, while moist Cuban-style roasted pulled pork caps the other.

Chez TJ ✿

Contemporary XX

E2

938 Villa St. (bet. Bryant & Franklin Sts.), Mountain View

Phone: 650-964-7466 Tue – Sat dinner only
Web: www.cheztj.com
Prices: **$$$$**

♿

Mark Leet / Mark Leet Photography

They like to kick it old school at Chez TJ—where antique pictures line the walls, and waiters, donned in formal vests and ties, still call you "sir". And that's just grand, because after 27 years on the local fine dining scene (Bruno Chemel is the new chef here), this venerable institution has earned the right to pass on trendy decor elements.

Set in a charming 19th century Victorian house in downtown Mountainview, Chez TJ has so much old-world charm that it has slid into a special-occasion-only sort of place, but what a shame. Preparing only the best from the local markets, Chez TJ's cuisine is acclaimed for its skill, style, and keen supervision. With delicious dishes like lobster tucked into cucumber rounds, then topped with mango and mint, or Alaskan halibut, kissed with lemon oil sided with a tangle of sautéed vegetables, do you really need an excuse to indulge?

Appetizers

- Beet Coloriage, Balsamic Gelée, Goat Cheese Foam, Lemon Oil
- Foie Gras Trio with Gastrique of Cassis and Maui Pineapple
- Artichoke Velouté and Palets de Cochon

Entrées

- "Pigeon Pie"- Squash, Swiss Chard, Star Anise Jus
- Niman Ranch Lamb, Potato Permentier, Fennel, Rosemary-Garlic Jus
- Seared Day Boat Scallop and Uni

Desserts

- Apple Mélange, Cinnamon Beignet, Caramel Panna Cotta
- Matcha-Framboise, Vacherin, Rose Water Nage
- Chocolate Zen Sakura Ganache, Yuzu Chiboust

Consuelo

377 Santana Row (bet. Olin Ave. & Olsen Dr.), San Jose

Phone: 408-260-7082 — Lunch & dinner daily
Web: www.consuelomexicanbistro.com
Prices: $$

Turn-of-the-19th-century Mexico comes to the swanky Santana Row shopping complex in the form of this charming cantina, decorated with iron chandeliers and rustic ceramics.

The food here hearkens back to tradition as well. Meals begin with homemade corn tortillas (not chips) and a trio of salsas. Richly flavored *mole poblano* served over chicken stays close to its Puebla origins in the blend of spices, dried chiles, nuts and chocolate. A delicacy prized in Mexico since the Aztecs, *huitlacoche* (corn fungus), or "Mexican truffle," lends its earthy sweetness to stuffed chicken breast and sautéed fish. Salute the past with your choice of the hundreds of tequilas and mescals, or a full range of Latin libations.

Dio Deka

210 E. Main St. (bet. Fiesta Way & Johnson St.), Los Gatos

Phone: 408-354-7700 — Sun – Fri lunch & dinner
Web: www.diodeka.com — Sat dinner only
Prices: $$$

Tucked into the Hotel Los Gatos on Main Street, Dio Deka is a lovely Greek tavern with a big, open kitchen, a crackling fireplace, and a whole lot of Greek hospitality. The brainchild of five Greek restaurateurs, the menu is a seamless blend of Greek and Mediterranean, with a heavy influence on fish and lamb.

Hunker down at the big communal table, and sink your teeth into grass-fed lamb chops. Served with lemony potato wedges and a scoop of silky spinach, the chops are a study in harmonious flavors—perfectly grilled and boasting a mouth-watering outer crust of spices. Don't miss the extensive 1,200-label wine list with its wide selection of Greek, Burgundian, Bordeaux, Californian varietals, and ace Ouzo selection.

Evvia

Greek XX

420 Emerson St. (bet. Lytton & University Aves.), Palo Alto

Phone: 650-326-0983 — Mon – Fri lunch & dinner
Web: www.evvia.net — Sat – Sun dinner only
Prices: $$

Equally popular sister to Kokkari Estiatorio in San Francisco, Evvia mirrors the delectable Greek fare, rustic ambience and friendly service of its big-city sibling. The casual dining room says country inn with wooden beams, a stone fireplace, copper pots and handmade pottery, and retractable floor-to-ceiling windows.

Whole fish is served grilled or roasted and the selection changes nightly. Lamb, a Mediterranean staple, comes in incarnations ranging from mesquite-grilled chops to meatballs. To end your meal on an authentic note, order a Greek coffee cooked over hot sand. Request it *sketo* (no sugar), *metrio* (medium sugar), or *glyko* (sweet), but however you like it, be mindful of the grounds at the bottom of the cup before you take that last swig.

Fook Yuen Seafood

C1

195 El Camino Real (at Victoria Ave.), Millbrae

Phone: 650-692-8600 — Lunch & dinner daily
Web: N/A
Prices:

Despite its name, Fook Yuen Seafood is foremost a dim sum restaurant. Servers parade around the room with trays and carts displaying an ever-changing variety of steamed buns, fried balls, noodle dishes, barbecue and stir-fried offerings. Be quick, decisive, and prepared to point and nod, for once an item has passed the table, it is unlikely to be seen again. Those who like to eat where patrons of the same culture flock should note that this is Chinese for the Chinese.

Arrive early to grab a seat and to be assured to see the full array of freshly prepared fare. Although there is no readily available price list, most dim sum items are priced under $5. In the evening, larger entrées range from braised abalone to sautéed scallops and chicken with vegetables.

Hong Kong Flower Lounge

Chinese

51 Millbrae Ave. (at El Camino Real), Millbrae

Phone: 650-692-6666 Lunch & dinner daily
Web: www.flowerlounge.net
Prices: $$

Decked in traditional green-tile pagoda-style roofs, the stunning façade of this Millbrae fixture is hard to miss.
Round up the extended family at midday—the bi-level dining space seats several hundred people—and come early for dim sum. Hong Kong Flower Lounge buzzes at peak times, much like the city for which it is named. And no wonder: dim sum carts and trays stream out of the kitchen, showcasing delectable items that run the gamut from the tried and true potstickers or light, fluffy steamed buns filled with tender, flavorful barbecue pork to the authentic and adventurous marinated duck tongue or jellyfish in chili bean sauce. Choose among these, or place an order with the friendly helpful servers, happy to accommodate your requests.

Hunan Home's

4880 El Camino Real (at Showers Dr.), Los Altos

Phone: 650-965-8888 Lunch & dinner daily
Web: www.hunanhomes.com
Prices: ⚭

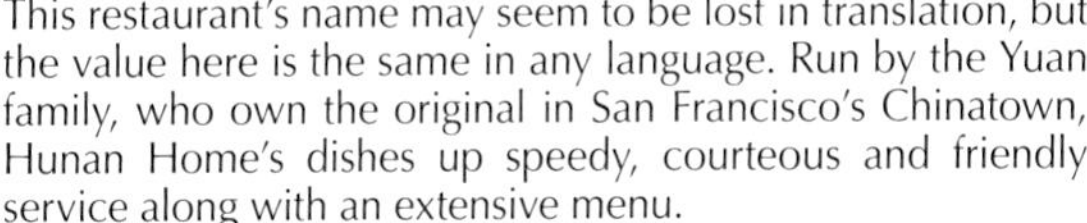

This restaurant's name may seem to be lost in translation, but the value here is the same in any language. Run by the Yuan family, who own the original in San Francisco's Chinatown, Hunan Home's dishes up speedy, courteous and friendly service along with an extensive menu.
Lunch brings the best bargains; midday specials include a choice of soup, salad or spring roll, entrée, steamed rice, dessert and tea for less than $10. Dinner is also reasonable, with an almost overwhelming array of items running the gamut from shredded pork to sizzling platters—and everything in between. Keep in mind the complimentary dishes, or you may end up with more food than you can eat.
Large tables in the middle dining room easily accommodate families and other groups.

Iberia

Spanish XX

1026 Alma Ave. (at Ravenswood St.), Menlo Park

Phone: 650-325-8981 Mon – Sat lunch & dinner
Web: www.iberiarestaurant.com Sun dinner only
Prices: **$$**

Located on the sleepy side of Menlo Park, Iberia is the brainchild of Chef/owner Jose Luis Relinque. At this amiable tapas bar, the chef adds his own spark to small plates that celebrate recipes from his native Spain, such as the savory *albondiguitas* of little meatballs in a saffron and onion sauce, and *patatas bravas* con *allioli*, spicy fried potatoes with garlic mayonnaise. On the other side of the portion spectrum, many of the specialties (paella) serve two or more and are priced accordingly.

Those who leave the table inspired can go next door to visit sibling The Rock of Gibraltar Comestibles and sign up for a cooking class. In addition to quality ingredients, the shop offers made-to-order sandwiches and a sampling of the restaurant's dishes to go.

John Bentley's

Contemporary XX

D2

2915 El Camino Real (bet. Berkshire Ave. & E. Selby Lane), Redwood City

Phone: 650-365-7777 Mon – Fri lunch & dinner
Web: www.johnbentleys.com Sat dinner only
Prices: **$$$**

Just off the seemingly never-ending corridor of El Camino Real, John Bentley's is an oasis of elegance. Whereas the original John Bentley's in Woodside centers on its historic setting in a c.1920s firehouse, the newer location displays an urban refinement. The comfortable dining space, with dark wood and colorful artwork, expands into several distinct sections.

Chef/owner John Bentley focuses on premium organic produce, sustainably raised meats, and environmentally sound seafood. Seasonal dishes are precisely prepared, as in the likes of seared foie gras teamed with sweet and sour cherries and candied kumquats; Dungeness crab artfully arranged atop slices of blood orange and avocado; or peppercorn-crusted Ahi with pickled ginger soba noodles.

Junnoon

Indian XX

150 University Ave. (at High St.), Palo Alto

Phone: 650-329-9644 — Tue – Sat lunch & dinner
Web: www.junnoon.com — Sun – Mon dinner only
Prices: **$$**

Pink and orange sheers filter a mysterious glow into Junnoon's Palo Alto dining room. Here Chef Kirti Pant (formerly of Tamarind in New York City) infuses contemporary Indian cuisine with passion, energy, and obsession, as the restaurant's Hindi name infers.

The Power Lunch, which allows you to order a light combination meal for less than $20, remains popular at this hotspot near Stanford University. Fans line up for the likes of aromatic Lucknow-style lamb *biryani* served with Punjabi chickpeas and mint *raita*; or paneer (farmer's cheese) and red pepper cake seasoned with cumin, ginger, and a spice blend called *garam masala*. A house signature, the moist tandoori halibut tempts taste buds with a delicious sauce flavored with coconut and ginger.

Kaygetsu

Japanese XX

325 Sharon Park Dr. (at Sand Hill Rd.), Menlo Park

Phone: 650-234-1084 — Tue – Sun dinner only
Web: www.kaygetsu.com
Prices: **$$$$**

Owned by sushi Chef Toshio Sakuma and his wife, Keiko, this "beautiful moon" (as the name translates from Japanese) hangs in the corner of the Sharon Heights shopping center. What shines here, amid the variety of sushi, nigiri, and maki, is the *kaiseki* menu. Harmonious balance of flavors, preparations, and artistry characterize this traditional meal, which has origins in the Zen tea ceremony.

Those who indulge in this option should plan to spend two to three hours feasting on a series of small sensuous courses. Flowers imported from Tokyo may grace the parade of items (roast duck with apple and tamari; yellowtail sashimi; rice cooked with salmon, fried tofu, and daikon radish) arranged on an array of attractive dishes, baskets, and platters.

Koi Palace

C1 — Chinese

365 Gellert Blvd. (bet. Hickey & Serramonte Blvds.), Daly City

Phone: 650-992-9000 — Lunch & dinner daily
Web: www.koipalace.com
Prices: $$

Don't let the size of Koi Palace intimidate you. This restaurant in Serramonte Plaza seats 400 and it's always mobbed at lunch with an Asian crowd taking tickets and standing in line for a table, but the excellent dim sum is well worth any hassle.

There's a staggering variety of these little bites, from savory (steamed fish maw and chicken; crabmeat Shanghai dumplings; suckling pig) to sweet (bird nest egg-custard tart). Indicate your order from the selections listed on the paper menu and wait for your food to be prepared to order and delivered to your table. In the meantime, servers will circulate around the room with additional items on trays and carts.

A word to the wise: If you're coming for dim sum at lunchtime, get here early.

La Forêt

F3 — French

21747 Bertram Rd. (at Almaden Rd.), San Jose

Phone: 408-997-3458 — Tue – Sun lunch & dinner
Web: www.laforetrestaurant.com — Mon lunch only
Prices: $$$

Built in 1848 as a boarding house for miners working to extract a local vein of cinnabar (aka quicksilver), this unassuming two-story structure tucks into a residential area south of downtown San Jose. Today the building houses a uniquely charming restaurant, La Forêt, named for the leafy surroundings visible through walls of windows.Here, an old-school approach to French-inspired cuisine means that a special of fallow deer tenderloin is couched in a cream-kissed Cognac reduction, with hints of ginger, Cabernet Sauvignon, and sage.

The décor seems arrested in the 90s, but what the place lacks in trendy design, it more than makes up for with its personable and well-informed staff that is there to accommodate diners at every turn.

Lavanda

B1

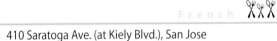

185 University Ave. (at Emerson St.), Palo Alto

Phone: 650-321-3514 — Mon – Fri lunch & dinner
Web: www.lavandarestaurant.com — Sat – Sun dinner only
Prices: $$$

Palo Alto goes Mediterranean at this pleasant spot, where white-cloth-draped tables huddle close together, light jazz animates the room, and a coterie of locals crowds the wine bar. Windows line the front wall and a lavender-streaked fabric mural decorates the wall opposite.

Start your meal here by mixing and matching a number of small tastes such as manchego cheese and preserves, shaved artichokes and parmesan, or chorizo and clams. The menu offers a choice of any three for $15. Still hungry? Pan-fried rabbit or roasted mahi-mahi all sing with the fresh flavors of the lands that border the Mediterranean Sea.

The wine list impresses with its extensive selection of international labels, which includes hard-to-find boutique producers.

Le Papillon

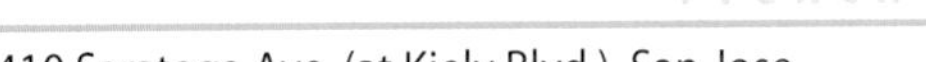

A3

410 Saratoga Ave. (at Kiely Blvd.), San Jose

Phone: 408-296-3730 — Sat – Thu dinner only
Web: www.lepapillon.com — Fri lunch & dinner
Prices: $$$$

Despite changes in Silicon Valley since this restaurant opened its doors in 1977, Le Papillon (French for "butterfly") maintains the tradition of sophisticated French cuisine that has long been its hallmark. Classic Gallic preparations take flight at the hands of Chef Scott Cooper. Tender buffalo tenderloin, for instance, is cooked to medium-rare and garnished with a well-seasoned Marchand du Vin sauce. A tartlet of bone-marrow custard adds a rich note to the dish.

A serious old-world atmosphere complements the food: tables are swathed in white linen, chairs covered with floral tapestry prints, and a lavish floral arrangement forms the room's focal point. Oenophiles' hearts will flutter when reading the lengthy list of French and California wines.

Lure

Seafood XX

C2

204-A 2nd Ave. (bet. B St. & Ellsworth Ave), San Mateo

Phone: 650-340-9040 Tue – Sat dinner only
Web: www.lurerestaurant.com
Prices: $$$

Black walls and tables meet sculptural white plaster etched with an undulating motif at this smart urban restaurant. Hip describes the vibe here from the dim lights and contemporary music to the sophisticated crowd, but where other places might stop there, Lure continues the theme all the way through to its cuisine.

Bustling and well-staffed, the glassed-in kitchen is stocked with the fresh shellfish offerings of the day, tantalizingly displayed on a mound of ice. You might wish to begin with the crudo tasting, a changing selection of fish with individual condiments (think tuna tartare with black sesame seeds, seaweed, garlic, and ginger; scallop sashimi topped with black and green *tobiko*; and Monterey sardines marinated in white wine).

Mantra

Indian XX

B1

632 Emerson St. (bet. Forest & Hamilton Aves.), Palo Alto

Phone: 650-322-3500 Tue – Fri lunch & dinner
Web: www.mantrapaloalto.com Sat – Mon dinner only
Prices: $$

Grounded in tradition, Indian dishes at Mantra are served with Californian panache. Roasted Kashmiri sea bass, marinated in cayenne pepper and mustard, and presented atop a nest of leeks, represents the variations on East Indian flavors at which this kitchen excels. Likewise, Anari steak (pomegranate-marinated flank steak served over Fuji apples and jicama with cilantro tequila cream) highlights Chef Sachin Chopra's varied experience as well as a nod to his current surroundings. Elegance and harmony pervade the sleek dining room, which showcases contemporary Indian artwork to maintain an urban feel. In the swanky Daru Lounge, pair a small plate of fresh *naan* pizza, Mantra chips, or the *dal* (lentil dish) of the day with an Indian beer or cocktail.

Manresa ✿✿

E3

320 Village Ln. (bet. N. Santa Cruz & University Aves.), Los Gatos

Phone: 408-354-4330 — Wed – Sun dinner only
Web: www.manresarestaurant.com
Prices: $$$$

Pim Techamuanvivit

Hidden down a narrow side street in the trendy shopping area of Los Gatos, Manresa possesses the kind of fresh ranch house charm that East Coasters think California is littered in—but locals know is a little harder to find done right. Consider this the aesthetic template—with its silk drapes, curvy fireplace, and exposed wood beams, Manresa is lovely through and through.

Chef David Kinch, who builds his menu around the biodynamic produce he procures from nearby Love Apple Farm, offers an ever-changing 4-course meal (selected by the customer from multiple categories) that might begin with a trio of plump, fried mussels resting in a rich broth with finely diced vegetables. For dessert, thin shards of dark chocolate layered with succulent blackberry gelée and fresh blackberries might top a mound of chocolate mousse. Capped with tiny *shiso* leaves, the result is heavenly.

Appetizers

- Creamed Corn and Garden Tomatoes with Assorted Basil
- Marinated Shellfish, Exotic Citrus and Olive Oil
- Into the Vegetable Garden

Entrées

- Wood Pigeon Baked in Savory Salt, Sunchokes
- Spot Prawns A la Plancha, Creamy Nasturtium Rice
- Roast Suckling Pig and Boudin Noir, Green Garlic with Vegetable Shoots

Desserts

- Jasmine Flower Pastille, Pea Tendrils with Grapefruit Sorbet
- Blood Orange with Sheep's Milk Ricotta, Red Beet Sorbet
- Dark Chocolate Crémeux with Wild Mint and Lime

Marché

A1 — Contemporary

898 Santa Cruz Ave. (at University Dr.), Menlo Park

Phone: 650-324-9092 — Tue – Sat dinner only
Web: www.restaurantmarche.com
Prices: $$$$

A change of chefs in spring 2008 has revitalized the menu at Marché. Other than that, not much is different. The dining room still looks sleek in shades of caramel and chocolate-brown, and the restaurant continues to be an elegant and popular place for dinner in downtown Menlo Park.

Revised daily, the menu anchors itself in Mediterranean and European recipes, with a nod to Californian cuisine tossed in for good measure. For instance, a loin of Berkshire pork might acquire a flavorful crust from crushed pistachios, before it is sliced and displayed beside a creamy onion fondue and a tangy apricot chutney.

Desserts fall into one of two categories: classic (dark chocolate crème brûlée) or contemporary (olive-oil cake with candy cap mushroom ice cream).

Naomi Sushi

A1 — Japanese

1328 El Camino Real (bet. Glenwood & Oak Grove Aves.), Menlo Park

Phone: 650-321-6902 — Tue – Fri lunch & dinner
Web: www.naomisushi.com — Sat – Sun dinner only
Prices:

Fresh fish are jumping at this Menlo Park Japanese eatery, where a sushi bar welcomes patrons as they enter. This is where Naomi's chefs create sushi, nigiri, and maki, displaying talent and subtle Japanese humor in naming special rolls. Raw-fish novices will appreciate the helpful explanations outlined on the menu, while regulars are encouraged to create their own maki combinations. Grilled entrées, daily specials, sake flights, and a chef's omakase (both large and small versions) round out the offerings. The staff will be glad to cater meals to children's finicky tastes.

Shelves around the room display an array of sake bottles and *Maneki neko* (ceramic cats bringing good luck). Murals of seaside landscapes and mounted game fish add a marine theme.

Navio

C2

1 Miramontes Point Rd. (at Hwy. 1), Half Moon Bay

Phone: 650-712-7040 — Lunch & dinner daily
Web: www.ritzcarlton.com
Prices: $$$$

Perched on a bluff overlooking the Pacific, the Ritz-Carlton Half Moon Bay (*see hotel listing*) is a breathtaking setting. So, too, is its restaurant Navio (whose name is Portuguese for "ship"). Though every detail in the dining room—wood-lined barrel-vaulted ceilings, alluring open kitchen, chairs with back pillows—is designed to please, the view through the picture windows steals the thunder.

Indeed, it can be difficult to focus on the food in front of you when the sun is slipping in all its rosy glory into the western horizon just outside. Local and seasonal items will nonetheless vie for your attention in preparations such as broiled Monterrey sardines with pickled fennel, and ravioli filled with rich duck meat braised in red wine.

Pampas

B1

529 Alma St. (bet. Hamilton & University Aves.), Palo Alto

Phone: 650-327-1323 — Mon – Fri lunch & dinner
Web: www.pampaspaloalto.com — Sat – Sun dinner only
Prices: $$$

Come hungry to this sophisticated churrascaria, where *passadors* circulate throughout the room carrying an unlimited parade of large skewers of spit-roasted meats that they slice at the table.

Quality is there in the rodizio dinner, 14 different types of meat, delivered piping hot to the table. Pork, beef, lamb, and chicken are seasoned with Brazilian dry rubs or spiced with combinations of garlic, ginger, mint, cumin, cracked pepper, paprika, and parmesan. Linguiça turns out tasty and sweet, while bacon lends a smoky flavor to pieces of turkey breast.

A buffet of side dishes kicks things up with the likes of coconut whipped sweet potatoes with yucca, ginger-glazed carrots, and a salad of chickpeas and olives.

Pasta Moon

Italian

C2

315 Main St. (at Mills St.), Half Moon Bay

Phone: 650-726-5125 Lunch & dinner daily
Web: www.pastamoon.com
Prices: $$

A winding half-hour drive south along the coast of San Francisco brings you to the sleepy, fog-licked beach hamlet of Half Moon Bay. A tapestry of independent restaurants and boutiques makes up the town's charming Main Street, where you'll discover Pasta Moon. An institution in these parts, the quaint and friendly Italian eatery packs tables tightly into a space scented with the heady aromas of garlic and spices.

Nilda's lasagne is pure pleasure, with layers of house-made noodles, Sicilian sausage, ricotta, parmesan, and zesty tomato sauce. Barolo-braised beef *brasato* satisfies hearty appetites, while antipasti and artisanal pizzas provide lighter fare. The selection of more than 45 Italian wines by the glass has oenophiles sipping with delight.

Pizza Antica

Pizza 

A3

334 Santana Row, Suite 1065 (bet. Stevens Creek Blvd. & Tatum Lane), San Jose

Phone: 408-557-8373 Lunch & dinner daily
Web: www.pizzaantica.com
Prices: 

Santana Row, San Jose's spiffy neighborhood complex seems to have something for everyone between its upscale shops, condominiums, spas, restaurants, and the chic Hotel Valencia (*see hotel listing*). At lunchtime pizza lovers line up at the extremely popular Pizza Antica, eager for a taste of the restaurant's thin-crust pies. The menu offers conceived combinations from "Our Pizza" or guests can customize their own pies with any mix of toppings from the section designated "Your Pizza" (roasted red pepper, arugula, salami, gorgonzola, marinated chicken, to name a few). A small selection of appetizers and salads rounds out the offerings.

Part of a small local chain, this bistro-style pizzeria appeals to families with its casual, kid-friendly attitude.

Plumed Horse ✿

Contemporary

E3

14555 Big Basin Way (bet. 4th & 5th Sts.), Saratoga

Phone: 408-867-4711 Mon – Sat dinner only
Web: www.plumedhorse.com
Prices: $$$$

James Fong

Nestled into the boutiques and artisan shops that line Big Basin Way, Plumed Horse is a worthy new contender for the attentions of daytrippers heading to Saratoga. In fact, there are enough slickly-appointed rooms to wander though here—including a jaw-dropping chef's table overlooking the kitchen—to warrant a weekend stay. Taking its name from the 19th century stable that once resided here, Plumed Horse cuts no corners with its cutting-edge design.

The good news is that Chef Peter Armellino's California-minded contemporary fare holds its own weight just as well. Try an oxtail consommé, enriched with snails and a green garlic flan; or a roasted California squab on a bed of spicy Moroccan harissa, garnished with candied kumquat crêpes.

Don't miss the dizzying wine selection. With over 24,000 bottles in inventory, no wonder the wine rack gets its own light parade.

Appetizers

- Artisan Foie Gras
- Sea Scallops, Pickled Ramps, Duck Confit, Le Puy Lentils
- Oxtail Consommé, Frog Legs, Burgundy Snails, Green Garlic Flan

Entrées

- Halibut, Pork Belly, Lemon-Caper Vinaigrette
- Venison, Yams, Almond-Shallot Vinaigrette
- Abalone, Pea Ravioli, and Lemon-Garlic Shoots

Desserts

- 2010, A Banana Split
- "Jalapeño Poppers"Jalapeño Jelly, Pineapple Salsa, Lime Gel
- Pain Perdue, Camembert, Candied Kumquat, Orange Gastrique

Red Lantern

Asian

808 Winslow St. (at Broadway St.), Redwood City

Phone: 650-369-5483 — Dinner daily
Web: www.redlanternrwc.com
Prices: $$

A redeveloped area of Redwood City is home to this newcomer, conveniently situated next to the Caltrain Sequoia Station. Asian artifacts, including a 20-seat communal table, adorn the soaring bilevel space. From the restaurant's high ceiling hangs a collection of huge red silk lanterns—red representing luck, happiness, and prosperity.

Local business people feel lucky indeed to have this place, judging from the crowds that come here for inexpensive lunch combinations spotlighting Southeast Asia. At dinner, the only option is the à la carte menu, where a "Taste of Paradise" might translate to Manila short ribs or adobo eggplant.

No matter what time of day you go, the food is fresh and flavorful, the atmosphere exotic-chic, and the vibe relaxed.

Saint Michael's Alley

Contemporary

B1

806 Emerson St. (at Homer Ave.), Palo Alto

Phone: 650-326-2530 — Tue – Sat lunch & dinner
Web: www.stmikes.com — Sun lunch only
Prices: $$

A Palo Alto fixture since 1959, Saint Michael's Alley has seen its share of social change. In the 60s, the management at the time gave then-unknown singers Joan Baez and Jerry Garcia an opportunity to entertain here. Since, the restaurant has seen new ownership; more recently, it was relocated and spiffed up with a California bistro style.

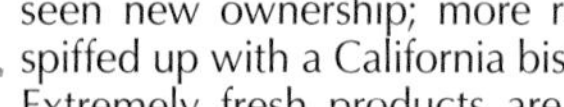

Extremely fresh products are handled with respect in the kitchen, where a salad of asparagus, favas, and toasted barley may be tossed with a lemon-dill vinaigrette; and sautéed leeks, wild mushrooms, green pea purée, and shaved parmesan combine beautifully in a spring pea risotto.

Accommodating service is just one more reason this place enjoys a loyal local following who thinks the world of it.

Sakae

C1

240 Park Rd. (bet. Burlingame & Howard Aves.), Burlingame

Phone: 650-348-4064 — Tue – Sat lunch & dinner
Web: www.sakaesushi.com — Sun – Mon dinner only
Prices: $$

No-frills describes the décor in this Burlingame sushi bar, but when you taste the fish here, you won't care about the absence of chic ambience. Reasonably priced combination meals are offered at both lunch and dinner, but it is the sushi that runs away with the awards.The superb freshness of the fish, some flown in direct from Japan, rivals that of some of the best sushi places in the country. This means that in the chef's sushi sampler the raw salmon is so pristine that it exhibits none of the astringency often present in this fish.

If you sit at the sushi bar you'll be restricted to raw offerings, and you can converse with the friendly sushi chefs. If you take a table seat, you can order off the menu of cooked items as well.

Sent Sovi

E3

14583 Big Basin Way (at 5th St.), Saratoga

Phone: 408-867-3110 — Tue – Sun dinner only
Web: www.sentsovi.com
Prices: $$$

On the main street of the charming town of Saratoga, Sent Sovi's entrance is tucked inside a brick-paved terrace. Natural light bathes the room inside, casting a warm glow on the copper wainscoting.

Chef Josiah Stone crafts his cuisine from naturally raised ingredients that hail from small local farms and ranches. In summer, à la carte items might include smoked-paprika-dusted scallops with Lemon Boy tomato coulis, or Niman Ranch pork tenderloin with yellow wax and Blue Lake beans. Other options include a six-course chef's tasting, a vegetarian menu, and a personalized Grand Tasting—which requires that you pre-order 48 hours in advance.

The upscale cadre of diners who favor this place don't seem to mind a bit of attitude from the servers.

Seven

B3

754 The Alameda (at Bush St.), San Jose

Phone: 408-280-1644 Mon – Fri lunch & dinner
Web: www.7restaurant.com Sat dinner only
Prices: $$

The trendy crowd jamming the narrow bar area is the first thing you'll notice upon entering this industrial-chic establishment just across from the HP Pavilion in downtown San Jose. Opened in 2003 by the Valdez twins, Curtis and Russell, Seven maintains the cool urban vibe that lures a young clientele. And the bar serves food until midnight, another draw for those looking for a bite after a concert or a Sharks game.

On the ceiling, a tangle of exposed ductwork and pipes overhangs the polished concrete floors. Curving booths and banquettes alternate in shades of Burgundy and Bordeaux against pale green walls. On the menu, an all-American cheeseburger and a classic chicken pot pie share space with French fare such as steak frites and duck cassoulet.

Sushi Sam's

C2

218 E. 3rd Ave. (bet. B St. & Ellsworth Ave.), San Mateo

Phone: 650-344-0888 Tue – Sat lunch & dinner
Web: www.sushisams.com
Prices: $$

Minimal décor leaves the attention on the wide variety of fresh fish at this unassuming sushi place, located on one of the busier blocks of downtown San Mateo. A favorite with local culinary professionals, Sushi Sam's boasts a well-trained team of chefs whose impressive knife skills are entertaining to watch from the three narrow seating areas (including the sushi bar).

Although there are only a few rolls on the menu, this spot has a more extensive array of fish—needlefish, butterfish, briny octopus, to name a few—than many other sushi joints in the area. Noodle bowls and hot specials are popular at lunch, while *ebi* tempura, beef teriyaki, and *saba shioyaki* (grilled mackerel) appear on the menu at dinner alongside special combinations.

Tamarine

B1

546 University Ave. (bet. Cowper & Webster Sts.), Palo Alto

Phone: 650-325-8500 — Mon – Fri lunch & dinner
Web: www.tamarinerestaurant.com — Sat – Sun dinner only
Prices: $$

A high-topped communal table, upholstered horseshoe-shaped booths, and modern music spawns a lounge ambience here. Set on an attractive strip of University Boulevard, Tamarine serves as a gallery for a changing display of contemporary Vietnamese art.

This theme also pervades the menu, with updated takes on traditional Asian cuisine. Artfully arranged plates emerge from the kitchen displaying such appetizers as savory shrimp cupcakes or grilled quail salad, and continue the parade in tri-squash scallop curry, clay pot cod, and cumin-spiced duck. Pair your entrée with a choice of aromatic rice from jasmine to Empress, the latter dotted with garlic, leeks, ginger, and egg.

Delectable Asian-influenced desserts merit the extra calories.

Tanglewood

A3

334 Santana Row (at Assylum Ln.), San Jose

Phone: 408-244-0464 — Lunch & dinner daily
Web: www.tanglewood.com
Prices: $$

Anchoring the north end of the posh Santana Row complex, Tanglewood adheres to the motto "dine in season; live in the moment." This is good advice, and under the aegis of Chef/owner Roland Passot, translates to innovative and ever-changing dishes, such as a salad of warm root vegetables dressed with saffron apple-cider vinaigrette; diver scallops roasted on a cedar plank; and spaghetti with no meatballs (a vegetarian take on the classic, made with roasted spaghetti squash, sweet pickled cherry tomatoes, fried wild rice balls, and tofu garlic cream). Served family-style, Sunday suppers spotlight a different special each week.

Tall retractable windows and elegant décor makes Tanglewood an equally classy roost for a business lunch or a respite from shopping.

The Village Pub ✿

Californian 

D2

2967 Woodside Rd. (off Whiskey Hill Rd.), Woodside

Phone: 650-851-9888 — Mon – Fri lunch & dinner
Web: www.thevillagepub.net — Sat – Sun dinner only
Prices: $$$

Frankie Frankeny

There's nothing pub-like about this sophisticated Woodside charmer, unless you count the fact that—like most good pubs—you don't really want to leave once you get a foot in the door. Guests are greeted by a beautifully designed room, with elegant, white-cloth tables and a great wood-burning oven. Get there early to relish a drink at the handsome bar, polished to a glossy mahogany and anchored by a crackling fireplace, before the crowds descend.

A stylish set pours in nightly for Chef Mark Sullivan's irresistible rustic fare, like a country pâté starter served with Port-soaked cherries; or a silky, delicately nutty chestnut soup that appears like a dream, with a delicious cloud of foie gras emulsion piled on top. For dinner, try the duck leg confit, served Perigord-style. Dancing with braised greens and sweet candied Kumquat, this is California cooking at its best.

Appetizers

- Shaved Foie Gras Torchon , Vanilla-poached Pears, Pomegranate Vinaigrette
- Maine Day Boat Scallops, Cauliflower Mousseline, Caviar Vin Blanc

Entrées

- Grilled Ahi Tuna, Gnocchi, Braised Short Ribs
- Tagliatelle, Fava Leaves, and Trumpet Mushrooms
- Grilled Angus Steak, Crispy Artichoke, Sauce Béarnaise

Desserts

- Citrus Panna Cotta, Lemon Soufflé, Caramelized Mandarin Tian
- Chocolate Soufflé, Grand Marnier Anglaise
- House-Made Ice Cream and Sorbets

Thea Mediterranean

Mediterranean XX

A3

3090 Olsen Dr. (at Winchester Blvd.), San Jose

Phone: 408-260-1444 — Lunch & dinner daily
Web: www.thearestaurant.com
Prices: $$

Expect good things from a restaurant named after a Greek goddess, and find them at this restaurant on the southern end of Santana Row. Named for the mythical mother of the sun and moon, Thea shines its light on Greek and Turkish specialties interpreted by Chef Rocio Gomez. To start, pita bread arrives warm from the oven; it makes an ideal way to scoop savory spreads like garlicky *melitzanosalata* (made from eggplant) and spicy *htipiti* (whipped feta and roasted red pepper).

A 20-foot olive tree forms the centerpiece of the dramatic, soaring dining room. The tall mahogany bar is lined with glass bottles in Mediterranean blues and greens that playfully reflect the light. To catch some direct rays from Thea's offspring, head for the outdoor patio.

231 Ellsworth

Contemporary XX

C2

231 S. Ellsworth Ave. (bet. 2nd & 3rd Aves.), San Mateo

Phone: 650-347-7231 — Tue – Fri lunch & dinner
Web: www.231ellsworth.com — Mon & Sat dinner only
Prices: $$$

At this South Bay darling, warm-toned wood paneling, seasonal flower arrangements, perfectly pressed linens, and a cobalt-blue barrel-vaulted ceiling set the mood. Service that is as polished as the setting is elegant makes this a winner for any special occasion.

Simple dishes with abundant flavors fill the seasonal menu. Thus plump crab cakes might roost atop a salad or multicolor beets get tossed with pistachio and smoked-paprika vinaigrette, while roasted pork loin pairs with a sauté of favas, morels, and sweetbreads.

As for the restaurant's sizeable wine collection, it stocks an impressive array of California labels as well as some serious Old World wines at sensible prices. A glassed-in cherrywood day cellar near the bar displays some 800 bottles.

Trevese ✿

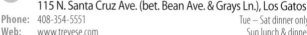

Contemporary XXX

E3

115 N. Santa Cruz Ave. (bet. Bean Ave. & Grays Ln.), Los Gatos

Phone: 408-354-5551 — Tue – Sat dinner only

Web: www.trevese.com — Sun lunch & dinner

Prices: $$$

Trevese

In the heart of quaint Los Gatos, where little boutiques and cafes hug the streets, sits a 19th century Queen Anne Victorian mansion on a mission—to introduce green fine dining to Northern California. Trevese is the brainchild of Chef Michael Miller, who cut his teeth at Spago before making his way north to open the critically regarded but now-defunct, Umunhum, in San Francisco.

In his new space, which he opened with his wife in 2007, Miller offers a beautifully sleek interior with a muted palette, modern leather furniture, and soft candlelight. And from the moment the 800+ bottle wine list hits your table, you know you're in for a treat. Kick things off with a press of duck leg confit and foie gras, topped with a sweet, earthy tuile of lentil and hazelnut. Below it, a tiny puddle of warm Dijon vinaigrette pools the plate—carrying the slightest hint of black truffle.

Appetizers

- Prawns, Toasted Almonds,Chili, Honey, Cilantro
- Scallops, Mirin, Soba and Seaweed Salad
- Duck Press, Foie Gras Center, Lentil Vadouvan Tuile, Dijon Cream

Entrées

- Cornish Game Hen with House Chorizo, Blue Cheese and Walnut Ravioli
- Halibut, Braised Spring Beans, Pancetta, Pea Jus
- Lamb Chop, Truffle Purée, Red Wine

Desserts

- Pistachio Sponge, Coconut Ice, Mandarin-Cardamom Syrup
- Brown Rice Pudding, Peanut Butter, Salted Caramel
- Ginger Bread, Carrot Foam

Xanh

Vietnamese

E2

110 Castro St. (bet. Evelyn Ave. & Villa St.), Mountain View

Phone: 650-964-1888 — Mon – Fri lunch & dinner
Web: www.xanhrestaurant.com — Sat – Sun dinner only
Prices: $$

In early 2008, Xanh moved down the street to bigger digs in this über-sleek lounge. Club music gets the groove on for an audience of thirty-somethings who applaud the liberties Chef Thuy Pham takes with Vietnamese cuisine. Crispy shrimp clouds, mellow yellow noodles, and ankle biters (crispy and spicy prawns) are all Xanh originals. Twists on traditional spring rolls, as in the Eskimo roll (pan-roasted catfish, rice noodles, and pineapple) and the Xanh Deuce (with pork tenders and crispy shrimp) further show off the chef's inventions.
Beaded mesh curtains, smoked-glass partitions, and a trickling waterfall bring a swanky feel to the three dining rooms.

Feast for under $25 at all restaurants with ☺.

Peter L. Wrenn / MICHELIN

Wine Country

Wine Country

Napa Valley and Sonoma County

Picnicking on artisan-made cheeses and fresh crusty bread amid acres of gnarled grapevines; sipping wine on a terrace above a hillside of silvery olive trees; touring caves heady with the sweet smell of fermenting grapes: this is northern California's Wine Country. Lying within a hour's drive north and northeast of San Francisco, the hills and vales of Sonoma County and Napa Valley thrive on the abundant sunshine and fertile soil that produce grapes for some of North America's finest wines.

FRUIT OF THE VINE

Cuttings of Criollas grapevines traveled north with Franciscan *padres* from the Baja Peninsula during the late 17th century. Wines made from these "mission" grapes were used primarily for trade and for sacramental purposes. In the early 1830s, a French immigrant propitiously named Jean-Louis Vignes (*vigne* is French for "vine") established a large vineyard near Los Angeles using cuttings of European grapevines *(Vitis vinifera)*, and by the mid-19th century, winemaking had become one of southern California's principal industries.

In 1857 Hungarian immigrant Agoston Haraszthy purchased a 400-acre estate in Sonoma County, named it Buena Vista, and cultivated Tokay vine cuttings imported from his homeland. In 1861, bolstered by promises of state funding, Haraszthy went to Europe to gather assorted *vinifera* cuttings to plant in California soil. Upon his return, however, the state legislature reneged on their commitment. Undeterred, Haraszthy persisted in distributing (at his own expense) some 100,000 cuttings and testing varieties in different soil types. Successful application of his discoveries created a boom in the local wine industry in the late 19th century.

THE TIDE TURNS

As the 1800s drew to a close, northern California grapevines fell prey to phylloxera, a root louse that attacks susceptible *vinifera* plants. Entire vineyards were decimated. Eventually researchers discovered they could combat phylloxera by replanting vineyards with disease-resistant wild grape rootstocks, onto which *vinifera* cuttings could be grafted. The wine industry had achieved a modicum of recovery by the early 20th century, only to be slapped with the 18th Amendment to the Constitution, prohibiting the manufacture, sale, importation, and transportation of intoxicating liquors in the US.

California's winemaking industry remained at a near-standstill until 1933, when Prohibition was repealed. The Great Depression slowed the reclamation of vineyards and it wasn't until the early 1970s that California's wine industry was fully re-established. In 1976 California wines took top honors in a blind taste testing by French judges in Paris. The results helped open up a whole new world of respectability for California vineyards.

M. Linda Lee / MICHELIN

COMING OF AGE

As Napa and Sonoma wines have established their reputations, the importance of individual growing regions has increased. Many sub-regions have sought and acquired Federal regulation of the place names as American Viticultural Areas, or AVAs, in order to set the boundaries of wine-growing areas that are distinctive for their soil, microclimate and wine styles. Although this system is subject to debate, there is no doubt that an AVA such as Russian River Valley, Carneros, or Spring Mountain can be very meaningful. The precise location of a vineyard relative to the Pacific Ocean or San Pablo Bay, the elevation and slope of a vineyard, the soil type and moisture content, and even the proximity to a mountain gap can make essential differences.

Together, Sonoma and Napa have almost 30 registered appellations, which vary in size and sometimes overlap. Specific place names are becoming increasingly important as growers learn what to plant where and how to care for vines in each unique circumstance. The fact that more and more wines go to market with a specific AVA flies in the face of the worldwide trend to ever larger and less specific "branded" wines. Individual wineries and associations are working to promote the individuality of North Coast appellations and to preserve their integrity and viability as sustainable agriculture.

DESTINATION WINE COUNTRY

In recent decades the Napa and Sonoma valleys have experienced tremendous development. Besides significant increases in vineyard acreage, the late 20th century witnessed an explosion of small-scale operations, some housed in old wineries updated with state-of-the-art equipment. Meanwhile, the Russian River Valley remains less developed, retaining its rural feel with country roads winding past picturesque wineries, rolling hills of grapevines, and stands of redwood trees.

With easy access to world-class wines, and organic produce and cheeses from local farms, residents of northern California's Wine Country enjoy an enviable quality of life. Happily for visitors, those same products supply the area's burgeoning number of restaurants, creating a culture of gourmet dining that stretches from the city of Napa north to Healdsburg and beyond.

Note that if you elect to bring your own wine, most restaurants charge a corkage fee (which can vary from $10 to as much as $50 per bottle). Many restaurants waive this fee on one particular day, or if you purchase an additional bottle from their list.

Which Food?	*Which Wine?*	*Some Examples*
Shellfish	Semi-dry White	Early harvest Riesling, Chenin Blanc, early harvest Gewürztraminer, Viognier
	Dry White	Lighter Chardonnay (less oak), Pinot Blanc, Sauvignon Blanc, dry Riesling, dry Chenin Blanc
	Sparkling Wine	Brut, Extra Dry, Brut Rosé
	Dry Rosé	Pinot Noir, Syrah, Cabernet
Fish	Dry White	Chardonnay (oaky or not) Sauvignon Blanc, dry Riesling, dry Chenin Blanc, Pinot Blanc
	Sparkling Wine	Brut, Blanc de Blancs, Brut Rosé
	Light Red	Pinot Noir, Pinot Meunier, light-bodied Zinfandel
	Dry Rosé	Pinot Noir, Syrah, Cabernet
Cured Meats/ Picnic Fare	Semi-dry White	Early harvest Riesling or early harvest Gewürztraminer
	Dry White	Chardonnay (less oak), Sauvignon Blanc, dry Riesling
	Sparkling Wine	Brut, Blanc de Blancs, Brut Rosé
	Light Red	Gamay, Pinot Noir, Zinfandel, Sangiovese
	Young Heavy Red	Syrah, Cabernet Sauvignon, Zinfandel, Cabernet Franc, Merlot
	Rosé	Any light Rosé
Red Meat	Dry Rosé	Pinot Noir, Cabernet, Syrah, Blends
	Light Red	Pinot Noir, Zinfandel, Gamay, Pinot Meunier
	Young Heavy Red	Cabernet Sauvignon, Cabernet Franc, Syrah, Grenache, Petite Sirah, Merlot, Blends, Pinot Noir, Cabernet Sauvignon
	Mature Red	Merlot, Syrah, Zinfandel, Meritage, Blends
Fowl	Semi-dry White	Early harvest Riesling, Chenin Blanc, Viognier
	Dry White	Sauvignon Blanc, Chardonnay, Pinot Blanc, dry Riesling
	Sparkling Wine	Extra Dry, Brut, Brut Rosé
	Rosé	Any light Rosé
	Light Red	Pinot Noir, Zinfandel, Blends, Gamay
	Mature Red	Pinot Noir, Cabernet Sauvignon, Merlot, Syrah, Zinfandel, Meritage, Blends
Cheese	Semi-dry White	Riesling, Gewürztraminer, Chenin Blanc
	Dry White	Sauvignon Blanc, Chardonnay, Pinot Blanc, dry Riesling
	Sparkling Wine	Extra Dry, Brut
	Rosé	Pinot Noir, Cabernet, Grenache
	Light Red	Pinot Noir, Zinfandel, Blends, Gamay
	Young Heavy Red	Cabernet Sauvignon, Cabernet Franc, Syrah, Grenache, Petite Sirah, Merlot, Blends
Dessert	Sweet White	Any late harvest White
	Semi-dry White	Riesling, Gewürztraminer, Chenin Blanc, Muscat
	Sparkling Wine	Extra Dry, Brut, Rosé, Rouge
	Dessert Reds	Late harvest Zinfandel, Port

Vintage	2007	2006	2005	2004	2003	2002	2001	2000	1999	1998	1997	1996	1995
Chardonnay **Carneros**	Above Average	Above Average	Above Average	Outstanding	Outstanding	Outstanding	Outstanding	Above Average	Above Average	Average	Outstanding	Above Average	Outstanding
Chardonnay **Russian River**	Outstanding	Above Average	Outstanding	Outstanding	Above Average	Outstanding	Outstanding	Above Average	Above Average	Average	Outstanding	Above Average	Outstanding
Chardonnay **Napa Valley**	Above Average	Above Average	Above Average	Above Average	Outstanding	Outstanding	Above Average	Average	Above Average	Above Average	Outstanding	Outstanding	Outstanding
Sauvignon Blanc **Napa Valley**	Above Average	Above Average	Outstanding	Outstanding	Above Average	Outstanding	Outstanding	Average	Above Average	Average	Outstanding	Above Average	Above Average
Sauvignon Blanc **Sonoma County**	Above Average	Outstanding	Above Average	Outstanding	Above Average	Above Average	Outstanding	Average	Above Average	Average	Outstanding	Above Average	Above Average
Pinot Noir **Carneros**	Above Average	Above Average	Above Average	Outstanding	Outstanding	Above Average	Outstanding	Average	Above Average	Average	Outstanding	Above Average	Above Average
Pinot Noir **Russian River**	Outstanding	Above Average	Above Average	Outstanding	Outstanding	Outstanding	Above Average	Above Average	Above Average	Above Average	Outstanding	Above Average	Above Average
Merlot **Napa Valley**	Above Average	Above Average	Outstanding	Above Average	Outstanding	Above Average	Outstanding	Above Average	Outstanding	Above Average	Outstanding	Outstanding	Outstanding
Merlot **Sonoma County**	Above Average	Above Average	Outstanding	Outstanding	Above Average	Above Average	Above Average	Above Average	Above Average	Above Average	Outstanding	Above Average	Outstanding
Cabernet Sauvignon **Napa Valley**	Outstanding	Outstanding	Outstanding	Outstanding	Above Average	Outstanding	Outstanding	Above Average	Outstanding	Above Average	Outstanding	Outstanding	Outstanding
Cabernet Sauvignon **Southern Sonoma**	Above Average	Above Average	Above Average	Outstanding	Above Average	Above Average	Outstanding	Above Average	Above Average	Above Average	Outstanding	Outstanding	Above Average
Cabernet Sauvignon **Northern Sonoma**	Above Average	Outstanding	Outstanding	Outstanding	Above Average	Outstanding	Above Average	Above Average	Above Average	Above Average	Outstanding	Outstanding	Above Average
Zinfandel **Napa Valley**	Outstanding	Outstanding	Above Average	Outstanding	Outstanding	Outstanding	Outstanding	Above Average	Above Average	Above Average	Outstanding	Outstanding	Above Average
Zinfandel **Southern Sonoma**	Outstanding	Outstanding	Above Average	Outstanding	Outstanding	Outstanding	Outstanding	Above Average	Above Average	Above Average	Outstanding	Outstanding	Above Average
Zinfandel **Northern Sonoma**	Above Average	Outstanding	Above Average	Outstanding	Outstanding	Outstanding	Outstanding	Above Average	Outstanding	Above Average	Outstanding	Outstanding	Outstanding

Napa Valley

Cradled between two elongated mountain ranges—the **Mayacamas** on the west and the **Vaca** on the east—the Napa Valley extends about 35 miles in a northerly direction from the **San Pablo Bay** to **Mount St. Helena**. The valley is home to some of California's most prestigious wineries, many of which cluster along **Route 29**. This road, the valley's main artery, runs up the western side of the mountains, passing through the commercial hub of Napa, and continuing north through the charming little wine burgs of **Yountville**, **Oakville**, **Rutherford**, **St. Helena**, and **Calistoga**—the latter known for its mineral mud baths. Other wineries dot the more tranquil **Silverado Trail**, which hugs the foothills of the eastern range and gives a more pastoral perspective on this rural county.

CLIME AND WINE

Throughout the valley you'll spot knolls, canyons, dry creek beds, broad stretches of valley floor, and glorious mountain vistas, all of which afford varying microclimates and soil types for growing wine. San Pablo Bay has a moderating effect on the valley's temperatures, while the influence of the Pacific Ocean—40 miles west—is lessened by the mountains.

Napa's success with premium wine has fostered a special pride of place. Fourteen American Viticultural Areas (AVAs) regulate the boundaries for sub-regions such as **Carneros**, **Stags Leap**, **Rutherford**, and **Spring Mountain**. As these sub-regions within the county are becoming better understood, more wineries are giving labeling prominence to specific sources of grapes, even down to the level of a specific vineyard. Certain sections are gaining reputations for specific grape varietals and even wine styles, and consumers are learning to look for the provenance of a certain vineyard or region rather than simply a type of grape.

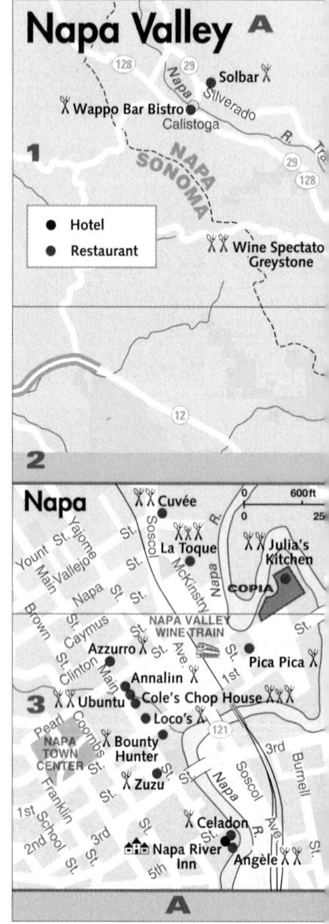

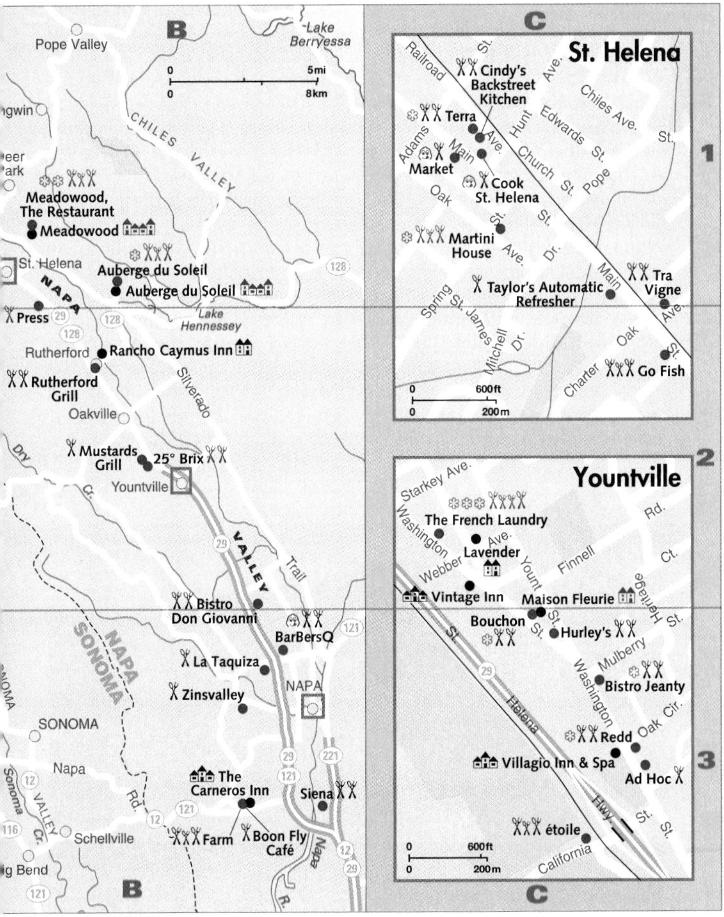

B

Pope Valley
Lake Berryessa
0 5mi
0 8km
CHILES VALLEY
Meadowood, The Restaurant
Meadowood
Auberge du Soleil
Auberge du Soleil
St. Helena
NAPA
Press
Lake Hennessey
Rutherford
Rancho Caymus Inn
Rutherford Grill
Oakville
Silverado
Mustards Grill
25° Brix
Yountville
Dry Cr.
VALLEY
Trail
Bistro Don Giovanni
BarBersQ
NAPA SONOMA
La Taquiza
Zinsvalley
NAPA
SONOMA
Napa
The Carneros Inn
Siena
Sonoma VALLEY Cr.
Schellville
Farm
Boon Fly Café
Napa R.
Rd.
B

C

St. Helena

Railroad
St.
Cindy's Backstreet Kitchen
Ave.
Chiles Ave.
Terra
Hunt
Edwards St.
St.
Adams
Main
Ave.
Market
Church St.
Pope
Cook St. Helena
Oak
St.
St.
Martini House
Ave.
Dr.
Main
Tra Vigne
Taylor's Automatic Refresher
Spring
St. James
Ave.
Mitchell Dr.
Oak
St.
Charter
Go Fish
0 600ft
0 200m

Yountville

Starkey Ave.
The French Laundry
Washington
Rd.
Ave.
Lavender
Webber
Yount
Finnell
Ct.
Vintage Inn
Maison Fleurie
Heritage
Bouchon
St.
St.
Hurley's
St.
Mulberry
St.
Washington
Bistro Jeanty
Helena
Oak Cir.
Redd
Villagio Inn & Spa
Ad Hoc
Hwy
St.
St.
étoile
California
0 600ft
0 200m

C

1
2
3

NAPA OLD AND NEW

Reclaimed 19th-century stone wineries and Victorian houses punctuate the valley's landscape, reminding the traveler that there were some 140 wineries here prior to 1890. Today, Napa Valley boasts 325 producing wineries (and nearly 400 brands), up from a post-Prohibition low of perhaps a dozen. The boom in wine production has spawned a special kind of food-and-wine tourism. Today, tasting rooms, tours, and farm-fresh cuisine are de rigueur here.

The **Napa River**, a trickle in most seasons, wanders the length of the valley floor culminating in the city of **Napa**, the largest population center in the valley. Once overlooked by visitors, Napa now holds its own as a destination. The city has been rapidly spiffing up its historic downtown starting with the old **Napa Mill**. Built in the late 19th century as part of a steamship wharf on the Napa River, the mill was restored several years ago. It now functions as an entertainment complex, holding an inn, shops, and restaurants. More recent development includes a pedestrian promenade skirting Napa Mill, and the mixed-use Riverfront complex that is being built on Main Street *(between Third & Fifth Sts.)*. Meanwhile, upscale hotels—a Ritz-Carlton and the 160-unit Westin Verasa Napa condominium hotel, for starters—are adding more luxury to the local hotel mix.

Opened in early 2008, **Oxbow Public Market** is a block-long, 40,000-square-foot facility that hopes to vie with the Ferry Building Marketplace across the bay. Oxbow brims with local food artisans and wine vendors, all from within a 100-mile radius of the market. Within this barn-like building, you'll find cheeses and charcuterie, spices and specialty teas, olive oils and organic ice cream, and, of course, a host of farm-fresh produce. The market is located next to **Copia, the American Center for Food, Wine and the Arts**, a $70-million cultural and educational center founded by winemaker Robert Mondavi.

MICHELIN

Ad Hoc

American

6476 Washington St. (bet. California Dr. & Oak Circle), Yountville

Phone: 707-944-2487 — Mon – Sat dinner only
Web: www.adhocrestaurant.com — Sun lunch & dinner
Prices: $$$

True to its name, Ad Hoc was intended to fill this space temporarily, until Chef Thomas Keller could realize his concept for a casual burger place here. Ad Hoc, however, took on a life of its own. The trendy bistro-style eatery now adds another good dining option to Washington Street's renowned restaurant lineup (which includes two other Keller enterprises: Bouchon and The French Laundry).

Locals flock here to eat and be seen. Judging from the animated atmosphere, the restaurant appears to be a local treasure. They are open for dinner daily and weekend brunch. The website posts the menu *du jour* by 2:00 P.M.; be it the acclaimed fried chicken or other yummy comfort food, you know it will be good.

Angèle

French

540 Main St. (at 5th St.), Napa

Phone: 707-252-8115 — Lunch & dinner daily
Web: www.angelerestaurant.com
Prices: $$

Napa Valley's commercial hub is finally coming of age in terms of its restaurants, thanks to places like Angèle. Located in the restored 1893 Napa Mill complex, Angèle sits at the end of the Hatt Building, overlooking the Napa River. Exposed wood beams of the vaulted ceiling recall the building's former use as a boathouse for the mill.

Refined French food prepared from market-fresh ingredients keeps diners coming back for more. A charcuterie plate of artisan salamis and country pâté, *magret de canard*, and house-made fettucine with spring vegetables are just a soupçon of what the menu offers.

Local winemakers enjoy this casual, family-friendly restaurant; at lunchtime the wine bar vies with the expansive riverfront patio as the place to be.

Annaliên

Vietnamese

1142 Main St. (bet. 1st & Pearl Sts.), Napa

Phone: 707-224-8319 — Tue – Sat lunch & dinner
Web: N/A
Prices: **$$**

Annaliên "Anna" Shepley fled to the United States from her native Saigon in 1975, and Napans are glad she did. Today the diminutive chef boasts her culinary heritage to crowds of diners at this cozy namesake restaurant in downtown Napa. Regulars are accustomed to seeing Shepley make the rounds; she is not shy about warmly greeting newcomers and inquiring how they are enjoying their food.

Tasty contemporary Vietnamese dishes reflect both French and Chinese influences, with a focus on pleasing the American palate. Selections may include *Dalat* spicy beef accompanied by a creamy slaw of shredded cabbage, lettuce, mint, and cilantro; or *Ha long* bread, a warm, pan-seared, green-onion-flavored flatbread served with curry dipping sauce.

Azzurro

Pizza 

1260 Main St. (at Clinton St.), Napa

Phone: 707-255-5552 — Mon – Fri lunch & dinner
Web: www.azzurropizzeria.com — Sat – Sun dinner only
Prices:

In early 2008, Chef Michael Gyetvan's Pizza Azzurro outgrew its space on Second Street and moved to this corner spot as the first tenants of a new building called Main Street West. The pizzeria's new digs are comfortable and classy with polished concrete floors, high ceiling, and wine-bottle pendant light fixtures.

In the gleaming open kitchen, a white-tiled, gas-fired oven turns out pies that are justly famous in the Valley for their thin crusts and imaginative combos (sweet onions, gorgonzola, and rosemary; fennel sausage, red onion, tomato sauce, and mozzarella). The expanded menu adds seasonal starters, pastas, desserts, and broader selection of beer and wine.

Be prepared to wait, as this lively, family-friendly scene fills up quickly.

Auberge du Soleil ✿

Californian ⑂⑂⑂

B1

180 Rutherford Hill Rd. (off the Silverado Trail), Rutherford

Phone: 707-963-1211 — Lunch & dinner daily
Web: www.aubergedusoleil.com
Prices: $$$$

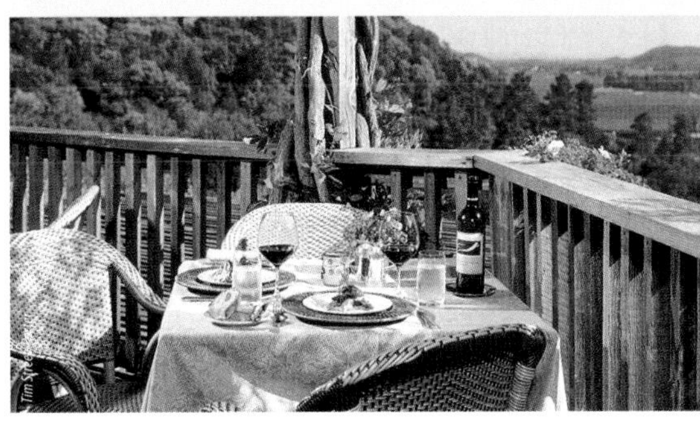
Tim Street

A view of the valley simply doesn't get more beautiful than the one from the terrace at Auberge Du Soleil, perched high above Napa Valley's Silverado Trail: a lingering meal at sunset is positively transformative. Adjoined to a gorgeous luxury inn of the same name, management is quick to remind people that the restaurant opened first (in 1981, as a matter of fact)—and the top-rate cuisine, enjoyed in the sunny dining room or on the outdoor deck, stands witness.

Chef Robert Curry turns out fresh California fare, with veggies, eggs, and other farm goodies filling his nightly prix-fixe and two tasting menus. A classic tuna tartare might kick off a dinner, arriving on a bed of green cucumber and topped with a tangle of ginger-touched wakame leaves. For a grand finale, you might be treated to a stack of pink rhubarb sticks, sided by a *blancmange* and a scoop of creamy ice cream.

Appetizers

- Sunchoke Soup, Fried Oyster, Rock Crab, Apple, Béarnaise Glaçage
- Hamachi Sashimi, Ruby Grapefruit, Soy Tapioca, Meyer Lemon
- Foie Gras, Poached Rhubarb, Pistachios

Entrées

- Bacon-wrapped Veal, Foie Gras Ravioli, Peas, Spring Garlic Jus
- Tuna, Hearts of Palm, Pork Belly, Quail Egg
- Lamb, Gnocchi, Goat Cheese, Squash Blossom

Desserts

- François Pralus "Trinidad"- Fondant au Chocolate, Coconut Streusel, Passion Fruit
- Crisp Filo-wrapped Chocolate Dumplings, Tarragon Ice Cream, Arbequina Olive Oil

BarBersQ

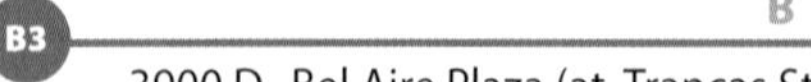

Barbecue XX

B3

3900 D., Bel Aire Plaza (at. Trancas St.), Napa

Phone: 707-224-6600 — Lunch & dinner daily
Web: www.barbersq.com
Prices: $$

Chef Stephen Barber, formerly of Mecca in the Castro District, plays with his name in the title of his barbecue place in Bel Aire Plaza. With a high-tech feel and a peppy vibe, the interior gets a boost from Italian marble, beveled mirrors, and stainless-steel—a bit more finesse than most barbecue joints.

The same is true for Barber's 'cue, which serves a packed house nearly every night. American heritage describes the menu, which journeys from grilled Drakes Bay oysters to Key West pink fried shrimp. Still, the real emphasis is on succulent Memphis-style barbecue.

Many of the fruits, vegetables, and herbs arrive on your table the same day they are picked. The all-California wine list further exemplifies the restaurant's commitment to the community.

Bistro Don Giovanni

Italian 

B2

4110 Howard Ln. (at Hwy. 29), Napa

Phone: 707-224-3300 — Lunch & dinner daily
Web: www.bistrodongiovanni.com
Prices: $$

A Napa Valley mainstay, Giovanni and Donna Scala's beloved bistro still pleases droves of tourists and locals with its rustic Italian fare. The large indoor space, warmed by a wood-burning pizza oven and ornamented by gleaming copper pots, is complemented by the outdoor terrace with its fountain, playful sculptures, and gardens. Views here stretch across miles of vineyard to the mountains beyond.

Fresh foccacia with olive oil for dipping start your meal. Next, perhaps, the Bouchot mussels with aïoli, Pastis, and leeks, or the sumptuous deep-fried olives and almonds. If it's on the menu, be sure to try the *polpetta d'agnello*, garlicky lamb meatballs with Tuscan beans. For dessert, the delicate tiramisu is the hands-down favorite.

Bistro Jeanty ✿

French ✕✕

C3

6510 Washington St. (at Mulberry St.), Yountville

Phone: 707-944-0103 — Lunch & dinner daily
Web: www.bistrojeanty.com
Prices: $$

Bistro Jeanty

Located on Yountville's restaurant row, Bistro Jeanty is the kind of beloved neighborhood bistro you might find anywhere in France—but this one has killer food to match. A splashy red-and-white striped awning lets you know straight away it doesn't take itself too seriously, as does the friendly hostess toting the blackboard tablet with the daily specials. The room is pure laid-back countryside charm, with a cracked, red floor, and butter yellow walls sporting French posters. Lest you worry about bistro-overkill, Jeanty is in on the joke—you're likely to see "Ratatouille" playing on the bar's television.

Authentic regional French fare built on ace ingredients defines the menu—a thick slice of coarsely-ground rabbit studded with two squares of silky foie gras pate is garnished with cornichons, julienned celery root, and apple, and then laced with a creamy Dijon dressing.

Appetizers
- Cured Pork Belly, Lentil-Balsamic Vinegar, and Foie Gras Ragout
- Pike Dumplings with Lobster Sauce
- Duck Paté with a Port-poached Pear

Entrées
- Mussels Steamed in Red Wine with Grilled Bread
- Cassoulet with Duck Confit, Sausage and Apple-smoked Bacon
- Black Pepper-crusted Tournedos

Desserts
- Warm Crepe Suzette with Orange Butter
- Chocolate Mousse Crème Brûlée
- Warm Caramelized Apple Tart with Crème Fraîche

Boon Fly Café

Californian

4048 Sonoma Hwy. (at Los Carneros Ave.), Napa

Phone: 707-299-4870 Lunch & dinner daily
Web: www.thecarnerosinn.com
Prices: $$

Tucked away amid 27 acres of grapevines and apple orchards off the Old Sonoma Highway, Boon Fly Café is part of the Carneros Inn. The more casual of the inn's two restaurants, this roadhouse-style cafe dishes up three square meals a day. Breakfast could be as simple as a cup of coffee and a couple of the cafe's signature homemade donuts, or as elaborate as Boon Fly Benedict with Hobbs ham and jalapeño hollandaise. For lunch, sandwiches and flatbreads (the house version of pizza) satisfy locals as well as inn guests. The dinner menu adds pasta dishes plus a handful of hearty entrées (grilled ribeye with garlic fries, roasted chicken breast).
If you have to wait for a table, stake out one of the swings or rocking chairs on the front porch.

Bounty Hunter

American

975 First St. (at Main St.), Napa

Phone: 707-226-3976 Lunch & dinner daily
Web: www.bountyhunterwine.com
Prices: $$

Reopened in spring 2008 after a significant kitchen expansion, Bounty Hunter retains much of the same historic warmth to match its worn wooden floors, exposed brick walls, and pressed-copper ceiling. An 1888 building houses this bar and bistro, which serves some 40 wines by the glass and 400 by the bottle. Patrons may choose among different wine flights, with whimsical names like Killer Cabs and Pinot Envy.
Once primarily salads and sandwiches, the lunch menu has blossomed with the addition of a new smoker. Fueled by hickory, apple wood and Cabernet barrel staves, it turns out spicy, slow-cooked ribs and brisket all day long—no longer just for dinner. These and signatures like the fantastic beer-can chicken, keep folks coming back for more.

Bouchon 

French XX

C3

6534 Washington St. (at Yount St.), Yountville

Phone: 707-944-8037 Lunch & dinner daily
Web: www.bouchonbistro.com
Prices: $$$

French Laundry/Deborah Jones

How the great Thomas Keller slums it—with an adorable, lively little bistro that oozes cozy-sweater charm and warms even the chilliest foodies with its easygoing attitude. But though these elements might appear like a casual afterthought, don't be fooled. A closer inspection unveils Keller's trademark perfectionism—and that's even before the meticulously-prepared food hits the table. Named for a traditionally meat-heavy cafe found in Lyon, Bouchon's menu is a goldmine of rustic French offerings, refined to sublime perfection by the master chef. Try a triplet of silky cod brandade beignets, served over tomato confit and topped with a single leaf of fried sage.

Even that most benign of bistro dishes, roast chicken, comes alive in Keller's deft hands—roasted to tender, golden perfection, and served with onion confit, celeriac, black truffle "tartlet," and chicken jus.

Appetizers

- Pâté de Campagne with Watercress
- Cod Brandade with Tomato Confit & Fried Sage
- Fresh & Smoked Salmon Served with Toasted Croutons

Entrées

- Leg of Lamb, Couscous, Olives, Mint- Lamb Jus
- Steamed Mussels, Garlic, Basil & Tomatoes, French Fries
- Pan-roasted Trout, Almonds & Beurre Noisette

Desserts

- Profiteroles, Vanilla Ice Cream & Chocolate Sauce
- Lemon Tart
- Pot de Crème

Celadon

International

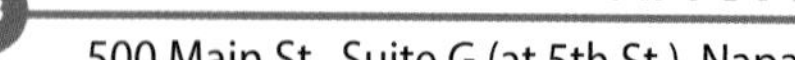

500 Main St., Suite G (at 5th St.), Napa

Phone: 707-254-9690 — Mon – Fri lunch & dinner
Web: www.celadonnapa.com — Sat – Sun dinner only
Prices: $$

Nestled in the Historic Napa Mill complex, Celadon presents the globetrotting menu of Chef/owner Greg Cole, who is currently splitting his time here with Cole's Chop House. He can often be found lending a hand in the dining room, chatting with guests in a genuinely caring manner. Dishes travel from sweet coconut fried prawns to Moroccan braised lamb shank, pleasing most every palate.

In addition to the celadon-green dining room, the large adjoining atrium provides covered "outdoor" seating in rain or shine. On cooler days, the atrium is heated and the raised brick fireplace adds coziness.

Be aware that the area around the restaurant is currently cordoned off with fencing and detours owing to ongoing development of the Napa riverfront.

Cindy's Backstreet Kitchen

American

C1

1327 Railroad Ave. (bet. Adams & Hunt Sts.), St. Helena

Phone: 707-963-1200 — Lunch & dinner daily
Web: www.cindysbackstreetkitchen.com
Prices: $$

Chef Cindy Pawlcyn continues her culinary legacy, which started with Mustard's Grill in Yountville and now includes Go Fish in St. Helena, in this early 19th-century house. Set a block off St. Helena's Main Street, Cindy's Backstreet Kitchen boasts flower-bedecked arbors on its terrace, while the modern, bistro-style interior sings with country charm. The long zinc bar attracts a local crowd who nosh on small plates while they sip house cocktails or savor some great Napa Valley wines.

The menu? It's a mix of classic and modern American dishes infused with Latin accents thanks to the influence of Pawlcyn's partner, Pablo Jacinto. Daily specials include a fish of the day as well as an item that's been smoked, braised or roasted in the wood-burning oven.

Cole's Chop House

Steakhouse XXX

A3

1122 Main St. (bet. 1st & Pearl Sts.), Napa

Phone: 707-224-6328 — Dinner daily
Web: www.coleschophouse.com
Prices: $$$$

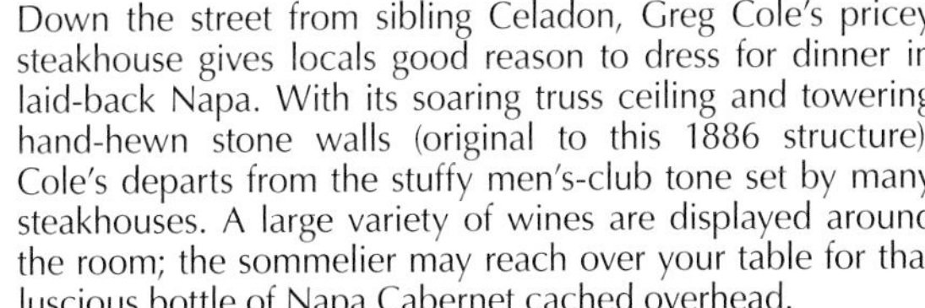

Down the street from sibling Celadon, Greg Cole's pricey steakhouse gives locals good reason to dress for dinner in laid-back Napa. With its soaring truss ceiling and towering hand-hewn stone walls (original to this 1886 structure), Cole's departs from the stuffy men's-club tone set by many steakhouses. A large variety of wines are displayed around the room; the sommelier may reach over your table for that luscious bottle of Napa Cabernet cached overhead.

On the menu, straightforward classics like oysters Rockefeller, Caesar salad, or formula-fed veal and New Zealand lamb compliment the main attraction: prime 21-day-dry-aged Angus beef.

Despite the Main Street address, the entrance is on the creek side, by the valet parking lot behind the restaurant.

Cook St. Helena

Italian X

C1

1310 Main St. (at Hunt Ave.), St. Helena

Phone: 707-963-7088 — Mon – Sat lunch & dinner
Web: N/A — Sun dinner only
Prices: $$

Located in the center of tiny St. Helena's commercial district, Jude Wilmoth's matchbox-size eatery really cooks with its all-day menu of Italian-accented fare. Local rock cod with Vidalia onion gremolata, handmade gnocchi with gorgonzola cream, and a moist chicken "chop" served with a mélange of corona beans, *cavalo nero*, and pancetta lardons paint an accurately delicious picture of the cuisine here. Reasonable prices and a friendly staff make this place all the more enticing.

Seating—whether it's at the low-slung marble bar, small white-linen and butcher-paper-topped tables, or on the black banquette that flanks the open kitchen—makes tight quarters that foster conviviality. The wine list leans toward labels from Italy and the Napa Valley.

Cuvée

A2 — American

1650 Soscol Ave. (at River Terrace Dr.), Napa

Phone: 707-224-2330 — Mon – Fri lunch & dinner
Web: www.cuveenapa.com — Sat – Sun dinner only
Prices: $$

Opened in May 2006, Cuvée sits adjacent to The River Terrace Inn with—despite its name—no wineries in sight. The elegant place fills the space with deep red hues and warm woods.

The classy bar/lounge includes seating for those wishing to dine, as well as comfy leather couches for patrons who just desire a cocktail. A unique concept normally reserved for wineries allows Cuvée's customers to sample wines poured straight from the barrel.

Modernized comfort food appears here in preparations like Chianti-braised short ribs, and potato-wrapped salmon served with herbed orzo in a light citrus-butter sauce. On a warm day, the secluded tree-lined courtyard makes the perfect spot for lunch.

étoile

C3 — Californian

1 California Dr. (off Hwy. 29), Yountville

Phone: 707-204-7529 — Thu – Mon lunch & dinner
Web: www.chandon.com
Prices: $$$$

As you walk up to Domaine Chandon winery past a landscape dotted with ponds and modern sculptures, you'll know you're in for a treat. Founded in Yountville in 1977 by the French Champagne house Moët & Chandon, Domaine Chandon stands out both for its sparkling wines and for its restaurant. And it's no coincidence that the latter was recently renamed after Chandon's most prestigious sparkling wine, étoile (French for "star").

Set off the tasting room, étoile sits under a wood-lined, barrel-vaulted ceiling—a visual reference to the oak casks in which wine is aged. Here, Chris Manning's vibrant seasonal cuisine pairs perfectly with the house wines.

Lunch is a delight on the stone terrace, where you can gaze out over the rolling grounds.

Farm

Californian XXX

B3

4048 Sonoma Hwy. (at Old Sonoma Rd.), Napa

Phone: 707-299-4882 — Lunch & dinner daily
Web: www.thecarnerosinn.com
Prices: $$$

Located just off Highway 121 between the towns of Sonoma and Napa, the Carneros Inn includes two dining options. Farm provides the fine-dining alternative, while the Boon Fly Café caters to more casual meals. In the former, cathedral ceilings, two large fireplaces, and a backlit display of wine bottles set the scene in this pleasant Wine Country retreat.
The finest local, organic, and sustainably raised products located within a 150-mile radius of the restaurant furnish the ingredients for the quintessential California cuisine here. Fresh flavors shine in such dishes as Pozzi lamb three ways (bone-in chops, boneless loin, and braised pulled lamb shoulder) served with a square of potato gratin. Most of the breads and artisan charcuterie offerings are made on-site.

Go Fish

Seafood XXX

C2

641 Main St. (bet. Charter Oak Ave. & Mills Ln.), St. Helena

Phone: 707-963-0700 — Lunch & dinner daily
Web: www.gofishrestaurant.net
Prices: $$$

Fishing for fresh seafood in Napa Valley? Cast your net no farther than Go Fish on Main Street in St. Helena. That's where you'll find Cindy Pawlcyn's (of Mustard's Grill and Cindy's Backstreet Kitchen) idea of a fish house.
With views of surrounding mountains and vineyards—best enjoyed from a seat on the large outdoor patio—Go Fish highlights its bright white dining room with hues of deep-sea blue, mustard and brown. A long Carrera marble sushi bar introduces the dining room, where a large chalkboard depicts a lone docked fishing boat.
A happy-go-lucky vibe pervades the upscale crowd who come here to taste wines and sample the bounty of the sea, from salt-crusted prawns with sweet-and-sour dipping sauce to wood-grilled Arctic char with saffron *vin blanc*.

The French Laundry ✿✿✿

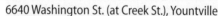

Contemporary 

C2

6640 Washington St. (at Creek St.), Yountville

Phone: 707-944-2380
Web: www.frenchlaundry.com
Prices: $$$$

Mon – Thu dinner only
Fri – Sun lunch & dinner

Deborah Jones

What is there left to say about the great Thomas Keller's legendary flagship? How about the fact that it still manages—even after years of topping the restaurant charts, expanding to the big, bad East Coast, and becoming a household name the world over—to be as exquisite and personable an experience as ever for anyone who enters its hallowed rustic interior. And with some careful planning (reservations should be made two months in advance; and jackets are required for men), you can step into this century-old stone laundry and see for yourself.

The two nine-course tasting menus (one is vegetarian) arrive like tiny rolling gifts from the Gods—with a nightly changing menu that might include a delicate and smooth Japanese sea scallop ceviche, paired with a blossom of *feijoa* flowers; or a thin slice of quickly-seared *kuroge* beef, dancing with white asparagus, shaved summer truffle, and wild local herbs.

Appetizers

- Oysters and Pearls: Sabayon of Tapioca, Oysters, Caviar
- "Foie Gras Terrine" Sunchoke, Orange Relish, Black Truffle Purée

Entrées

- Poularde Wrapped in Bacon, Little Gem Lettuce, Peas, Glazed Pearl Onions
- Sweet Butter-poached Maine Lobster
- Ribeye of Elysian Field's Farm Lamb

Desserts

- "Soufflé aux Noyaux d'Abricots", Wildflower Honey Ice Cream
- "Pavé de Chocolat Blanc au Thé Vert"
- Pistachio "Pain de Gênes" and Passion Fruit

Hurley's

Californian XX

C3

6518 Washington St. (at Yount St.), Yountville

Phone: 707-944-2345 — Lunch & dinner daily
Web: www.hurleysrestaurant.com
Prices: $$

For all its tiny size, Yountville claims a remarkable number of renowned restaurants along Washington Street, the town's main thoroughfare. The fact that Bob Hurley's kitchen has been holding its own here since 2002 speaks volumes for this casual place, where locals populate the friendly bar scene and the long wooden communal table.

Hurley, whose kitchen experience includes Domaine Chandon (now called étoile) and Napa Valley Grille, plays riffs on California cuisine with Mediterranean flair. Horseradish-crusted salmon with basil potato purée or Moroccan beef skewers served with hummus give you the idea.

You may feel more like you're in Tuscany as you bask on the sunny terrace flanked by olive trees, but locals will tell you this is vintage Yountville.

Julia's Kitchen

Californian XX

A2

500 1st St. (bet. Silverado Trail & Soscol Ave.), Napa

Phone: 707-265-5700 — Wed – Sun lunch & dinner; Mon lunch only
Web: www.copia.org
Prices: $$$

Although Julia Child, the beloved chef who introduced America to French cuisine in the 1960s, died in 2004, her indomitable spirit lives on in the Napa restaurant named for her. Couched within COPIA, the American Center for Food, Wine & the Arts—worth a visit in for its food-and-wine-related exhibits, tastings and cultural events—Julia's Kitchen displays a contemporary design enlivened by a large oil portrait of Julia herself.

Inspired by Julia's recipes, the seasonal menu includes distinctively fresh ingredients, cooked, of course, with a French twist. COPIA's edible organic garden provides much of the produce and herbs used to flavor salads and other dishes. Both an à la carte and a chef's tasting menu are available at lunch and dinner.

La Taquiza

Mexican 

2007 Redwood Rd. (at Solano Rd.), Napa

Phone: 707-224-2320 Lunch & dinner daily
Web: N/A
Prices: ⊜

A patio lined with leafy potted palms provides prime seating on this corner of Redwood Plaza, home to this delectable fresh-Mex taqueria. Inside, polished concrete floors, black metal furnishings, and local artwork create a stylish perch any time of year.

Fresh coastal ceviches, chilled seafood *coctels*, and bountiful bowls—or *tazons*—brimming with your choice of meat, seafood, or grilled vegetables prove that this is no mere taco stand. The celebrated fish tacos come either Baja-style (fried) or California-style (flame grilled), making it easy to eat light and still leave satisfied.

The complimentary fresh salsa bar offers varying levels of heat and bold flavors to suit all tastes. A small menu selection for *niños y niñas* (kids) is also available.

La Toque

Contemporary 

1314 McKinstry St. (at Soscol Ave.), Napa

Phone: 707-483-7512
Web: www.latoque.com
Prices: $$$$

For years La Toque has been delighting those trekking to Rutherford for an evening-long event. Chef Ken Frank and La Toque are settling into their sparkling new location in Napa, at the Westin Verasa. Hungry Napans look forward to Chef Frank's consistent attention to detail to elevate the Southern Napa Valley dining scene.

A unique, seasonal prix-fixe tasting menu debuts weekly, and the spacious new kitchen will allow for expanded offerings and the ability to display even more of the kitchens' talent.

Scott Tracy and their extraordinary global wine collection have made the move as well. The talented sommelier's passion for wine shows as he painstakingly explains each pairing, and even offers maps of wine regions to those who show interest.

Loco's

Southwestern

A3

1040 Main St. (bet. 1st & Pearl Sts.), Napa

Phone: 707-251-8058 Tue – Sat lunch & dinner
Web: N/A
Prices: ⊕

Charm and good Tex-Mex fare is what brings diners back to this family-run spot overlooking Behren's Creek in downtown Napa. Facing the creek behind the Napa Opera House, Loco's is a bit difficult to find, but that's part of its mystique.

You'll usually see owner Mike Van Duyn behind the grill, and his smiling wife, Donna, greeting guests warmly. The spirit of the Old West lingers in the framed pictures of cowboys that line the walls.

Gallop over for some crab enchiladas, barbecue beef brisket tacos, or shrimp burritos. If the weather cooperates, the lure of the creekside deck may spur you to enjoy some fresh guacamole with roasted jalapeño salsa while you quench your thirst with one of the many Mexican *cervezas* available here.

Market

C1

1347 Main St. (bet. Adam & Spring Sts.), St. Helena

Phone: 707-963-3799 Lunch & dinner daily
Web: www.marketsthelena.com
Prices: $$

If only life were as simple as a box of Market's buttermilk fried chicken—simple, comforting, not too fussy. It's a concept that pervades the whole restaurant, which was recently turned over to head chef, Eduardo Martinez. Martinez is a bit of an American success story himself—having started as a dishwasher in 1993, and worked his way through the Napa kitchen circuit before landing his newest role as owner.

In keeping with Douglas Keane and Nick Peyton's original concept, Martinez takes his cue from the local market, spinning fresh, seasonal ingredients into lip-smacking comfort food like plump Dungeness crab cakes, or wildly good butterscotch pudding, made with real Scotch and whipped to an ethereally smooth consistency.

Martini House

Contemporary

1245 Spring St. (bet. Main & Oak Sts.), St. Helena

Phone: 707-963-2233
Web: www.martinihouse.com
Prices: $$$

Mon – Thu dinner only
Fri – Sun lunch & dinner

Dennis Anderson

Music to anyone's ears—there's a table for two with your name on it, in a historical bungalow in downtown St. Helena. If you don't fancy the shaded terrace, with its lovely rose garden and gently lapping koi pond, try the countrified fairy tale interior, filled with stained-glass lanterns and a crackling fireplace come winter.

Once you've settled in, you'll want to turn an eye to Chef/co-owner Todd Humphries' menu—a wild, galloping tour of America's homegrown ingredients. Take the mushroom tasting menu, for example, that begins with a mushroom carpaccio of a thinly-sliced king trumpet, garnished with shaved celery, radishes, soft parmesan and crispy mushroom chips—and then laced with a light and sweet Meyer lemon aioli. To end, a bouncy candy cap mushroom bread pudding, studded with golden raisins and currants, and glossed with a maple sugar crème anglaise.

Appetizers

- Marinated Ahi Tuna, Enoki Mushrooms, Tuna Confit, Fried Ginger, Lemon Aïoli
- Beef Carpaccio, Himalayan Truffles, Arugula
- Maine Lobster Salad

Entrées

- Black Bass, Shrimp, Pea Tendril, Ginger-Shiitake Mushroom Dumpling
- Roasted Duck Breast, Glazed Butternut Squash, Hobbs Smoked Bacon

Desserts

- Meyer Lemon Crêpes, Citrus Fruit, Mascarpone Mousse
- Coffee Panna Cotta and Spiced Butterscotch Sauce
- Warm Chocolate Fondant, Crème Fraîche Ice Cream

Meadowood, The Restaurant 

Contemporary XXX

B1

900 Meadowood Ln. (off Silverado Trail), St. Helena

Phone: 707-967-1205 Mon – Sat dinner only
Web: www.meadowood.com
Prices: $$$$

Meadowood Napa

Just outside of St. Helena, off the Silverado trail and tucked deep into the mountain perch that holds the secluded, luxurious Meadowood resort, sits a beautiful little cottage. In the winter, a cozy bar greets customers with a roaring fireplace; in the summer, patrons follow the host to a patio overlooking the hotel's rolling golf course.

A polished service staff is efficient and discreet, reading customers minds with minimal fuss. And at the center of the beautiful, elegantly-appointed room, customers set their sights on Meadowood's top-flight cuisine, orchestrated by newly welcomed chef, Christopher Kostow.

The ultra-fresh ingredients draw on the local California bounty in utterly unique ways. A slow-smoked Jidori egg served over a toasted English muffin sports a feather-light mousseline; or an olive-oil poached wild black cod simmers in a fish and saffron sauce.

Appetizers

- Asparagus and Egg "En Cocotte", Smoked Salt Mousseline
- Parsnip Soufflé, Crispy Sweetbread, Maitake, Black Truffle
- Chilled Carrot Purée, Lobster, Lime

Entrées

- Konpachi, Braised Lettuce and Peas, Mint
- Suckling Pig, Caraway-scented Cabbage, Pickled Apple
- Scallop, Hawaiian Prawn, Cauliflower Purée, Quail Egg

Desserts

- Grapefruit Curd and Chestnut Croustillant, Rosemary Ice Cream
- Coconut Sorbet, Grilled Pineapple, Sichuan Pepper
- Butterscotch Soufflé

Mustards Grill

B2 — Contemporary

7399 St. Helena Hwy. (at Hwy. 29), Yountville

Phone: 707-944-2424 — Lunch & dinner daily
Web: www.mustardsgrill.com
Prices: $$

These days, Mustards' founder, Cindy Pawlcyn, divides her time between her 1983 flagship and newer ventures, yet her original restaurant continues to draw crowds seeking new American cuisine in true Wine Country style.

Daily specials scribbled on a blackboard announce the seafood tostada, the fresh catch, and the "truckstop deluxe" of the day, with their garden providing much of the menu's produce. Just as enticing, the signature Mongolian pork chop, tea-smoked duck, and sweet corn tamales with wild mushrooms have been winning raves for 25 years. The oak-wood smoker turns out succulent barbecue ribs, smoked quail, and duck, as well as a homey aroma.

Despite its age, this roadhouse has not waned in popularity over the years, so be sure to book in advance.

Pica Pica

A3 — Latin American

610 First St. (at McKinstry St.), Napa

Phone: 707-205-6187 — Mon – Sat lunch & dinner
Web: www.picapicakitchen.com — Sun lunch only
Prices: ⊖⊖

A lesson in Latin American food awaits you at this new restaurant in the Oxbow Public Market. Napa's answer to San Francisco's Ferry Building Marketplace, Oxbow is lined with shops and stalls selling array of produce and gourmet items. Navigating this luscious labyrinth is not to be done on an empty stomach.

That's where Pica Pica comes in. Catering largely to a take-out crowd, this "corn-centric kitchen" will teach you the ABCs of its menu beginning with *arepas* (a white corn flatbread, grilled and stuffed with a choice of fillings), *bululú* (a salad of corn, red bell pepper, jicama, and pineapple), and *cachapas* (a sweet yellow corn pancake filled with cheese or meat). Refreshing frozen drinks like the coconut lemonade will energize you for more shopping.

Press

Steakhouse XXX

B1-2

587 St. Helena Hwy. South, St. Helena

Phone: 707-967-0550 Wed – Mon dinner only
Web: www.presssthelena.com
Prices: $$$$

The simple warehouse façade visible from Highway 29 hides this posh steakhouse, where vaulted ceilings and natural light flooding through greenhouse-glass panels create an airy, luxurious space. A dark wood wine cabinet towers behind the bar, and an oversized fireplace and rotisserie form the focal point of the dining room. The swanky outdoor patio features long wooden tables and lush foliage.

Most of the beef is hand-selected, USDA Prime Angus, but the prized Japanese Kobe Kuroge Wagyu beef also appears on the menu. Dry-aging for 28 days enhances the taste of the meat—a grill fueled by cherry and almond woods does the rest.

The list of exclusively Napa Valley wines uncovers local gems from well-known vintners and small-batch wineries.

Rutherford Grill

American XX

B2

1180 Rutherford Rd. (off Hwy. 29), Rutherford

Phone: 707-963-1792 Lunch & dinner daily
Web: www.houstons.com
Prices: $$

Delectable aromas from the open kitchen and the rotisserie oven entice you as you enter this friendly, casual Wine Country restaurant, a member of the Hillstone Restaurant Group. The menu may be a bit lacking as far as first courses go, but the skillet cornbread is sure to jumpstart your appetite. Follow it up with meltingly tender barbecue pork ribs, a hardwood-grilled Rutherford ribeye with homemade Worcestershire sauce, or a succulent rotisserie-roasted chicken and you'll understand why there's often a line out the door.

Located at the intersection of Highway 29 and Rutherford Road, the grill is popular with locals who work at the surrounding wineries and who appreciate the restaurant's no-corkage policy. The large, U-shaped bar welcomes solo diners.

Redd ✿

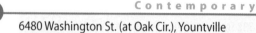

C3 — Contemporary XX

6480 Washington St. (at Oak Cir.), Yountville

Phone: 707-944-2222 — Lunch & dinner daily
Web: www.reddnapavalley.com
Prices: $$$

A warm welcome kicks off dinner at Redd, and things just keep getting better from there. Located on Yountville's ever-blossoming restaurant row, Redd's offers two good seating options—a sun-soaked dining room washed in minimalist white walls and pale wood, or a large courtyard dining area accented with a gently lapping fountain. Either way, you're in for a treat with Chef Richard Reddington's (formerly of Auberge du Soleil) globe-trotting contemporary cuisine.

Start with a tender *hamachi* sashimi on a mound of sticky rice, studded with fresh edamame and drizzled with a lime and ginger dressing. Later, make your way to an entrée of fresh, delicate skate wing set atop a mound of spinach purée, pocked with silky, sautéed wild mushrooms. Served with a few delicately fried artichoke hearts laced with aioli, and ringed with a black truffle jus—the result is just spectacular.

Appetizers

- Glazed Pork Belly, Apple Purée, Soy Caramel
- Caramelized Scallops, Cauliflower Purée, Balsamic Reduction
- Yellowfin Tartare, Avocado, Chili Oil, Fried Rice

Entrées

- John Dory, Jasmine Rice, Mussels, Chorizo, Curry Nage
- Duck Breast, Swiss Chard Crepe, Chocolate
- Braised and Roasted Lamb, Favas, Garam Masala

Desserts

- Meyer Lemon Cake, Tangerine Float, Grapefruit S'more
- Peanut Butter, Milk Chocolate Gianduja, Peanut Parfait
- Chocolate Tart, Dulce De Leche Ice Cream

Siena

Contemporary XX

B3

875 Bordeaux Way (at Napa Valley Corporate Dr.), Napa

Phone: 707-259-0633 Lunch & dinner daily
Web: www.themeritagehotel.com
Prices: $$$

Couched inside The Meritage Resort at Napa (at the crossroads of highways 29 and 221), Siena takes its name and the inspiration for its interior design from the stunning Tuscan city. The open kitchen acts as a focal point in the dining room, where framed photographs and colorful hanging banners recall Il Palio (the celebrated horse race that takes place annually in Siena).

Wine Country travelers happily recount their day over a complimentary glass of sparking wine and contemporary American entrées such as herb-roasted Alaskan halibut served with roasted corn and fava bean succotash, or Niman Ranch lamb osso buco accompanied by mascarpone mashed potatoes. For dessert, a white nectarine crostada tastes deliciously sweet and tangy.

Solbar

Californian X

A1

755 Siverado Trail (at Rosedale Rd.), Calistoga

Phone: 707-226-0800 Lunch & dinner daily
Web: www.solagecalistoga.com
Prices: $$$

No need to stay at Solage Resort and Spa to indulge in the spirited dishes at this refined yet casual restaurant. Solbar is open to the public, but expect to see resort guests relaxing at neighboring tables, wrapped in their terrycloth robes.

Their spa cuisine nourishes with light, healthy fare, such as hot and cold endive salad with avocado, tarragon, and ruby red grapefruit. Heartier appetites can indulge in buttermilk fried green tomatoes with Dungeness crab and Creole remoulade; or Hereford flatiron steak with blue cheese potato croquettes.

The airy, loft-like space fosters a tranquil feel with rustic, polished wood tables and huge windows flanked by sage velvet curtains. Outside, the palm and olive tree-lined terrace completes the serene mood.

Taylor's Automatic Refresher

C1 American

933 Main St. (at Charter Oak Ave.), St. Helena

Phone: 707-963-3486 Lunch & dinner daily
Web: www.taylorsrefresher.com
Prices: ⓈⓈ

This St. Helena stalwart, opened in 1949, was here long before anyone came to Napa Valley for the wine. A piece of American pop culture, Taylor's was remodeled in 1999 but it still looks the part of the classic roadside drive-in.

A trip to Taylor's provides a welcome break from the valley's haute cuisine. Here you'll find no fancy fare; basic burgers (including an Ahi tuna version), garlic fries and hot dogs are menu mainstays. You can get wine at Taylor's, but you might find a thick chocolate milkshake a more satisfying accompaniment. Bring the family and enjoy a casual meal at one of the umbrella-shaded picnic tables.

Taylor's younger sibling in San Francisco's Ferry Building features the same menu and enjoys a following of its own, but the newest location in Napa is at the Oxbow Public Market.

Tra Vigne

C1-2 Italian 

1050 Charter Oak Ave. (off Hwy. 29), St. Helena

Phone: 707-963-4444 Lunch & dinner daily
Web: www.travignerestaurant.com
Prices: $$$

On the south side of St. Helena, this vine-covered complex styles itself after an Italian village. Tra Vigne, the fine-dining gem of the collection, enfolds diners in a soft gray room decorated with contemporary artwork and chocolate-brown leather booths. A menu revamp now spotlights the likes of handmade rigatoni alla carbonara (with guanciale bacon and organic eggs), smoked and braised beef short ribs with soft polenta, and wood-oven-roasted Dungeness crab.

If you're not up for a big meal, stop by the Cantinetta for antipasti or panini, washed down with a host of wines by the glass. Or you can sit in the lovely brick courtyard—a coveted spot in warm weather—and snack on a crisp-crusted pie fresh from the handmade brick oven at the Pizzeria.

Terra ✿

C1 — Contemporary XX

1345 Railroad Ave. (bet. Adams & Hunt Sts.), St. Helena

Phone: 707-963-8931 — Wed – Mon dinner only
Web: www.terrarestaurant.com
Prices: $$$

Hiro Sone

Housed in a late 19th century historical foundry off of Main Street in St. Helena, Terra's exterior is all arched windows and old stone walls. Inside, two cozy rooms sport lofty, wood-beamed ceilings, red smoke tiles, and cozy little tables, giving Terra a lovely rustic ambience. Locals and tourists alike pour in nightly for co-owner and chef, Hiro Sone's, creative, globe-trotting fusion fare like foie gras tortellini and Alaskan black cod. His Japanese touch is deliciously evident, but once you enter the domain of his pastry-chef wife and partner, Lissa Doumani, the only dominating factor is sugary bliss. Dip your fork into a warm, crusty rhubarb pie, served over a gorgeous swirl of strawberry and vanilla sauce, and sided with smooth vanilla ice cream.

Don't miss the wine list, which pays homage to the local artisanal scene from Dry Creek, Alexander Valley, and the Russian River Valley.

Appetizers

- Foie Gras Tortelloni in Game Jus with Winter Black Truffles
- Panko-crusted Miyagi Oysters, Pork Belly "Kakuni," Black Vinegar Sauce
- Panzanella with Burrata

Entrées

- Grilled Duck Breast, Nettle Cavatelli , Duck "Sugo"
- Lamb Chops, Puntarella, Cauliflower Fritters
- Sake-marinated Black Cod, Shrimp Dumplings in Shiso Broth

Desserts

- Chocolate Bread Pudding with Sundried Cherries and Crème Fraiche
- Eureka Lemon Cake with Meyer Lemon Ice Cream and Huckleberry Sauce

25° Brix

Californian

B2

7377 St. Helena Hwy. (at Washington St.), Yountville

Phone: 707-944-2749 — Lunch & dinner daily
Web: www.25degreesbrix.com
Prices: $$$

A new contender in the farm-to-table movement appears with the sleek, beautifully redesigned 25° Brix. The refreshed digs, owned by the Kelleher family, take over where the old Brix left off—with every intention of utilizing the 16 acres of fertile wine land it calls home. Executive Chef Carlos Cañada takes the wheel in the kitchen, spinning out fresh California garden cuisine with bright, seasonal produce doing most of the leg work on a rotating menu that might include grilled prawns with corn custard; avocado mousse and cilantro crème fraîche; or an Alaskan halibut with pea ravioli and baby squash-Parmesan broth.

The restaurant has several private dining options, including a reserve wine cellar and a gorgeous patio overlooking the vegetable gardens.

Ubuntu

Vegetarian

A3

1140 Main St. (bet. 1st & Pearl Sts.), Napa

Phone: 707-251-5656 — Mon – Thu dinner only
Web: www.ubuntunapa.com — Fri – Sun lunch & dinner
Prices: $$$

Ubuntu combines a restaurant and upstairs yoga studio; but diners are only meditating on Chef Jeremy Fox's (formerly of Manresa) thoughtful organic vegetarian dishes. Omnivores and herbivores alike are satisfied by the mélange of roasted, puréed, and raw cauliflower cooked with Indian *vadouvan* spice, presented in a mini cast-iron pot with toasted croutons; or marinated ruby iceplant beets laid atop a pool of Asian pear purée.

In keeping with the Zulu concept from which the restaurant takes its name (which translates to "humanity towards others"), the chef and his wife, Pastry Chef Deanie Fox, harvest farm-fresh produce daily from their biodynamic gardens.

Wappo Bar Bistro

International

A1

1226 Washington St. (at Lincoln Ave.), Calistoga

Phone: 707-942-4712 Lunch & dinner daily
Web: www.wappobar.com
Prices: $$

Follow Highway 29 to the north end of Napa Valley and you'll come to Calistoga, famed for the healing properties of its mineral-rich mud. Before you take that mud bath, though, head for this wine bar and bistro.

"Eclectic" is the best way to categorize Wappo's globe-trotting cuisine, which roams from India to Thailand, Brazil to Singapore, skirts the Mediterranean and ends up back in California. It's challenging to keep up with all these different flavors, but the kitchen in this redwood-lined dining space manages it well. Products are well selected and the execution is serious for such dishes as tandoori chicken, Thai coconut curry with prawns, and *vatapa* (Brazilian seafood stew).

Try to snag a table on the adorable patio.

Wine Spectator Greystone

Californian

A1

2555 Main St. (at Deer Park Rd.), St. Helena

Phone: 707-967-1010 Lunch & dinner daily
Web: www.ciachef.edu
Prices: $$$

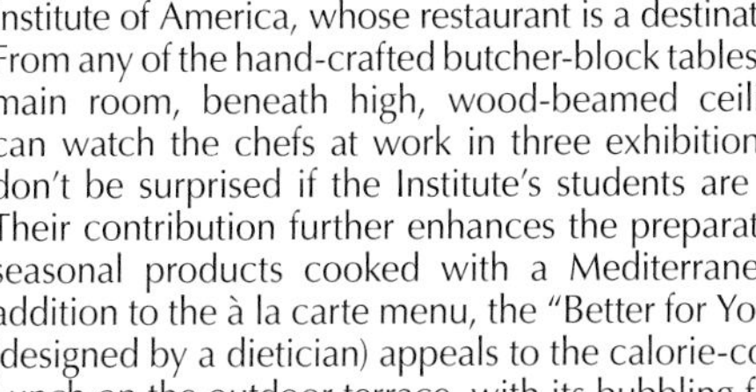

Inside this imposing stone chateau (built in 1889 as Greystone Cellars winery) is the West Coast campus of the Culinary Institute of America, whose restaurant is a destination in itself. From any of the hand-crafted butcher-block tables in the rustic main room, beneath high, wood-beamed ceilings, guests can watch the chefs at work in three exhibition kitchens—don't be surprised if the Institute's students are pitching in. Their contribution further enhances the preparation of local seasonal products cooked with a Mediterranean spin. In addition to the à la carte menu, the "Better for You" selection (designed by a dietician) appeals to the calorie-conscious.

Lunch on the outdoor terrace, with its bubbling fountain and vineyard view, is a Wine Country classic.

Zinsvalley

Californian

B3

3253 Browns Valley Rd. (bet. Austin & Larkin Ways), Napa

Phone: 707-224-0695 — Mon – Fri lunch & dinner
Web: www.zinsvalley.com — Sat dinner only
Prices: $$

Set within a strip mall on the West side of Highway 29, Zinsvalley attracts a clientele of largely locals, owing to its location slightly off the beaten path. The small dining room wears a rustic look, with wood beams, plank flooring and a brick fireplace. Outside, the shady patio overlooks a creek and provides a pleasant respite on a warm, sunny day.

If you're in a hurry at noon, the Fast Lunch option includes a half-sandwich, soup and salad for one low price. At lunch or dinner, creative Californian cuisine embraces the season with such dishes as a crispy Dungeness crab cake sandwich with citrus aïoli, or a lamb sirloin plated with ratatouille "hash."

Of the two wine lists, one cites only Zinfandels; as an added benefit, there's no corkage fee.

Zuzu

Spanish

A3

829 Main St. (bet. 2nd & 3rd Sts.), Napa

Phone: 707-224-8555 — Mon – Fri lunch & dinner
Web: www.zuzunapa.com — Sat – Sun dinner only
Prices: ⊜

One of the few tapas bars in the Valley, Zuzu was serving small plates before the fad reached its current level of trendiness. The varied fare featuring tastes of Spain, Portugal, and elsewhere in the Mediterranean makes this a great place to go with a group. Sharing dishes in the casual environment is de rigueur, and a good way to save a few dollars. At $14, Moroccan barbecue-glazed rack of lamb with mint and curry oil stands at the high end of the price spectrum, while *boquerones* with white anchovies, hard-boiled egg, and remoulade on grilled bread ring up at only $6.

Zuzu is open later than most downtown Napa restaurants, so you can go to grab a late-night nosh, sway to the beat of the Latin music, and hang out in the well-stocked wine bar.

Sonoma County

Bordering Marin County on the north and located a short trip (traffic permitting) 50 miles northeast of San Francisco, Sonoma County claims 76 miles of Pacific coastline. The picturesque and scenic landscapes here have served as film locations for Hollywood classics like *The Birds, American Graffiti*, and *Peggy Sue Got Married*, among many others. More famously, the area is home to 250 wineries that boast some of the best grape-growing conditions in California. Thirteen distinct wine appellations (AVAs) have been assigned in the county, where vintners produce a dizzying array of wines in an area slightly larger than the State of Rhode Island. Along Highway 12, heading north from the town

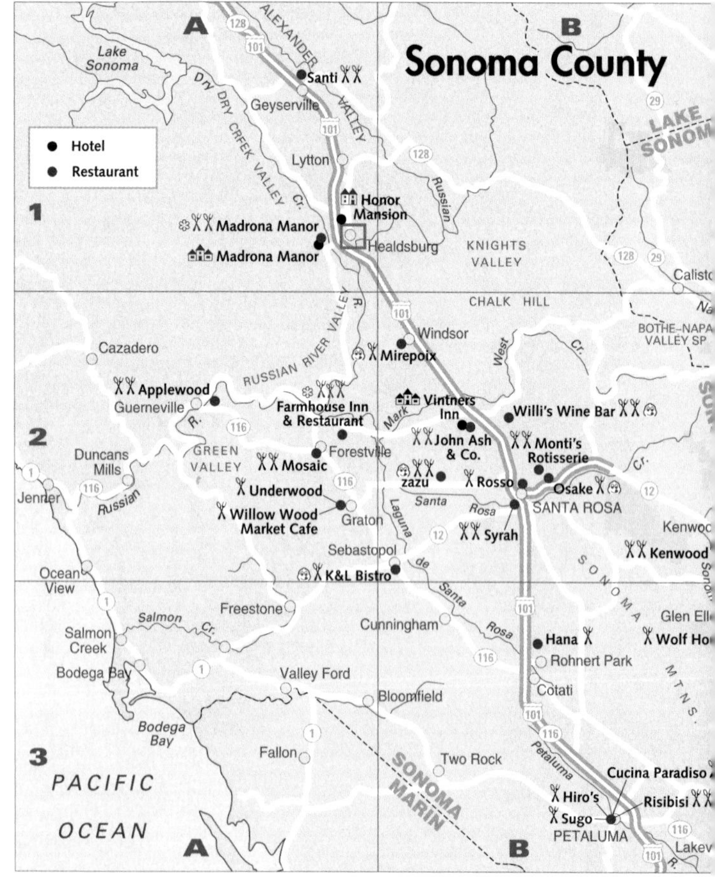

of Sonoma through Santa Rosa to Healdsburg, byroads lead to out-of-the-way wineries, each of which puts its own unique stamp on the business of winemaking.

VITICULTURAL VALLEYS

The **Russian River Valley** edges the river named for the early Russian trading outposts that were set up along the coast. This is one of the coolest growing regions in Sonoma, thanks to the river basin that offers a conduit for cool coastal air. Elegant Pinot Noir and Chardonnay headline here, but Syrah is quickly catching up. At the upper end of the Russian River, the **Dry Creek Valley** yields excellent Sauvignon Blanc, Chardonnay, and Pinot Noir. This region is also justly famous for its Zinfandel, a grape that does especially well in the valley's rock-strewn soil. Winery visits in Dry Creek are a study in contrasts. Palatial modern wineries rise up along the same rural roads that have been home to independents for generations,

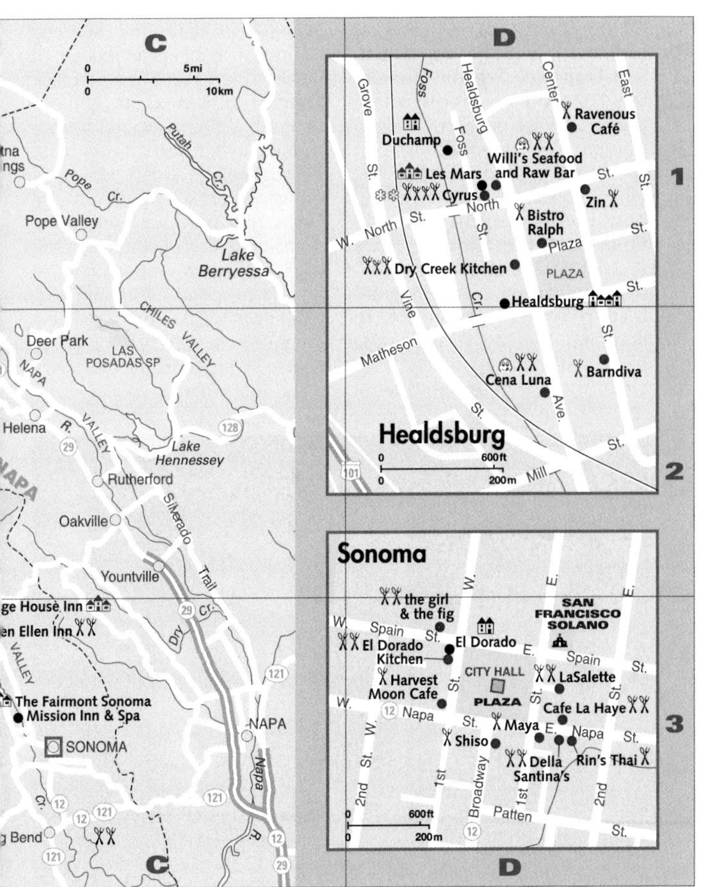

and young grapevines trained into laser-straightened rows are broken up by the dark, gnarled fingers of old vines.

Sonoma County's inlandmost AVAs are **Knights Valley** and **Alexander Valley**, the latter named for Cyrus Alexander who planted the area's first vineyard in 1846, is also an area along the Russian River perfectly suited for canoeing. These two warm regions both highlight Cabernet Sauvignon.

Nestled between the Mayacamas and Sonoma ranges, the 17-mile-long **Sonoma Valley** dominates the southern portion of the county. At its center is the town of **Sonoma**, site of **San Francisco Solano Mission**, the last and northernmost of California's 21 missions along *El Camino Real*, founded in 1823 and once included a thriving vineyard before secularization and incorporation into the **Sonoma State Historic Park** system 102 years ago, when the vines were uprooted and transplanted elsewhere in Sonoma. The town's eight-acre plaza is still surrounded by 19th-century adobe buildings, most of them now occupied by shops, restaurants, and inns.

Just below Sonoma lies a portion of the **Carneros** district, named for the herds of sheep (*carneros* in Spanish) that once roamed its hillsides. Carneros is best known for its cool-climate grapes, notably Pinot Noir and Chardonnay.

WAY BEYOND WINE

There's history in these hills. Northern California's first premium winery, **Buena Vista**, was established just outside the town of Sonoma in 1857 by Agoston Haraszthy. Sonoma County also bears evidence of historic figures such as writer Jack London and Mexican general Mariano Vallejo, whose former homes are open to visitors. Throughout the county, vineyards rub shoulders with orchards and farms that produce everything from apples and olives, to organic eggs and artisan-crafted cheeses. Be sure to spend some time here foraging at local farmers' markets for picnic supplies—to pair, of course, with some of the area's wonderful wines.

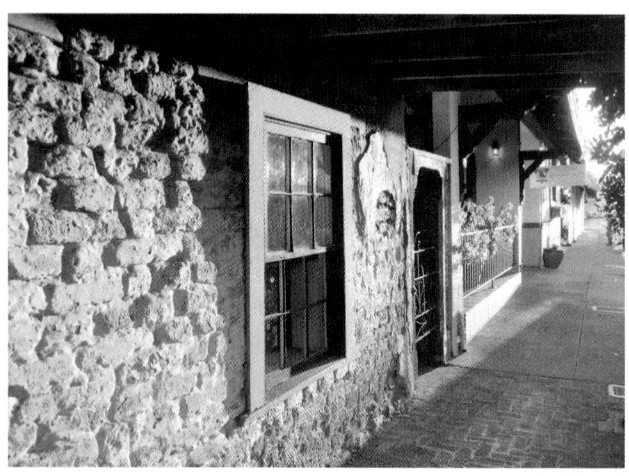

Peter L. Wrenn/MICHELIN

Applewood

Californian XX

A2

13555 Hwy. 116, Guerneville

Phone: 707-869-9093 — Tue – Sat dinner only
Web: www.applewoodinn.com
Prices: $$$

A romantic Wine Country weekend awaits visitors to the Applewood Inn, located on winding Highway 116. A mile from Guerneville, this tile-roofed B&B sits on a knoll surrounded by manicured gardens and orchards. Dinner guests are welcome at the inn's barn-like restaurant, warmed by soaring stone fireplaces set at either end of the room. An enclosed sun porch affords lovely views of the woodsy environs.

California sensibilities marry French and Italian flair in the cuisine of Chef Bruce Frieseke, whose talent speaks for itself in the likes of a fennel-crusted Ahi tuna loin nesting on a bed of fava beans, with cilantro blossoms scattered on top.

Call to reserve one of the inn's 19 rooms if you plan to partake in the liquid assets of the Wine Country.

Barndiva

Contemporary X

D2

231 Center St. (bet. Matheson & Mills Sts.), Healdsburg

Phone: 707-431-0100 — Thu – Sun lunch & dinner
Web: www.barndiva.com — Wed dinner only
Prices: $$$

Despite the name, you'll find no prima donnas here. Instead, a block off Healdsburg's square, Jil and Geoffrey Hales' soaring mahogany barn houses a chic urban boîte with a pastoral soul. Vivid artwork and funky wire sculptures of fish and game cling to the white walls inside. If it's sunny, go straight for the garden terrace, where raked sand and manicured flora beget the feel of a posh country club—*sans* the attitude or dues.

The seasons inspire eclectic dishes that look to local purveyors and food artisans for their ingredients. Dessert adds a graceful ending with such creative contemporary confections as a lemon-black pepper angel food cake with blood orange gelée.

The beauty of this place motivates many couples to hold their nuptials here.

Bistro Ralph

Californian

D1

109 Plaza St. (bet. Center St. & Healdsburg Ave.), Healdsburg

Phone: 707-433-1380 — Mon - Sat lunch & dinner
Web: www.bistroralph.com
Prices: $$

California cuisine laced with French influences triumph at Chef Ralph Tingle's laid-back bistro, set just off Healdsburg's shady central plaza. Menus are concise and seasonal. Lunch may feature a smoked salmon BLT on toasted sourdough, or a plate of chicken livers with caramelized onions and fried polenta. Dinner entrées may pair Liberty Farm duck confit with figs and balsamic sauce, or grilled wild salmon with chanterelles and creamed corn. Complete your meal with a selection from their mostly local wine list.

The dining room, with its tall whitewashed brick walls, teems day and night with locals and tourists. Take some time before or after a meal to explore the elegant shops and winery tasting rooms that surround the plaza.

Cafe La Haye

Californian

D3

140 E. Napa St. (bet. 1st & 2nd Sts.), Sonoma

Phone: 707-935-5994 — Tue – Sat dinner only
Web: www.cafelahaye.com
Prices: $$

A Sonoma favorite since Saul Gropman opened it in 1996, Cafe La Haye maintains an artsy spirit in its quaint and comfortable space. Exhibits of work by local artists grace the walls of the soft yellow dining room in this two-story house off Sonoma's square. Here happy diners crowd the little white-butcher-paper-covered tables or hobnob with the chefs at the counter facing the tiny open kitchen.

Local and seasonal are the watchwords for the cafe's dishes, which showcase California savoir faire coupled with a down-home sensibility. Expect the likes of baked almond-crusted goat cheese, grilled Arctic char accompanied by mashed potatoes and tender asparagus, and Wolfe Ranch quail served over olive quinoa to titillate your taste buds.

Cena Luna

Italian XX

D2

241 Healdsburg Ave. (bet. Matheson & Mill Sts.), Healdsburg

Phone: 707-433-6000 — Mon – Sat dinner only
Web: www.cenaluna.com
Prices: $$

This family-run Northern Italian eatery is warm and welcoming in all the right ways. Set just off the main square in Healdsburg, Cena Luna (which translates to "dinner moon" in Italian) is the brainchild of co-owners and chefs, Yvette Peline-Hom and Stuart Hom. Together, they've put together a delicious menu, minus the wine country pretension.

Colorful salads filled with roasted beets, oranges, and goat cheese get things started—but save room for one of the house made pastas, where you might come across tender pockets of veal and duck ravioli; or a soft tangle of chicken and prosciutto fettuccini, laced with preserved lemon and fresh mozzarella. For dinner, try the chicken stuffed with prosciutto and *crescenza*, or roast duck with mascarpone.

Cucina Paradiso

Italian X

B3

56 E. Washington St., Petaluma

Phone: 707-782-1130 — Mon – Sat lunch & dinner
Web: www.cucinaparadisopetaluma.com
Prices:

A local favorite cached away in the Golden Eagle Shopping Center, Cucina Paradiso livens its strip-mall space with opera music, terra-cotta-colored walls and artwork from a local gallery. Husband-and-wife team Dennis (he's the chef) and Malena Hernandez opened this place in 1998, and since then Petaluma residents have been touting the restaurant for its tasty Italian cuisine and gracious service.

Much-requested grilled calamari salad shares menu space with other popular picks such as homemade ravioli filled with roasted duck in a sauce marrying sun-dried tomatoes, basil and pine nuts; roasted breast of Petaluma duck glazed with balsamic vinegar; and last, but far from least, classic tiramisu. And it all comes at prices that won't break your budget.

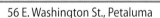

Cyrus ✿✿

Contemporary

D1

29 North St. (bet. Foss St. & Healdsburg Ave.), Healdsburg

Phone: 707-433-3311 Dinner daily
Web: www.cyrusrestaurant.com
Prices: $$$$

Cyrus/Andy Katz

Just off the posh Les Mars Hotel lobby, Cyrus lets you know its brand of pedigree right away. There's the seamless service that starts the moment you enter the door; and the space itself, with its cloistered ceilings, curving banquettes, and wooden armoires. Then there's the caviar and champagne cart gently wheeled your way—and did we mention jackets are favored?

The food is worth it. You can piece together a prix-fixe menu from different options, or put yourself in Chef Douglas Keane's very capable hands with his nightly tasting menu. Dinner might begin with a perfectly-seared single scallop atop a large quenelle of savory lentils, shot with cream reduction, and a black olive puree pocked with juicy blood orange. For garnish, a delicate lobe of sea urchin roe is draped over an orange supreme. And that's just the appetizer. Keep a lookout for Cyrus' new bakery next door.

Appetizers

- "Gazpacho" with Fluke Sashimi and Basil
- Summer Squash with Hijiki Noodles, Miso Stuffed Blossom and Sea Stock
- Roasted Porcini Risotto with Parmesan Broth

Entrées

- Scallop, Uni and Olive, Cara Cara Reduction
- Crispy Poussin, Potato Purée, Haricots Verts, Morels
- Veal Loin, Rösti Potatoes, Sweetbreads "Grand Mere"

Desserts

- Tart 'N Tangy Theme
- Flowers Theme
- Carnival Theme

Della Santina's

Italian XX

D3

133 E. Napa St. (bet. 1st & 2nd Sts.), Sonoma

Phone: 707-935-0576 — Lunch & dinner daily
Web: www.dellasantinas.com
Prices: $$

This cozy little Italian dining room exudes hominess, with family photographs and framed lace napkins adorning the walls, and rustic Tuscan dishes that keep fans returning. A sprawling back patio is equipped with heaters and canopies to accommodate alfresco dining on cool days.

The kitchen offers a variety of spit-roasted meats, including duck, chicken, pork, and rabbit; as well as pastas like fresh pappardelle in a hearty rabbit ragù; lasagna Bolognese; or linguini with pesto. Both the *gnocchi della nonna* and the veal *della casa* change daily, and a set four-course dinner delivers good value. The Californian-Italian wine list covers all the bases from A to Z, starting with Amarone from the Veneto region to Sonoma Zinfandel.

Dry Creek Kitchen

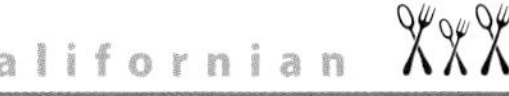

Californian XXX

D1

317 Healdsburg Ave. (bet. Matheson & Plaza Sts.), Healdsburg

Phone: 707-431-0330 — Mon – Thu dinner only
Web: www.charliepalmer.com — Fri – Sun lunch & dinner
Prices: $$$

Located in the Hotel Healdsburg *(see hotel listing)*, Dry Creek Kitchen borders the town's historic plaza. The restaurant, another notch in the belt of the Charlie Palmer Group, boasts an elegant dining space that echoes the colors of the vineyards. Many of the well-spaced tables here peer out onto the plaza through large windows in the front.

Palmer's menu favors meats, cheeses and seasonal produce from local purveyors—even the wine list gathers only Sonoma County vintages. While an à la carte menu offers the likes of Idaho red rainbow trout with a ragoût of braised greens; or spice-crusted Sonoma duck breast with local fava-bean "cassoulet," another way to experience the cuisine here is to go for the chef's multicourse tasting.

El Dorado Kitchen

Californian XX

D3

405 1st St. W. (at W. Spain St.), Sonoma

Phone: 707-996-3030 Lunch & dinner daily
Web: www.eldoradosonoma.com
Prices: $$

Brought to you by the proprietors of Auberge du Soleil in Rutherford, El Dorado Kitchen premiered in June 2005 inside the El Dorado Hotel *(see hotel listing)* on Sonoma's plaza. Country-casual meets contemporary-chic in the large, airy dining space, where whitewashed walls contrast with dark woods. The room's focal point is a communal table fashioned from a single slab of 200-year-old wood.

Executive Chef Justin Everett distills the essence of seasonal products in what he bills as superb contemporary California cuisine. His enticing menu is just as likely to feature an albacore tuna Niçoise tartine for lunch as it might Niman Ranch pork osso buco at dinner. On a warm evening, the stone courtyard sets the scene for an intimate tête-à-tête.

Glen Ellen Inn

Californian XX

C3

13670 Arnold Dr. (at Warm Springs Rd.), Glen Ellen

Phone: 707-996-6409 Fri – Tue lunch & dinner
Web: www.glenelleninn.com Wed – Thu dinner only
Prices: $$

For a romantic getaway, head for the hamlet of Glen Ellen. The secluded Glen Ellen Inn promotes serenity with a cozy fireplace on the enclosed porch and a trickling waterfall in the back garden. Inside, tones of gold, green and burgundy prevail, and homemade biscuits and focaccia get your meal off to a tasty start.

Oysters and designer martinis are a big draw. The former come fire-grilled, crispy fried, or raw on the halfshell. But don't stop there. Artichoke and stilton ravioli, or Sonoma duck with orange-ginger glaze and soba noodles satisfy as entrées. And don't overlook the seasonal desserts; the likes of spiced pumpkin baked Alaska make a sweet ending indeed. Can't bear to leave? Book one of the six "Secret Cottages" set alongside a burbling creek.

Farmhouse Inn & Restaurant ✿

Californian 

A2

7871 River Rd. (at Wohler Rd.), Forestville

Phone: 707-887-3300 Thu – Mon dinner only
Web: www.farmhouseinn.com
Prices: $$$

The Farmhouse Inn & Restaurant/Andy Katz

Wind your way through the Russian River Valley's curving River Road, with its rolling green hills and soaring Redwood trees, and eventually you'll stumble upon an adorable little cluster of pale yellow clapboard buildings. This little hideaway is the Farmhouse Inn—a collection of cottages and home to Chef Steve Litke's acclaimed restaurant.

Drawing on local, market-fresh ingredients, Litke fashions his Californian menu to the season—but might include a fresh, roasted sea bass, dancing in a light champagne butter sauce, and served over whipped potatoes, woodsy morel mushrooms, fava beans, and bright peas; or a velvety starter of delicate bison carpaccio, drizzled with a fruity olive oil and dusted with coarse sea salt, and served with shaved porcini mushrooms, edible wild flowers, and micro-greens.

Don't miss the excellent Sonoma-heavy wine list, fat with local varietals.

Appetizers

- Asparagus and Potato Salad, Truffled Araucana Egg
- Fava Leaf Lasagnette, Serrano Ham, Parmesan Fonduta
- Sautéed Foie Gras, Pineapple Confit, Brioche

Entrées

- Chicken "Sotto Mattone," Preserved Lemon-Olive Salsa
- Rabbit : Bacon-wrapped Loin, Roasted Rack, Confit of Leg
- Black Olive Rosemary Salt-crusted Lamb

Desserts

- Pistachio Crème Brûlée, Lemon Pistachio Biscotti
- Michel Cluizel Chocolate Soufflé, Bourbon Crème Anglaise
- Meyer Lemon Olive Oil Cake

Hana

Japanese

B3

101 Golf Course Dr. (at Roberts Lake Rd.), Rohnert Park

Phone: 707-586-0270 — Tue – Sat lunch & dinner
Web: www.hanajapanese.com — Sun dinner only
Prices: $$

Double Tree Plaza, off Highway 101 in Rohnert Park, may not be the most glamorous location, but connoisseurs from near and far know to come here for some of the area's best sushi. The menu offers impeccable freshness, value for money, and good selection, ranging across udon and soba noodle dishes to *nigiri* sushi and rolls to bento box combinations. Main courses also deserve attention, like *yakitori don*, flavorful chicken meatballs and grilled chicken breast served in a bowl of steamed rice, sparked by red wine teriyaki sauce.

Although Chef Ken Tominaga splits his time between Hana and his St. Helena restaurant, Go Fish, any of the jovial sushi chefs will regale you with humorous anecdotes while preparing your meal.

Harvest Moon Cafe

Californian

D3

487 1st St. W. (bet. Napa & Spain Sts.), Sonoma

Phone: 707-933-8160 — Dinner daily
Web: www.harvestmoonsonoma.com
Prices: $$

A relaxed feel and light-hearted approach have put this little family-run place on Sonoma's culinary map. Husband-and-wife team Nick and Jen Demarest's respect for locally grown produce is evident in the handful of appetizers and entrées that comprise the daily changing menu of Californian cuisine. Cooked with care and creativity, the food here is homey and comforting. Tastes of the Mediterranean enliven the likes of a simple yet impressive rainbow of heirloom beets paired with leeks and sautéed shrimp, or Moroccan-style braised lamb alongside spiced carrots, couscous, *harissa*, and *charmoula*.

Set on Sonoma's historic plaza, the serpentine dining space seats about 40 people and is augmented by a large garden patio furnished with tiny red metal tables.

Hiro's

B3 — Japanese

107 Petaluma Blvd. (bet. Washington St. & Western Ave.), Petaluma

Phone: 707-763-2300 — Lunch & dinner daily
Web: www.hirosrestaurant.com
Prices: $$

Japanese businessman Hiro Yamamoto came to Sonoma County from Japan in 1988, fell in love with the quality of life here, and the rest is history in the making. Set in the heart of downtown Petaluma, Hiro's restaurant serves some of the freshest sushi around.

Sushi and sashimi are plated to please the eye, and innovative maki rolls are presented with a twist (as in a Dynamite roll done with salmon and fresh crab salad baked over a California roll with a creamy piquant sauce). If you don't see a roll you like on the menu, the sushi chefs will customize one for you. Many nights, Hiro himself works the floor, seeing to the satisfaction of his guests. Unique wood-block prints by Naoki Takenouchi add an artistic element to the room's casual studio feel.

John Ash & Co.

B2 — Californian

4330 Barnes Rd. (at River Rd.), Santa Rosa

Phone: 707-527-7687 — Dinner daily
Web: www.vintnersinn.com
Prices: $$$

A true California wine country retreat, John Ash & Co. is part of the Vintner's Inn on the north side of Santa Rosa. Launched by Chef John Ash in 1987, the rustic restaurant's earth-colored walls, wooden beams, and wrought-iron chandeliers lend the feel of a Tuscan country house. Its location, amid the vines of the Ferrari-Carano vineyard, adds to this illusion.

The Executive Quick Lunch selections, featuring a cup of soup, small salad, and sandwich, are designed as a quick, delicious bargain. Those wishing to linger among the grapevines can relish the trellis-shaded patio while enjoying the likes of savory squash soup with pumpkin-seed pesto, or a salmon fillet layered with pancetta, avocado and basil pesto aïoli on foccacia.

Kenwood

International

9900 Hwy. 12 (at Warm Springs Blvd.), Kenwood

Phone: 707-833-6326 Wed – Sun lunch & dinner
Web: www.kenwoodrestaurant.com
Prices: $$

Both locals and wine trail travelers (Highway 12 from Sonoma to Santa Rosa) trust Kenwood to dish up country charm with a side of urban sophistication. The bright spacious interior is divided into three distinct areas, including a bar and a private dining room. In the main room, French doors open onto a vineyard landscape bounded by the Sugarloaf Mountains.

Not content to confine itself to one continent, the menu roams from Asia to Europe and back to North America. This may translate into escargots with parsley butter, veal piccata with artichokes atop porcini ravioli, and crisp, rich duck spring rolls with mango salad and tangy ponzu sauce.

A relative rarity in Wine Country, Kenwood's courteous service, atmosphere, and menu are all kid-friendly.

K & L Bistro

French 

119 South Main St. (bet. Burnett St. and Hwy. 12), Sebastopol

Phone: 707-823-6614 Mon – Sat lunch & dinner
Web: www.kandlbistro.com
Prices: $$

The K and L stand for Karen and Lucas Martin—the husband-and-wife team who own this little French bistro. You should get to know their names, because come here often enough and they'll very likely get to know yours. It's that kind of cozy, neighborhood place, where red brick walls display the work of local artists, and where the day's desserts and wines are scrolled on a blackboard.

The menu is a casual French affair laced with a few American staples. But the care and attention given to the food is obvious. A tender asparagus salad with brown butter is paired with thin slices of Parmesan, and a perfectly-poached egg. A filet of Petrale sole is sautéed in a dust of flour with parsley and butter, meuniere style, and sided with a stack of crispy frites.

LaSalette

Portuguese XX

D3

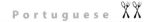

452-H 1st St. E. (bet. Napa & Spain Sts.), Sonoma

Phone: 707-938-1927 — Lunch & dinner daily
Web: www.lasalette-restaurant.com
Prices: $$

Mustard-colored walls and dark wood columns inside this quaint little place direct your attention to the wood-burning oven used to do much of the cooking (whole roasted fish is a delicious example). Contemporary Portuguese fare fills the remaining menu with the likes of cod cakes (fried dumplings of salt cod and onion served with cilantro-flavored olive oil) and copper bowls filled with the signature *cataplana de Marisco* (a traditional seafood and white bean stew). Save room for satisfying sweets such as fig cake layered with hazelnut ice cream, topped with crème anglaise and chocolate sauce.
Self-taught Chef Manuel Azevedo named his restaurant after his mother, whose secret recipe is used to make LaSalette's tasty cinnamon and honey-spiked dinner rolls.

Maya

Mexican X

D3

101 E. Napa St. (at 1st St.), Sonoma

Phone: 707-935-3500 — Mon – Sat lunch & dinner
Web: www.mayarestaurant.com — Sun dinner only
Prices: $$

Located on a corner facing Sonoma's historic town square, Maya pays homage to contemporary Mexican food and adds a dash of Californian flair. Flash-fried baby artichokes with tequila cream dipping sauce pave the way for entrées like plantain-crusted sea bass, pan-seared and set on *pasilla*-pesto corn risotto; and *carne asada* tacos made with marinated hanger steak dusted with a Yucatan spice rub and served with fresh pico de gallo.
Of course, the place to start is at the "temple of tequila," as the tiered central bar is called, with a margarita or a shot of premium tequila. Spicy toasted pumpkin seeds make a tasty accompaniment.
Bright hues, exposed stone walls, heavy wood furniture and hammocks hanging from the ceiling give the room character and warmth.

Madrona Manor ✿

Contemporary XX

A1

1001 Westside Rd. (at West Dry Creek Rd.), Healdsburg

Phone: 707-433-4231 Wed – Sun dinner only
Web: www.madronamanor.com
Prices: **$$$**

Lenny Siegel

Old world sophistication is the name of the game at Madrona Manor. Located just off of Healdsburg's downtown area, the romance hits you the second you pull into the magical 8-acre forest that surrounds this 19th century Victorian house. The sweeping garden, designed by Geno Ceccato, is worth a detour alone—and you'll have plenty to walk off if Chef Jesse Mallgren has anything to say about it.

The menu is divided into four whimsical categories—clean and crisp, soft and delicate, smooth, and meaty—and the nightly tasting menus truly come alive when paired with the Sonoma County wine list. You can wander out to the carriage house porch for a drink, or stay put in the lovely dining room with its roaring fireplace, gilt-framed pictures, and dripping chandeliers. Between that and 1930's French music, you'll feel like you've landed in a traditional European guesthouse.

Appetizers

- Oh-Toro "Crudo", Estate Beets, Daikon, Ponzu, Celery Leaf Salad
- Onion Velouté, Banyuls Vinegar, Egg, Parmesan
- Foie Gras Tasting

Entrées

- Skate "Cuit Sous Vide", Nettle Spaetzle, Lobster Brown Butter
- Local Petrale Sole, Potato Purée, Fennel, Watercress Emulsion
- Lamb Loin, Spring Onions, Fava Bean Falafel

Desserts

- Crème Fraîche Panna Cotta, Blackberries, Lavender Sorbet
- Valrhona Chocolate Soufflé, Crème Anglaise
- Cart "à Glace" Ice Cream Sundae Hand "Churned" Tableside

Mirepoix

French

B2

275 Windsor River Rd. (at Honsa Ave.), Windsor

Phone: 707-838-0162 — Tue – Sat lunch & dinner
Web: www.restaurantmirepoix.com
Prices: $$

Between Santa Rosa and Healdsburg, the tiny burg of Windsor embraces the spirit of the medieval French market town of Mirepoix, for which this restaurant is named.

A little brown house, complete with a front porch and umbrella-shaded terrace, holds the 24-seat dining space. Though Chef Matthew Bousquet's presentations appear rustic, this is food that deserves recognition. A double-cut pork loin chop harmonizes deliciously with cooked cabbage that retains a slight acidity from vinegar to balance its subtle sweetness. Atop the meat, a dollop of roasted-apple butter proves a perfect counterpoint to the syrupy cider reduction below. The full menu is served all day, in true bistro-style.

The wine list of smaller, hard-to-find labels changes every few days.

Monti's Rotisserie

American

B2

714 Village Court (bet. Farmer's Ln. & Hardmand Dr.), Santa Rosa

Phone: 707-568-4404 — Lunch & dinner daily
Web: www.montisroti.net
Prices: $$

Hungry shoppers in Santa Rosa's Montgomery Village complex crowd Monti's long, zig-zag, wooden bar to lunch on succulent, mouth-watering meats from the large, wood-burning rotisserie that forms the dining room's focal point amid the eclectic Mediterranean-meets-Southwest décor. Aside from the rotisserie items and grilled entrées, choose from pizza, pasta, raw bar selections, and small plates of Tunisian Dungeness crab "briks" with tomato chutney; or risk the addictive house-made fries tossed with blue cheese and rosemary.

This American bistro is the third sister in a family of restaurants operated by Chef Mark Stark and his wife, Terri. Weather permitting, the spacious, trellis-covered patio makes a great place to take a break from shopping.

Mosaic

Californian

6675 Front St. (at Mirabel Rd.), Forestville

Phone: 707-887-7503 — Lunch & dinner daily
Web: www.mosaiceats.com
Prices: $$

Chef/owner Tai Olesky grew up in Sonoma County, so he's no stranger to the bountiful farms and vineyards whose products star in the Mosaic's locally focused cuisine. The self-taught chef stirs global notes into many of his entrées, as in crispy prawns with a chile-lime glaze, or coffee-crusted filet mignon. At lunch, the humble hamburger is transformed when made from ground beef tenderloin and Italian sausage. Crown it with manchego cheese, watercress, and horseradish mayonnaise and you've got a mouth-watering masterpiece.

The painted-brick building sits on the main drag in sleepy Forestville. A rustic canvas, the interior incorporates glazed concrete floors and velvet drapes. Out back, the trellised garden patio invites repose any time of day.

Osake

Japanese 

B2

2446 Patio Ct. (at Farmer's Ln.), Santa Rosa

Phone: 707-542-8282 — Mon – Fri lunch & dinner
Web: www.garychus.com — Sat dinner only
Prices: ⚭

Located at the end of the Montgomery Village outdoor mall, this spacious restaurant satisfies shoppers and other locals with a good variety of tasty Japanese dishes amid a sleek, minimalist, gray and black décor.

Count on Chef/owner Gary Chu's artful presentation to spark your appetite and his scrumptious food to seal the deal. On the generous menu, octopus carpaccio drizzled with olive oil and warmed with cayenne pepper; mushrooms stuffed with crab and avocado breaded in panko and crispy fried; or bright, tender, grilled giant calamari with soy-honey ginger sauce provide a respite from sushi and nigiri. At lunch and dinner, fairly priced Bento box combinations, offering a range of delicate and refreshing flavors, are available with sake pairings.

Ravenous Café

Californian

D1

420 Center St. (bet. North & Piper Sts.), Healdsburg

Phone: 707-431-1302 — Wed – Sun lunch & dinner
Web: N/A
Prices: $$

Husband-and-wife chef team Joyanne and John Pezzolo found bigger digs for their little cafe across the street from its original location, a couple of blocks from Healdsburg's historic plaza next to the Raven Theater. In this case, "bigger" is relative, since the tiny restaurant still only has a smattering of tables.
Even so, locals love this homey place where the menu is elegantly handwritten every day and they can count on the fresh Californian cuisine to be interpreted with a rustic touch. Who could pass up the likes of sautéed Arctic char cakes served with ginger, lemon and cilantro aïoli, or the Ravenous burger cooked just the way you like it?
If you expect you'll be ravenous when you arrive, be sure you make a reservation in advance.

Rin's Thai

Thai

D3

139 E. Napa St. (bet. 1st & 2nd Sts.), Sonoma

Phone: 707-938-1462 — Lunch & dinner daily
Web: www.rinsthai.com
Prices:

Warm hospitality engulfs you upon entering this quaint family-run place just off Old Sonoma Plaza. Bright yellow walls are hung with wooden carvings and colorful ceremonial masks under a high-pitched ceiling, and one of the owners is always on hand to make sure guests are handled with care.
Moderately priced dishes blend California products in nimble preparations with sauces that complement rather than dominate. Be sure to try the pleasantly plump "puffys," fried wontons stuffed with chicken, onion, and potato that have been simmered in yellow curry.
Flavorful food, coupled with the intimate ambience in this charming Victorian cottage make for an ideal first date; the place is sure to linger in your memory, even if the relationship does not.

Risibisi

B3 Italian

154 Petaluma Blvd. N. (bet. Washington St. & Western Ave.), Petaluma

Phone: 707-766-7600 Mon – Fri lunch & dinner
Web: www.risibisirestaurant.com Sat – Sun dinner only
Prices: $$

Although founding chef and partner Fabio Flagiello departed from this place in early 2008, the kitchen hasn't missed a beat in his absence. Remaining owner, Marco Palmieri—who hails from the Adriatic seaport of Trieste, Italy—ensures for now that the cuisine Flagiello inspired remains. Northern Italian recipes are interpreted with California freshness in the likes of a rustic pumpkin ravioli with Swiss chard and sage brown butter; and *pollo Boscaiola*—a moist, pan-roasted Fulton Farms chicken accompanied by sautéed crimini mushrooms, watercress, grilled potatoes, and zucchini. The restaurant's namesake *risi e bisi*, a Venetian risotto dish, changes daily.
Soothing eclectic music complements the colorful abstract paintings that line the sunny-hued walls.

Rosso

B2 Pizza

53 Montgomery Dr. (at 3rd St.), Santa Rosa

Phone: 707-544-3221 Lunch & dinner daily
Web: www.pizzeriarosso.com
Prices: $$

Fans of soccer and thin-crust pizza, rejoice: the flat-screen TV over Rosso's bar is broadcasting a match, and pizzas are emerging from the wood-burning oven. Since Rosso supports local farms and sustainable agriculture, blistered-crust pies are crowned with ingredients sourced within 100 miles, whenever possible.
Pizzas come with red or white bases, and range from the red "Goomba" topped with hand-crafted meatballs and spaghetti, to the "Funghi" of taleggio and fontina cheeses, local mushrooms beneath shaved fresh artichokes and thyme. Complete your meal with a selection from their respectable list of international wines.
Reservations are only accepted for six or more, so be prepared to learn about European "football" as you wait.

Santi

Italian

A1

21047 Geyserville Ave., Geyserville

Phone: 707-857-1790
Web: www.tavernasanti.com
Prices: $$

Wed – Fri lunch & dinner
Sat – Tue dinner only

It's worth the short drive north from Healdsburg to discover the quaint little wine village of Geyserville. On its main street you'll find Santi, couched inside a landmark 1902 building.
Farmers' markets dictate the menu at this Alexander Valley tavern, where both the décor and the food clearly express the concept of "country." Grilled Monterey Bay sardines stuffed with fennel, pine nuts and bread crumbs, then wrapped in crispy prosciutto, joins the seasonal appetizers, while a boneless half-chicken cooked under a brick with house-cured pancetta, chickpea *inzimino* and Swiss chard show that Santi's rustic fare hits the mark.
On a sunny day, the vine-shaded patio is the place to linger and appreciate hard-to-find vintages from local wineries.

Shiso

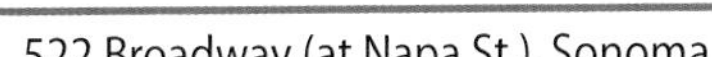

Japanese

D3

522 Broadway (at Napa St.), Sonoma

Phone: 707-933-9331
Web: www.shisorestaurant.com
Prices: $$

Wed – Sat lunch & dinner
Tue & Sun dinner only

Named for the aromatic Japanese herb, Shiso arrays itself in minimal fashion with bamboo floors, lime-green tones, and round white paper lanterns that hang like moons down the center of the long room.
The well-thought-out menu offers high-quality sushi and a whole lot more. The kitchen crew's skill comes to light in creative choices such as poke nachos with wasabi aïoli, tobiko and green onions; and the unique Ahi Sunkist maki roll made with Ahi tuna, cilantro, avocado and orange, and topped with peanuts and sweet eel sauce. For lunch, try the softshell crab BLT if it's in season; this sandwich comes with wasabi mayonnaise and Japanese potato salad.
Desserts (banana mousse crêpes; flourless chocolate cake; coffee crème brulée) take on a Western attitude.

Sugo

Italian 

5 Petaluma Blvd. (at B St.), Petaluma

Phone: 707-782-9298 — Tue – Sun lunch & dinner
Web: www.sugopetaluma.com
Prices: $$

The strip-mall location is nothing to brag about, but the unglamorous environs melt away once you enter this welcoming spot. Softened by music, candlelight, and large wood-framed mirrors, Sugo does Petaluma proud. The restaurant is set in the town's theater district, and keeps pace by screening black-and-white movies on a wall above the kitchen.

Freshly made Italian fare at reasonable prices keeps the locals—and anyone else who is lucky enough to stumble upon this place—coming back for more. Homemade goodness fills every bite of a chicken artichoke piccata or a simple grilled salmon dressed with lemon, garlic, and wine. Pastas, panini, and thin-crust artisan pizzas are also available. Pick any glass of wine for just $5.

Syrah

Californian 

205 5th St. (at Davis St.), Santa Rosa

Phone: 707-568-4002 — Tue – Sat lunch & dinner
Web: www.syrahbistro.com — Sun – Mon dinner only
Prices: $$$

This bistro celebrates and cultivates a love of wine. Chef Josh Silvers and his wife, Regina, feature a carefully selected wine list that spotlights nearly 50 different labels of Syrah, with a host of other French and California varietals.

Pair the namesake syrah with this approachable cuisine dictated by the season. Try one of the ever-changing offerings from sea, lake, or stream. The menu is balanced by dishes such as Josh's crab cakes spiked with tarragon aioli; a Riesling-braised Petaluma half-chicken accented by mushrooms, spinach, and pappardelle; or a Madras curry butternut squash stew enriched with coconut milk and sugar pumpkin. Just be sure to save room for a dessert or cheese plate.

On your way in or out, visit their sibling next door, a wine shop named Petite Syrah.

the girl & the fig

Californian XX

D3

110 W. Spain St. (at 1st St.), Sonoma

Phone: 707-938-3634 — Lunch & dinner daily
Web: www.thegirlandthefig.com
Prices: $$

Tucked inside the 1880 Sonoma Hotel (*see hotel listing*) on Sonoma Plaza, you will find this convivial restaurant decorated with warm hues and colorful paintings throughout.

Fresh produce, artisanal cheeses, cured meats, grass-fed beef, and house-smoked trout imprint the menu with Californian style. Of course, figs play a starring role in the well-composed signature dish: a fig and arugula salad tossed with toasted pecans and diced pancetta, drizzled with port vinaigrette. Set-price *plats du jour* represent a good deal, with or without the wine option. Desserts may include a tart and refreshing Meyer lemon cheesecake, finished with a dollop of crème fraîche.

As an added bonus, the shop in the front bar area offers cookbooks, food items, and Wine Country gifts.

Underwood

International

A2

9113 Graton Rd. (at Edison St.), Graton

Phone: 707-823-7023 — Tue – Sat lunch & dinner
Web: www.underwoodgraton.com — Sun dinner only
Prices: $$

The tiny town of Graton (located about an hour north of San Francisco) centers on this block of restaurants and shops, where you'll find Underwood. Here, townspeople and local vintners gather over good food and wine. The nickel-topped bar lends a saloon feel, while the rest of the place sports a bistro ambience. In warm weather, the patio that wraps around the side and back of the building is the preferred place to dine.

Variety is the hallmark of Underwood's menu, which travels from fresh local oysters and a selection of cheeses to Spanish-style tapas (Serrano ham with Manchego cheese and capers), meaty hoisin-glazed baby-back ribs, and a Moroccan lamb sandwich.

Directly across the street, the Willow Wood Market Cafe is run by the same folks.

Willi's Seafood & Raw Bar 

D1 — Seafood XX

403 Healdsburg Ave. (at North St.), Healdsburg

Phone: 707-433-9191 — Lunch & dinner daily
Web: www.willisseafood.net
Prices: $$

One block north of Healdsburg's square, a wrought-iron archway announces this upscale tavern. Make your way through the hedge-lined heated patio into the main room, where a pressed-tin ceiling hangs over dark wood tables and booths are tucked into raised nooks framed by painted wooden shutters.

Drop by the bar for local wines and fresh oysters or the *crudo* of the day. Small plates dominate the menu, in iterations such as clam and garlic flatbread, or Dean's tender salt and pepper baby back riblets with sautéed chilies and onions. Bright, fresh flavors and good technique are exemplified in offerings such as lobster with garlic butter and sautéed fennel, or marinated spicy chicken skewers from the grill, served atop a bed of cooling cucumber and feta salad.

Willi's Wine Bar 

B2 — Contemporary

4404 Old Redwood Hwy. (at River Rd.), Santa Rosa

Phone: 707-526-3096 — Wed – Sat lunch & dinner
Web: www.williswinebar.net — Sun – Mon dinner only
Prices: $$

Like its Healdsburg sibling, Willi's Wine Bar continues Mark and Terri Stark's concept of international tapas-style dishes. You could easily miss this small roadhouse as you drive by on tree-lined Old Redwood Highway, but the jammed parking lot will clue you in to Willi's locale and the yummy aromas from the kitchen will draw you inside.

The gracious waitstaff hands out smiles along with Tuscan pork riblets, and "Moo Shu" bacon (sliced into strips to resemble the Chinese pork dish) served with Hoisin barbecue sauce and chive pancakes. A couple of these small plates will satisfy, but several make it a party. All the wines at Willi's are available by the glass and the bottle as well as the 2-ounce pour, so you can sample to your heart's content.

Willow Wood Market Cafe

Californian

9020 Graton Rd. (at Edison St.), Graton

Phone: 707-823-0233 — Mon – Sat lunch & dinner
Web: www.willowwoodgraton.com — Sun lunch only
Prices: $$

Good, down-home comfort food is dished up with genuine country hospitality at this tiny roadside eatery. Your first impression may be of an old-fashioned soda fountain, but it also doubles as a general store, brimming with local food items, wines, and kitschy souvenirs.

Sister to Underwood across the street, kid-friendly Willow Wood serves breakfast, lunch and dinner, focusing on the kind of food you expect from a friend's mom in the good old days. Although a plentiful selection of salads and hot sandwiches is always at the ready, locals know to order a bowl of creamy polenta, with accompaniments such as goat cheese and house-made pesto, rock shrimp and roasted tomatoes, or even pork tenderloin ragout. For dessert, the fresh fruit cobbler is unbeatable.

Wolf House

American

13740 Arnold Dr. (near London Ranch Rd.), Glen Ellen

Phone: 707-996-4401 — Lunch & dinner daily
Web: www.jacklondonlodge.com
Prices: $$

Adjoining the c.1905 Jack London Lodge, Wolf House restaurant is named for the mansion of lava boulders and redwood logs that author Jack London and his wife began building in the hills above Glenn Ellen in 1911 (you can visit the ruins of the house, which burned in 1913, at nearby Jack London State Historic Park).

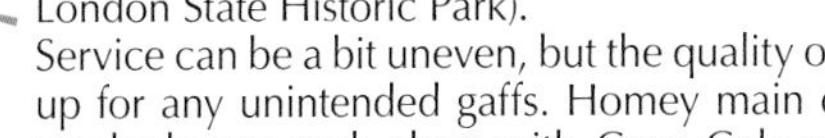

Service can be a bit uneven, but the quality of the food makes up for any unintended gaffs. Homey main dishes such as a smoke-house pork chop with Coca-Cola yams and apples sautéed in brandy; English-style fish and chips; and house-made country meatloaf served with warm potato salad leave no doubt as to the skill in the kitchen.

The windows overlook serene tree-lined Sonoma Creek, and the outdoor patio accommodates diners as weather permits.

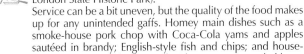

zazu

Californian

3535 Guerneville Rd. (at Willowside Rd.), Santa Rosa

Phone: 707-523-4814 — Wed – Sun dinner only
Web: www.zazurestaurant.com
Prices: $$

This quaint little red roadhouse outside Santa Rosa may seem out of the way but is well worth the trip to sample California cuisine that comes straight from farm to table. A successful duo both in and out of the kitchen, Chefs/owners John Stewart and Duskie Edwards funnel their passion into every rustic dish. They harvest a wealth of fruits and vegetables from the organic garden behind the restaurant, and go hog-wild making their own sausages, bacon, and salumi. A select network of other purveyors fills in any voids with sustainably raised meats for the Rincon Valley "sloppy goat" sliders or Southern fried Cloverdale rabbit.

Here, the staff's friendliness is genuine, the narrow room is softly illuminated by boat lights, and a good meal is guaranteed.

Zin

American 

344 Center St. (at North St.), Healdsburg

Phone: 707-473-0946 — Mon – Fri lunch & dinner
Web: www.zinrestaurant.com — Sat – Sun dinner only
Prices: $$

Winter, spring, summer, and fall each lend their bounty to the eclectic, seasonal cuisine at this Healdsburg staple, located one block north of the town square. Co-owners Jeff Mall and Scott Silva are both sons of farmers, and their pastoral upbringing shines forth in the kitchen's fresh twists on American classics, featuring produce often grown in the restaurant's own organic garden. A different Blue Plate special marks each day of the week and celebrates Americana with dishes such as chicken 'n dumplings, Yankee pot roast, or spaghetti and meatballs.

True to the restaurant's name, the wine list focuses on the best local examples of the Zinfandel varietal, a grape that thrives in the soil of the surrounding Dry Creek Valley.

Peter L. Wrenn/MICHELIN

Where to **stay**

© Tim Pannell/Corbis

Alphabetical list of Hotels

O

P

R

S

T - V

W

MICHELIN

Stanyan Park

A1

750 Stanyan St. (at Waller St.)

Phone: 415-751-1000
Fax: 415-668-5454
Web: www.stanyanpark.com
Prices: $$

30 Rooms

6 Suites

Stanyan Park's handsome three-story Queen Anne-style turret marks the corner of Stanyan and Waller streets, overlooking Golden Gate Park to the west and the Haight-Ashbury neighborhood to the east.

Inside, all (smoke-free) rooms are quietly decorated in conventional Victorian style. Families and longer-term guests will appreciate the spacious suites (up to 900 square feet), fully equipped with kitchens and large living rooms. Free wireless Internet access and voice mail provide modern convenience in the historic atmosphere. The hotel's staff serves up a warm welcome, along with a complimentary breakfast and afternoon tea daily.

With Golden Gate Park at its front door, the Stanyan provides wonderful access to all of the park's cultural and natural attractions. Visitors to nearby hospitals and the University of San Francisco will find this hotel particularly convenient. While hardly hip, the Stanyan affords a comfortable stay at a reasonable price.

Inn at the Opera

333 Fulton St. (at Franklin St.)

Phone: 415-863-8400 or 800-325-2708
Fax: 415-861-0821
Web: www.innattheopera.com
Prices: **$$**

35 Rooms

12 Suites

♿

Inn at the Opera

At the heart of San Francisco's arts district, within a couple of blocks of the Opera House, Symphony Hall, and the San Francisco Ballet, this small hotel has been popular with musicians, stage performers, and audience members alike since 1927. Its 47 guestrooms are plain in their old-fashioned styling and furnishings, and they are on the small side. They do include microwaves, wet bars, small refrigerators, CD players, and bathrobes. The Ballet Studio, Concerto, and Symphony suites offer lounge or living room areas, bigger bathrooms, and kitchenettes. Ovation at the Opera, the hotel's fine-dining restaurant, puts up traditional French cuisine nightly, and a continental breakfast buffet comes gratis with your room.

The Inn at the Opera is also convenient to business and government offices in the Civic Center, while just a stone's throw away, funky Hayes Street is a good place to dine or shop. Boutiques sell unique glassware, pottery, and other crafts; eclectic restaurants and cafes provide a variety of lunch and nightlife options.

Phoenix

601 Eddy St. (at Larkin St.)

Phone: 415-776-1380 or 800-248-9466
Fax: 415-885-3109
Web: www.thephoenixhotel.com
Prices: $$

41 Rooms

3 Suites

Joie de Vivre Hospitality

Hip and vibrant, the Phoenix bills itself as the city's "rock and roll hotel," and indeed it is popular with entertainers in the industry as well as a cool young clientele. The building retains its 1956 motel atmosphere, though updated with high-volume color and styling. Once inside, guests will feel miles away from the seedy Tenderloin district that surrounds the hotel.

The 41 guestrooms are done up in tropical bungalow décor, aglow in bright hues, bamboo furnishings, and works by local artists. Though the rooms are ample in size, the bathrooms can be tiny (renovated bathrooms are larger). Three modern one-bedroom suites are also available. In true motel style, the rooms face—and open onto—a lushly planted courtyard where funky sculptures, Indonesian-style lounging areas, and a heated swimming pool that is itself a work of art (check out the underwater mural) offer a boisterous oasis for schmoozing or sunning.

Amenities include free parking and hotel-wide wireless Internet access. Nearby clubs and concert halls offer guests a variety of nightlife choices, from cutting-edge to classical.

Adagio

550 Geary St. (bet. Jones & Taylor Sts.)

Phone: 415-775-5000 or 800-228-8830
Fax: 415-775-9388
Web: www.thehoteladagio.com
Prices: $$$

171 Rooms

2 Suites

Catering to the Internet-cafe set, the Adagio displays a modern minimalist décor that appeals to young travelers from the U.S. and abroad. The impressive Spanish Colonial Revival structure was built in 1929 as the El Cortez, and knew several different names and owners before it was refurbished and reopened in 2003 by the Joie de Vivre Hospitality group (whose properties include the Carlton, Hotel Kabuki, and the Hotel Vitale among others).

Rooms are dressed in a contemporary and sober style with earthy tones and clean lines; many of the rooms have city views. All guests enjoy complimentary high-speed Internet access, CD players, 24-inch Sony TV's, and Egyptian cotton linens, plus double-paned windows to screen out the street noise. On the Executive Level, rooms boast downtown views, Frette bathrobes, hookups for iPod/MP3 players, and DVD libraries. You won't need to miss your workout here; the on-site fitness center offers Cybex equipment.

Off the lobby, Cortez restaurant *(see restaurant listing)* delights diners with Mediterranean-inspired cuisine.

Bijou

111 Mason St. (at Eddy St.)

Phone: 415-771-1200 or 800-288-6005
Fax: 415-346-3196
Web: www.hotelbijou.com
Prices: $

65 Rooms

♿

Joie de Vivre Hospitality

Hollywood comes to San Francisco at the Hotel Bijou, where Art-Deco inspired décor and a jewel-tone palette recall the golden years of the silver screen. Movies shot in San Francisco take center stage, and each of 65 small and simple guestrooms is named for one. Still photographs from the films decorate the boldly colorful walls, done up in rich reds and yellows. Bathrooms with full tubs and showers are utilitarian and well maintained; well-kept rooms offer dataports and two-line phones, with wireless high-speed Internet access available throughout the hotel. Although rooms at the back of the five-story building have no view, they are quieter than those at the front. Pastries, coffee, and tea are served gratis each morning.

Just off the handsome purple and red lobby, the Petit (and it is) Bijou Theatre screens two locally set movies each evening, from *48 Hours* to *Lady from Shanghai*. The hotel is convenient to cable-car stops, the streets around Union Square, the neighborhood's posh retail district, as well as to the business center of the city.

Clift

A2

495 Geary St. (at Taylor St.)

Phone: 415-775-4700 or 800-697-1791
Fax: 415-441-4621
Web: www.clifthotel.com
Prices: **$$$**

338 Rooms

25 Suites

Clift

Dark meets light, antique goes modern, and eccentric cajoles conservative at this high-style hostelry. Built in 1913 and reconceived for the 21st century by Philippe Starck, the Clift surprises at every turn. Dramatic lighting, soaring ceilings, a cacophony of textures, and eclectic furnishings dress the public areas in a sleek elegance that takes equal cues from Surrealism, Art Deco, and a style uniquely Californian. The legendary Redwood Room, with its original 1933 redwood paneling and huge bar (said to be carved from one tree) may be the ne plus ultra, especially as reinterpreted during the renovation.

By contrast, the guestrooms are swathed in quiet tones of foggy gray, beige, and lavender. Acrylic orange nightstands and wooden wheelbarrow armchairs add whimsy to the minimalist sophistication. Standard rooms measure only 260 square feet, but more expensive chambers are larger, with deluxe one-bedroom suites topping out at 925 square feet. All of them feature luxuries from Egyptian cotton 400-thread-count sheets to DVD and CD players with an in-room disc library.

Off the lobby, glamorous Asia de Cuba *(see restaurant listing)* serves tasty fusion fare.

Diva

440 Geary St. (bet. Mason & Taylor Sts.)

Phone: 415-885-0200 or 800-553-1900
Fax: 415-885-3268
Web: www.hoteldiva.com
Prices: $$

116 Rooms

2 Suites

Hotel Diva

Edgy Euro-tech style pervades the Diva, where stainless steel and cobalt blue set the tone. Renovated rooms feature wired and wireless high-speed Internet access, and CD and VCR players; you can even rent iPods at the front desk. Streamlined furnishings of metal and blond wood, and rolled-steel headboards furnish the rooms, which are done in a hip black and gray color scheme. Bathrooms are small but complete. Kids will love the Little Diva suites, tailored to the young traveler with pop-art colors, bunk beds, kid-friendly movies, and a microwave oven stocked with popcorn.

No buffet breakfast is offered, though guests can order a breakfast box in their rooms or visit the Starbucks located in the same building. PCs and laser printers are available in the business center, where copy and fax services come with a fee. The hotel occupies a favorable location facing two of the city's main playhouses, the Curran Theatre and the American Conservatory Theater (ACT), and steps from the city's fashionable Union Square shopping district.

Out front, the Diva Sidewalk of Fame displays the signatures of celebrity guests like Tony Curtis, Stevie Wonder, and Lily Tomlin.

The Inn at Union Square

440 Post St. (bet. Mason & Powell Sts.)

Phone: 415-397-3510 or 800-288-4346
Fax: 415-989-0529
Web: www.unionsquare.com
Prices: $$

24 Rooms

6 Suites

Perfectly located just steps away from Union Square, this laid-back inn is a relatively inexpensive hotel option in the high-rent heart of the city. Its 24 adequately sized rooms, decked out in regal gold and red, all come equipped with down pillows and duvets, flat-screen TVs, a work desk, and free wireless Internet access. Compact bathrooms are equipped with hair dryers, robes, and Aveda products. In the two-room penthouse suite you'll find extra luxuries such as a wet bar, a wood-burning fireplace, and a whirlpool tub.

Each floor has a small sitting area where coffee, tea, and fresh fruit are available throughout the day. Small fireplaces in these nooks are often lit with crackling fires in the evening, when wine and hors-d'oeuvres are offered on the house. Each morning, a complimentary continental breakfast (including cereal, pastries, fruit, yogurt, hard-boiled eggs, and toast) is set out here as well. The hotel also provides valet parking and access to a well-equipped fitness club with a heated pool.

Much more traditional than trendy, the Inn at Union Square stands out for its tranquility and prime location near some of the city's best shops and restaurants.

King George

A2

334 Mason St. (bet. Geary & O'Farrell Sts.)

Phone: 415-781-5050 or 800-288-6005
Fax: 415-391-6976
Web: www.kinggeorge.com
Prices: $

151 Rooms

2 Suites

King George Hotel

The charmingly painted façade of the 1912 King George adds a bit of fun to this Anglophile's hideaway. Inside, the lobby welcomes with its warm yellow, beige, and gold color scheme, and, of course, a full-size portrait of King George. Most of the guestrooms have been recently renovated with pleasing fabrics, inviting green walls, classic wood furniture, and new bedspreads to create a European feel; all include high-speed Internet access, safes, irons, and ironing boards. Executive rooms on the second floor are larger than the rest. Count on the concierge to arrange airport shuttles, restaurant reservations, and theater tickets.

Enjoy breakfast on-site at the Windsor Tearoom, which also serves tea on Saturdays and Sundays. Winston's Bar and Lounge specializes in wines, Champagne, specialty beers, and appetizers. For a small fee, guests can enjoy access to a nearby health club. The hotel is highly accessible to Union Square and the theater district, as well as the Moscone Convention Center and the San Francisco Museum of Modern Art.

Mandarin Oriental

C2

222 Sansome St. (bet. California & Pine Sts.)

Phone: 415-276-9888 or 800-622-0404
Fax: 415-433-0289
Web: www.mandarinoriental.com
Prices: $$$$

151 Rooms

7 Suites

Mandarin Oriental Hotel Group

From this superb hotel's ground-floor entry, high-speed elevators whisk guests to their aeries, located in the towers of the city's third-tallest building, between the 38th and 48th stories. Glass-enclosed sky bridges connect the two towers on each floor, offering spectacular views of the city and beyond. Guestroom views dazzle as well (binoculars are provided), from every angle, though corner rooms and those with a "bridge-to-bridge" perspective take top honors. Choose a city or bay view, and if tub-to-ceiling bathroom windows delight, reserve a Mandarin King room. Handsome Asian design elements, elegant fabrics, and warm colors lend a refined air to the recently refreshed rooms and suites; spacious marble bathrooms are perfectly equipped.

Spacious and comfortable, the lobby includes a pleasant lounge area, a sushi bar, and live piano music beginning at 5:00 P.M. daily. The hotel features its own fitness center, and passes can be purchased for a nearby health club. In-room high-speed Internet access is available, with WiFi in the hotel's public areas.

On the second floor, Silks restaurant *(see restaurant listing)* features contemporary cuisine with pan-Asian influences.

Monaco

501 Geary St. (at Taylor St.)

Phone: 415-292-0100 or 866-622-5284
Fax: 415-292-0111
Web: www.monaco-sf.com
Prices: **$$$**

177 Rooms

24 Suites

Kimpton Hotels and Restaurants

You can count on the Kimpton group to deliver luxury, and the Monaco is no exception. Located in the midst of the theater district, and just two blocks from Union Square shopping and dining, this hotel occupies a beautifully renovated 1910 Beaux Arts building. The lobby sets the tone for travel with a check-in desk styled like a steamer-trunk, and hand-painted ceiling frescoes depicting whimsical skyscapes of hot-air balloons and planes. On the landing of the grand staircase, a painting aptly entitled *Celestial Lady* clearly illustrates that the sky is the limit.

In the guestrooms, bright fabrics drape over canopy beds, cheery striped paper covers the walls, and Chinese-inspired furnishings add exotic flair. Flat-screen TVs come with a yoga channel, and there is no fee for the high-speed Internet access. Frette robes, in-room safes, hairdryers, irons and ironing boards, and L'Occitane bath amenities should provide everything you need; but if you forgot something, items like toothbrushes and razors are just a phone call away.

Enjoy a meal in the impressive surroundings of the Art Deco-style Grand Café (*see restaurant listing*), in the building's former ballroom.

Nikko

222 Mason St. (bet. Ellis & O'Farrell Sts.)

Phone: 415-394-1111 or 800-248-3308
Fax: 415-394-1106
Web: www.hotelnikkosf.com
Prices: $$

510 Rooms

22 Suites

Hotel Nikko

Though large, the Nikko offers a comfortable and convenient stay, with a choice of 12 different types of rooms and suites in various sizes. At 280 square feet, the Petite queens are best for single occupancy, but may also suit two people in search of a good deal. Deluxe rooms, both king and double/doubles, occupy floors 6 through 21. The Nikko Floors (22, 23, and 24) offer added services and amenities, including restricted access, complimentary high-speed Internet, and breakfast served in a private lounge. At the top end, the two-bedroom, two-bath Imperial Suite measures in at 2,635 square feet. City views are divine, especially from the higher floors. Public areas showcase changing exhibitions of paintings, sculpture, and media arts curated by the Baxter Chang Patri Gallery.

A lovely swimming pool, together with a fitness room and sauna, occupy the large and very bright fifth-floor atrium. For your business needs, the well-equipped business center can arrange printing, binding, faxing, translation, and secretarial services, along with other office functions. Stop by Nikko's fine-dining restaurant, Anzu (*see restaurant listings*), for sushi, prime cuts of beef, and a sake martini.

Omni

500 California St. (at Montgomery St.)

Phone: 415-677-9494
Fax: 415-273-3038
Web: www.omnisanfrancisco.com
Prices: $$$$

347 Rooms

15 Suites

Omni Hotel, San Francisco

Located in the heart of the Financial District with a cable-car stop right outside, this Omni opened in 2002 in an elegantly renovated 1926 bank building. Though only the original stone and brick façade has been preserved, the spacious wood-paneled lobby, floored in rosy marble, takes its cue and its stylishness from a bygone era.

Spread over 17 stories, the 347 rooms and 15 suites follow suit. They are large and classic in style, with details to match, including Egyptian cotton sheets and well-equipped bathrooms decorated in marble and granite. Most guestrooms feature T-1 high-speed Internet access and three phones; one is cordless. For upgraded amenities, reserve on the 16th "signature" floor, where rooms come with a Bose Wave radio and CD player, DVD player, wireless Internet, and a color copier/printer. Specialty accommodations such as Get Fit rooms (furnished with a treadmill and healthy snacks) and a Kids Fantasy Suite, where bunk beds and kids rule in the second bedroom, are also available. Bob's Steak and Chop House will draw the meat-loving guests.

Every Saturday at 10:00 A.M., a guided walking tour departs from the hotel for an overview of city history.

Prescott

545 Post St. (bet. Mason & Taylor Sts.)

Phone: 415-563-0303 or 866-271-3632
Fax: 415-563-6831
Web: www.prescotthotel.com
Prices: $$

132 Rooms

32 Suites

David Phelps/Kimpton Hotels & Restaurants

This boutique hotel blends old and new, whimsy and tradition into an attractive whole. Especially in the comfortable lobby, playful designs and colors create a welcoming space that includes cozy armchairs and a fireplace. Guestrooms are situated in two separate but connected older buildings, one featuring Deluxe rooms and the other, known as the Club Level, offering rooms with upgraded amenities, including access to a private lounge, express check-in and departure, and complimentary breakfast. Club Level guests also enjoy an evening cocktail party with hors d'oeuvres from Postrio *(see restaurant listing)*, the on-site restaurant.

Rooms are stylishly, if soberly, decorated with hints of the Louis XVI and French Empire styles. They feature Italian linens and Ralph Lauren fabrics, and the well-equipped bathrooms are trimmed in marble. High-speed wireless Internet access, laptop-size safes, and CD-player clock radios add convenience. A 450-square-foot fitness room is located on the eighth floor, and in-room spa services offer massages, facials, and hand and foot treatments. The Brown Sugar Massage might be just the ticket after a hectic day.

Rex

562 Sutter St. (bet. Mason & Powell Sts.)

Phone: 415-433-4434 or 800-433-4434
Fax: 415-433-3695
Web: www.thehotelrex.com
Prices: $$

94 Rooms

Joie de Vivre Hospitality

One block off Union Square, the Rex provides a great location for a reasonable price. This member of the Joie de Vivre group styles itself after the art and literary salons rife in San Francisco in the 1920's and 30's. The lobby feels like a gentleman's study, with its dark paneling, comfortable seating, and shelves brimming with books. Quotes from various regional authors adorn the walls of the different floors as well as the hotel's cozy bistro, Café Andrée, where breakfast is served to hotel guests each morning.

In the bedrooms, gingham bedspreads and curtains lend a country feel to spaces brightened by large windows and sunny-colored walls. Pillowtop mattresses, bathrobes, CD players, and mini-refrigerators add some of the comforts of home. Writing desks and complimentary high-speed Internet access accommodate business travelers, as does the hotel's business center, aka The Study.

Other reasons to stay here? A complimentary wine reception in the lobby bar each evening, guest access to a nearby fitness center, and even a get-oriented tour with a San Francisco Greeter—on the house.

Serrano

405 Taylor St. (at O'Farrell St.)

Phone: 415-885-2500 or 866-289-6561
Fax: 415-474-4879
Web: www.serranohotel.com
Prices: **$$**

217 Rooms

19 Suites

Serrano Hotel/David Phelps

Centerpiece of this 1924 Spanish Revival building is its two-story lobby, where the majestic fireplace, beamed ceilings, wood-paneled columns, boldly patterned carpet, and leafy potted plants create a charming Old World atmosphere. It's all fun and games at the Serrano, and the games begin with the Check-In Challenge. If you can beat "the house" in a quick game of 21, you could win a free room upgrade. The fun continues once you settle in your room; you can call to order a board game from the hotel's library to be delivered to you. You can also find more board games in the lobby.

Fresh and well-maintained, rooms are adorned in sunny colors with red-and-yellow-striped drapes and Moroccan accents; leopard-print terrycloth robes add another exotic touch. If you're in the city on business, you'll appreciate the large glass-topped desk, comfy swivel chair, a two-line cordless phone, and an Internet access port. There's also a 24-hour business center on-site (accessible with your room key) that keeps computers, scanners, printers, and fax machines at the ready.

And best of all for pet lovers, the Serrano—like most Kimpton properties—will welcome your four-legged friend in style.

Sir Francis Drake

B2

450 Powell St. (at Sutter St.)

Phone: 415-392-7755 or 800-795-7129
Fax: 415-391-8719
Web: www.sirfrancisdrake.com
Prices: $$$

410 Rooms

6 Suites

John Rizzo/Kimpton Hotels & Restaurants

Named for the English explorer who landed in the Bay Area in 1579, "The Drake" enjoys a long and colorful history as one of San Francisco's landmark hostelries. When it opened in 1928, the hotel boasted such high-tech wonders as ice water on tap, an indoor golf course, and a radio in every room.

A recent $20-million restoration has put a fresh face on this dowager—now part of the Kimpton group—don't worry, the doormen retain their trademark Beefeater uniforms. Touting tons of marble, the swanky soaring lobby recalls the grandeur of a bygone era. Off the lobby, hip Bar Drake proffers cocktails with a Prohibition-era twist.

Rooms are moderately priced, given the hotel's enviable location near Union Square and the Theater District. Your accommodations will sport a sage and cream color scheme, plush carpeting, and a yoga channel on the flat-screen TV. Frosted globe overhead light fixtures are studded with gold stars—a nod to the hotel's legendary Harry Denton's Starlight Room, located on the 21st floor—where views of the city span 360 degrees. Make sure your plans include a visit to the scrumptious Scala's Bistro (*see restaurant listing*).

Triton

B2

342 Grant Ave. (at Bush St.)

Phone: 415-394-0500 or 800-800-1299
Fax: 415-394-0555
Web: www.hoteltriton.com
Prices: $$

140 Rooms

Awash in hipness from its in-your-face décor to its eco-friendly guestrooms, this "unhotel" will startle some and delight others. Undulating columns sheathed in gold, psychedelic murals, and funky, eclectic furniture sets the tone in the lobby. The hotel's 140 rooms offer a variety of styles. Designed for one guest, Zen Dens provide incense, a Book of Buddha and your own bamboo plant to nurture. The 7th-floor Eco rooms feature water and air filtration, energy savers, and all-natural linens, as well as a restful monochromatic palette. While the Triton welcomes pets, none are allowed on this floor to keep it allergy free.

The hotel's Celebrity Suites (really just larger bedrooms) have been decorated by the likes of Carlos Santana and Woody Harrelson. Even the usual queens, kings, and double/doubles are quirky, artistic, and comfortable. All include eco-friendly bath products, flat-screen TVs, pillow-top mattresses, and luscious linens. Next door to the hotel, Café de la Presse *(see restaurant listing)* serves breakfast and provides room service.

The Triton sits outside the Chinatown gate, within a few minutes walk from Union Square and the Financial District.

Westin St. Francis

335 Powell St. (at Union Square)

Phone: 415-397-7000 or 866-500-0338
Fax: 415-774-0124
Web: www.westinstfrancis.com
Prices: $$$$

1195 Rooms

29 Suites

Resorts and Great Hotels

This luxury hotel deserves its legendary status. Regally situated at the head of Union Square, the St. Francis, opened in 1904, was modeled on the grand European hotels of the period. Barely surviving the earthquake and fire in 1906, the hotel went on to build two more wings, and in 1972 a 32-story tower was added behind the main structure. Today the St. Francis remains the grand dame of West Coast hotels; visitors and residents alike rendezvous in its lobby as they have for generations.

For full effect, you may want to reserve a room in the main building, where historic materials decorate the large hallways. Rooms here are decorated in a charmingly old-fashioned Empire style, and many have good views of Union Square. More contemporary tower rooms all have bay windows for sweeping city and bay vistas. Westin's signature Heavenly Bed™ and Heavenly Bath™ come in every room. Between the spa and the acclaimed Michael Mina restaurant *(see restaurant listing)*, you won't want for much here.

The stately 10,700-square-foot Grand Ballroom lends itself equally to society galas and business functions.

Drisco

2901 Pacific Ave. (at Broderick St.)

Phone: 415-346-2880 or 800-738-7477
Fax: 415-567-5537
Web: www.hoteldrisco.com
Prices: $$

29 Rooms

19 Suites

Joie de Vivre Hospitality

Comfortably at home in tony Pacific Heights, this 1903 hotel offers elegant accommodations surrounded by beautiful residences and quiet streets, removed from the bustle of downtown. Well dressed throughout in shades of beige accented by rich wood tones and mellow colors, this member of the Joie de Vivre group possesses a charming atmosphere that permeates each of its rooms. Accommodations, including 19 suites, vary in size but are consistently graceful in style, and well furnished with robes and slippers, VCR and CD players, and wireless high-speed Internet access. Some rooms offer nice city views; others overlook the building's tiny courtyard.

Guests can enjoy a complimentary breakfast buffet in the sunny first-floor dining room, and coffee, tea and newspapers are available 24 hours in the hotel's lovely lobby. Each evening, wine and hors d'oeuvres come compliments of the house. An on-site workout room and complimentary access to the Presidio YMCA will appeal to fitness fiends, while the small business center provides basic services for business travelers.

Kabuki

1625 Post St. (at Laguna St.)

Phone: 415-922-3200 or 800-533-4567
Fax: 415-614-5498
Web: www.hotelkabuki.com
Prices: $$

218 Rooms

Cesar Rubio

The heart of Japantown beats right outside the door of this reasonably priced hotel. Formerly the Miyako, the property was purchased and renovated in 2007 by the Joie de Vivre group. The result appeals with a design that blends Asian and Western elements.

Clean and spacious, rooms are appointed with attractive contemporary furniture, including new Serta mattresses. Electronic amenities run from flat-screen TVs to free wireless Internet access. Corner rooms have sliding-glass doors that open onto a private balcony.

Although this hotel lacks some of the little luxuries you'll find in more expensive properties, the Kabuki offers unique features such as a welcome tea service delivered to your room after check-in, and complimentary sake and wine set out in the lobby weekdays between 5:00 P.M. and 6:00 P.M. In keeping with Japanese tradition, guests have access to the nearby Kabuki Springs and Spa communal baths. Or you can reserve ahead with a bath butler (call 72 hours in advance), who will prepare a comforting bath for you in the deep soaking tub in your room. Afterwards, stop in at O Izakaya Lounge downstairs for a glass of sake and small plates, Japanese-style.

Laurel Inn

444 Presidio Ave. (at California St.)

Phone: 415-567-8467 or 800-552-8735
Fax: 415-928-1866
Web: www.thelaurelinn.com
Prices: $$

49
Rooms

Joie de Vivre Hospitality

The Laurel Inn, built in 1963, embraces its mid-century pedigree with gusto and good taste. Bold strokes of color enliven the interior, particularly in the artist-inspired area rugs that decorate the rooms and public spaces. Furnishings throughout are sleek and not fussy. Large windows grace the newly renovated guestrooms, which include 18 larger units with kitchenettes, much in demand by guests planning extended stays. Each room offers wireless high-speed Internet, CD and VCR players, a two-line phone with dataports, and an iron and ironing board. Rooms on the back side of the hotel feature pleasant city panoramas and are quieter than those facing the street, though all are efficiently soundproofed.

Guests traveling with cars and pets will appreciate the free indoor parking and pet-friendliness of the Laurel. A small continental breakfast is served in the attractive lobby each morning. If you're content not to be in the center of downtown action, the Laurel Inn, located in residential Pacific Heights, offers good value.

Majestic

1500 Sutter St. (at Gough St.)

Phone: 415-441-1100 or 800-869-8966
Fax: 415-673-7331
Web: www.thehotelmajestic.com
Prices: $

49 Rooms

9 Suites

Hotel Majestic

The Edwardian elegance of the Majestic dates from 1902, when it was built as a private residence. Already a hotel by 1906 when the earthquake struck, the building survived to become San Francisco's oldest continuously operated hotel. Lavish public areas, set about with French and English antiques, marble columns and wrought-iron balustrades, recall a bygone era of domestic luxury which extends to the 58 rooms and suites.

Though the standard rooms are on the small side, the suites are large, pleasant and reasonably priced for their size. Sumptuously swagged canopy beds furnish each room, and bathrooms are completely equipped and beautifully tiled and marbled. All rooms come with Turkish robes and turndown service featuring cookies before bed. Though old-fashioned in style, the hotel offers modern electronic amenities, including wireless high-speed Internet and a laptop computer for guests' use.

A complimentary continental breakfast and afternoon wine and hors d'oeuvres are served in the dining room. Check out the butterfly collection in the Avalon Room off the lobby. A meal is a must at the elegant Café Majestic which ladles innovative fare.

Carlton

1075 Sutter St. (bet. Hyde & Larkin Sts.)

Phone: 415-673-0242 or 800-738-7477
Fax: 415-673-4904
Web: www.hotelcarltonsf.com
Prices: $

161 Rooms

Joie de Vivre Hospitality/Scott Brooks

The unassuming exterior of this 1927 hotel belies the charming and cheerful atmosphere that awaits inside. Renovated and reopened in 2004, the Carlton now features a globetrotting theme realized through furniture, photographs and objects from around the world. The eclectic result is colorful and eccentric though not overdone.

Rooms are neat and tasteful, decorated in soft colors splashed with exotic accents, and the higher of the building's seven stories afford unobstructed views of the city. Though they lack air-conditioning, each room features a large ceiling fan for those rare hot days. Those on the top three floors, for a higher price, provide complimentary high-speed Internet access.

Hotel employees—an international team that speaks more than a dozen languages—are singularly dedicated to the comfort of their guests. The convenience, friendliness and style of this hotel make it a good value for the money.

The Fairmont

950 Mason St. (at California St.)

Phone: 415-772-5000 or 800-257-7544
Fax: 415-772-5013
Web: www.fairmont.com
Prices: $$$

528 Rooms

63 Suites

The Fairmont Hotel San Francisco

Flagship of the Fairmont hotel group, this Gilded Age palace overlooks the city from atop Nob Hill as it has since construction began in 1902, despite earthquake and fire. Recently returned to their past glory, the hotel's public spaces sparkle with turn-of-the-century splendor. The lobby alone is worth a visit, especially to see the restoration of architect Julia Morgan's original Corinthian columns, alabaster walls, marble floors, and vaulted ceilings trimmed in gold. Guests can soak up the atmosphere over a meal in Laurel Court, the hotel's original dining room. Or, for a different kind of nostalgia, visit the Tonga Room, a tiki hideaway, complete with thatched umbrellas and live music.

Rooms have been refurbished in pale yellows, refined fabrics, and dark wood furnishings. With their 14-foot vaulted ceilings, those around the exterior of the original seven-story structure are particularly spacious and boast nice views of city and bay. For panoramic skyline views, choose a room in the 23-story tower, opened in 1961. All guestrooms include extra-long mattresses and have been updated with modern business amenities, though high-speed Internet comes with a fee.

Nob Hill

B3

835 Hyde St. (bet. Sutter & Bush Sts.)

Phone: 415-885-2987 or 877-662-4455
Fax: 415-921-1648
Web: www.nobhillhotel.com
Prices: $$

52 Rooms

Nob Hill Hotel

Decorated in a plush crush of Victoriana, the elegant Nob Hill Hotel combines stained glass, velvety fabrics, and ornate furnishings to create a cozy turn-of-the-century hideaway. The hotel was built in 1906 and restored in 1998; its 52 rooms are generally small but nicely kept and well appointed with marble baths, brass bedsteads, and richly colored wallpapers. Each is romantic and intimate, and some rooms, including two penthouse suites, have beautiful private terraces. Several suites feature whirlpool tubs. Small refrigerators and microwaves are provided, along with CD players, hairdryers, and coffeemakers—not to mention the reassuring teddy bear on each bed. The atmosphere is hushed and the rooms are quiet, whether they face the courtyard or the street.

Rates include an evening wine tasting, access to a 24-hour fitness center, and a continental breakfast. Outside, all the attractions of Nob Hill await, from historic buildings to glorious views.

Orchard Garden

466 Bush St. (at Grant Ave.)

Phone: 415-399-9807 or 888-717-2881
Fax: 415-393-9917
Web: www.theorchardgardenhotel.com
Prices: $$$

86 Rooms

Orchard Garden Hotel

You can feel good about staying here in more ways than one. California's first hotel built to U.S. Green Building Council standards, Orchard Garden is environmentally friendly through and through, from the construction materials and modern, light wood furnishings to the carpets and linens. The 86-room, smoke-free hotel uses organic cleaning products, recycled paper, and an innovative key-card system that reduces energy consumption by 20 percent.

The environment is amenable as well as sustainable. Soft earth tones (a lot of green, naturally) create a serene atmosphere; the well-insulated design keeps even the street-side rooms quiet. Those eco-sheets are soft Egyptian cotton, and Aveda organic toiletries stock the bathroom. Natural and high-tech comforts—including WiFi Internet access and high-definition LCD TV with DVD—co-exist peacefully here.

The hotel restaurant, Roots, on occassion will offer a complimentary breakfast buffet. It also serves lunch and dinner using local organic produce and natural meats, and features an American Farmstead Cheese Cart.

Casually calming, comfortable, and convenient (only a few blocks from Union Square), Orchard Garden makes it easy to be green.

The Ritz-Carlton

600 Stockton St. (bet. California & Pine Sts.)

Phone: 415-296-7465 or 800-241-3333
Fax: 415-291-0288
Web: www.ritzcarlton.com
Prices: $$$$

276 Rooms

60 Suites

The Ritz-Carlton, San Francisco

This imposing Neoclassical building began life as an insurance company in 1909, and since 1991 it has housed San Francisco's finest hotel. For pure class, luxury, and service, the Ritz-Carlton reigns supreme. A multimillion-dollar renovation in 2006 enhanced its cachet with upgraded technology, guestroom amenities, and new personal services for travelers with children, pets, and computers.

Decorated with a rich collection of 18th- and 19th-century antiques and paintings, the hotel's lobby includes a gracious lounge that serves afternoon tea, cocktails, and sushi. On the second level, the Terrace Restaurant offers breakfast and lunch, and dining alfresco in the courtyard is among the hotel's great pleasures. For elegant suppers, the Dining Room *(see restaurant listing)* serves contemporary cuisine in a lavish setting.

Each of the guestrooms has been carefully restored with European charm and luxury in mind. All include wireless Internet access and high-definition, flat-screen TVs; marble bathrooms come with rain showerheads, double sinks, and separate water closets. On the upper floors, the amenities of the Club Level provide unexcelled ambience, privacy, and pampering.

Argonaut

495 Jefferson St. (at Hyde St.)

Phone: 415-563-0800 or 866-415-0704
Fax: 415-563-2800
Web: www.argonauthotel.com
Prices: $$

239 Rooms

13 Suites

Kimpton Hotels and Restaurants

There's no doubt about which hotel has the most character in this part of the city. Perfectly located near Ghirardelli Square, the cable-car turnaround and Fisherman's Wharf, the Argonaut occupies a 1907 waterfront warehouse at The Cannery. It shares the space with the Maritime National Historic Park Visitor Center.

There's no doubt, either, about the theme of this pet-friendly hotel: its solid, primary colors, maritime artifacts, and nautical design motifs give it away, beginning in the lobby where a lovely celestial clock hangs over the fireplace. Exposed brick walls and massive wooden beams and columns also reflect the hardworking heritage of the historic building.

Rooms and suites remain solidly in character: bold stripes and stars decorate walls, furniture, and carpets. The rooms are well soundproofed and have modern amenities including flat-screen TVs, CD-DVD players. and complimentary high-speed Internet access. Some of them offer views of the bay and Alcatraz. A Kimpton Group signature, six "Tall Rooms" come with extra-long beds and raised showerheads for tall guests.

Bohème

444 Columbus Ave. (bet. Green & Vallejo Sts.)

Phone: 415-433-9111
Fax: 415-362-6292
Web: www.hotelboheme.com
Prices: $$

15 Rooms

Hotel Boheme

This quaint boutique hotel at the foot of Telegraph Hill in the heart of North Beach takes its inspiration from the bohemian Beat Generation of the 1950s. And well it might, as poet Allen Ginsberg once slept here. Next door you'll find Vesuvio Cafe and City Lights Bookstore (founded by poet Lawrence Ferlinghetti), two hangouts still haunted by Beat spirits.

Built in the 1880s and rebuilt after the earthquake, the Victorian structure has been nicely adapted to its current role. Its 15 rooms reflect a certain 1950s countercultural style in their bright colors and eclectic furniture; they are small, romantic, and meticulously clean. Each has a private bath, and all the rooms offer wireless Internet access. About half face Columbus Avenue, which makes for good people-watching, but not much peace and quiet. The surrounding neighborhood is great for strolling and sipping coffee; from here you can walk up Telegraph Hill to Coit Tower and explore up and down the Filbert Steps.

The courteous staff at the Hotel Bohème is glad to help make reservations for restaurants, theater performances, and tours.

Four Seasons

757 Market St. (bet. Third & Fourth Sts.)

Phone: 415-633-3000 or 800-819-5053
Fax: 415-633-3001
Web: www.fourseasons.com/sanfrancisco
Prices: $$$$

231 Rooms

46 Suites

Four Seasons Hotel, San Francisco

A testament to the burgeoning neighborhood south of Market Street, this sophisticated, modern luxury hotel opened in 2001. Occupying the first 12 stories of a residential highrise in the Yerba Buena Arts District, the Four Seasons is convenient to Union Square, the Moscone Convention Center, and the San Francisco Museum of Modern Art.

The lobby, on the fifth floor, balances modern and classic design, blending golden wood tones with artwork for a quiet, contemporary effect. Art is everywhere, as the hotel showcases throughout its public spaces a considerable collection of paintings, sculpture, and ceramics by Bay Area artists.

Rooms, as they ascend from the 6th to the 17th floor, offer more and more stunning views of the city. Restful tones and residential touches decorate each one, the smallest of which measures a generous 450 square feet. All rooms feature large baths with a deep soaking tub and separate shower. In-room amenities include fluffy terrycloth robes, down pillows, high-speed Internet access, a CD sound system, and Playstation. Guests have complimentary access to the on-site Sports Club/LA, with its junior Olympic-size pool and full-service spa.

The Mosser

B2

54 4th St. (bet. Market & Mission Sts.)

Phone: 415-986-4400 or 800-227-3804
Fax: 415-495-4337
Web: www.themosser.com
Prices: $

166 Rooms

The Mosser

The Mosser successfully overlays a fresh modern look against the backdrop of its historic building, originally opened as a hotel in 1913. It offers a good price in a great location accessible to destinations north and south of Market Street. Best of all, the helpful, friendly staff really sets this economical property apart.

Though they are small and lack a view, the rooms on the courtyard are quiet (all have double-pane windows) and less expensive. The clean, crisp décor includes platform beds, white-washed walls, and geometrically patterned carpet for a comfortable Danish-modern effect. Some rooms feature lovely bay windows with window seats that overlook the street.

For a particular bargain, 54 of the hotel's 166 rooms share well-kept bathrooms—no more than three rooms per bath—though sinks, vanities, and bath amenities furnish all the rooms. Extras include CD players, cable TV, ceiling fans, dataports, and voice mail. Wireless Internet access is available for a fee. The hotel even has its own professional recording studio, in case you need help mixing your new CD.

InterContinental

888 Howard St. (at 5th St.)

Phone: 888-811-4273
Fax: 415-616-6501
Web: www.intercontinentalsanfrancisco.com
Prices: $$$

536 Rooms

14 Suites

InterContinental Hotels/Rien van Rijthoven

San Francisco's newest InterContinental hotel rose on the scene in February 2008, piercing the SoMa skyline with its 32-story blue-glass tower. The eye-catching landmark on the corner of Howard and Fifth streets sits adjacent to the Moscone Convention Center, and just a few blocks away from Market Street—equally well situated for those visiting for business or pleasure.

Contemporary in style and voluminous in size, the hotel offers friendly, personalized service that helps make up for its corporate feel—though abundant meeting facilities do draw a large business crowd to the property.

In the rooms, colors are neutral, so as not to distract from luxuries such as feather pillows and comforters, wood paneled headboards, flat-screen TVs, and large windows for surveying the downtown landscape. Standard bathrooms are on the small side, yet well-equipped with marble countertops, Floris bath products, and fluffy towels and bathrobes.

An indoor lap pool and state-of-the-art gym are located on the 6th floor, next to the 10-room I-Spa, with a lovely terrace that wraps around the building. Off the lobby, Luce restaurant creates tastes of Tuscany using California products.

Palace

2 New Montgomery St. (at Market St.)

Phone: 415-512-1111 or 888-625-5144
Fax: 415-543-0671
Web: www.sfpalace.com
Prices: **$$$$**

518 Rooms

34 Suites

Palace Hotel

Another of downtown San Francisco's grand dames, the Palace symbolized the city's meteoric rise from boomtown to world-class metropolis when it opened in 1875. Today, through earthquake, fire, and 130-plus years, the hotel withstands the test of time. Its centerpiece is the sumptuous Garden Court, beautifully restored to its 1909 condition. Here, guests can have breakfast, lunch, or brunch under a stunning canopy of intricately leaded art glass hung with Austrian glass chandeliers. In a different mood, the Pied Piper Bar displays a mural painted especially for the Palace by American illustrator Maxfield Parrish in 1909.

Classically elegant guestrooms and suites were refreshed in 2002 and are now done up in pale sunny tones with broad accents of color. With 14-foot ceilings and windows that open, they are spacious and airy. For business travelers, work areas are ample and well lit, with high-speed Internet access (wireless is available in meeting spaces), two-line phones, and laptop safes. The fitness center features a beautiful skylit lap pool, workout room, and spa services.

Palomar

12 4th St. (at Market St.)

Phone: 415-348-1111 or 866-373-4941
Fax: 415-348-0302
Web: www.hotelpalomar-sf.com
Prices: $$$

179 Rooms

16 Suites

Palomar/David Phelps

Edgy, urban, artful, tranquil: this downtown addition to the Kimpton family of properties offers just enough of each in a great location. At home on the 5th through the 8th floors of a landmark 1908 building, Hotel Palomar comprises 198 guestrooms, including 16 one- and two-bedroom suites.

Some of the rooms overlook Fourth and Market streets (they are well soundproofed) while the rest face the interior courtyard. Rooms are quite spacious and strike a good balance between contemporary style and restful atmosphere, though every one sports a sassy leopard-print carpet. Rooms provide complimentary Aveda bath amenities, two plush robes, wireless Internet access, CD and DVD players, and an expanded work area. Suites and luxury rooms feature Fuji spa tubs and turreted windows with circular seating areas.

Guests can enjoy the on-site fitness center 24 hours a day, and complimentary yoga baskets are available upon request. Morning coffee is served in the lobby, and the stylishly redecorated Fifth Floor Restaurant *(see restaurant listing)*—acclaimed for its French-Gascon cuisine—is open for breakfast and dinner.

St. Regis

C2

125 3rd St. (at Mission St.)

Phone: 415-284-4000 or 877-787-3447
Fax: 415-442-0385
Web: www.stregis.com
Prices: **$$$$**

214 Rooms

46 Suites

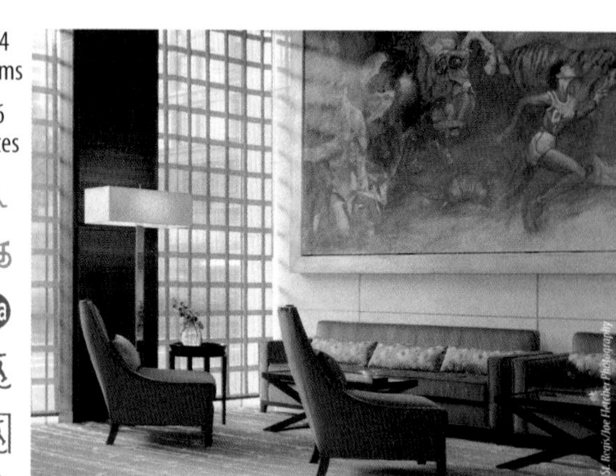

St. Regis/Joe Fletcher Photography

The historic St. Regis' first incarnation in the City by the Bay is anything but stuffy. Occupying the first 20 floors of a handsome new highrise designed by Skidmore, Owings, and Merrill, the new hotel epitomizes the look and feel of classic contemporary. The oxymoron works, and it doesn't stop there. The complex also includes condos on the upper floors, a 1907 building, and the Museum of the African Diaspora. Next door is the San Francisco Museum of Modern Art.

Throughout, the hotel cultivates neutral colors, from the striated Zebrano wood of the lobby to the rich cocoa and foggy gray tones of the guestrooms. A striking 16-foot open fireplace greets guests as they enter the lobby, which also features a sleek lounge area. Cool, comfortable, spacious rooms, and suites overlook Yerba Buena Park, or have expansive city views. On the ground level, Ame *(see restaurant listing)* serves Hiro Sone's modern fusion cuisine.

Plasma-screen TVs are standard, and a touchscreen on the nightstand controls the room's temperature, curtains, and lighting. Those familiar with St. Regis service will be cheered to know that the signature personal butlers are alive and well here.

Vitale

8 Mission St. (bet. Steuart St. & The Embarcadero)

Phone: 415-278-3700 or 888-890-8688
Fax: 415-278-3750
Web: www.hotelvitale.com
Prices: $$$

179 Rooms

20 Suites

A relative newcomer to San Francisco, the self-proclaimed "post-hip" Vitale occupies a prime location on the city's waterfront in the revitalized Embarcadero. Across the street, the Ferry Building Marketplace offers a panoply of gourmet delights, and San Francisco Bay laps at the front yard.

A fresh and natural luxury permeates public spaces and guestrooms. Rich wood paneling, rough-hewn stone columns, large softly curtained windows, and simply designed furniture in muted hues give the lobby a modern Scandinavian look. Natural light streams into the airy guestrooms, where all the details have been carefully planned with a sumptuous touch: luxurious linens, flat-screen TVs, CD players, and complimentary wireless Internet access. About half the 199 rooms on the hotel's eight floors have waterfront views; suites in the circular tower offer 180-degree panoramas of city and bay.

Among the offerings at the dog-friendly Vitale are free yoga classes for guests, and an on-site spa with rooftop tubs for soaking up fabulous views. Americano restaurant *(see restaurant listing)* serves breakfast, lunch, dinner, and weekend brunch; the circular bar makes a comfortable place to hang out.

W - San Francisco

181 3rd St. (at Howard St.)

Phone: 415-777-5300
Fax: 415-817-7823
Web: www.whotels.com
Prices: **$$$**

410 Rooms

W San Francisco

Equally well-situated for business or pleasure, the W San Francisco sits next door to the Moscone Convention Center, the San Francisco Museum of Modern Art, and Yerba Buena Gardens. Built in 1999, this W recently received a fashion-forward facelift. The octagonal, three-story lobby now offers everything a hip, young professional could desire: contemporary artwork, a bar serving organic cocktails; live DJ music; and comfortable seating around a fireplace.

Most of the rooms boast an unobstructed view of the city, along with details such as an iPod docking station, a well-appointed mini bar, and marble baths with Bliss amenities—courtesy of the hotel's new 5,000-square-foot Bliss Spa. Refreshed accommodations sport a modern minimalist design with Asian accents. Options range from "Wonderful"—W-speak for standard—to "Fabulous," not to mention the two levels of suites. Laid-back and polite, the young staff is eager to help guests at any time of day or night; and the hotel's Pets Are Welcome policy means you don't have to leave your best friend at home.

Continuing the alphabetic W theme, XYZ restaurant (*see restaurant listing*) indulges diners with modern Californian cuisine.

Claremont Resort & Spa

41 Tunnel Rd., Berkeley

Phone: 510-843-3000 or 800-551-7266
Fax: 510-843-6239
Web: www.claremontresort.com
Prices: $$$

263 Rooms

16 Suites

Conceived in the grand tradition of 19th-century resort spas, the Claremont in its present configuration opened for business in 1915. For more than 90 years, it has pampered guests with comfort, cuisine, and spa services par excellence. Today the gleaming white castle-like edifice houses 279 luxurious rooms and suites, three restaurants, a world-renowned spa, and a spectacular health club open to all guests. Surrounded by 22 beautifully landscaped acres in the hills overlooking San Francisco Bay, the Claremont promises classic resort indulgence and luxury.

Rooms offer three degrees of comfort, all sumptuous; about half of them face the stunning skyline vista of San Francisco and the Bay Bridge. Amenities include Internet access and in-room entertainment centers; some bathrooms feature whirlpool tubs.

With so much to do around the resort, however, you may not spend much time in your room. At the on-site private health club, 10 tennis courts (6 lit for evening play), 2 outdoor heated pools, fitness equipment, and 65 weekly classes from yoga to hula will keep you busy. Relaxing treatments, wraps, and massages at the 20,000-square-foot Spa Claremont ice the cake.

Casa Madrona

801 Bridgeway, Sausalito

Phone: 415-332-0532 or 800-288-0502
Fax: 415-332-0528
Web: www.casamadrona.com
Prices: $$$

63 Rooms

Casa Madrona Hotel & Spa

Whether you prefer contemporary or historic surroundings, Casa Madrona has a room for you. Tucked into a hillside rising from the Sausalito waterfront, the complex includes a 19th-century mansion, a covey of quaint cottages, and a modern hotel building. From its elevated vantage point, the Victorian Mansion, built in 1885, offers lovely bay views.

Nineteenth-century atmosphere pervades its small but charming guestrooms, each decorated individually with antique furniture and period wallpaper. Cottage-style accommodations built into the hillside since 1976 include the mid-size Garden Court rooms (decorated in contemporary or historic styles), and the Bayview rooms, each of which features a distinctive decorating theme—from the Rose Chalet to the exotic Katmandu room. Most of these offer fireplaces and large private balconies. Brick pathways and outdoor stair steps set about with gardens and scented plantings connect these chambers. Californian contemporary-style rooms occupy the most recently opened addition to the hotel in a building perched on the waterfront.

Downstairs, Poggio *(see restaurant listing)* dishes up authentic Italian fare.

The Inn Above Tide

30 El Portal (at Bridgeway), Sausalito

Phone: 415-332-9535 or 800-893-8433
Fax: 415-332-6714
Web: www.innabovetide.com
Prices: $$$

29 Rooms

©Marco Ricca, NY

You can't get much closer to the bay than at The Inn Above Tide, where balconies extend out over the lapping water. Also nearby the attractive shingled building is the San Francisco ferry landing and the Sausalito Visitor Center kiosk.

The hotel's small lobby accommodates only the reception desk; complimentary continental breakfast is served in the adjacent guest lounge—or the staff will deliver it to your room, if you prefer. Also included in the room rate is complimentary wine and cheese from 5:00 P.M. to 7:00 P.M. Each of the 29 renovated rooms faces the water and offers stunning views of San Francisco, Sausalito, and Angel Island. Floor-to-ceiling windows bring the outdoors in, and binoculars come standard in each room.

Small superior rooms offer no deck, but deluxe rooms feature terraces and wood- or gas-burning fireplaces, and a host of amenities that increase as you upgrade from queen to king to grand. All rooms offer wireless Internet access. Interiors are styled in sober but soothing beige tones, with nature providing a vivid blue accent just outside.

Cypress

10050 S. De Anza Blvd. (at Stevens Creek Blvd), Cupertino

Phone: 408-253-8900 or 800-499-1408
Fax: 408-253-3800
Web: www.thecypresshotel.com
Prices: **$$**

224 Rooms

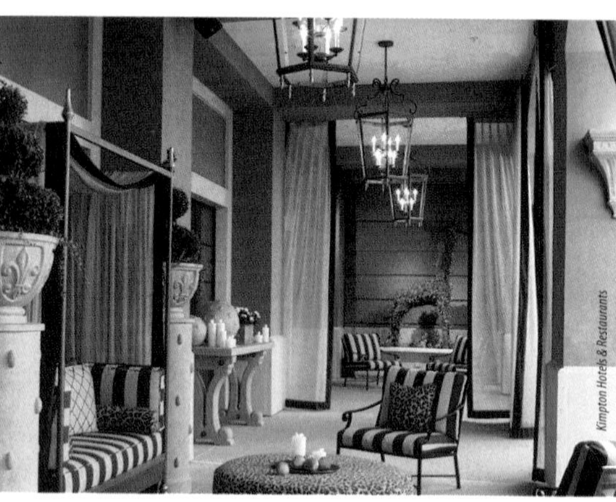

Kimpton Hotels & Restaurants

This member of the Kimpton Group is set in the heart of Silicon Valley, close to major interstate arteries and a convenient launching pad for accessing local high-tech companies as well as the area's attractions.

Bold contemporary style is a Kimpton signature, and the Cypress follows suit with rooms decked out in a mélange of colors and textures, including animal-print carpeting and polka-dot wallpaper. Large windows let in natural light, but if it's tranquility you seek, simply draw the thick curtains and block the outside world. Down duvets, ample fluffy pillows, leopard-print robes, L'Occitane bath amenities, and free WiFi Internet access appeal to both leisure and business travelers.

There's a 24-hour fitness facility on-site, but if swimming is your thing, you'll have to walk a few minutes to a nearby lap pool (part of a neighboring residential complex). A complimentary wine reception each evening is part of the program here.

This pet-friendly property offers a special package that pampers your pooch with yummy treats and his own dog bed, while it caters to you with complimentary valet parking.

De Anza

233 W. Santa Clara St. (bet. Almaden Blvd. & Notre Dame Ave.), San Jose

Phone: 408-286-1000 or 800-843-3700
Fax: 408-286-2087
Web: www.hoteldeanza.com
Prices: $$

80 Rooms

20 Suites

Hotel De Anza/Mark Nichols

A complete renovation in 1990 brought this Art Deco gem back to life, where it most decidedly remains. Behind its unmistakable pink façade, the Hotel De Anza exudes a genuine period charm, from its spacious and comfortable lobby to its pleasant guestrooms and suites. Its ideal location in downtown San Jose makes it convenient for business or pleasure.

Neutral taupes and browns with blond wood furniture warm the bedrooms without overdoing it. And though most rooms face a busy street, they are adequately soundproofed. Bathrooms are decorated in green marble. High-speed Internet (with wireless in the public areas), two TVs, and a VCR with complimentary videos furnish each room, along with three phones.

Check out La Pastaia restaurant for Italian cuisine served in a colorful taverna atmosphere. Late-night snackers can "Raid Our Pantry" for free deli sandwiches between 10:00 P.M. and 5:00 A.M. In the morning, a full buffet featuring cold and hot items is served in the brightly hand-painted breakfast room. Don't miss sipping a cocktail at the Hedley Club Lounge, accented by an exotic Moorish-Spanish décor.

Montgomery

211 S. 1st St. (at San Carlos St.), San Jose

Phone: 408-282-8800 or 800-738-7477
Fax: 408-282-8850
Web: www.hotelmontgomerysj.com
Prices: $$

80 Rooms

6 Suites

Joie de Vivre Hospitality

This 1911 Renaissance revival-style building was moved 186 feet from its original location in 2002, in order to save it from the wrecking ball. Today, as the Hotel Montgomery, the edifice has been refitted inside with a chic contemporary design featuring low sofas upholstered in geometric-patterned fabrics and faux-fur-covered armchairs in the lobby.

In the rooms, a warm color scheme of gold and brown is accented with Burberry plaids and splashes of red. Egyptian cotton linens and down comforters dress the beds, and the bathrooms are elegantly appointed with beige marble. Conveniences, including free high-speed Internet access, safes that fit laptops, and a 24-hour fitness center make the accommodations in this historic property thoroughly modern.

Since downtown San Jose attracts more corporate types than tourists, the low-key Montgomery attracts a lot of business travelers. In this regard, the hotel is well-located near the convention center and next to the local VTA (Valley Transportation Authority) light-rail track that heads up to Mountain View. (For a quiet stay, ask for a room that doesn't face the track.)

The Ritz-Carlton, Half Moon Bay

C2

1 Miramontes Point Rd. (at Hwy. 1), Half Moon Bay

Phone: 650-712-7000 or 800-241-3333
Fax: 650-712-7070
Web: www.ritzcarlton.com/hmb
Prices: $$$$

239 Rooms

22 Suites

Elegant décor, luxurious amenities, impeccable service—everything you would expect from a Ritz-Carlton is here. But as good as this hotel is, everything pales next to the view. And that's exactly how it was planned. Sitting atop a bluff overlooking the Pacific coastline, the resort takes full advantage of its setting. Guestroom décor in subdued tones creates a calming frame for the coastal views that most rooms feature. Baths follow suit in white polished marble. Some rooms have terraces with fire pits.

Navio restaurant *(see restaurant listing)* offers formal dining, while The Conservatory Lounge dishes up more casual fare with its floor-to-ceiling ocean vistas. Keep your eye on the Pacific in the custom-built wine room, where 5,000 bottles await, or on the Ocean Terrace. If all the drama at sea gets to be too much, afternoon tea is served in the paneled library.

Nearly flawless service makes it challenging to do anything yourself here. If you must be on the go, tennis courts, jogging trails, a fitness center, a full activity schedule, and two oceanside golf courses oblige. Or relax in the spa's Roman bath. Better yet, just sit back and enjoy the view.

Stanford Park

100 El Camino Real (at Sand Hill Rd.), Menlo Park

Phone: 650-322-1234 or 888-322-7788
Fax: 650-322-0975
Web: www.stanfordparkhotel.com
Prices: $$$

134 Rooms

29 Suites

Situated next to Stanford University and the Stanford Shopping Center, this English Colonial-style hotel offers a civilized retreat from research or retail. Stately palm trees and a fountain announce the entrance to the four-story hotel. Cedar shingles and white trim cover the exterior, while antiques and museum-quality objects d'art grace the lobby. The latter, incidentally contains a library of literary masterpieces for guests' use—this is still Stanford, after all.

Spacious guestrooms, some with fireplaces, canopied beds, and vaulted ceilings radiate traditional elegance. Bathrooms boast granite counters and make-up mirrors. Other appointments include full-length mirrors, large closets, and separate dressing areas. Put on one of the plush robes and curl up with a book—or your computer and complimentary Wi-Fi access.

With manicured garden courtyards blooming with bright flowers and lush foliage, the public grounds of the Stanford Park make a serene park-like setting in which to relax. If active is your style, you can swim laps in the heated pool, pump some iron in the on-site gym, then savor the American fare at the Duck Club Restaurant.

Valencia

355 Santana Row (bet. Olin Ave. & Tatum Ln.), San Jose

Phone: 408-551-0010 or 866-842-0100
Fax: 408-551-0550
Web: www.hotelvalencia.com
Prices: $$

195 Rooms

16 Suites

Spa

Hotel Valencia/Thuy Saliba

This charming hacienda, punctuated with Asian accents, is located in Santana Row, San Jose's new upscale "urban oasis" where shopping, dining, living, and entertainment venues share 42 acres near downtown. The hotel spans an entire block and evokes a gracious Old World atmosphere done up in chic California style.

Visitors enter through the large main lobby and take an elevator to the third-floor reception area, which is warmly decorated in rich tones of red and ochre. Outside, the hotel floors rise around a charming courtyard, complete with a central fountain and an open fireplace. Dine on this cozy patio at Citrus, the hotel's sleek steakhouse. Or, for a spectacular view with your Shiraz, ascend to the seventh-floor terrace of Cielo bar.

Accommodations are generously sized; deluxe rooms feature balconies overlooking Santana Row or the hotel's courtyard. Deep yellow walls, dark wood furniture, and trim give rooms a European feel. Perfectly equipped bathrooms include robes and oversized plush towels. High-speed and wireless Internet access are complimentary. For relaxing, Valencia offers an Ayurvedic spa and a lovely outdoor pool on the fifth floor.

Auberge du Soleil

B1

180 Rutherford Hill Rd. (off the Silverado Trail), Rutherford

Phone: 707-963-1211 or 800-348-5406
Fax: 707-963-8764
Web: www.aubergedusoleil.com
Prices: $$$$

31 Rooms

21 Suites

Spa

The quintessential Wine Country hideaway, the "Inn of the Sun" tucks into 33 hilly acres overlooking the Napa Valley. It was the valley's first luxury hotel when it opened its rooms to guests in 1985. More than 20 years later, silvery olive trees and sunny colors still create a rustic Mediterranean feel, while flat-screen TVs, DVD players, and complimentary wireless Internet access provide all the modern amenities you could desire.

Scrambling down the hillsides, newly renovated rooms and suites, all housed in "sun and earth" cottages, feature Italian linens, down pillows and duvets, robes, slippers, private terraces, and mini-bars stocked with beverages and snacks—compliments of the house. Spacious bathrooms are equipped with skylights, separate showers, and LCD flat-panel TVs to watch while you soak in the tub.

Be sure to savor a meal at The Restaurant at Auberge du Soleil *(see restaurant listing)*, which is renowned as much for its breezy terrace and sweeping views as for its excellent Cal-Med cuisine. And pamper yourself with a Napa-themed treatment (a warm grapeseed-oil massage or the Vineyard Head to Toe) at the 7,000-square-foot Spa du Soleil.

The Carneros Inn

4048 Sonoma Hwy. (Napa)

Phone: 707-299-4900 or 888-400-9000
Fax: 707-299-4950
Web: www.thecarnerosinn.com
Prices: **$$$$**

76 Rooms

10 Suites

Mark Hundley

Perched at the crossroads between Napa and Sonoma, the Carneros Inn is a PlumpJack resort—part of the group that owns the PlumpJack winery as well as Jack Falstaff restaurant and Plumpjack Café in San Francisco (*see restaurant listing for both*).

The concept here takes its cue from the surrounding countryside, fitting a complex of individual cottages into a 27-acre vineyard setting. Natural light bathes tastefully decorated cottages, with French doors leading out to an enclosed patio. Here, reclining lounge chairs promote stargazing, and a table with a heat lamp over it makes the ideal stage for a private alfresco wine tasting.

In the bathrooms, heated slate floors warm your feet, and sunken tubs provide places for soaking. Guests even have the option of indoor or outdoor showers. Two pool areas, a spa, and a terrific gym featuring yoga and fitness classes (schedule changes seasonally) will keep you in top shape.

With its breathtaking view, Hilltop restaurant is the place for breakfast, while fine-dining Farm (*see restaurant listing*) has a great outdoor lounge for cocktails. Boon Fly Café (*see restaurant listing*) dishes up a casual menu of sandwiches and flatbread pizzas.

Lavender

C2

2020 Webber St. (bet. Yount & Jefferson Sts.), Yountville

Phone: 707-944-1388 or 800-522-4140
Fax: 707-944-1579
Web: www.lavendernapa.com
Prices: $$

8 Rooms

Four Sisters Inns

Nested in a profusion of lavender and roses, this country inn offers a comfortable, rustic stay in the heart of Napa. A wraparound porch embraces the main farmhouse, and inside, the small entry parlor and sunny breakfast room welcome guests. A full complimentary meal is served each morning, to be enjoyed here or in the lovely terrace garden.

Two guestrooms also occupy the main house, one with a private spa tub tucked onto an enclosed outdoor deck. Six cottage rooms surround the house and garden, each with its own private entrance and patio. All the accommodations are spacious and decorated with sophisticated country charm in the Provençal style; they include king beds and fireplaces. Glazed tile glistens in the gracious bathrooms, set off pleasingly by brightly painted walls. Double sinks and a generous-size tub make these baths particularly pleasant, though soaking tubs have no showers. Wireless Internet access is available throughout the hotel.

Guests at Lavender can borrow house bicycles for a spin, and enjoy pool privileges (for a fee) at nearby Maison Fleurie *(see hotel listings)*. Or, try your hand at *boules*, the French version of lawn bowling.

Maison Fleurie

6529 Yount St. (at Washington St.), Yountville

Phone: 707-944-2056 or 800-788-0369
Fax: 707-944-9342
Web: www.maisonfleurienapa.com
Prices: $$

13 Rooms

The "flowering house" has given itself over to a lush French country style, with Provençal-inspired fabrics, furnishings, and atmosphere. Located in three buildings set amid beautifully landscaped gardens and overlooking vineyards, the 13 rooms of the Maison Fleurie spell charm and comfort.

A homey lobby/lounge complete with a fireplace welcomes visitors in the main building, where seven of the guestrooms are located. These include king and queen rooms, along with two very small rooms without televisions. The two Carriage House rooms have private entrances, and those in the Bakery Building all include fireplaces, king beds, and whirlpool spa tubs. Breakfast (with home-baked muffins and bread) and evening wine and hors d'oeuvres are complimentary for all guests, and every room features wireless Internet access.

On the grounds, the small heated swimming pool and outdoor hot tub are pleasant, and the vistas delightful. Guests can borrow bicycles for a spin in the countryside or an exploration of the surrounding town of Yountville, known for its trendy boutiques and excellent eateries.

Meadowood

B1

900 Meadowood Ln. (off the Silverado Trail), St. Helena

Phone: 707-963-3646 or 800-458-8080
Fax: 707-963-3532
Web: www.meadowood.com
Prices: **$$$$**

41 Rooms

44 Suites

Spa

Meadowood Napa

Set on 250 exquisite acres a mile east of downtown St. Helena, this world-class resort off the Silverado Trail nestles amid wooded hills, where accommodations take the form of individual cottages. A country-club ambience pervades this recently renovated Relais & Châteaux property. White wainscoting, wood-burning fireplaces, spacious bathrooms, and French doors leading onto private terraces highlight the room décor. (The resort doubles as a private country club for Napa Valley residents.)

While Meadowood makes the perfect perch for Wine Country adventures, between the 9-hole golf course, 7 tennis courts, 2 croquet lawns, 2 lap pools, the fitness center, and the new full-service spa, you may never want to leave the grounds. There's even a wine center (ask the staff to arrange vineyard picnics), where the resort's wine tutor holds tastings and seminars for guests. Meals can be either casual at The Grill (where an English-style breakfast is served) overlooking the golf course, or more formal at the excellent Restaurant at Meadowood *(see restaurant listing)*, lauded for its refined California cuisine.

Napa River Inn

500 Main St. (at 5th St.), Napa

Phone: 707-251-8550 or 877-251-8500
Fax: 707-251-8504
Web: www.napariverinn.com
Prices: $$$

68 Rooms

Napa River Inn

The Historic Napa Mill (1884), with its present-day complex of shops and restaurants, forms a convenient setting for this downtown boutique hotel. Rooms at the Napa River Inn are divided among three structures and are distinguished by three different design themes. Full of vintage charm, eight rooms in the 1884 Hatt Building are done in Victorian style with canopy beds, fireplaces, and old-fashioned slipper tubs. In the Plaza Building, 34 rooms sport a rustic wine country décor and creature comforts such as marble bathrooms and balconies with river views. The remaining quarters are housed in the 1862 Embarcadero Building, where they are decked out in a maritime motif, complete with cherrywood wainscoting, porthole mirrors, and carved-rope frames.

All rooms offer amenities such as complimentary daily newspaper, bottled water, irons, ironing boards, terrycloth robes, nightlights, and make-up mirrors. Grapeseed-oil-based bath products are de rigueur for this wine country inn.

The town's points of interest lie close by, and if you don't feel like walking, the city trolley stops in front of the hotel every 15 minutes to transport you around the downtown area.

Rancho Caymus Inn

1140 Rutherford Rd. (off Hwy. 29), Rutherford

Phone: 707-963-1777 or 800-800-1777
Fax: 707-963-5387
Web: www.ranchocaymus.com
Prices: $$

25 Rooms

1 Suites

Rancho Caymus Inn

Well located between St. Helena and Yountville, Rancho Caymus Inn blends a bit of old California with Wine Country convenience and unpretentious western hospitality. All the rooms and suites are housed in the rambling hacienda-style building. Each bears the name of a Napa Valley personality, from Lillie Langtry to Black Bart.

Mexican-style wooden furniture, hand-carved walnut bedsteads, wrought-iron details, and colorful woolen rugs impart a genuine Old West ranch feeling to the spacious rooms. Massive century-old oak ceiling beams and trim of walnut, fir, and redwood add a natural warmth. Designed as "split levels," the sleeping areas are set up a step in each room. Standard amenities include televisions, air conditioning, wet bar, and refrigerator, and some rooms have mission-style fireplaces and private outdoor balconies or sitting areas. More elaborate Master Suites feature whirlpool tubs against a stained-glass backdrop in their bathrooms. All the rooms are quiet, well maintained, and clean, and breakfast is included in the room rate.

Villagio Inn & Spa

6481 Washington St., Yountville

Phone: 707-944-8877 or 800-351-1133
Fax: 707-944-8855
Web: www.villagio.com
Prices: $$$

86 Rooms

26 Suites

M. Linda Lee/MICHELIN

Villagio brings to mind a Tuscan village; two-story villas range through lush gardens and vineyards that share a 23-acre family-owned estate with the Vintage Inn. A stroll around the grounds here reveals tranquil pools and fountains, vivid flowers, and cypress, olive, and Meyer lemon trees.

Accommodations are done in Tuscan style with warm tones, wrought-iron accents, plantation shutters, and wood-burning fireplaces. Rooms on the upper levels have domed ceilings and furnished balconies (ground-level rooms have patios). Villagio accommodates business functions with 10,000 square feet of meeting space. In the morning, breakfast takes the form of a complimentary gourmet buffet (complete with Champagne) served in the lobby. Also included in the room rate is the afternoon tea and Friday evening wine tastings, sponsored by local vineyards.

At the end of a long day spent cycling or visiting wineries, a Napa River stone massage at the Spa at Villagio is a great way to unwind. (A new expanded spa is in the works.) Weddings are memorable events at Villagio, especially with the addition of the new outdoor pavilion surrounded by grassy lawns and bright plantings.

Vintage Inn

6541 Washington St., Yountville

Phone: 707-944-1112 or 800-351-1133
Fax: 707-944-1617
Web: www.vintageinn.com
Prices: $$$

72 Rooms

8 Suites

Opened in 1985, this lovely property lines Yountville's main street with French Country charm. Paths and footbridges connect the two-story buildings, where French antiques, toile de Jouy fabrics, plush robes, and down duvets set the tone for luxurious comfort. Each room features a wood-burning fireplace, and bathrooms are equipped with dual sinks and an oversize whirlpool tub; suites add wet bars and eating areas.

Rates include a bottle of wine in your room, a gourmet breakfast buffet, and afternoon tea. If you tire of touring wineries, the inn offers an outdoor heated lap pool, tennis courts, and bicycle rentals. Not to mention the fact that guests have access to the spa at sibling Villagio and to the Yountville Fitness Center (at no charge). Pets are welcomed here with their own goodies (no wine, but some yummy treats).

Shoppers can stroll next door to explore "V Marketplace." Once the Groezinger Winery, this brick complex now houses shops, galleries, and eateries. Foodies will love the fact that some of Napa Valley's most renowned restaurants—Bouchon, Bistro Jeanty, Redd, The French Laundry *(see restaurant listings)*—lie within easy walking distance of the resort.

Duchamp

421 Foss St. (at North St.), Healdsburg

Phone: 707-431-1300 or 800-431-9341
Fax: 707-431-1333
Web: www.duchamphotel.com
Prices: $$$

6 Rooms

This unusual small hotel is located within minutes of Healdsburg's downtown plaza, convenient to the wineries of the Russian River, Dry Creek, and Alexander Valley. The owners also run a small winery of the same name. Their affection for French Dada artist Marcel Duchamp manifests itself in wonderful, whimsical ways at both locations.

The hotel comprises seven small bungalows: one for reception and six housing one guestroom each. The grouping surrounds a heated swimming pool equipped with a sundeck and Jacuzzi. Each room is large, but minimalist in style, with whitewashed walls and decorative murals to add just a touch of color. Floors are polished concrete, the furniture contemporary. French doors let in the light, and each cottage features a private patio. King beds furnish the rooms, along with a high-definition flat-screen TV, a CD player, and free wireless Internet access. White walls and tiles dress the very large bathrooms, which include two washbasins and a roomy shower.

Guests are treated to a continental breakfast buffet in the reception cottage, and the hotel staff will gladly arrange for private tours and tastings at Duchamp Estate Winery.

El Dorado

405 1st St. W. (at W. Spain St.), Sonoma

Phone: 707-996-3220 or 800-289-3031
Fax: 707-996-3148
Web: www.eldoradosonoma.com
Prices: $$

27 Rooms

El Dorado Hotel

The El Dorado occupies a spot at the heart of historic Sonoma, located directly on Spanish Plaza in a recently renovated historic building. Laid out by Mariano Vallejo in 1835, the eight-acre site is the largest Mexican-era plaza in California.

Light and color set the hotel's 27 rooms aglow, while cool tile floors suggest the town's Spanish origins and four-poster beds made up with fine linens add romance. French doors open onto private balconies or terraces and admit a wash of sunlight into the rooms. Some look over the historic plaza; others face the restaurant terrace, which is shaded by a fig tree. Though most bathrooms offer only showers, they are well appointed. Electronics include a flat-screen TV, along with DVD and CD players, cordless phone, and dataport.

If you don't mind casual service, the El Dorado presents good value for the money, as well as an alternative to the Provençal or Tuscany style that predominate in other Wine Country hostelries. Savor seasonal California cuisine at El Dorado Kitchen *(see restaurant listing)*.

The Fairmont
Sonoma Mission Inn & Spa

100 Boyes Blvd. (bet. Arnold Dr. & Hwy. 12), Sonoma

Phone: 707-938-9000 or 800-441-1414
Fax: 707-938-4250
Web: www.fairmont.com/sonoma
Prices: $$$

166 Rooms

60 Suites

Tile roofs, adobe walls, and the historic character of a Sonoma Valley mission create the perfect backdrop for a relaxing weekend getaway or a visit to Wine Country. Originally built around an ancient hot springs in 1895, the resort was rebuilt in 1927 after fire destroyed the property. Renovated and greatly expanded since then, the facility retains its gracious 1920s atmosphere with all the comforts of a modern hotel and spa.

Nowadays, guests can still "take the waters," as well as enjoy the many services offered at the luxurious spa. They can also play the private 18-hole championship golf course, hike the countryside, lounge by the pool, take fitness classes, or join bike tours. The sprawling resort comprises a central "living room" with a variety of accommodations spread among an assortment of buildings. Done up in French country décor, standard rooms tend to be small; wood-burning fireplaces furnish about half of them. Signature Mission Suites, the most recent additions to the property, foster romance with two-person Jacuzzi tubs and private patios or balconies.

Gaige House Inn

13540 Arnold Dr. (at Railroad St.), Glen Ellen

Phone: 707-935-0237 or 800-935-0237
Fax: 707-935-6411
Web: www.gaige.com
Prices: $$$

12 Rooms

11 Suites

The Gaige House Inn offers a complete departure from typical Wine Country accommodations. Here, serenity trumps country or western charm; Japanese influences replace French and Spanish inside an 1890 Queen Anne Victorian. Tucked away on three wooded creekside acres, this intimate inn features a full menu of spa services, a particularly fine breakfast, and a lovely swimming pool.

Guests can reserve a room in the main house or a garden or creek suite in separate cottage settings. Though all 23 rooms and suites share a similar palette of earthy browns and grays with design details inspired by nature, each one has been thoughtfully furnished, decorated, and arranged individually. In some, tatami mats cover hardwood floors, and rice-paper screens decorate the walls; others feature fireplaces. In the eight spa suites, beautifully hewn granite soaking tubs, and Japanese *tsubo* gardens for massage services turn your room into a spa. All cottage rooms feature private terraces or a little garden by the creek. This secluded inn promises quiet nights and peaceful days.

25 Matheson St. (at Healdsburg Ave.), Healdsburg

Phone: 707-431-2800 or 800-889-7188
Fax: 707-431-0414
Web: www.hotelhealdsburg.com
Prices: **$$$$**

51 Rooms

4 Suites

Facing Healdsburg's century-old town plaza, Hotel Healdsburg fills two connecting buildings with a warm, contemporary décor. Start in the lobby, with its clean lines, comfy seating, and adjacent screened porch for refreshments. Then it's off to your spacious room, where you'll be greeted by Tibetan rugs, teak furniture, fine linens, and French doors leading to your own private balcony.

Oversize bathrooms are outfitted with walk-in showers and separate soaking tubs. Outside, the pool beckons from its olive- and cypress-tree-shrouded nook.

Pamper yourself at the hotel's spa, where you can unwind with a Thai massage or a wine and honey wrap. For an amorous afternoon, indulge yourself and a loved one in a massage and soak *à deux*, complete with sparkling wine and chocolates. After your spa treatment, finish off the day right by enjoying contemporary cuisine at Charlie Palmer's Dry Creek Kitchen *(see restaurant listing)*. A kicked-up continental breakfast is included in the room rate.

Honor Mansion

14891 Grove St. (bet. Dry Creek Rd. & Grand St.), Healdsburg

Phone: 707-433-4277 or 800-554-4667
Fax: 707-431-7173
Web: www.honormansion.com
Prices: **$$$**

13 Rooms

Honor Mansion

Romance awaits behind the unassuming façade of this restored 1883 house, located less than a mile away from the tony boutiques, tasting rooms, and fine restaurants lining Healdsburg's downtown plaza. Owners Cathi and Steve Fowler have anticipated guests' every need in the 13 individually decorated rooms and suites. Rooms in the main house vary in size and style, while four separate Vineyard Suites (the priciest accommodations) foster *amore* with king-size beds, gas fireplaces, and private patios complete with your own whirlpool (robes and rubber ducky included). On the four-acre grounds, landscaped with rose gardens and Zinfandel vines, you'll find a lap pool, a PGA putting green, bocce and tennis courts, a croquet lawn, and a half-basketball court.

The multicourse breakfast, which will steel your stomach for a day of sampling wine at area vineyards, is included in the room rate. Following the Fowlers' hospitable lead, the staff will pack you a picnic lunch, and make arrangements for everything from private winery visits to poolside massages, all with equal aplomb.

On weekends, count on a minimum stay of two nights in low season, and four nights in high season.

Les Mars

D1

27 North St. (bet. Foss St. & Healdsburg Ave.), Healdsburg

Phone: 707-433-4211 or 877-431-1700
Fax: 707-433-4611
Web: www.lesmarshotel.com
Prices: $$$$

16 Rooms

Les Mars Hotel

Picture the limestone façade of a 19th-century French chateau just off Healdsburg's plaza, and you've got Les Mars. Step inside and you'll be instantly awash in luxury, from the 17th-century Flemish tapestry that hangs in the lobby to the hand-carved walnut panels and leather-bound books that line the library.

Sumptuous antiques fill the 16 individually designed rooms with the likes of Louis XV armoires, draped four-poster beds, and chaise longues. Italian linens, reading lights, and switch-operated fireplaces provide extra thoughtful touches. In the bathrooms, lined with salt and pepper marble, you can pamper yourself with deep soaking tubs, lavender bath salts, and Bulgari amenities. Third-floor rooms boast high ceilings with exposed wood beams. Yes, the prices are steep, but this level of luxury doesn't come cheap.

The adjoining Cyrus restaurant, a separate venture *(see restaurant listing)*, makes an equally elegant setting in which to linger over Chef Douglas Keane's contemporary cooking.

Note that there's a minimum stay of two nights on weekends, and this family-owned hotel is not recommended for children under 12 years of age.

Madrona Manor

1001 Westside Rd. (at West Dry Creek Rd.), Healdsburg

Phone: 707-433-4231 or 800-258-4003
Fax: 707-433-0703
Web: www.madronamanor.com
Prices: $$$

17 Rooms

5 Suites

Eight wooded acres form the backdrop for Madrona Manor. A short drive from downtown Healdsburg, this 19th-century estate oozes with romantic cachet. It's a serene place to retire to after a day of wine tasting.

Built for San Francisco businessman John Paxton, the stately, three-story Victorian mansion has graced this site since 1881. Of the 22 handsome rooms on-site, 9 are located in the mansion itself; all of these have king-size beds and fireplaces. The remainder of the rooms and suites are scattered around the grounds in buildings such as the original carriage house. All rooms are individually decorated and fitted with soft linens and terry robes. WiFi is available in most areas of the inn, and rates include a buffet breakfast each morning. If it's seclusion you seek, reserve the Garden Cottage with its own private garden and sheltered deck. And be sure your stay includes an intimate dinner at the mansion's lovely restaurant *(see restaurant listing)*.

To foster romance, there are no TVs in any of the rooms, but with a heated pool on-site, the boutiques of Healdsburg, and the Dry Creek Valley wineries so close by, you won't want for things to do.

Vintners Inn

B2

4350 Barnes Rd. (at River Rd.), Santa Rosa

Phone: 707-575-7350
Fax: 707-575-1426
Web: www.vintnersinn.com
Prices: $$$

44 Rooms

Nestled in 92 acres of vineyards, Vintners Inn welcomes guests with a bottle of wine. The inn, owned by Dan and Rhonda Carano of Ferrari-Carano Winery, is located just north of Santa Rosa and convenient to Highway 101.

Four two-story Tuscan-style buildings with red-tile roofs range around a landscaped courtyard. Each room enjoys its own private balcony or small patio. Country décor is rustic and refined, and Internet access and a copy of the local newspaper come compliments of the house. Rooms on the second floor boast vaulted ceilings with exposed wood beams; some are equipped with fireplaces. If you want a bit more space, reserve a junior suite, outfitted with a king-size featherbed, a fireplace, and a sitting area with a sleeper sofa. A 32-inch television with a VCR and CD player, two-line phones, and a dataport add to the modern amenities.

Rates include a buffet breakfast each morning; for lunch or dinner, you need only walk next door to John Ash & Co. *(see restaurant listing)* for a meal that highlights Sonoma County products.

In 2006 the inn opened an Event and Conference Center, which offers more than 6,000 square feet of meeting space.

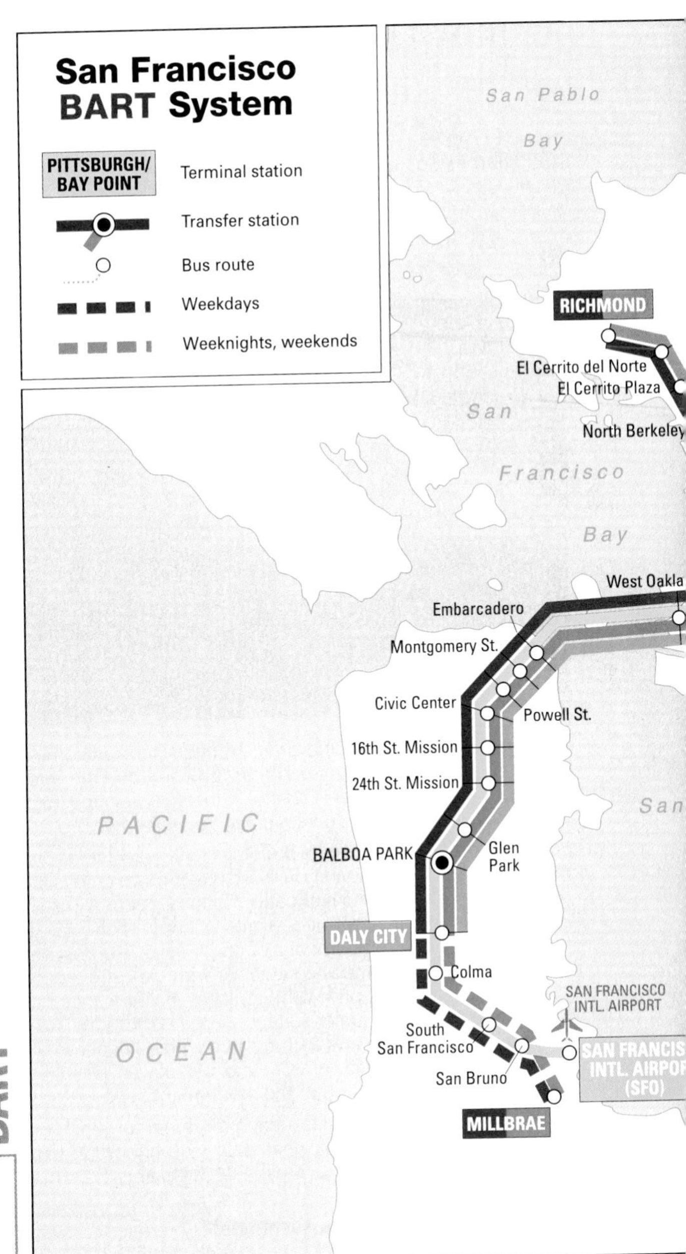
San Francisco BART System
PITTSBURGH/ BAY POINT
Terminal station
Transfer station
Bus route
Weekdays
Weeknights, weekends
San Pablo Bay
RICHMOND
El Cerrito del Norte
El Cerrito Plaza
North Berkeley
San Francisco Bay
West Oakla
Embarcadero
Montgomery St.
Powell St.
Civic Center
16th St. Mission
24th St. Mission
PACIFIC OCEAN
Glen Park
BALBOA PARK
DALY CITY
Colma
SAN FRANCISCO INTL. AIRPORT
South San Francisco
San Bruno
MILLBRAE

BART